The Refiner's Fire

The Refiner's Fire

An Odyssey of Faith

*"See, I have refined you, though not as silver;
I have tested you in the furnace of affliction.
For my own sake, for my own sake, I do this."
Isaiah 48:10*

RICHARD BASTEAR

Copyright © 2016 Richard Bastear
All rights reserved.

ISBN-13: 9781534881235
ISBN-10: 1534881239
Library of Congress Control Number: 2016910520
CreateSpace Independent Publishing Platform
North Charleston, South Carolina

*To my father who taught me,
the love of language,
and
To my children and grandchildren,
that they may experience the
Joy of the Lord in reading this
as I found in writing it.*

Contents

Introduction ix

Chapter 1	A Defining Moment	1
Chapter 2	Once Upon A Time	5
Chapter 3	A New Home	28
Chapter 4	The Home Front	38
Chapter 5	Coming of Age: Life With Father	67
Chapter 6	High School Days	71
Chapter 7	Adventures In Learning	85
Chapter 8	Road Trips	95
Chapter 9	Introduction To The Adult World	107
Chapter 10	Joe College	121
Chapter 11	Highs and Lows	135
Chapter 12	Lessons Learned on the Mountain	142
Chapter 13	In And Out Of Love	155
Chapter 14	Life Against Death	161
Chapter 15	Peaches	167
Chapter 16	Planes	176
Chapter 17	Army, 1952-1954	181
Chapter 18	A New Beginning	227
Chapter 19	The Indelible Footprint	251
Chapter 20	A Full Time Ministry	270
Chapter 21	Rip Tides and Cross Currents	290
Chapter 22	On the Edge of a Volcano	314

Chapter 23	Moving On	331
Chapter 24	The Rhinoceros & The Pussy Cat	360
Chapter 25	The Beast	378
Chapter 26	Recovery	406
	Epilogue	417
	Bibliography	425

Introduction

The community I grew up in no longer exists. Oh, the town is on the map, but when I return there for a visit there is no one that I know. Familiar places of my childhood are gone or transformed into something new. I am a stranger in my hometown. I drove to my secret hiding place in the San Gabriel Mountains where as a youth I could be alone with my dog Christopher. We ate lunch with the beauty of Sturtevant Falls surrounding us. Now there is a public parking lot that is jam packed with people who want to picnic or hike to the falls. The quiet mystique of the place is gone. The little Methodist Church where I was baptized is now Vietnamese and I can't even read the bulletin board. I came to a harsh realization that change is everywhere.

We long for a place where we can find companionship, recognition, touch, and laughter. Or does such a place really exist? Perhaps that is why escape through drugs is so popular. I want to share my story because I actually found such a place. There are dangers along the way, and places where a person can get lost and confused. It is why I call this journey an odyssey. Yet, it is a journey worth taking just because the cause is so great, and if we persist, we find our meaning and purpose. Along the way I also found what it means to be a person. Telling that story is one of the goals of this book.

On this odyssey I found that I was my own worst enemy. How could I ever clear my head of the baggage my parents gave to me? How could I free myself from dependence on them to a interdependence with them? How could I calm my many fears? It seemed as though I always had to prove myself to others. I carried a host of secrets in my head that I shared with no one: my low self-esteem and a need to be inconspicuous.

I refused to ask anyone for help or let anyone know how I felt. I forged ahead doing things my way, stubbornly believing that my way was best. I began to find that there were consequences for that kind of behavior. I began paying a price for an insistence on my way. That brings me to the second goal of my story. I want to share my testament of faith. For I found that through those consequences God was reaching out to me in love and showing me that there is a better way.

The possibility of a turnaround came when my neighbor began inviting me to the new San Gabriel Presbyterian congregation. Later I attended our local Methodist Church and joined their youth group, and the choir. The pastor baptized me at age 20 and challenged us to go fly with him to Russia, bail out, and proclaim the gospel to the communists. I raised my hand, signaling an affirmative response. I was ready to go.

That led to a move out into the larger world. I went to U.C. Davis, then to the U.S. Army. After basic training I was sent along with six others to Trieste, Italy for peacekeeper duty. While there I led a double life. I was our chaplain's assistant and company guidon, but I also sought the companionship of local ladies of the night. The result was a deep burden of guilt that I was a hypocrite of the worst type. Returning to U.C. Davis to study I experienced a defining moment in my life. I found God's forgiveness, and my guilt rolled away. Overcoming my past fears on my own was impossible. But in slow, halting steps of sweet surrender to God's grace, I began to regain my footing. If you read through to the conclusion you will find my secret of a joyous life, my testament of faith.

Thirdly, I want to talk about the Refiner's fire, and how it influenced my life. I was so bound up in myself that I couldn't see nor hear any clear sense of direction for my life. I knew I was alone, but couldn't see a way out. But, as I experienced consequences for my stubbornness it also seemed as though someone was trying to get my attention. Slowly

INTRODUCTION

I came to the dim awareness that God wanted to play a significant part in my life. He was using those consequences to show me a better way. Finally, through friends and counseling, and surrender to God's grace I found the love of God was the source of the Refiner's fire. I share that story with you now.

There is another dimension to this story. I was raised in a home where the knowledge of sex was forbidden. Growing up as a boy, however, Nature had a way of reminding me of my sexuality. Consequently there are frequent allusions to those times when I stumbled upon the reality of our human libido and had to make sense of it. It was not an easy task, and several times as an adult I chose the wild side in order to learn about the forbidden. Thankfully, with good counseling and by God's grace, I learned to sublimate my sexual drive and turn it to the purpose for which God intended it. I want to suggest now that this story that I tell is not for children, but is written for adults who are seeking a better way of living.

I want to thank the three mentors who tried to teach me their writing skills: Diane Runion, Linda Trapp, and Howard Lachtman. If there are errors here they are mine. My teachers bear no responsibility, but to point the way to the great art of writing. The rest is up to the student. Linda and Howard patiently read and corrected errors in the chapters of this book. My daughter Suzanne designed the cover, and Deborah Soares helped me solve a multitude of computer problems along the way. I thank my wife Marilyn for the many ways she supported me through this effort. She too spent many hours editing my typos and my grammar. I could not have completed this without her gracious love. If you find pleasure here on these pages it will bring me joy to find out. Be my guest and read on.

ONE

A DEFINING MOMENT

The bedroom was dark and the early morning air carried a chill. I was planning to get up early and make sure my grandson, Austin, got to school on time. I could hear my wife's slow, deep breathing in the morning darkness. I lay quietly for a minute and offered an early morning prayer: "This is the day the Lord has made, let us rejoice and be glad in it." I fumbled for my small LED flashlight, and suddenly I felt a strange sensation in my chest. It was unlike anything I had ever felt before. I could feel a deep heaviness in my chest and with it a squishing as my heart lost its regular rhythm. I laid back and quietly rested for a minute waiting for the heaviness to subside and the rhythm to normalize. Neither happened in the succeeding five minutes so I decided that the best thing to do was to get up and begin preparing for the day, as if nothing had happened.

By afternoon a feeling of anxiety was slowly creeping from my stomach into my chest. Something was wrong. I called my cardiologist and talked to his technical assistant. She suggested that my wife Marilyn bring me to their clinic and the TA would administer an EKG. I deferred, and told her I would drive myself to the clinic. Guys just stubbornly persist that they don't need help. *I will do this myself.* My streak of independence was as strong now as before. But my chest was heavier and the strange rhythm of my heart was even more intense. After the technical assistant completed the EKG she told me that she was requesting a wheelchair to take me across the street to St. Joseph's Hospital to admit me for further tests. I insisted that I could walk across the street and admit myself, still persisting in my independence. Reaching the admissions desk at the hospital, I suddenly began to collapse. I grabbed a chair and kept myself from hitting the floor. A nurse touched an alarm and suddenly twelve nurses and staff surrounded me. They brought a wheelchair and eased me into it. Now I was a patient, and my time for denial was over.

Things were moving quickly at the hospital. My cardiologist determined that I was having an atrial fibrillation. He gave me an anesthetic. After I lost consciousness, he used a defibrillator to shock my heart back into a regular pattern of contraction. When I awoke Marilyn was at my bedside along with Dr. Lim. Dr. Lim told me his sobering diagnosis: "The atrial fibrillation means that you need open-heart surgery." I already knew that my heart's mitral valve was not functioning properly, but I wanted to avoid open-heart surgery to repair it. I was shocked at the news. I had hoped that it would never come to this. The thought of a world-class surgeon sawing open my chest and holding my heart in his hands in order to repair it demoralized me. "Isn't there some way out of this?" I asked. "Not unless you are willing to jeopardize your chances of survival," came the doctor's response.

I called Stanford Hospital on the campus of the university in Palo Alto and set up dates when I could come for a full body MRI and other tests. We set the date for surgery for October 6, 2011. My children, Suzanne and Steve, asked if there was anything they could do. "Yes," came my reply, "come and be with me at the hospital. I need you." Steve brought his daughter Jessica. My wife Marilyn, and Suzanne came too. We rented rooms at a nearby motel on October 5 and began what was an anxious vigil. The surgery was scheduled for early morning on the 6th but a phone call from Stanford warned of a delay.

Finally a call came from Stanford at 5:00 pm: "Come immediately. We are preparing for you." We dashed to our cars and drove straight to the cardiac surgical center. Once again I looked at the beautiful garden of flowers planted at the hospital entrance, but this time wistfully. *Would I survive this surgery to see them again?* Sent to a room where I filled out paperwork, I was then allowed to return to my family. At 10:00 pm a nurse came for me. We knew this was now a defining moment and we shared hugs and kisses all around. The nurse escorted me to a separate room and gave me a hospital gown to put on, the kind where your butt shows through and leaves you feeling strangely exposed. A technician shaved my chest and then swabbed it with some kind of dark antiseptic. I was now on a gurney and wheeled toward surgery. One last time my kids and grandkids came and gave me hugs. My mind was working overtime with fear, *"Can I leap off the gurney now and make a dash for the familiar things of my family? Yet, my butt will show!"*

By now I could see in the distance the massive lights in the ceiling of the operating room. They were intimidating. My anesthesiologist walked over and said calmly, "Would you like a cocktail?" My response was immediate, "Of course." He injected me in the arm and asked me to start counting. I think I got to three and dropped off into a drug-induced sleep. My family laughed as they saw how quickly I faded away. I remembered nothing of the surgery.

In ICU after surgery the nurses discovered internal bleeding in my chest. Marilyn and Suzanne came to my bedside the next morning and gave approval to reopen my chest. Fortunately, I was still under the influence of anesthesia and didn't have the anxiety of the first time around.

By 2:00 pm I was returned to ICU and spent three days there. Then in a regular nursing room the nurses urged me to stand up by my bed and take a few hesitant steps. Then I walked to the bathroom. Later that day with some support from the nurses I walked to the nurse's desk and back to my bed. I was shaky and unstable, but I did it. The nurses kept prodding me to walk further. One week later I was released and Marilyn drove me home to Stockton.

Feeling good to be headed home was moderated by the awareness that I was as weak as a newborn puppy. I didn't like being so helpless. I was now going to endure being a patient and chafed at the thought.

Surviving major surgery was an awakener for me. Awakened to my own mortality, I was aware that I was allowed only a finite life span. I began to consider my own death. But even more importantly I wanted to thank God for bringing me through all this. *What did God want of me? I had to find out, and then live that life.*

I was aware that there was no one other than me to tell the story of my family. Those realities gripped my mind and confirmed a decision I had made after my previous wife, Gayle, died. I wanted to tell my story. I began getting up at 5:30 or 6:00 am each morning to write, edit or do research on letters and photographs that I had squirreled away over the years.

This book is the result of that decision.

Two

Once Upon A Time

What's in a name? Shakespeare asked that question 500 years ago and it intrigues me now. Does our name give a clue as to our character? Is there a heritage in our names that has fixed certain behaviors to us for good and for ill? Does our DNA have some unknown strands so that some of our behavior is predetermined? Somewhere in all of this lies a truth about whom we are. I told my students at Delta College that we are not biological accidents on the face of the earth, doomed to be galley slaves on some one else's ship. In our mysterious mix of nature and spirit there is a realm of freedom of choice. We have that freedom of choice even while inheriting chromosomes from our ancestors. Thus while I affirm my freedom, I want to know my ancestry; to know more about the name Bastear, where we came from, and what kind of people we are. And if my origins are shrouded in unknowns, then I want to clarify them.

The Bastear saga began in Bohemia, a region in central Europe, now called the Czech Republic. Only slowly did I come to know of my father's origins. He never talked of his beginnings in Bohemia. But he did speak of his father and mother, brother and sister, aunts and uncles. Those were strange names to me. As a young man I met a few of them. That set my curiosity in motion to find out who I was and where my family came from. I discovered that I was the third generation in the New World, and the third generation, according to author Will Herberg, are interested in their family heritage, but also lose their original language. I regretted that I had not met my father's family, who lived in Chicago. I never met his father, who died in Chicago when I was 14. I met his mother once on a train trip through Chicago as a teen-ager of 17. Most of the others were strange names to me. Ditto on my mother's side.

My father, called a "polack" or "bohunk" by his schoolmates and neighbors, chafed under their derision. He learned to fight back with his fists, and that would stop the problem for a while. But there were others ready to call him names. He decided on a policy of renunciation with his past. His father changed his name from Bastyr (pronounced Bas-teech), to Bastear. With a neutered name like that no one could guess his origins.

Dad gave up any Bohemian words that he had learned, for fear they might give him away. He gave up his ethnic foods just as soon as he could, and he quit the Catholic Church, thus creating a great divorce with his origins. He then became an American by blending into his new country. He never looked back. As my sisters and I grew up we had no idea of our European ancestry. By my teenage years I began to ask my first few questions about our past. I needed to know these things. I wanted to find answers.

We are Bastyrs. We are Bohemian in origin. Josef, my grandfather, and Josef, my great grandfather were born and baptized in the village Catholic Church of Kostelec nad Orlici. Great grandpa was born about 1848, and Josef Jr. was born March 4, 1878 or 1879. Teaching Western Civilization at San Joaquin Delta College in Stockton I was drawn to the region of Bohemia. The capitol of the Holy Roman Empire in the Middle Ages was Prague. Prague was also the capital of Bohemia. Bohemia became a great Kingdom. "Good King Wenceslaus," the patron saint, ruled here. Jan Hus preached here in the Bethlehem Chapel in Prague. From his pulpit he protested the lax morality of priests and pope, condemned indulgences, and finally attracted the attention of authorities. The pope ordered Hus to come to Constance, Switzerland in 1414. There the doctors of the church found him guilty of heresy, and set a date for him to be burned at the stake. He became a symbol of protest and hope to those wanting reformation in the church.

Am I proud of my origins? Of course I am! I have been tempted to revert to the original spelling of our name. In Bohemia Bastyr meant sheepherder. It reminded me of our family's humble beginnings in a peasant home. My ancestors lived under the lord of the manor, and were ministered to by the village priest who helped peasant families meet the crises and tragedies of failing health and death. Peasants also shared in the festival days sponsored by the church, and of course in services of marriage, baptism and burial of the dead. But the cocoon in which they lived was broken open by Napoleon Bonaparte when he carried the watchwords of the French Revolution eastward in his conquests: "liberty, equality, and fraternity." (1799-1815). Those words resonated across Europe, and in 1848 there was a revolt in Prague, the capital of Bohemia.

The revolt was put down, but Napoleon had planted a seed that continued to grow.

My great grandfather Josef Sr. finally made a once-in-a-lifetime decision to leave home and all of its familiar attractions. The Austro-Hungarian Empire now required all young men to register for the draft. Josef Jr. was 13 and would soon have to register.

Letters had come from America and the peasants who had emigrated earlier wrote stories about available land, where there were no nobility to lord it over them. America was a land bursting with opportunity. "Come," they wrote. There were now modern steel ships to take them to America from Hamburg, Germany. Josef Sr. took all of that information, talked to his family, his relatives and friends and came to a momentous decision; he and his family would pull up stakes and travel to America.

Spring in Bohemia is lovely. But the spring of 1892 also created anxiety for the Bastyr household. They loaded their wagon with suitcases and a large chest brimming with family heirlooms. Everything else was sold or given away. Oscar Handlin in his classic book about European immigrants, "The_Uprooted," tells how every step of the way to America was steeped in wrenching change. Saying goodbye to all that was familiar, they traveled by train to their port of embarkation. For them that was Hamburg, Germany. They had their passports carefully checked at each frontier. Then, they stood in long lines to purchase tickets at the port city, and bought tickets for passage on the Normannia. (The information on the year of emigration, and the name of the ship come from my uncle in Santa Barbara, California who vouches for their authenticity.)

They loaded on board and were promptly ushered by crew members into the deepest hold of the ship, called "steerage," reserved for peasants going to America. Wealthy travelers were put in cabins on the main deck where they got all of the first class privileges. Those in steerage were served cheap food, stacked in bunks one above the other, were provided with inadequate bathing facilities, and were only allowed on deck for fresh air twice a day. Many became sick but had to endure their illness with whatever home remedies they had brought.

New York City was bustling with activity. Ellis Island opened for business on January 1, 1892. New immigrants were processed there. All those arriving had to be checked by Public Health doctors and approved for entry. Breadwinners had to have marketable skills so as to find jobs and not be a burden on society. Anyone too ill to come ashore might be turned back.

Once they passed inspection they were ferried across the harbor to New York City itself. On the way they could see the Statue of Liberty, recently given by the people of France to America to celebrate the 100th anniversary of the French Revolution. In the city they faced daunting challenges. There were those wanting to exploit the inexperience of the immigrants. The immigrants faced immediate prejudice against newcomers. They had to find cheap housing in the tenements as they arranged transportation by rail to Chicago, their final destination.

Chicago had a large population of Bohemians, and amongst them were families with names like Pinc, Hajic, Kubs, and Studik. All of them would, by marriage, become interlinked with the Bastyrs. The Bohemians had their own enclave in the great city. In their enclave the Bohemians had their own restaurants, newspapers, churches, dance halls, breweries, and drinking establishments. Josef Sr. drank heavily of the local pilsner beer as did the other men in their neighborhood. Solace and friendship bubbled in the beer after a hard days' work.

Many of them had seen the "Great White City" that was the Columbian Exposition of 1892 in Chicago, celebrating the discovery of America by Christopher Columbus in 1492. It was a marvel to behold, all lighted with hundreds of thousands of new electric bulbs, the invention of Thomas Edison just a few years before. The gleaming white city contained wonderful architecture, and a new feature in America: a Ferris wheel. Nothing like this existed in the Old World.

Josef Sr. soon established himself as a bricklayer and a carpenter. He hired out quickly to nearby contractors. Homes, apartments, redesigned mansions being turned into apartments, sprang up along the west side. Emigrants were arriving daily and provided a cheap and a plentiful source of labor to build the greatest city in the west of America. Josef had to work hard to keep his job.

Josef Jr. enrolled in the local high school, and soon followed his father into the building trades. He opened a bank account, came of age, and after graduation from high school, went to work full time as a carpenter. At St. Vitus Catholic Church he met the girl he wanted to marry, Elizabeth Hajic. She was born in 1878 in Chicago, to Josef Hajic and Anna Pinc. Josef was 21 and Elizabeth was 22. Josef appealed to Elizabeth's parents for their permission to marry her. He could promise to provide a home and full time work to support her. His zeal prevailed.

They were married on August 6, 1901 at St. Vitus Church. Josef looked debonair in his rented tuxedo, a distinct pride in his achievement. Elizabeth wore a traditional white wedding gown, her veil pulled back, a bouquet in her right hand, as she stood by Josef for their wedding photo. She showed a quiet strength and grace in the lines of her face. My father, Edward Frank, was born one year later, August 21, 1902.

Their wedding marked a turning point for this new couple. Their certificate of marriage revealed that Josef had modified his name. He changed his first name to Joseph, and his last name to Bastear. Those simple changes took the hard edge off the pronunciation of our name. It Americanized it so that they could blend in with this dynamic new world.

My father, Edward, being the first born of five, carried a heavier load of responsibility than his brothers and sisters. Joseph raised him to be the leader so he could care for the others. Due to the health standards of the day, one son, George, born in 1907, died five years later, in 1912. Dad remembered that it was probably the dreaded scourge of diphtheria that took his life. Another son, Henry, was born stillborn. Thus, the Bastear children consisted of my father, his brother Harry, born in 1912, and sister Gladys born in 1915.

Edward appeared in photos at the age of eight. He looked unhappy, even morose. In one photo Dad stood in front of the grocery store that Joseph bought at 569 Laflin Street, and had Elizabeth, my grandmother, manage from 1906 to 1909. The store was small, and behind Elizabeth were stacked quaint barrels of food items for sale. Dad's mother stood in the doorway keeping a watchful eye on him. Dad had a stick in his hand with which he was ready to roll a barrel hoop down the street. Next door was a butcher shop, and the butcher's son was a bully. Edward got regular doses of name-calling: "Polack," for instance. Eventually the butcher boy started shoving and dad shoved back, and hit him in the face. Bullying from the boy next door stopped that day.

What elementary school he attended remains a mystery. He was silent on such matters, (or maybe we didn't listen well). He left the impression that those were years he would rather forget. Carol, my sister, wrote a letter to me in 1959 after she had gone through psychotherapy, and shared her thoughts about our father:

> *"I was always scared to death of Dad. I can't remember receiving a hug or a kiss or kind word from him, ever. I can't imagine what kind of childhood he had, but it must have been terrible. He won't even talk about it now. And we know Mom's must have been terrible."*

The value of work was impressed on him at an early age. He referred to it often as we grew up and were reminded by Dad of growing up under Joseph. After school his father taught him how to deliver beer to the workers at construction sites. Joseph worked as a cabinetmaker by 1911. Young Edward was instructed to go to the local brewery and buy a bucket of beer, then bring it to Joseph's construction site.

The workers would take a break, find seats amongst the building materials, and produce a mug. Dad would ladle beer into their mugs, collect a nickel (and maybe a tip), and go around the circle pouring beer until each man was served. A nickel for each beer did not seem like much to me, but this was the turn of the century and a nickel was worth much more then than now. The bucket of beer did not cost much either. Dad performed this service until dinnertime.

At home, Elizabeth, or Lizzie as she was called, often served chicken and dumplings, a favorite in the Bohemian community; Bohemian was still spoken along with English. Joseph was lord of his household, and ordered Dad to empty his pocket of nickels and put them on the table. Joseph put them into two equal piles. One half was for the family savings, and the other half was for Dad. Any other money he made was also distributed in the same way.

There was no discussion of the matter. It was non-negotiable. Life with his father was hard. Joseph had sacrificed everything to come to America. He worked diligently to support himself and his father's family, and the old world standards were equally applied to my father. Joseph worked hard, and drank hard and kept those expectations of his firstborn son.

As a teen-ager Dad enrolled in Harrison Technical High School. By his own admission he was a dreamer. He wanted to go on to college and get a degree in engineering. He dreamed of becoming a football star like his uncle, Edward Hajic, at St. Stephen's College (now DePaul). In fact, Dad was named after him. Dad sang a song playfully from those years: "You've got to be a football hero to get along with a beautiful girl." That was a part of his romantic nature.

My father loved tales of adventure. Was that a part of his Bohemian heritage? Growing up with father often included listening to pirate stories. His favorite book was Ralph Paine's "Four Bells, Tales of the Caribbean." Other favorites were Robert Service's, "Spell of the Yukon." How many times, when Dad felt expansive, did we hear a few lines from "*Dangerous Dan McGrew?*" There were tales of Simon Girty, who during the Revolutionary War, with British help, sold rifles to the Indians in the Ohio River Valley. The tribes used those rifles to fight against the expanding American frontier.

There was another world to contend with: the reality of Chicago's mean streets. Dad wrote this letter to Carol and described one of his street fights.

> *"My worst battle was when I took on two Polish boys at the same time and ended up getting stabbed in the back; lucky the Post Man came along and broke it up and that eve my pop went after the Polish boys' Pop. Pop could handle his dukes nifty. Great stuff. Occasionally I feel like setting down my life story for the grand chilluns to read from the time I was a curly headed boy to cruising around the dance halls of the 20's in Ohio, etc., and almost getting thrown out of a couple except my Navy buddies threatened to clean up the joint in that case. That was in the days we used to drink Dr. Ed Pinauds Toilet Water (alcohol content) for kicks and rode around in a Ford Lizzie. Well, sorry I got turned on and let loose. Over and out. Pops."*

Dad played football in the neighborhood leagues. He excelled at quarterback, and was in demand as a player. Glowingly, he spoke of playing with guys twice his size and wearing no pads while he did so. This was the fulfillment of a dream, to prove his manhood. He could do anything he set out to do.

He wrote a letter regarding one of his football heroes, George Gipp, of Notre Dame:

> "He came into my orbit as a great B.F. man (Back Field). (A natural but also as a heck of a poker player and Crap Shooter and not much of a student. Don't think he was too regular at Class attendance). Spent six months in South Bend in '22 and got to know a few things about Notre Dame and the golden Dome. Also it was one of my boyhood fantasys (sic) to attend Yale and be close to greatness. S'all for now. Dad. (Fantasy, fantasies, Fantasys, The Dictionary not clear on this)."

In the summer months he and some of the family went to Aunt Lottie's farm (Elizabeth's sister) in Lowell, Indiana. The boys had plenty of places to play, hide out, and swim in nearby Cedar Lake. A flock of geese had made the lake their home. One afternoon the boys went swimming in the nude.

One of Dad's cousins was floating on his back when suddenly a nearby goose saw what it thought was food in the water. The goose made a swift lunge to seize the prize but the choice morsel turned out to be his cousin's penis. Both the goose and his cousin were equally shocked by this outcome. His cousin cried out in fright while the goose squawked and swam away to a safer place. The cousin came ashore to inspect and nurse his wounds. My father and the rest of the boys roared with laughter, and followed him to the lake's edge. Dad told that story many times as we grew up, and closed it with his Bastear chuckle as he relived the fun each time he told the story.

In another letter he spoke of,

> *"Throwing hay, moving horses, sparking the country Gals (except I had ideals then), Boy Scout work and Camps, (and) some years also as a Sunday School teacher (actually a cover for coaching a boys Junior Basketball team), ---."*

But there was another side, a darker element that also made up his character. The summer before he entered his Junior Year, he and his father had a long talk. Can we surmise how it went?

Joseph: "This beer is good. Bring me another mug. Now son, how is it going at high school?"

Dad: "I have learned basic mathematics, English, American History, Algebra, and am getting good grades. Have you seen my grade report?"

Joseph: "No. I am too tired to read it right now. I will read it later. But I have some important news for you. You will not be returning to high school in the fall. After you spend some time with your Aunt Lottie in Lowell this summer, I want you to find full time work and help support our family. You will share your wages with us 50-50 as before. Do you understand?"

Dad: "I am ready to enter the 11th grade and begin my classes in engineering and drafting. Please, I want to finish high school."

Joseph: "Sorry, I hate to do this. But, you will quit high school."

Dad: "Why?"

Joseph: "Because I said so! I want no complaints from you. And I don't want to hear anything more about it. Now do as I say!" My father's dream was emptied of meaning on that day with repercussions that neither anticipated.

Another incident changed his relationship to the Catholic Church for the rest of his life. As a teen-ager he looked for pick-up games in nearby churches or parks. On this particular afternoon he saw a game of basketball at a local church. There was an opportunity to play and he took it. However, from out of the rectory came an old priest walking with a cane. He saw dad as an outsider, not one of his students, and he whacked Dad across his back with the cane and ordered him off of the premises. Dad left, but the pain he felt was more than physical; his feelings were deeply hurt. Never again did he go to a Catholic Church.

After dropping out of W. H. Harrison High School in 1916, he went to work for Western Electric. The company had entered the booming new business of manufacturing telephones. He started at the lowest level. He ground telephone parts, taking off burrs, at 29 cents for 1000 parts. From there he advanced to "Inspector."

Once Upon A Time

In 1920 the company sent him to Austin, Texas. There he supervised a crew of 35 men installing telephones. From Austin he was transferred to Dallas supervising 12 men. They tested circuits for automatic telephone exchanges. Weekends were wild and unforgettable.

Oil drilling was big business. "Roughnecks" were hired to build the platforms from which the drilling would take place. When oil was struck, wild cheering erupted from the oil-spattered men. On Saturday nights the roughnecks took baths, combed their hair, shaved, and prepared for some fun in town. They rode into town in their new tin lizzies, and when they got there the men fired their six shooters into the air with lusty glee. The men scattered to find saloons, card halls, and the dance halls where some ladies would be waiting. The fun lasted into the morning hours. These were Texas boomtowns and the spirit of the old west emerged on Saturday nights.

Dad told these stories as we grew up. His sense of pride kicked in as he relived those stories, glad that he had been there to witness it all. He liked to go downtown and be a part of the excitement. Sometimes he watched from his hotel window. He loved to, "cut a rug" at the dance hall, inviting the bargirls to dance. He knew how to drink with the guys. His Dad had introduced him to beer at an early age, and whiskey soon followed. In his own words, "he was in the pink." It never occurred to me to ask my father if he ever "crossed the line" on Saturday nights. Boys didn't ask questions like that.

He and his crew set up telephone exchanges next in Mexia, Texas, then in Dennison, New Mexico, and finally in Longview, Texas.

Riding horses along the Rio Grand River with local women was a Sunday activity that he relished. He called them "sweet magnolia blossoms." He loved their company, but found that he couldn't go far with a good girl unless he went to church with her. Then there followed an attitude adjustment and such a lady might cozy up to him.

Western Electric had found a good man. My father knew his electric equipment, and he knew how to supervise his crew. Some of them remained his friends even after he moved to California. I watched him pour over blueprints of company equipment until he was sure how a telephone exchange worked.

Alliance, Ohio, was his next assignment, then on to Zanesville, Ohio. There he supervised a crew that cross-connected cables for telephones. (What that meant I failed to ask). Photos of him during those years show him and his buddies playing football in city leagues and industrial leagues. He looked so sharp in his three-point football stance, even posing in a vested suit, minus his coat.

On his football team, fights broke out when a lineman would slug an opponent, and a free-for-all occurred. Dad, as quarterback, helped restore order so the game could continue. In those years of fistfights and mayhem he wrote that, "Never did he allow a personal injury keep him from a game."

In the spring and summer baseball was on his mind. He continued to cut a hole in the palm of his mitt so there was more certainty that a caught ball stayed in his mitt. (and showed a certain toughness). While playing pitcher in an industrial league in Cincinnati, Ohio, he struck out 14 players in one game. That was one of his proudest moments.

Yet no matter how well he performed on the athletic field there seemed to be a sense that it was not quite enough. As he moved upward in his career, engineers with PhD's who graduated from prestigious universities, surrounded him. He, on the other hand, was a high school dropout. He performed well with his knowledge of blue prints and how to repair company equipment. But it was always in the shadow of these university men. Little did his father, Joseph, know that forcing his son out of high school would leave Dad to wrestle with a personal demon of what might have been had he finished his education.

An unspoken fear lurked somewhere in the back of his mind. When my father was in a tight or threatening situation where he felt vulnerable he would say, "Nobody's going to make a chump outta me!" Why did he say that when he was so smart? Only later did it occur to me that Dad had a fear of failure that could morph into a fear of stupidity. He had heard that word on the streets of Chicago over a lifetime. Somehow he applied it to himself in the recesses of his mind. He always had to prove himself. Who he was, what he was, never seemed to be enough.

By 1923 he quit Western Electric and started work with Western Union, where there was better pay and more opportunities for advancement. His roving eye settled on a girl named Lillian McFarland. She worked as a clerk for a prestigious law firm in Chicago's "Loop." On weekends she attended Millard Avenue Presbyterian Church along with her grandmother, Phoebe Ann Stanton.

She was a beautiful young lady of 19. Her photos reveal a soft, lovely glow that my father found irresistible. No one could have guessed that just three years earlier she was a cross-eyed teen who underwent surgery to correct the defect in her eyes. At age three she caught a severe case of measles, the same year that her mother died. She was left with cross-eyes.

Dad was invited to attend the church by a friend who promised that, "Lots of pretty girls attended there." Dad saw Lillian and knew he wanted to get acquainted. Meeting her evoked memories of horseback rides along the Rio Grande River with pretty young ladies. He had to go to their church and meet their parents if he wanted significant time with them. Dad became active at the Church. He played on their basketball team. He coached their boys' basketball team. Then he took a bolder step. He started teaching a Sunday school class. Lillian was pleased. However, years later he confessed that he did it solely to impress her. They began dating, but always under the watchful eye of Phoebe Ann.

Grandmother Stanton took the responsibility to raise the three girls when their mother, Grace McFarland, died on Mom's third birthday. The three were: Minetta (b. 1898), Laurine (b. 1900), and Lillian (b. 1903). Their father, William McFarland, took the three girls to their grandmother's house after Grace died, and hightailed to a ranch in Montana. Abandoned by their father, their mother dead, is it possible that Lillian's cross-eyes after measles were a classic Freudian response to too much trauma in one year?

Phoebe Ann dedicated herself to raising her three granddaughters at her home in Battle Creek, Michigan. Later they moved to 2924 Van

Buren Street in Chicago. Of Scottish lineage and a staunch Presbyterian, Phoebe Ann was born in Ohio in 1844, and grew up attending to prayer, hymn singing, and Bible study. Born during Queen Victoria's youthful reign, Phoebe became an exemplar of the Victorian era; women were expected to be virtuous and remain virgins up to their wedding day. Men were expected to develop into gentlemen and treat ladies with respect, as the weaker sex.

When the Civil War began two of her seven brothers enlisted into Ohio Regiments and served in cavalry units, tending mounts. Living conditions were primitive; the men were exposed to rain and snow, ate decayed meat and stale bread, shared in the long marches, and often slept in wet blankets. The boys returned from the war in poor health. They came home to Phoebe Ann's house, moved in, and lived out their days under her care. Phoebe Ann was expected to be strong.

One of the boys, named Ezekiel, became Lillian's favorite. She affectionately called him "Uncle Ekie." He took the cross-eyed girl under his wing and comforted her when she came home from school bruised by the teasing she took because of her cross-eyes. Lillian absorbed lessons on how to survive under difficult conditions, plus she adopted Phoebe Ann's Presbyterian faith and Victorian virtues.

They attended the Presbyterian Church in Battle Creek, singing revival hymns that roused the congregation to new faith. Growing up years later with my mother at our home in San Gabriel, I could hear her singing and humming the gospel hymns she had learned in her youth. One of her favorites was, "Bringing in the Sheaves," a hymn she sang as she mopped the kitchen floor. Singing gospel hymns made household drudgery a little easier.

In Edward and Lillian we have a meeting of two different worlds. My father's world consisted of his athletic abilities, where he earned respect by playing hard, taking risks, and participating in fights. He loved the new field of electronics, and knew that it would become his career. He could flirt with pretty girls and dance far into the night. My mother's world, on the other hand, was conservative. A paragon of virtue, she knew nothing of flirtation, or of dancing and drinking. She was now on the edge of a momentous decision; meeting a man she was deeply attracted to, but who was so much her opposite. Little did Dad know that Lillian was suspicious of men.

After her father abandoned her and her sisters, she vowed never to talk to her father again. Phoebe Ann taught her the dangers of "unregenerate men." Here lay all the potential for a major collision, as well as the possibility of a love match. Common knowledge says opposites attract. Dad was 20; Mom was 19. Like two magnets in proximity, they attracted each other when brought together. But opposites also quarrel.

Dad had the common sense to become a part of her church. But her church was a means to an end, a way to win her trust. Her photos show her at this time a thing of beauty: soft eyes, a lovely face, warm lips, and hair coiffed in a 1920's wave. Her dress fit comfortably, not too tight or loose, with no plunging necklines, and no cleavage showing. Here was a lovely plum ready to be picked, ripe, but some of the sweetness was not yet fully developed.

Dad knew how to dress to impress his lady. He wore dark suits with a tie, vest, and coat, polished shoes, and a grin that revealed his happiness in this new relationship. Sometimes in his photo album, he leaned against his own Tin Lizzie, showing a pride of ownership. He gave his prime time after work to Lillian. They were married July 19, 1924 at Millard Avenue Presbyterian Church in Chicago.

They left on their honeymoon with Mom's sister, Laurine, and her new husband, Frank Larned. They requested a month off and drove north in Dad's new model T Ford to Wisconsin, Michigan, and Minnesota. Their first stop was Kellogg, Minnesota, where Minetta had married Horace Tresselt, a veteran of WWI. There the Tresselts bought their first farm.

The newly weds in their chugging model T had fun all the way, especially Mom and Laurine. They would laugh and giggle at their perspective on life, or at shared memories of growing up together. They sat side by side in the back seat; one would laugh, and the other responded with a belly laugh, until their bodies shook with a crescendo of joy at the fun they had created. They had rollicking good times together. I have never seen two women who enjoyed each other so much, full of spontaneous laughter. Years later I grinned just listening to them bounce funny stories off each other. The men learned to tolerate the sisters' antics. Frank, especially passive and taciturn, simply smiled as he sat in the passenger seat beside my father, while Dad drove. The two men had little in common.

Their first destination was the Kellogg farm. Photos show the men with Horace's team of plow horses; also in the photo appeared Grandpa McFarland in a big straw hat, who had left Montana to help Horace with his farm. Mom did not appear in the photos. Apparently, she did not feel kindly toward him. She would not forgive his act of abandoning them.

Dad could hardly tolerate Frank. Frank, raised by a wealthy family in Chicago, knew none of the hard life that my father experienced. Frank's family owned a button factory in Chicago. Frank lived a sheltered life, didn't play sports, refused to have children, and had gone to college to get a degree in chemistry. Frank, a non-drinker, and a passive man, was not Dad's type to spend time with. Yet here they were, brought into proximity by their wives.

Dad learned a lesson the hard way with Laurine; in a playful way he slapped her on the fanny. She turned, confronted him, and told him, "Never ever do that again." After that he considered her "strange" that she did not enjoy his kind of playfulness.

Back in Chicago, family issues flared. Some of Joseph's brothers were not to be trusted, as Dad found out the hard way. Uncle John had made it big in real estate investments. He made so much money that he was able to buy Frank Lloyd Wright's home in Oak Park, outside Chicago. Then John invested in a Florida land scheme, part of a land boom in Sebring, and invited Dad to put significant money into it and "get rich." Unfortunately, the scheme was bankrupt by 1925, and Dad lost several hundred dollars. Uncle John was penniless by 1930. There was a bitter aftertaste in the Bastear household. John's search for power and wealth had failed and he had pulled my father into it.

My sister Sybil was born April 30, 1925. Carol was born March 8, 1928. In 1929 Western Union made plans to expand their Los Angeles office. Dad was asked to transfer there with his family of four. His response was a refusal unless Western Union paid their moving expenses. The chief of the Chicago office agreed to that, and Dad and Mom began packing. They left for Los Angeles during the summer of 1929 and traveled cross-country on a train to Los Angeles.

They selected a home in San Gabriel, a mission town southeast of Los Angeles. The reason for that choice? Laurine and Frank had already come west and purchased a nearby chicken farm off of San Gabriel Boulevard, a mile south of Garvey Boulevard, at that time a sparsely settled valley surrounded by hills. Both families were now located in the San Gabriel Valley.

Our little home on Daroca Street was a quiet section of San Gabriel. I was born at Voorbeck Maternity Hospital in Monterey Park, January 30, 1930. Dad had been at the hospital all night waiting for Lillian to complete her agony of delivery, and at 6:00 am the next morning my father held me in his arms after the nurses had bundled me in blankets. Dad then handed me to Mom, and left for work.

Mom was left to fill out formal papers regarding her live birth. One of the questions was, "Father's occupation." In her weariness she listed him as "Ticker man." When she listed my name she wrote, Richard Allen, though it was supposed to be, Richard Alan, reflecting my Scottish heritage by way of the Stantons. Dad's indignation burned brightly when he found out that he was listed as a Ticker man. He had worked hard to become a Western Union engineer, and that was "lese majesty," i.e., beneath his dignity.

However, there was no going back to correct the error. The birth certificate had already been sent to the County for recording. Years later Dad reminded his friends of my mother's mistake. She remonstrated that it was an all night ordeal and she had been exhausted, but to no avail. "Ticker man" stood.

Our new home was one-half block from Las Tunas Boulevard. Dad soon developed a routine. After breakfast he walked to Las Tunas, caught the Pacific Electric Red Car, and took it downtown to Spring Street where Western Union maintained their headquarters. Mom thus got the use of our Model A Ford. It was black. Henry Ford had proclaimed that customers could buy any color they wanted as long as it was black. Mom could bundle us and take us with her in our Ford when she had to shop. Of course, everyone else's car was black, so we were part of the great American melting pot.

The Depression was deepening and growing worse. Twenty five percent of the labor force was out of work, but Dad's job was secure, and we were so grateful that Western Union needed him, even though his wages were cut. For a lower rental he moved us to 138 Segovia Street, but with banks failing and Wall Street in collapse, my father finally moved us to the outskirts of Los Angeles, to a stucco home on Somerset Street in a place called El Sereno. It was 1932 and F.D.R. stumped the country pleading for my parents' votes and an end to the "Hooverville" shantytowns that sprang up everywhere. He won my parents' votes, and they became solid Democrats from then on.

Those were precarious years for us and for many others. To have a full time job was a blessing. We never lacked for food or shelter. Mom's refrain at dinner was, "Clear your plate, they are starving in China." To this day I am uncomfortable if I leave food at my place. Pennies and nickels were precious. A Coca Cola cost five cents, candy was a penny.

Hungry men came to our door for a bite to eat. Mom, with her soft heart, could not refuse a hungry man's request. While an unemployed man waited on the front porch, she would make a tuna sandwich to go. Word must have traveled quickly among the indigents that our home was a "good stop." We had visitors throughout the Depression years.

While in El Sereno I began having nightmares. Along with that I had severe earaches, and fluid would ooze out of my ear. Asthmatic attacks began. Some nights Mom would stay up late rubbing mentholatum copiously on my chest. She followed that with mentholatum dissolved in a pan of boiling water. With a towel over my head and the boiling water, I could inhale deeply of the vapors and find relief.

Around my neck she tied a dirty sock in hopes it would ward off germs. My socks were smelly and sent a foul odor to my nose. Was it also hard on the germs? My mother, convinced of the prophylactic value of my dirty socks, used that home remedy just as she learned it from Grandma Stanton. That was all the testimony she needed to apply it to me. I had to wear a dirty sock every night that I was sick.

On top of that, I had to take a dose of cod liver oil each morning to fortify me. It tasted like dead fish in my mouth, and sometimes I gagged on it. "Here, drink some orange juice to help it down," Mom would say. She completed the medicine routine by giving me a spoonful of chopped walnuts drizzled with honey. That was a sweet treat that made the rest bearable. I loved that. These were home remedies that she used when we could not afford a doctor visit.

During those years my parents purchased a ten-volume set of books called "Journey's Through Bookland." Volume one contained nursery rhymes. Mom sat me on her lap and when I was sick or ready for bed, she read page after page of rhymes to me. By the time I grew up the pages were worn thin with use.

When I was alone I browsed the rest of the volumes, age-graded for young people. How I lingered over the paintings and drawings of heroes like Beowulf, and Siegfried, great sword in hand, poised to strike an enraged dragon with a deathblow. Then Sir Walter Scott's "Ivanhoe" beckoned, with a full color plate of a mysterious Black Knight (King Richard the Lion Hearted incognito) attacking an enemy castle single-handedly. With battle-axe held over his head, he stood ready to smash the front portal. Those stories awakened my imagination, and I loved such tales of bravery. Thus began a lifelong joie de vivre in reading.

Kindergarten began in 1935. In preparation, Mom took me shopping and bought me a pair of short pants, a white shirt, and Buster Brown shoes. What a bold outfit for such a modest neighborhood! Sierra Park School was nearby and I was allowed to walk with Sybil and Carol to our school. We had no fear of danger. There didn't seem to be such a thing in our part of town.

The teacher gave our class a project for our first Lent. We carefully took the half-shells of eggs given to us by our mothers, and filled them with a planter mix. The teacher gave each of us a nasturtium seed to plant into our half-shell. We watered it lightly until the seed germinated and reached several inches in height. Then we carried our plants home during Easter week as a resurrection message of new life. There were no questions asked about crossing the line between church and state. We simply enjoyed our project. Mom showed me where I could plant it in the garden. The plant soon produced flowers and adorned our garden all summer.

My mother insisted that I come straight home after school. I wanted to stay after school and play. Instead I went home so she could watch over me. At first it was no problem, but as I grew older the order remained the same. When I resisted, the reply came from Mom, "You are sickly." It felt like old-fashioned control to me.

Somerset Street was built on a gently sloping ravine where a creek drained excess water, and flowed to the Los Angeles River. The creek provided numerous opportunities for play. Crawdads abounded in the murky water and we learned how to catch them. Attaching a piece of bacon to an open safety pin, we tied that to a string, then the string to a wooden pole, and we were bona fide crawdad hunters. Dipping the line into a quiet pool of water we could feel a tug on the line as one of them would catch a scent, and seize the bacon in his claw. Then, with a jerk we hauled our catch to shore. It would hang on to the bacon even as we lifted it out of the water.

Under Somerset Street a long tunnel had been dug to allow the creek water to continue its course to the sea. It was lined with cement, and the farther we went in the darker it became. What an opportunity for exploration and adventure! We would dare one another to go farther and farther into the darkness and see what we could find. Neighborhood rumors abounded that there was some sinister creature hiding in there.

We felt like Tom Sawyer exploring a cave along the Mississippi River, and were fearful of finding, like him, some terrifying "Indian Jim," or a refugee from the law, hiding in the tunnel.

Deeper and deeper we walked into the darkness, dismayed, yet excited, about what we would find ahead. In the blackness one of our group would scream that they had come upon an ogre, a phantom, or some outlaw. Startled and frightened, we would turn and run as fast as we could back toward the pinpoint of light at the entrance to our cavern.

One big problem occurred as we hastily retreated. The homeless and the unemployed, after they had eaten one of Mom's tuna sandwiches, headed for the tunnel for some rest, and to relieve themselves. The smell of their deposits wafted through the tunnel, leaving a pungent odor to my nose. But worse followed. Occasionally, someone would step on a pile of poop, evoking groans and childhood curses at the stumblebum who had left his mark there. Back in the light, we found a stick to clear our shoes of the stickiest, smelliest poop on earth.

One blessing was that the guys wore black and white U.S. Keds, the only color available in those days. Like our Model A Ford, I could have any color I wanted as long as it was black. I wore my Keds for play, for school, and for tunnel trips. Fortunately, they washed easily. I found a hose bib, and washed them free of all the foul stuff, then put them on again for more play.

The only time I did not wear Keds was on Sunday mornings, when it was an absolute rule that I wear my Buster Brown shoes. Never was I to wear those shoes into our nearby tunnel, nor for play. Dire consequences were predicted if I did so.

All of our precious possessions were black in color: our Model A Ford, my US Keds, my father's suit, our family Bible, and finally the Bible I was awarded by our church on Easter Sunday. They were each in a funereal black. Perhaps it was a sign of the times. We were in the Great Depression and black symbolized the mood of the country.

We went into downtown Los Angeles that summer, my first such trip. Walt Disney Studios had produced their big hit "Snow White and the Seven Dwarfs." Emery Rutledge, our neighbor, got two cars and filled them with our neighborhood friends. We drove to a huge theater, beautifully decorated, and were fascinated with the Disney production. Afterwards he took us to a wonderful restaurant called Clifton's, a premier eatery. Inside were waterfalls, tropical trees and plants, creating an ambiance that roused our senses to amazement and to good eating.

We played many games together on Somerset Street. One was cross-dressing. The girls delighted in putting dresses on the guys, then laughing and pointing at their creations. Mr. Rutledge built a playhouse in his back yard, and the cross-dressing took place there. In the front yard we played a new game called MONOPOLY. Those games lasted all day as we bargained for properties, and for some kind of advantage over the rest of the players.

At lunchtime Mom made us tuna sandwiches and lemonade. Then we slipped into her new 1936 Dodge sedan, turned on the radio, and listened to "Portia Faces Life." A dramatic musical introit alerted us that another challenging episode was on the way. Portia endured many hardships, but then she prevailed against great odds. Perfect listening for the Depression years. Sometimes I think those radio shows became the building blocks for a later development called television.

On summer evenings we played "Hide and Seek" or "Kick the Can." One evening while playing "Kick the Can" I ran across Somerset Street to hide on the front porch of a house on the other side. Without looking, and full of excitement, I plunged forward. Just then a Model A Ford came down the hill toward us, and I was first in the path of danger. The driver accidentally hit me while I carelessly ran across the street.

Dad rushed out of the house as he heard yelling and screaming. He picked me up, laid me on the back seat of our Dodge, and sped to the nearest hospital. A doctor examined me and found no broken bones, and no apparent internal damage. But he ordered two days of rest for me. Mom's response was another of her classics, "All's well that ends well." She had a ton of folk wisdom available for every situation.

We built homemade skateboards and propelled ourselves up and down the hills, going farther and farther from home each day. The other guys nicknamed me "Daredevil" because I would go farther, faster than the rest of them. I relished that name, and like my father, wanted to prove myself. Sometimes we spotted a home under construction, and if no carpenters were present we would climb up the framework to the rooftop. Someone cried out, "Jump!" No one jumped but me. The Daredevil label was now fixed on me.

A defining moment occurred at this time. Mom and Dad had purchased a two-masted model sailing ship for me on my birthday. After the party was over and friends had gone home, I stepped into the back yard to put rigging on the ship so the masts were secured and sails could be attached. Cord had come with the ship and it should have been obvious what with directions and all to know how to attach the rigging and the sails. But the directions were back in the house, and instead of going back inside I plunged ahead to do it myself.

Soon I hopelessly tangled the rigging so that I could not proceed, and could not turn back and start over. Frustration turned to anger; I took the ship in my left hand and threw it down on the concrete driveway. Smashed to pieces it was now useless. Then I kicked the remnants aside. I looked back on that incident and saw a behavior pattern emerging where I gave up too easily and quit the task at hand.

My parents took the three of us to Sunday School at the First Presbyterian Church of El Sereno. I was cleaned and scrubbed, and wore my short pants and Buster Browns. They would drop us off at the church and return home while we went to class. However, on Christmas and Easter Sundays they would attend church with us. That was always special. Afterwards we took family photos in the front yard. During Easter Week of 1939 the church awarded us kids King James Bibles for our good attendance. We were off to a good start in life. But we knew nothing of the war fever that Hitler created in Europe, and that on September 1, WWII began for the European powers, and war would soon suck us into its fiery furnace.

Three

A New Home

1939 was a year of dark clouds and bright sunshine. My parents decided to move back to San Gabriel to a new subdivision going up on the north side of town. Hitler was preparing to invade Poland and spark WWII. Like most Americans we were isolationists: let the war fever remain in Europe. In today's world America plays world policeman in places like Iraq and Afghanistan. But that would have been unthinkable in 1939.

We were excited at the prospect of a new home. The home had just been completed and smelled of new wood and fresh paint. It had conveniences we had never seen before: a built in floor heater, crank windows, and a slot on our front porch for mail delivery to come directly into our house. There was a cabinet in the outside wall where the milkman could place our quarts of milk without ringing our doorbell. Checking everything, we kids dashed about, marveling at what we saw. We were no longer renters. We were now a part of the American dream. We owned our own home. Here was the future America laid out before us. This was the beginning of suburbia, the movement away from the city. The new mood was leave the city, come to suburbia. Our street looked so new, so bright, so clean, that we fell in love with it. So did the rest of America.

Dad had to act decisively to make it happen. It was still the Great Depression and loans were hard to come by. Dad asked uncle Frank for a loan of $500 to make the down payment on our $5,000 home. Frank demurred and wiggled out with an excuse. Behind his back Dad called him "an old tightwad." Dad expanded on that later with a more sardonic comment. He pulled out his pipe, tamped in his favorite Heine's Blend tobacco, took out a match, lighting it with a flick of his thumbnail on the match head. Holding the flaming match up to his pipe, he took several long draws, and then blew smoke rings into the air. His choice words were right out of his Chicago days, "He's tighter than the bark on a tree." Dad had a steady job and a bright future, and he finally found a bank that would loan him the whole amount. $500 seemed like a king's ransom to us in those days. What a contrast with America now!

We came together as a family to make our house into a home. Both front and rear were bare ground. We planted flowers and shrubs. Dad put in iron pipes in the front yard to create a sprinkler system, another new advance in home ownership. After that we put in grass seed, then spent months removing weeds from the grass.

Slowly, the empty lots on Milton Drive began to fill in with other new homes. We became a pretty neighborhood. Cars drove by to look at this new creation of California.

But over on the south side of San Gabriel was a community of Mexican-Americans. They had older homes with no sidewalks. The homes were often in disrepair, but some had beautiful gardens with white picket fences. Not far away was the San Gabriel Mission, built in 1771 by missionary fathers from Mexico, acting for the King of Spain.

We were living in the shadow of history with the Mission reminding us of our heritage. Yet few took the time to explore our heritage. Now south San Gabriel was populated by refugees from the Mexican Revolution. They came here to start a new life. They hoped for acceptance in this land of opportunity, but found instead segregation and suspicion. I was nine years old and I thought: *Mexicans live on the south side of the tracks. None of them went to our elementary school, and none went to our high school. They lived in a separate world apart from us.* It didn't occur to me to question that arrangement. I simply accepted it as *de facto*. Only many years later as an adult did it become clear to me that structuring neighborhoods like this wasn't accidental. It was planned. Some one in the City Hall created two separate communities believing it would be better for everyone that way. Segregation was alive in San Gabriel, and we chose to ignore it.

Sometimes we ventured south of the tracks and went to a restaurant by the Mission called El Poche. That was as much as we knew or wanted to know about "the other side." El Poche served great Mexican food, had beautiful gardens with fountains, and hosted a mariachi band on weekends. Dad would take us there on Friday nights and treat us to frijoles, rice and enchiladas. That was the extent of our knowledge of those who lived on the south side.

Many of the men toiled in our fields planting and harvesting local fruits and vegetables. Brown hands provided for our daily sustenance. Because they lived on the south side it was as if they were invisible. In twelve years of growing up in San Gabriel I never met a Hispanic youth in school or elsewhere. We paid no heed to the south side mostly out of ignorance and separation. We were the poorer for it. When I finally signed on for a class in Spanish at high school there was not a Spanish speaking person to be found. Occasionally one of our teachers did mention the great adventure of Spain colonizing its northern frontier of California with 21 Missions, and the friars who came along to bring civilization to this unknown land. When segregation settles into an area everyone loses. We grew up in separate worlds.

Meanwhile, at home a dynamic emerged in our family. Dad became close to Sybil, the oldest of we three kids. Mom drew close to me, the youngest, originally because I was so sickly and she wanted to take care of me. Carol became the in-between child and suffered from the lack of attention that inevitably followed. Dad started giving Sybil tennis lessons. She was a natural athlete. She caught on fast and soon won trophies playing tennis on the Alhambra High School team.

A New Home

Carol had no talents or interest in that direction and neither did I. I am sure that Dad must have felt some disappointment that I did not emerge as a jock like he did in his youth. Dad's discomfort came to a head on New Year's Day, 1941. Stanford was to play Nebraska in the Rose Bowl and we had tickets. I decided I did not want to go. I wanted to stay home and read a good book. Dad shook his head woefully as he went out the front door to our car.

Sybil soared at Alhambra High School in both athletics and in scholastics. Meanwhile, Carol and I fought each other. We didn't know terms like sibling rivalry, but we had such a rivalry, and it was intense. We got in fights regularly. We exchanged hostile words, and one of us would lash out in response. She tried to scratch my face with her fingernails. I punched her in the face and chest. She would cry out tearfully that I hurt her and soon our parents arrived to break it up. We both wanted our parent's love and did not know how to get a fair share and equal treatment with Sybil. The sibling fights settled nothing. Sybil was the star of our family, and Carol especially trailed far behind.

Winter nights had a wonderful charm. The best part was lying in bed and listening to a crackling fire. I collected eucalyptus wood from San Marino Park and brought it home on my bike. The eucalyptus wood was saturated with natural oil, and as it burned it gave off a popping sound and a unique fragrance throughout my bedroom. My room was at the back of the house and was the only room without an attic. Thus when it rained I could hear the staccato beat of raindrops on the roof. The cadence of raindrops created a rhythm that joined with the fire and the eucalyptus smell from the fireplace. It made me feel cozy and secure. Then I either turned on the radio for one of my favorite programs or read a book.

There was a powerful sense of quietness and strength in those winter nights. I learned to let my mind wander in free association. My imagination kicked in as I thought about traveling the world some day. One of the upshots of those winter nights was that I became something of a loner. I liked the ambience and the solitude of my room. There was no thought of loneliness. If I turned on my radio and tuned in to "Gangbusters" I became a crime fighter for 30 minutes. Or I could turn to "The Shadow" who knew the evil that lurks in the hearts of men. I could imagine what it was like to have knowledge like that. If I turned to "Grand Old Opry" I could sing along with Roy Acuff and the Smokey Mountain Boys and learn new songs. If I took one of my books I could read about Tom Sawyer and Huckleberry Finn. There were adventures there for a lifetime. I joined with Huck Finn on a raft trip down the Mississippi River. I was finding that the best moments in life occurred in that solitude.

But, I was socially awkward, especially around girls. I was attracted to a blond girl in Ms. Wallason's class named Mary Jane. But as close as I ever got to knowing her was to give her candy on Valentine's Day. Emblazoned on the candy were the words, I LOVE YOU. That is all she knew of my attraction to her. I got no response from her except an occasional smile.

The one person besides my Mom that I could talk to was Sybil. We had wonderful times together where she would tell me what girls like in a guy. She taught me to be respectful of the opposite sex. But I also wanted to know how to play with girls, and couldn't find out about that. Add to that the fact that I was sickly. Mom insisted that I come home immediately after school so she could "take care of me." Her heart was in the right place, but what I really needed was time with the guys after school. I was learning to be a loner just at a time in my life when I needed to develop socially.

Mom became protective of me. When Dad wanted to "bear down on me," because I was slow getting up on Saturday morning, she would intervene and say, "Now, Ed!" He would back off. It is no wonder that his nickname for Mom was "the Chief." In subtle ways she ran the household. Anytime he wanted to discipline me he had to get around Mom's control. That was not easy to do. I enjoyed the protection that she offered me, but it came with a price. It meant that I became mama's boy. I didn't recognize it at the time. I didn't understand such things. Slowly I intertwined with her in her protective cocoon.

I believe it was frustrating for Dad. He still tried to draw out the athlete that he hoped was inside of me. He bought a genuine pigskin football for me for Christmas. I liked it. Now when the neighborhood guys wanted a game I got selected first. I had the only pigskin football on the street. He also bought me a new Montgomery Ward bicycle. With that I began some riding trips with guys on the street. But in reality Dad spent more and more time with Sybil on the tennis courts at Alhambra. Mom drew ever closer to me. That dynamic was now in place.

I believe that Mom wanted me to grow up to be a Victorian gentleman. Her father had abandoned her and her sisters when she was three. I don't think she trusted men after that. So she was going to make sure that I turned out differently. I also think that in her heart she wanted me to become a minister. When Emery Rutledge, our neighbor, helped start a new Presbyterian congregation on Las Tunas Avenue, he extended an invitation to me to go with him each Sunday.

Mom would wake me up and say, "You look like the wild man of Borneo. Go clean up." I got out my new Buster Brown shoes while she ironed a freshly laundered shirt for me. I could hear the sizzle of the hot iron on cotton cloth, and smell the fragrance as she neatly pressed the shirt to perfection. The fragrance it created clung to my nose. I was now ready for church, and the only one in our family who went to church. At the very least, she thought, I could become a Christian man. That was fine with me. I enjoyed the trips with Emery to the Women's Clubhouse where the new church rented space on Sunday mornings.

There was another dimension to the emerging relationship between Mom and me. It was unspoken, but oh so subtle and so powerful. Sometimes I think what wasn't said is just as powerful as what is said. Mom established that sex, or the knowledge of sex, was prohibited in our household. No one mentioned it, and no one spoke of it. It was as if it did not exist. It became like a proverbial elephant in the front room. No one spoke of it, but it was there. I grew up in a neutered household. I was already shy with girls, and the prohibition exacerbated that shyness all the more.

Nature has a way, however, of speaking up. I began having bed-wetting episodes. I couldn't explain it. I would wake up in the morning and the sheets would be soaked. I was embarrassed. Mom would quickly come in, gather up my wet sheets, and take them to our service porch and wash them in our new Sears-Roebuck washing machine. It made a terrible clatter as it washed the sheets, but they came out clean. Later, another problem began. I awakened other mornings and my PJ's were soaked with semen. That was even more embarrassing. Mom would again gather my wet PJ's and wash them. I didn't understand what was happening. But it went on for months. I felt uncomfortable as I watched Mom change sheets once again.

Finally in desperation Dad walked me over to the historic Church of Our Savior Episcopal Church, a block away, and enrolled me in their Boy Scout Troop. I got a uniform, a Boy Scout axe, and a handbook. I soon became a proud Tenderfoot. One day Dad dog-eared a page in the handbook. He furtively handed it to me, and asked me to read it. This was hush-hush, something to be quietly perused in the privacy of my room.

Once alone, I opened to the page and found it was titled, "Nocturnal Emissions." This was a brand new concept to me. I read on and found out that young boys sometimes ejaculate in their sleep. But the book hurried on to point out that such emissions are "normal," and not to worry. But it didn't seem quite normal to me. I felt the sting of embarrassment about it as Mom washed my PJ's so many mornings. Now I was being inducted into the secret and prohibited world of sex, and I found out that it is a powerful thing, and not easily repressed. I kept what I learned to myself since no one in our home spoke openly of such realities. Sex and sexual knowledge was prohibited, but kept intruding.

The summer of 1941 held a special treat for us. Aunt Laurine and Uncle Frank, our only relatives on the west coast, invited us to join them at Santa Anita racetrack. Mom was not interested in betting on the races, but Dad and Laurine relished the opportunity to gamble. Laurine and Frank drove over from their new home in Whittier, and we met them at the front gate to the track. Just outside the entrance to the grandstands was a life-sized statue of the world's greatest racehorse, Sea Biscuit. We stood to marvel at the horse's grace and power.

The mid-day break was special. The track announcer told us to please stay in our seats; a special show was on the way. Suddenly, from out of the north came the sounds of huge motors bearing down on us. A P-38 interceptor plane flew over the rooftops and straight toward the track. The plane flashed silver in the sunlight, but it was actually unpainted aluminum. It was America's newest warplane. It looked and sounded formidable. I was eleven years old, and this was unlike anything I had ever seen before. I was awed.

At mid-field the pilot pulled back on the stick and the P-38 shot straight up into the sky. The powerful engines created a backwash over the track. The pilot kept climbing, hanging by his propellers in the sky. We thought surely the fighter plane must fall out of the sky and crash to earth. But, upwards he went, and we were breathless at the show. Then, almost out of sight, he leveled off, made one more swoop over the track, and raced back to his base in Burbank. That was our introduction to American air power. What an impact he made on us! There were only a few of those fighter planes in production, because America was officially isolationist. But within a couple of years planes like the P-38 would help turn the tide of war. I was now more in love with airplanes than ever before. I wanted to see all that I could of them, and dreamed of the day I would become a pilot and fly one.

Mom and Dad paid more attention to the news. They listened eagerly to President Roosevelt's speeches calling for America to be "the arsenal of democracy." If we couldn't build aircraft for our own forces, we could build them for the British, who were now being blitzed by Hitler's air power. Mom and Dad listened to the President's "fireside chats." Dad chuckled when Roosevelt referred to his political opponents as "those Republicans." He also liked the president's line as he campaigned against a Republican candidate, he would say, "Let us look at the record." My father loved the felicitous use of words.

Dad would let Roosevelt's favorite expressions roll off of his tongue. That and Dad's penchant for nicknames, and quotes from his favorite books made him a wordsmith. I picked up on this trait and learned to memorize key phrases, just like my father. My relationship to my mother was crucial in my formation, but in many ways I picked up on my father's traits, such as his fun with words. I also became a Democrat, just like my parents. I remained faithful for the rest of my life. Aren't decisions like this made when a child is young and impressionable? Later, as an adult, I found that getting my parents out of my head was a formidable task, as I tried to let go and get ready to move on with my own life.

I appealed to Dad to drive us out to Burbank and visit the Lockheed aircraft factory. Perhaps, I thought, I could see up close some P-38's coming off the production line. On Sunday morning December 7th, Dad and I packed into our new, 1941 Plymouth (for which he paid a princely sum of $600.00) and drove to Burbank. We got there fairly early. There were no freeways then, and Sunday morning traffic was light. Dad parked as close to the factory as possible. I urged him on so we could stand at the place where newly minted aircraft come off the line.

Congress had passed Roosevelt's Lend Lease Program, and Lockheed began a 24-hour production of a twin-engine bomber for the British. It was called the "Hudson." Inside the factory I could see workmen painting British insignia onto the wings, fuselage, and tail of each bomber. Camouflage paint had already been applied. Workers then fueled each bomber with high-octane gas. These machines of war were wheeled out on to the tarmac.

A pilot and co-pilot appeared and checked the flaps on the wings and tail section. When they were assured that everything was in working order, the pilots mounted a stepladder and disappeared into the plane. They checked all the gages of their front panel, and then their flight plan. They gave a thumbs-up to the crew outside, and the engine on the starboard side coughed, sputtered and smoked as the engine roared to life. Then after the same sequence on the port side, both engines blasted us with their backwash. The pilot checked his ailerons and flaps once again, waved at the ground crew, and headed out on the field.

Suddenly the pilot applied full throttle and the bomber roared down the field, heading to the east coast, and thence to the Battle of Britain. There I was eleven years old, goose bumps up and down my spine, my eyes filled with stars, as I pondered seeing history in the making. Dad said nothing, but I think he was thrilled as I was at the sight and sound of such power.

Suddenly a loud speaker crackled, and an authoritative voice announced in clear tones, "All visitors must leave the field IMMEDIATELY!" We turned and headed back to the car to listen to our radio. Every channel was urgently broadcasting the same amazing message: The Imperial Japanese Navy had bombed Pearl Harbor. All citizens were to stay tuned for further developments. All service personnel were to return to their posts at once. All military leaves were cancelled. The next day we listened as President Roosevelt asked Congress for a Declaration of War, calling December 7th "A day that will live in infamy." Our parents had a clearer fix on what all of this meant for America. All we kids knew was that excitement was in the air. Our home, along with millions of others, would soon feel the impact of war. World War II had finally come to America, and it would change our lives forever.

Four

The Home Front

The New Year opened with bad news. In the Pacific the British, Dutch and Americans were suffering huge losses to the Japanese. On the east coast German subs sank American ships at an alarming rate. My father was offered a commission in the Signal Corps of the United States Army as a second lieutenant. He was ready to serve his country along with millions of other men who volunteered for the armed forces. He was not in line to be drafted because of his age. But he compared Army pay with what he got at Western Union and decided our family could not survive on military pay. He declined the Army's offer.

I watched him from a distance as he wrestled with that decision. I was a child in a man's world, barely 12 years old. The world began to look more threatening. I asked him, "Are you going away?" hoping his answer would be "No." I needed him in ways that he did not understand. He said "No" to the Army, but offered me no reassurance of his care. That was not his to give.

Sybil and her boyfriend Jim spent countless hours together that spring dating and talking about their future. Jim knew he would be drafted into the Army just as soon as he graduated in June of '42. But he had already decided that he wanted to become a pilot in the Army Air

Corps, and he volunteered for that before the local draft board called his number. Sybil had decided that she would go to Pasadena City College after she graduated in June. She wanted to become a nurse and be ready to serve in the military after her training was completed.

Wartime rationing began. Along with our neighbors we received stamps that allowed us to purchase restricted amounts of sugar, meat, gas, and tires. It was my job to save our empty Folger's coffee cans. After breakfast each morning I poured our bacon grease into the can and set it aside. When the can was full we took it to a collection station where it was processed into an ingredient for TNT. We were asked to grow our own vegetables by planting "Victory Gardens."

However, my crops were paltry, undersized, and not tasty. I liked growing vegetables, but I found that they are like people. They need lots of attention if they are to thrive. I lacked people skills and maybe that is why I was deficient in our victory garden. I planted a victory garden every summer of the war and never got good results. Finally, I quit trying when the war was over.

Jim and Sybil decided to go dancing at the famous Hollywood Palladium. I wanted to go too. Jim and I had become buddies and he agreed with Sybil to take me along. I really liked Jim. He had a big, boyish grin, a friendly disposition, and was deeply in love with Sybil. I looked up to him as a role model. The big band era was in full swing, and as we entered we could hear the loud syncopation of dance music. Were we hearing Tommy Dorsey? Harry James? Or was it Glenn Miller? All I heard was a big band sound. Songs like "American Patrol" echoed through the dance hall.

Patriotism rose to the surface as men and women danced to the music. *Am I really seeing this?* I thought. *Yes, this is real.* I was surrounded by a sea of uniforms that shimmered and swayed like a field of wheat on a breezy day. Most would soon be shipped out to training bases or to other wartime assignments. When a slow dance played they held their sweetheart's ever so closely. They knew they might not see each other again. For fast dances they did the jitterbug. We found a table and I watched as my sister and Jim held each other romantically while they danced. In the swirl of music and uniforms, I felt that the war, which seemed so remote, had finally come home to all of them and to me. Now I too was a part of this great world war.

There was fear along the California coast. Our neighbors spoke openly of a possible Japanese invasion. The Japanese Navy had attacked Pearl Harbor successfully, and we thought they could do it again along our coast.

Behind our back yard fence was a small farm where a Japanese-American raised gladioli flowers for commercial sales. The flowers were a field of beauty in the spring. But in the spring of '42 the FBI came and took him and his family into internment. They were put into hastily built tarpaper shacks at Santa Anita racetrack, and held until some could be sent elsewhere further inland. Around the perimeter of Santa Anita a barbed wire fence was put up with gun towers to enforce their incarceration. All Japanese Americans were held in such camps for the duration of the war. Wartime fears were spreading and my neighbors no longer called them "Japanese," but now they were labeled "Japs." Garish cartoons appeared in our newspapers that portrayed them as buck-toothed monkeys.

Somehow in wartime one of the great casualties of war is the truth. That casualty appeared now. I was too young to understand how the Constitution was trampled in 1942, but years later I came to see it as a travesty of justice to arrest American citizens without cause and hold them in armed camps for the duration of the war. When Americans are frightened they can do ugly things to the Constitution. My patriotism kept me from seeing it at the time.

My neighbor's farm was put up for auction due to failure to pay property taxes. (Impossible to do when he was behind barbed wire.) His property was purchased by a group of doctors and built into a retreat where they could relax. Our Japanese neighbor could never come home again.

There are parallels here with American responses to Muslim extremism. In cartoons Muslims are portrayed as gangsters. We have a tendency to put them into piles, labeling them as bad guys. We see them as the bad guys and we the good guys. Once again the Constitution is being stretched because of our fears. Will we rue the day that we allowed some Muslims to be tortured as our prisoners? Sometimes the Detention Center at Guantanamo Bay in Cuba reminds me of the tarpaper shacks at Santa Anita. Will we later regret the denial of due process of law to them as we did with Japanese Americans?

Spotter Stations were hastily built up and down the California coast. The stations looked like lifeguard outposts, but they were different. They existed in a chain right up the coast to Oregon. A spotter was located in each post and was charged with looking for saboteurs coming ashore from enemy submarines, and for enemy aircraft.

To help spot aircraft correctly we were asked to build scale models of wartime airplanes. The spotters used our models in their stations to help them distinguish friendly aircraft from the Japanese. I decided to build a twin engine B-25 Billy Mitchell bomber. I bought a kit with a diagram showing how to build it to scale. I then took a piece of pine and whittled the fuselage to shape. On the way to Washington Elementary I sanded it to a smooth finish. As I approached the woodshop the guys standing on the front stoop burst into laughter when they saw me. As I sanded the 6" fuselage it looked like I was masturbating. My face turned red when I realized what had happened. I decided to finish the sanding later. I completed the model later and sent it off to the spotters after I applied olive drab "dope" and American insignia.

One night in February a spotter swore he saw a "Jap" bomber coming in over Los Angeles. He reported it and soon antiaircraft batteries opened up on the "enemy" plane. We had a battery two miles away located in San Marino Park. They started firing too, creating a roar that rattled our windows and shook our home. Christopher, our dog went crazy. We waited anxiously in the front room, but no bombs fell. An all clear sounded and the "raid" was over. There was no Japanese bomber after all. That night revealed how afraid we were of the Japanese.

I developed a savings habit. I had a cedar wood chest in my room, and I filled it with left over change at the end of each day. The government asked all Americans to show their patriotism by purchasing war bonds that would help finance our war effort. I rode my bike over to the Post Office and picked up a war bond savings book, and purchased 25-cent stamps to paste into it. When the total number of stamps reached a value of $18.50 the postmaster gave me a Series E War Bond worth $25.00. It matured in 10 years. By the end of the war I had taken my first steps not only into patriotism, but had learned the rudiments of investing for the future. I carried the savings habit into adult life and it has served me well.

On Main Street in Alhambra Uncle Sam brought in a captured German Messerschmitt ME 109 fighter plane shot down during the Battle of Britain. It was placed in the center of the street where it would block traffic and encourage people to get out of their cars, look, and hopefully buy war bonds.

To me it was like looking at the P-38 that I saw at Santa Anita racetrack in 1941. Only the Nazi fighter plane had wing-mounted guns that probed menacingly forward. The nose was painted yellow. German insignia were prominent on the wings, fuselage and tail. Here was the enemy, tamed for the moment, and it aroused fear and loathing in the crowd. It was a visible symbol of Hitler's tyranny over Europe, the most feared weapon in his aerial arsenal. The sale of war bonds heated up. Americans were now in this fight, and it was a great cause against Hitler's tyranny. We too wanted to be a part of such an effort. I was right there with them, and felt proud that I had already purchased war bonds. My patriotism blossomed.

The dynamic at home deepened. Dad spent a great deal of time with my oldest sister Sybil playing tennis on Saturday mornings. She became captain of Alhambra High's tennis team. He celebrated her tennis trophies with the men at Len's tennis shop at Alhambra Park. Sybil became the star of our family. When I went to Alhambra High two years later her teachers remembered her and asked me to be a good student like her. I said nothing, but felt uncomfortable. "Syb," after all, was my forever buddy. In my eyes every woman should be like Sybil: strong, smart, a good athlete, and an outstanding student. She was like a universal woman. She could do whatever she set her mind to.

Was this a kind of "sister worship?" Perhaps. But at this point in time I needed role models. Sybil was my ideal female. Not surprisingly, I didn't find any girls like her in the neighborhood.

Mom spent more time with me, taking care of me, while Carol, the middle child, remained on the margins. Head colds were a frequent complaint with me, each one held in check by a dirty sock around my neck. I also had all the typical childhood illnesses. I continued to come home right after school so Mom could make sure I was under her watchful eye. I chafed at what looked like control to me, but I was also drawn to the cocoon of protection that she offered. I willingly submitted to her care. I think my father began to non-verbally resent me for intruding into his relationship with Mom. I sensed it, but made no comment.

I noticed that Mom and Dad no longer spoke terms of endearment to one another. Dad nicknamed Mom "Chief," and he used it for general conversations. But when he felt more sentimental he called Mom "Liza." I never saw them hold hands. I never saw them kiss. I did not hear the precious words spoken, "I love you." Maybe their generation learned not to show affection openly. Perhaps those things happened only behind closed doors. I only know that I did not see it or hear it. My bedroom door was 10 feet down the hall from their bedroom door. In those wartime years I did not hear the bedsprings squeak. I couldn't put my feelings into words. But I knew that something was missing in our home; I just couldn't name it. Maybe I could call it love.

The summer of '42 turned out to be a disaster for our family. Mom became severely ill. A doctor came to our home to examine her. His diagnosis of Rheumatic Fever hit us hard. I didn't know what that was, but I knew my mother was seriously ill. She was ordered to complete bed rest, and we were to take care of her needs until further notice.

We kids learned to get up in the morning, get a box of cereal, a bowl and spoon and pour on some milk. Dad reversed a lifelong process and cooked bacon and eggs for Mom and himself. Sybil, as the oldest child, would take the plate to Mom and help her eat breakfast in bed. I learned to take care of myself. I put together a peanut butter sandwich, an apple, and a thermos of milk for a lunch. It fit snugly into my black metal lunch pail.

Mom remained bedridden into the fall months. When she was finally able to get up her health was seriously impacted. Rheumatic Fever morphed into rheumatoid arthritis, the most severe type of arthritis, and held her body hostage for the rest of her life. Slowly, year-by-year, her body began to change. The toes on her right foot splayed to the right. The toes on her left foot splayed to the left. No longer could she wear shoes. Only slippers would fit her feet. Her hands began to stiffen. Her knees swelled to twice their normal size. Eventually she started walking with a cane. Later, she got around in a wheelchair. Her heart was impacted also. She did not give an exact name for her heart problem, but it did not function normally again.

Crippled, she did her best to carry on with her duties. She did all of her household chores as before, but now much more slowly. When she sat down to rest she took out her Bible to read. She read and prayed for a half hour at a time. Her favorite verse was Ecclesiastes 11:1, "Cast your bread upon the waters, and you will find it after many days." As she went back to her household chores, she mopped the kitchen floor with her rag mop, and sang or hummed the old gospel hymn "Bringing in the Sheaves."

I never heard her complain about the pain the arthritis caused her, or the limits placed on her life. Was that another quality that she learned from Grandma Stanton? Or was that something that she learned at her childhood Presbyterian Church? Whatever the source, she learned to quietly endure the worst that life had to offer. Her doctor prescribed gold shots. That and Aspirin helped moderate the pain somewhat. She remained stoic in the midst of pain. I was too young to realize what an amazing gift of grace she possessed.

Whatever I learned of sensitivity toward people, I learned from my mother. Whatever I learned of love for books, I learned from my mother. Whatever I learned about cherishing gospel hymns, I learned from her.

Many years later when I felt called to ministry, somewhere in my heart I knew it was what Mom wanted for me.

Sitting at her bedside after school, she revealed to me several times that her arthritis was God's punishment on her for some past sin. She could not explain to me what her mortal sin was. But she carried the burden of that "sin" quietly for the rest of her life. I could not talk her out of it. Later, I found that other adults harbored the same fear. Like Mom they did not deal with it openly, but silently suffered from such ideas in their mind.

I learned, like Mom, to keep my feelings to myself. As I emerged into teen years I avoided complaints. I kept my frustrations to myself. However, I found that such decisions could also become a handicap. My friends did not always understand my behavior. I was more of a loner when I kept my fears to myself.

We were regular subscribers to the "Los Angeles Times" newspaper. The Times began printing colorful full-page maps of war zones. The map of the Solomon Islands campaign caught my eye. I cut it out and posted it on the wall of my room. I followed the war stories of valiant Marines who built a perimeter around Henderson Field on Guadalcanal. The Japanese attacked again and again trying to break through the Marine defense. They failed as the Marines beat back each attack. Offshore, the allied fleet and the Japanese fleet clashed in titanic battles. Sailors called the area "Iron bottom sound" for all ships that were sunk there.

Those war stories sparked my imagination. I begged my parents to let me enlist in the Marines, even though I was only 12. I saw myself as offering my services to the men on the front lines. I could bring ammo and C-rations to the men fighting on the perimeter. Mom's response was always the same, "Don't be foolish!" Sometimes to reinforce her response she called me "Dickie," a reminder that I was still a child. I hated that name. "Mom," I called out, "Don't call me that." I was reaching out to be big like Jim Pettit.

Maybe I should have walked right over to the nearest recruiting office and offered myself to the Marines. What if I had presented myself to the recruiting sergeant in charge and requested permission to enlist? Perhaps he would have made me an honorary Marine. Maybe he would have made me a poster boy for home front morale. I certainly was full of encouragement for the Marines. I would have been proud to wear the dress blue uniform, and then switch to battle fatigues to bring supplies to the front lines. I loved to dream thoughts like that.

At the same time Dad began bringing home books about the war. I read William L. White's book, "Queens Die Proudly" just as soon as Dad finished it. That was the story of a B-17 squadron stationed at Clark Field in the Philippines in 1941. Then he brought home the book "They Were Expendable," the saga of P. T. boats based in Manila Bay in 1941. Against overwhelming odds these tiny boats carried the fight to the Japanese Navy. But they finally had to retreat to bases in Australia. I read those stories with deep interest, and wanted more. My friend Stan Henry and I rode our bikes to Vroman's bookstore in Pasadena and perused for hours for more war stories. My sense of patriotism blossomed.

My childhood illnesses and problems mounted. I had boils, asthma, hay fever, head colds, nocturnal emissions, and bed-wetting. Mom's remedies were the same: a dirty sock around my neck for head colds, and home after school for my other illnesses so she could check on me. I think she must have sensed that I had self-esteem problems, because now she began to quote Emile Coue's dictum "Every day and every way I am getting better and better." Then she asked me to repeat it back to her. Mom asked, "Do you believe it? Yes, Mom, I believe you," I responded. She sounded like the woman in a radio program who stood at the door and called with the voice of a Jewish mother, "Henry, Henry Aldrich." That was her signal for me to come and take my medicine.

I also developed a slouch. I was getting taller, but didn't want to be noticed. A slouch seemed to me a good way to deal with my tallness. Mom could see that and her response was to throw her shoulders back and tell me to "Stand up straight!" I did so, but later reverted to a slouch again. At other times she threw her shoulders back, looked at me with grave determination and said, "Be a man!" That put more emphasis into my mind, and I held my shoulders straight for a longer period of time. It took me a long time to learn that my eventual height (6'1/2") could be an asset rather than a liability. I still need to remember to throw my shoulders back and stand tall. It is too easy to fall back into a slouch.

I was ready to earn some money and began delivering the Los Angeles Times every morning. I got up at 4:30 am and quietly brought in the bundle of papers from our driveway and into the kitchen. I shut all the doors to the kitchen and folded the papers. Then I could throw them for delivery to each driveway. As I folded the papers the headlines jumped out at me: great sea and island battles in the Pacific, and fierce fighting in North Africa. General Rommel, the "Desert Fox," kept outflanking the British. The men of the Afrika Corps sang "The Ballad of Lili Marlene." So did the Tommies. So did I. Music became a part of the battlefield. It resonated with me. I began to develop a historical awareness of the war. I have carried it ever since then. Now as I listen to world news I see modern conflicts in the context of history. It bothers me that my fellow Americans are so deficient in remembering our past. George Santayana said it well, "Those who fail to learn from history are doomed to repeat it."

Printer's ink was all over my hands by the time I finished folding papers. But that ink smelled of the work I was doing, and the learning going on in my mind of the tides in human history and their impact on us. I came to love history through that smelly ink on my hands, and it is no wonder that some day I would teach history in college.

When I was 13 I had my first anxiety attack. I didn't know the word "anxiety," but I knew how I felt. My heart began to race, and I felt ill at ease at a moment when nothing was present to threaten me. I didn't understand what was happening to me. And, of course, just like Mom, I told no one, but held my fears inside. I jumped up and down, but my heart wouldn't stop racing. So I quickly walked around the block. However, the anxiety did not go away.

Finally, I developed a remedy. By now our fledgling Presbyterian Church had a full time pastor, although he was a senior retired minister with a shock of white hair. The regular pastor had enlisted as a Chaplain in the U.S. Army for what we called "the duration of the war." I rode my bicycle to our pastor's home after school. He graciously invited me inside. I slowly got to the point, and I tried my best to describe a feeling that I really did not understand. I felt foolish trying to explain such deep discomfort when nothing was present to warrant such fear. I am not sure that he understood what I was trying to say. Finally, to help bring the conversation to a close he said, "Let me pray for you." Afterward I said "Thanks for the prayer." I felt better for the prayer, but I did not feel understood.

When I was not understood I felt a depth of loneliness that is hard to express. There was little communication in our home, and touching was always limited. Now to feel misunderstood by my pastor was an added burden that I did not handle well. My pastor was the only person I talked to about my anxiety, and if he didn't comprehend what I was trying to tell him, who would? I was alone, and I didn't know what to do about it.

Because of Mom's illness I was charged with the task of shopping at the nearby Market Basket store for our groceries. Mom would make a shopping list and I would fill her order. Market Basket had a Holland Dutch bakery and it was easy to purchase Dad's favorite treats: bear claws, or a velvet crumb coffee cake. I got to know the grocery aisles pretty well and filled the basket with canned food.

At the cash register there were numerous wartime posters. There was one that announced "Smokes for the Boys." We would put spare change into a box that would go toward cigarettes for our troops. Even though Dad's Lucky Strikes choked me when I had asthma, I went ahead and put in change "for the boys." The cashier also had decals of American divisions serving in the war. I bought some and applied them to my bicycle. Nearby were wartime posters designed to inspire us and to warn us, "Loose Lips Sink Ships." If ever I knew anything about Jim's movements in the Army Air Corps, I was to keep that to myself. Another said, "Keep 'Em Flying." One showed Uncle Sam pointing straight at me and said, "Buy War Bonds." *Thanks Uncle Sam, but I already do that.*

Then I got a treat. On the east side of the store was a drug counter with a large magazine rack. Supervising the area was an old druggist with a tic in one eye. As I gazed at the latest edition of "Air War" magazine, he kept a beady eye on me. The more he spied on me the more urgent became the tic. Then his mouth curved into an inverted crescent as I opened the magazine. On the cover of the magazine an artist painted a lurid picture of a wounded "Jap" pilot, hit by bullets from an American fighter plane, going down in flames. The old druggist didn't approve of my browsing in his magazines. He always glowered at me. Silently, I felt sorry for the old geezer with the upside down grimace. But I felt as though I had earned the right to look at wartime magazines. After all, I thought, I will fly a war bird some day and shoot down "Japs" too.

Aircraft factories blossomed all over southern California. They made the wartime aircraft for our armed services. The nearest factory was built by Consolidated-Vultee, and they made basic trainers for the Army Air Corps. Those were the planes that student pilots used to learn their flying skills. I wrote a letter to the president of the company and asked if I could have a job helping to produce the planes. I planned to ride my bicycle about 20 miles to get there and work for them during the summer vacation of 1943. Or maybe I could find someone from our neighborhood that worked there and could give me a ride.

The company wrote a polite refusal, thanking me for eagerness to serve, but reminded me that to hire a 13 year old would be a violation of the law. I wanted a tangible way to serve my country, but had to settle for reading books, planting a victory garden, and buying war bonds. Still, I got the consolation of listening to warplanes flying overhead. Their engines had a deep-throated roar that I learned to quickly identify.

Jim Pettit was stationed at Luke Field in Tucson, Arizona for more training. While on leave to see Sybil, he gave me a belt of six, live 50-caliber bullets that I mounted upright on the mantle over my fireplace. They were huge, and reminded me of the killing power of our bullets. Whoever got hit by one of these would not live long. It never occurred to me that putting them over the fireplace was a very dangerous place for live ammunition. He also brought me one of his khaki uniforms that I proudly wore whenever I could. Lastly, he sent me a subscription to "Flying" magazine. The magazine had a section of color photos of American military aircraft in service overseas. Each month I cut them out and mounted them into albums. I turned my room into a military ready room to stay abreast of the war.

I also needed a quiet place where I could be alone. Most Sundays I chose to go to Sunday school with Mr. Rutledge to the new Presbyterian Church he was organizing. But some Sundays I loaded Christopher, our black cocker spaniel, into the box I had built on top of the rear fender of my Montgomery Ward's bike. Then I tied a bright aluminum cup to his ID collar. If Chris got thirsty along the way, I could stop, fill his cup with water, and give him a drink.

We rode down Longden Avenue and followed it all the way to Santa Anita racetrack, about five miles away. When I pedaled fast Chris' long floppy ears caught the wind and flapped gaily, much like Dumbo's when he learned to fly. Together, we made a funny sight. Sometimes at boulevard stops folks would pull alongside, reach out from the passenger side of their car, and put coins in Chris' cup. Chris woofed and wagged his tail. We all laughed and continued down the boulevard.

However, at the Santa Anita racetrack I always paused to look at the barbed wire and the gun towers that kept Japanese-Americans locked inside. The tarpaper shacks looked flimsy. The gun towers looked menacing. One of those citizens inside was my neighbor, and I didn't know what to say. I looked for him, but all I saw were people quietly shuffling from one tarpaper shack to another. They were humiliated by their imprisonment. It felt strange to me as I took in the scene.

Civil rights and liberties were unknown to me. Yet to know that my neighbor was locked inside and guarded by armed American soldiers did not seem right. But we didn't question our president when he ordered Japanese-Americans interned. Security was the key phrase. So America set the Constitution aside, and as a youth in a man's world, I quietly watched it happen. But, at the same time I also failed to see the incongruity between my concern for my Japanese-American neighbor, and my desire to become a fighter pilot so I could shoot down some warplanes in the Pacific. That came later.

After a pause I pedaled on toward Sierra Madre Boulevard, a broad, sweeping street leading into the San Gabriel Mountains. I turned onto the boulevard and headed several miles up the mountain. It got so steep that I got off my bike and walked the bike while Chris got to ride. At Chantry Flats I parked, grabbed our supplies, and lowered Christopher to the ground so he could sniff and pee. Off to the side a trail headed down into the canyon below. "C'mon Chris," I called, urging him away from a bush he inspected before he saluted it.

The deeper into the canyon I went the cooler the trail became. At the bottom of the canyon was a stream that bubbled down from the mountain above. Pausing, I could hear the sound of silence. Then I could hear birds singing, and see frogs sunning themselves along the creek. I listened as the water made a pleasing gurgle while winding its way down the mountain. The air held an aroma of the surrounding trees and bushes. The sun broke through in shafts of light, and trees created cool shadows. The war became very distant in this place.

Off to the left I saw a snake quietly approaching the stream. His beady eyes were on a frog that sat on a rock at the water's edge. The frog looked out over the water. The snake edged behind the frog, opened his mouth, and with a swift strike, clamped his jaws on the frog's hindquarters. Once he had secured the frog he began slowly to draw the frog ever deeper into his gullet. The frog remained silent, and stared straight ahead without blinking an eye, even though he was doomed. Surely he would croak in distress as he was slowly sucked into the mouth of the snake. But no, he remained silent.

I had thought my secret hiding place was the Garden of Eden. Here was a paradise, unlike anything else in our valley, but the snake turned it into a fallen world of death, and of warfare. The world was at war. All of us had taken sides. Here was a war of survival even in this paradise. This place of beauty was very much a part of the world. Who was the poet who said dolefully, "Even in Arcadia there is death"? I quietly watched, disappointed that the frog met such a fate, and disappointed that this too was part of Creation. I asked myself, but got no response, "Why did God make it that way?"

Up and deeper into the canyon we went. We followed the trail. No one else was there. Shadows increased. Moisture hung in the air. Finally, I heard the distant sound of a waterfall, the sound I had come to listen to. We arrived in the shadows surrounding Sturtevant Falls, the best-kept secret in the San Gabriel Mountains. It was a shimmering cascade of water falling to the rocks below, in a shady corner of the mountains. This is what we came for. I stood and took in the scene, and the tranquility of it all. I let the sight, the sounds, and the coolness sink into my senses; the rushing, cascading water created music for my soul. Christopher and I found a flat rock, and sat down to enjoy the solitude and the peace. There I found that nature heals. I don't know how, but this was a mystical place for me.

I fed Chris from the bag of dog food that I had brought. The peanut butter sandwich made a good lunch for me. The cool water at the foot of the falls was so sweet that I drank it without hesitation, and wanted to drink more. Up above was Mt. Wilson, where winter snows had melted to create this idyllic waterfall. We stayed and lingered as long as we could. Every kid, I thought, needs a secret hiding place, a place where he can dream dreams, and let his imagination roam free. Without that kind of time, life is just activity without meaning.

Finally, reality intruded. We had to turn around and head for home. Riding downhill on Sierra Madre Boulevard with Chris' Dumbo ears flopping in the wind, his mouth open to take in the fresh air, was another treat. But it was time to return to the real world. My inner world at home was in shambles. I was physically growing up, but I was not maturing. I kept my dilemmas myself, and now paid for it with anxiety attacks. Sturtevant Falls was my escape. But the escape was only temporary.

Another incident on that same trail had an impact on my patriotism. I took Chris toward my secret hiding place several weeks later. Along the trail I met two soldiers who were stationed at Santa Anita. Their task was to guard the Japanese-Americans interned at the racetrack. They invited me to join them. One soldier gave me his garrison cap and I wore it proudly. We followed the trail around the falls and continued up the mountain. We stopped to rest and drink from the cool water. After we had drunk and refreshed ourselves, one of the soldiers stepped to the stream's edge and urinated into the pristine water.

That was the same water from which we drank! That was pure water, coming down the mountain from melting snow above, or from some hidden aquifer deep in the heart of the mountain. That was water flowing from the depths of creation, and it was clear. Shocked, I said nothing, but I was offended. *Can't you go pee on a rock, or like Chris, let fly on a nearby tree? Even my dog has enough sense to do that.* That is what I wanted to say.

He, on the other hand, was nonchalant, as if this was a common occurrence. In my eyes he had polluted not only the stream, but had poisoned the well of God's Creation. That soldier became a symbol to me of the cleft in our human nature that affected all of us. I had been idolizing the men who went off to war to fight against fascist tyranny. But now I found a new reality that impacted my wartime patriotism, and my naiveté. In that moment I realized that all of us participate in what my Sunday school teacher called, "original sin." My wartime patriotism took a hit, and I got another glimmer of life in a fallen world. I turned around with Chris at my side and went down the trail without them. My paradise had been cracked open again.

I rode home with my new garrison cap firmly mounted on my head. I pedaled furiously, creating a breeze that kept Christopher's ears flopping in the wind. That and a grin, which seemed to appear on his face as he gulped fresh air, kept cars honking and passengers waving as we headed home. I think people needed a diversion from the heavy war news, and from the gold stars that appeared in more windows. Each gold star stood for a family member killed in action. Chris and I would have made a good painting for Norman Rockwell on the cover of "Saturday Evening

Post." What a light-hearted scene we made as I pedaled down the streets: a boy and his dog out for a day in the sun.

In January 1944 I was set to graduate from Washington Elementary School. Our teacher, Ms. Hutchinson, gave each of us an opportunity to give something to the war effort. We made a list of each class member's contribution, and read it to our proud parents at the graduation ceremony. My contribution was: "Dick wills his Keds to the U.S. Army in hopes that they will be used for de-feat." That created a ripple of laughter across the audience, and nicely moved me out of elementary school and into high school.

On the opening day for Alhambra High School, John Maize and I stood at the bus stop on Roses Road. John and I got into an argument as we waited for the big yellow school bus driven by a man named Slim. Dad had brought home a set of illustrated books about dinosaurs. I was fascinated by the illustrations inside. For Dad, the books confirmed his skepticism about how creation happened. It was by evolution, not by divine fiat.

For me the information simply revealed that God took the long way around to create the apex of his wonderful work: Adam and Eve. Maybe God was a creative evolutionist. My book of dinosaurs insisted on the verity of evolution. But I refused to kowtow to those scientists. Albert Schweitzer once said that the fly in the ointment of all theories is that they try to prove too much and carry their conclusion too far. I saw truth in the scientific explanation, but simply refused to believe that we were biological accidents on the face of the earth.

The book of Genesis made the greatest statement of faith ever made when the author, a biblical author, said, "In the beginning God created the heavens and the earth." Then he wrote that we are "made in the image of God." I held to that faith. But how can I explain that? I told John about the book of dinosaurs, but before I could go on with the truth of Genesis, John reacted. "Well," he angrily replied, "God created the world in seven days, and the book of Genesis says so. You're wrong if you believe that other book. I don't want to see it."

Soon we were hurling words back and forth at each other. The school bus arrived and Slim flipped open the doors of the bus for us. He saw trouble brewing. He had on a pair of brown, unfinished leather gloves that gave him an air of authority. With his steely-eyed look we quit arguing to climb aboard. Slim motioned for us to sit in front row seats, on opposite sides of the bus. Slim kept a watchful eye on us. He always maintained control and would stop the bus if necessary to keep the peace. John and I settled into a fragile silence. Years later we went to our high school reunions together, but we didn't talk about the age of dinosaurs any longer.

The first day of classes at Alhambra High was misery for me. Unknown to me, a jock on the football team, Bill Storey, hung a condom on the rear pocket of my new corduroy pants. All the jocks wore faded Levi's, white T-shirts, and penny loafers or a pair of Mexican sandals. I, on the other hand, wore a bright, colorful homemade shirt of blues, reds and white. Mom had sewn it just for this occasion. With my new corduroys and shirt I became a marked man, but I did not know it.

Like Joseph and his famous coat of many colors, who became an object of scorn to his brothers, so did I. Joseph was sold into slavery by his brothers. I think I know what he felt like. I wasn't sold into slavery, but it felt just as bad to me. I must have worn the condom draping off my back pocket, for at least an hour. No student bothered to tell me, but instead giggled behind my back. The embarrassment of discovery was beyond description.

The next hurdle on opening day was roll call in each class. Except for the teachers who had taught Sybil and Carol, the others mispronounced my name. Imagine for a moment how the name Bastear can be mangled. Usually my name was called so strangely that the class laughed while I corrected the teacher.

A gauntlet of bullying followed in the boy's gym class. We had to take showers after class. Dubbed "knobby knees," or "string bean," special treatment waited for me and other freshmen in the shower room. As we emerged from our showers we proceeded to the drying room. As we exited from the showers, upper classmen would stand at the entrance to the drying room with wet towels and snap us on the butt until we could scoot out of range. They howled with laughter as we lowly freshmen endured their torment. They thought it was great fun. "Hey, I got one," shouted an upper classman as he snapped his wet towel across my butt. Another upper classman shouted, "Look, I got the skinny one. He runs like a bunny rabbit. Hee, Hee." For us it was misery.

We dared not complain to the coaches. That would have marked us for even more maltreatment. The coaches sauntered to their offices on the other side of the gym while all of this was going on. I came to hate the coaching staff. If I could have graded them they would have all received F's. They developed a statewide championship football team, and we went out to cheer the team to victory. But in my mind the coaches' failure to supervise the locker room after class cancelled what they did with the football team.

Some adults may casually reply, "Boys will be boys." However, there was much more going on in the minds of our antagonists. The upperclassmen learned to be arrogant and domineering. We on the receiving end became victims. Neither outcome served them or us very well. Yet no one on campus put a stop to the bullying.

Often I fantasized that Jim Pettit would come home on leave in his full dress uniform as an Army Air Corps officer, and walk across campus with me. My peers would see me with an authentic war hero, and then they might have some respect for me. But Jim was never able to walk across the campus with me. I had to learn to gain respect on my own.

Things were heating up for Sybil. She had dated Jim all through high school. But our next-door neighbor was also an attractive young man named Bill Yates. He entered the submarine service soon after Pearl Harbor. Up to that point he disdained any meaningful time with Sybil. All she got was a doleful "Hi" from him, and no more.

But she had become president of the Girls Athletic Association, a member of the Girls League, president of the Tennis Club, a life member of the California Scholastic Federation, and the winner of a Nursing

Scholarship. Sybil morphed into a lovely lady, attractive and smart. Bill came home from a tour of duty in the north Pacific where his submarine patrolled, looking for Japanese ships to sink. Sybil was now attending Pasadena City College and looked sharper than ever. Bill took a fresh look at this girl next door and suddenly decided he really wanted to get acquainted. He came to our house for visits and spent more time with Sybil than he did with his mother next door.

I got acquainted with Bill too. I was part of the drama of his meeting Sybil. Bill shared stories of his submarine service. He told how he served on what was called "a pigboat," a leaky WWI diesel submarine. Because the crew was crowded together, he had to sleep on a torpedo. That information boggled my mind. Now, in my estimation, Bill was a hero also. It was soon obvious that Sybil and Bill were falling in love. Bill stood tall, and in his Navy white ducks created an aura of strength and purpose. When Bill walked into the room all eyes turned to him. "Hello. How are you?" he would ask, as he stood tall and straight, and looked each person in the eye. He instantly commanded respect. He was the polar opposite of Jim. Whereas Jim was boyish and had an easy going "Hi," Bill was a take-charge kind of guy.

While on leave Bill applied to his Congressman for an appointment to the U.S. Naval Academy in Annapolis, Maryland. He was granted entrance with the next class. That meant decision time for him and Sybil. Like other wartime romances, Bill proposed. Sybil hesitated. Her question became, *Can a woman love two men at the same time*? She loved both of them. But Jim held on to her with a boyish amore, while Bill came on solid and strong. Sybil needed Bill's strength, and accepted his proposal. Jim was crushed. Boots on the ground triumphed over propellers in the air.

Bill played football on an intramural team at the Academy. Once while on leave, he showed me a three-point stance that he used on the team. He told me to take a stance opposite him. We used my pigskin football for this demonstration. Crouching and facing me he asked, "Are you ready?" Foolishly I blurted back, "Sure." He snapped the football, then slammed into me, and knocked me on my back. I felt like I had been run over by a Mack truck. In that instant I found that assertiveness ran deep in his blood. "You OK?" he asked, as he stood over me. I covered my bruised feelings with a simple, "Yes." Jim would not do that without giving me instructions first. Consequently, I felt much closer to Jim than to Bill.

Sybil graduated from Pasadena City College in June 1944 with an AA degree in nursing. She then applied to Johns Hopkins School of Medicine in Baltimore, Maryland. She was accepted and made plans to begin classes in nursing that summer. She could be much closer to Bill. They could see each other in what scant spare time they had.

Vignette: A Defining Moment

On a warm night in June 1944, soon after Allied troops stormed ashore on Normandy beaches, in a titanic battle that would determine the fate of Europe, my sister Sybil stood close to us in our little corner of the world. We were at the train station in Pasadena, California. Her bags were packed. She wore high heels that accented her height and legs, and carried her gracefully to the loading platform. Dad and I carried her bags. She was to board the train for Chicago, and thence to Baltimore. Her sweetheart, Bill would meet her at the station there.

Another wrenching change faced our family. We felt it, but none of us knew how to articulate our feelings. So we stood waiting in silence. The train engineer gave a blast of his horn, announcing his approach. The huge train rolled into the station, hissing steam, tired brakes squealing as it came to a stop. The platform shuddered as the train rolled to a stop, as if hit by an earthquake. We stood on the platform hugging and kissing, not knowing when we would ever see her again. She was the magnet of our family, the one whom all of us cherished. She was my best friend, and the one person I could talk to about personal matters. Now the war was taking her away. Mom cried, but could only say, "Be sure to write." Dad was on the verge of tears, but stifled any show of his emotions. Sybil and I hugged. I was learning one of the contradictions of life and love. The one I loved the most was leaving. Suddenly, the engineer let out a blast of steam with a great roar, and a cloud of steam engulfed us. It symbolized the kind of fog in which our family had been living. The conductor called in a loud voice, "All Aboard! Last call, All Aboard!" Sybil turned and walked to her coach, taking her seat. We exchanged waves and blew kisses. One more blast of the horn and the engineer signaled that the train was leaving. We stood there until the train rounded a curve heading eastward, and then disappeared from view. We drove home in silence. Once again the war came home to us.

That summer war news poured in. Jim Pettit had been assigned to a squadron of P-47 Thunderbolt fighter-bombers in England. They were to fly close support for General Patton's divisions as they made a breakout from Normandy. Jim wrote us a letter that after one mission over northern France he flew his Thunderbolt fighter plane in victory laps around the Eiffel tower. He felt proud to tell us about that. Then in late August came bad news. As of August 20, Jim was reported by the War Department as Missing in Action. We found out later that he had been shot down in aerial combat by a German fighter plane.

Mom had just returned from shopping for groceries. Ellen Pettit, Jim's mother, called to tell us the news. I was going outside to help carry in the groceries. Instead, as Mom poured out the sad news, we stood there staring at each other. We were stunned. Only slowly did the reality of the news sink in. We might never see his happy smile again or hear his boyish laughter. We felt sadness because of the broken relationship between Jim and Sybil. Jim had never loved anyone but my sister, and grieved that she had gone to Baltimore to be close to Bill. Later, the Red Cross informed Ellen that Jim had been killed in action.

Now the blue star in her window became a gold star. It was hung side by side with the gold star for her husband who was killed in action the previous year in New Guinea. Gold stars were multiplying in our neighborhood. The war became very real, and very painful for us. Jim had been a friend to me when I needed someone like him to look up to. He was my hero and I missed him. So did my parents. At least I had one of his khaki uniforms that I could wear in his memory. The shirt fit perfectly. With the pants I had to roll up the legs for a good fit. For the rest of my life I have honored Jim on Memorial Day by flying our American flag in remembrance of him.

That fall Dad got orders to repair the teletype machines at Muroc Army Air Base (later renamed Edwards Air Force Base). We left early to drive in the cool of the day across the Mojave Desert. When we got there B-24 Liberator squadrons had finished practicing bombing and aerial gunnery. Mojave Desert was the perfect place for them to practice. We checked in at the front gate. Dad showed his I.D., and the M.P.'s ushered us into the base. What a thrill to be there!

After years of cutting out photos of military aircraft, I was looking at the real thing. The huge bombers were parked in rows across the field, squat and olive drab. "Look Dad, have you ever seen anything like this?" I asked. "Can we go take a closer look at them?" "Not right now," came his businesslike reply. The bombers looked like hornets when they sit on their nest. When nesting they make a pervasive humming noise. But agitate them and the hum turns to a sharp buzz, and they attack. There was a low hum from the field that morning, and I knew these bombers were capable of great destructive power.

We drove to the operations hut, parked and walked in. The building was full of pilots in flight gear checking in after their morning practice runs. I couldn't believe what I was seeing. This was a kid's dream come true. Mom had said, "The early bird catches the worms." It proved true that morning. Here I stood surrounded by pilots in their combat gear. This was a "Wow" experience and I found it hard to put it into words. I was barely a teen-ager, and was standing next to men in combat gear that would soon ship off to war zones around the world. *"Is this a motion picture or is this reality?"* I thought to myself.

The Officer of the Day broke into my reverie by taking Dad and me to a back room where the teletype machines were housed. I sat in a corner and peeked out a window while Dad worked. I watched B-24's taking off for more practice. With a roar of their engines they lifted into the morning sky to prepare themselves for combat. Dad outdid himself when he brought me along that day.

Many years later I read Stephen Ambrose's book, "The Wild Blue." He told the story of the heroism of men like Lt. George McGovern with the 15th Air Force stationed in Italy during WWII. McGovern and his crew flew dangerous missions over occupied Europe in B-24 Liberators. The 15th Air Force suffered 50% losses. Perhaps, I thought, some of the men that I saw training at Muroc were assigned to the 15th Air Force. I wondered, *"How many of them came home when the war was over?"* I couldn't help but ask the question.

I took a second newspaper route, this one in the afternoon for the "Pasadena Star News." Right after classes I took Slim's bus home, then pedaled my bike to Huntington Drive to pick up my bundle of papers. I got the usual coating of black printer's ink on my hands as I folded papers, and another important lesson. My assigned route took me up the hill to the Huntington Library, once the home of multi-millionaire Henry Huntington. His uncle, Collis P. Huntington, Charles Crocker, and Leland Stanford were partners in creating the Central Pacific Railroad that punched through the Sierra Nevada Mountains, and across the desert to Promontory Point, Utah.

Henry Huntington also became a millionaire. He bought rare art and books from palaces in Europe to decorate his home. Then he created a world-class botanical garden around his home. Now his home was owned by the state of California and open to the public. Directly across the street a long row of fine homes were built, stately in their opulence and beauty. They became my assigned route.

Dad reminded me in his inimitable way that we were "hoi polloi." He loved to verbally play with words, and this phrase was one of his favorites. That phrase meant that we were common garden variety of citizens, quite apart from "them," the rich. They were "rich," while we struggled to survive. He intimated that they were arrogant, and from their mansions would not mix with the hoi polloi.

So it was that at the end of the first month of delivering the Star News I had to collect their monthly payment. With some trepidation I went down long, rose-lined pathways to expansive front porches. I had my spiel all ready, "Hello, I am your delivery boy for the Star News. I am collecting for a month's delivery." I took my best stance, stood tall, crossed my fingers and hoped for the best.

I expected some sort of ogre to answer, but instead it was the lady of the manor, and in a polite way she listened to my reminder, went to get her purse, and counted out the correct number of dollar bills. Then, for good measure, she counted off one more dollar as a tip for me. I had never been tipped before, and surprised by her response, I said, "Thanks!" One dollar was a generous tip. *Where was the ogre? Was this not millionaires' row?* Other homeowners were equally generous with me. What I expected was far different from what I got. Wealthy people can be generous and friendly human beings like the rest of us. I did not forget that lesson.

Sometimes Jay Stevens and I rode our bikes to the Huntington Library, now a public museum, and went inside to view Mr. Huntington's collection of art. As we walked past Greek and Roman statues, they stood nude in all their glory. We giggled when we saw male and female statues revealing classical nude bodies with grace and beauty, without any hint of embarrassment. Coming from a home where sex was prohibited, this was all new and wonderful to me. "Look Jay," I whispered, "at those nude Greek males. They have pointy-heads on their penises." Mine wasn't shaped like that. I suddenly realized what it meant to be circumcised. That was a revelation to me. It was the distinguishing difference between the Greeks and us. The teacher of my Sunday school class referred to the Greeks as, "uncircumcised pagans." Now I knew I wasn't a pagan.

The female statues also revealed more information to my primitive sexual knowledge. The females lacked an extension like the males.

I now knew the difference in plumbing between the male and female. The females had graceful orbs above their waist and we were entranced with the sight. "Whew" said Jay, "will you look at that? Have you ever seen anything like that before?" In a hushed and whispered reply I said, "No, never." Now I was gaining information previously denied to me, and I was obviously enjoying the experience. There is something impish when teens get to do something they are not supposed to do. Now was that kind of moment for me. I'm sure the docents had their eyes on two bumpkins who were giggling too much in a palace of fine art. What I didn't know was what happened between males and females when they were alone. That was a vast unknown.

Stan Henry and I decided to ditch school one day that spring. Harassed in the locker room by the bullyboys, both of us wanted a break from the misery. We rode the Pacific Electric "red car" down Huntington Drive to the corner of 6th and Main in downtown Los Angeles. That was the seedy side of town. We were sophomores (translated as, wise fools) out for adventure. We were going to be big and explore our world.

The previous year there had been riots between sailors and Mexican-American "Pachucos" on these streets. The young, angry Mexicans dressed in "zoot suits," and were out to prove themselves to "gringos" in the area. The pachucos were protesting against discrimination, and being treated like second-class citizens. We saw plenty of sailors but no pachucos that day.

On the corner of 6th and Main was a large burlesque theater. Outside, under a large marquee, stood colorful photos of women who wore only pasties and G-strings, striking sensuous poses. We purchased tickets, and the vendor at the ticket booth asked no questions as to our age, though I'm sure he could see our youthful naivité. Sailors from the Long Beach Navy Base, finding no pachucos to fight, came in and occupied the seats closest to the stage.

The show opened with a monologue of off-color sexual jokes, none of which impressed me. Then, the curtain was opened to reveal a buxom peroxide blonde, clad in a loose silken gown. At school we called such blonds "convertible blonds." Sailors whistled and shouted, "Take it off!" She shed her flimsy cover. The sailors shouted all the more, "Take it off!" She then removed her bra. Now the sailors were ecstatic. "More!" they cried, "More!" Off came her panties. Then she curled her legs around a shiny brass pole that stood on stage, and began gyrating her body on the pole. Sailor hats flew into the air. Sailors stood and shouted with delight.

She tantalized them with her moves, extracting feverish responses as long as she could. The sailors got their money's worth. I do not remember being sexually aroused by the show, but rather fascinated by the sailor's response. It was comical, foolish, and absurd all at the same time. Was it Shakespeare who said, "What fools these mortals be?" Sex was taboo at our home in San Gabriel, but now I was getting little snippets of what sex was all about because of trips like this.

We then walked to a nearby theater and saw a war movie showing American pilots shooting down Japanese pilots. When a "Jap" pilot was hit by American bullets, blood spurted from his mouth, and he cried out, "Damado!" as he went down in flames. The audience cheered. Everyone referred to the Japanese as "Japs." Sometimes I think we did that to our wartime enemies so that it would be easier to watch them be killed in Hollywood movies. Then we could cheer while our consciences were dulled to the horror that is war.

On April 12 President Roosevelt died at his retreat in Warm Springs, Georgia. Our teachers were speechless when they heard the news. So were we. We couldn't imagine America in a world without his leadership. The principal cancelled all classes, and we were summarily dismissed. Students milled around asking questions of each other, none of which we could answer. His death was like a jab to the solar plexus. How could we go on without him? There was no bus to pick us up so I walked the five miles to my home in San Gabriel. How sad, I thought, that he would not be able to witness the surrender of Hitler's Third Reich a month later.

On August 6 the Times headline literally screamed as I folded newspapers, "Atomic Bomb Dropped on Japs." I had no idea what an atomic bomb was, but the reports stated it was the most powerful weapon ever devised. Soon after, the Japanese accepted unconditional surrender, and the war was over. We called it, "VJ Day."

Suddenly cars were honking their horns, the church bells on the old mission San Gabriel and the historic Church of Our Savior rang out, and people stepped outside to savor this moment of triumph. I pedaled my bike to Las Tunas Drive. There I saw people spontaneously dancing in the streets, strangers hugging and kissing one another, and people pouring out of their homes to celebrate the news. Drivers along the boulevard formed into a line, honking, shouting, and waving to crowds who gathered curbside. Some men tossed their hats into the air. All of the pent-up emotions of wartime privation were released. All the telegrams sent home alerting families of the death of a loved one, were set aside. 12 million young men and women would come home from military service. The killing was over. We would have peace.

The entire town was ecstatic. Who could remain calm in a situation like this? It was impossible. As Jesus said, "Even the rocks will cry out." That is what was happening. Those who had been silent for four years burst into joy. I could not remain silent. I shouted for joy and waved at whomever I could see. Along with the multitude I jumped up and down with tumultuous enthusiasm. The power of group dynamics took over.

We danced and cried out together in a crazed passion such as I had never seen before. I worked my way to curbside so I could see a spontaneous parade of cars that lined up and honked their way down Las Tunas Drive. This was a moment of triumph that I could feel in my bones. The photo that soon appeared in "Life" magazine of a sailor wildly kissing a woman in Times Square, New York, summed it up for me.

Dad had been critical of some of our wartime commanders who had ordered our men into costly, terrible battles on islands in the Pacific. He thought there was a better way to win the war. I listened to what he said. Our local Veterans of Foreign Wars organized a hasty parade to "lead" the celebration. Vets from WWI passed their hats among us for free-will donations of cash. A veteran approached me with his old, battered garrison cap outstretched in his hand. "Something for the boys," he said. I refused his request. He stared at me in disbelief, then cursed me, turned, and walked away. My wartime patriotism had frayed.

Mom, Dad and I began going to the movies together on Friday nights. The war was over and we found more time for recreation. Preceding the featured movie were cartoons followed by newsreels of world events. In newsreels we saw scenes that caused us to gasp in horror. General Patton and his men liberated German concentration camps. The faces of the survivors were blank, and their bodies emaciated to skin and bones. Army engineers brought in bulldozers and scooped up thousands of lifeless bodies, pushing piles of bodies into hastily dug pits, and then covering them over. The pain written on the faces of the dead was more than we could endure. American officers ordered the citizens of nearby German towns to leave their homes and help feed the survivors with emergency rations. We witnessed these scenes over and over.

We were forced to ask, "How can things like this happen in a civilized world?" Had we become animals? Hitler's surviving officials were put on trial and drew our wrath. But a question simmered in our minds: What kind of creature is man? My pastor picked up the theme and drove home sermons on the nature of sin. We listened.

I could relate to "sin" when I saw it so vividly displayed in the collapse of Nazism. But as the pastor preached and carefully pointed out our separation from God, I understood it only as a general concept. I was still an infant when it came understanding the behavior inside me that often distanced me from His grace.

The family dynamic that began years before had now become entrenched. At the theater Dad sat on one side of Mom and I on the other. Mom was always between us, physically and mentally. The wedge between my father and me was in place and would remain that way for years to come. Dad and I began WWII together at the Lockheed Aircraft factory on December 7th, 1941. We ended the war sitting in a theater watching newsreels of the Nazi defeat. But Mom was between us. Both of us vied for her love. That was our story thus far.

Five

Coming of Age: Life With Father

Why is it that growing up through the teenage years is so difficult? Is it because of our parents' unrealistic expectations of us? Or is it the expectations that we place on ourselves? Or is it that we struggle to figure out who we are? Mark Twain said there are two major events in a person's life. One is birth. The other is when we find the reason why we were born. I was still trying to find my "why." Life with father was part of that search.

My time with Dad kept getting more interesting. As I reached my teens he used unique words to define himself and our relationship. We were not close, but life with Dad was never dull. A part of our relationship was his use of language. He liked to use words just as a juggler uses balls. The juggling of words got my attention. I liked that. Doing his ten to twenty chin-ups after work, he was "in the pink." When his day went well, he described it as "copasetic." When office politics or rivalries bothered him, surrounded as he was by Ph.D. engineers from USC/UCLA, he would quote Job 5:7, "Yet man is born to trouble, as surely as sparks fly upward." When his relationship with Mom appeared tentative, he called her "Chief." There rang a note of accuracy in this name; Mom was the quiet head of our home. Only occasionally did Dad use the more intimate "Liza."

Dad's habits were fixed and he brooked no alterations. When he got home from work, he took off his hat and tossed it on the kitchen bench. He laid down any blue prints from work. He stepped out to the yard for his chin-ups on our clothes line pole, dusted his hands, and walked back to the cabinet at the entrance to our kitchen. Inside were several bottles of his favorite whiskey and several bottles of mixers. He took down two tall glasses, put in ice cubes, then a healthy shot of whiskey in each, and blended that with mixer. He called these his "Highballs."

Taking one in his hand, he took a stool and sat in a corner by the sink, always alone. He sipped, slowly turning the glass in his hand as he did so. He seemed to be holding an elixir that would cause his problems at work to fade away. He let the drink pass over his tongue, savoring it. He always followed that glass with another, but never more. Two glasses was standard, and he did not exceed it. I never saw my father drunk. This was his transition time. Then after 15-20 minutes of silent drinking, he put the bottles away, and began to face our family. We knew that we were not to interrupt his ritual.

My nicknames increased with the years. In Yosemite I was "Hatchet Hezzie," because I liked to cut firewood. At Lake Arrowhead I was "Silent Sam." When exercising, "Joe Bonomo." And for everyday use I was "Moe." I never quite knew what to make of "Moe." I simply knew that "Moe" was one of the "Three Stooges." I did not ask Dad, but simply accepted his monikers. When I was slow at eating my oatmeal for breakfast, his comment was, "It'll put hair on your chest." When slow getting out of bed, he would say, "Get the lead out!" or "Up and at 'em, my hearty!" or "Gotta get going," usually in a tone of invitation mixed with a tone of command. When I was on the verge of an unknown, or had made a good decision, his comment was, "Moe can see through a ladder." *What in the world did that mean?* I did not ask him. When ready to go to U. C. Davis, he called me "Joe College."

And when Dad met a lady he liked, he took off his hat, and held it with both hands behind his back. Then, waiting for the right moment, he would say, "How's about you and me, Sugarloaf?" Both would laugh, and part company. When he met a person who seemed peculiar he would later comment that the person was "pixilated." When he was in an expansive mood, he liked to quote the closing lines of the poem "Invictus:" "I am master of my fate, I am the captain of my soul." Or if he was in a jocular mood, he liked to quote from Robert Service's book, "Yukon Poems," especially "The Shooting of Dan McGrew".

Dad held on to skepticism that he blended with his own sense of humor. In his personal philosophy, he chose to see the dark side of human nature, and the tragic sense of life. He avoided any concept of God, but did take us to church on Christmas and Easter.

One Easter Dad decided to take us to Riverside for an Easter Sunrise service. We piled into the car at 4 a.m. We arrived in darkness. Dad and Mom had flashlights ready for us. Mom urged us to stay together in the darkness, so Sybil, Carol and I held hands. Slowly we formed into a line with other worshippers and began the ascent of Mt. Rubidoux. We followed a pathway upward with our little beams of light probing the encircling darkness. I felt like a pilgrim. We walked quietly and steadily. At the top a level place had been created around a giant cross. We formed a circle around the cross, and someone led us in a hymn, and then another. Then, as the first light of the sun appeared splitting the darkness, we sang "Christ the Lord is Risen Today, Hallelujah!" As the morning light gilded the hilltop, and as we sang more hymns, I experienced God's presence. This was my first Easter Sunrise Service, and stood out as the most authentic that I ever attended. Did Dad know how this would touch my heart so deeply? Dad was a labyrinth of moods, not easy to understand. Perhaps what I sensed in him is true of all of us. We are a complex blend of contraries.

For humor Dad had his favorite radio shows: "Jimmy Durante," "Groucho Marx," "Fibber McGee and Molly," "Charley McCarthy," and "Amos and Andy." (And in his later years, "Archie Bunker.") For mellow moods he turned to "Hawaii Calls" on Sundays, and longed to visit the Islands. He never got there. Guy Lombardo personified "the sweetest music this side of heaven," and so did Lawrence Welk. To appease the

"Chief", he turned in later years to the "Hour of Power" with Reverend Schuller. Mom read her Bible daily and asked Dad to watch this television show with her. Mom also sang or hummed old gospel hymns as she puttered around the house. Dad kept a respectful silence.

Once in his later life Dad used a term of endearment with me. My daughter Suzanne and I flew down to San Gabriel the week after Christmas to clean his house. Then, we got ready to take him to "Goody's," his favorite restaurant. As Dad and I waited in the driveway for Suzanne, Dad looked over to me and pushed back his pork-pie hat and said, "Son, I want you to know I do believe in the man upstairs." It was the only time he called me "Son", and the only time he ever affirmed his faith in God. I caught my breath, hardly expecting such an amazing confession. Was it because Dad was 87 years old now and facing the possibility of death at any time? I don't know. Perhaps he had wanted to say it for a long time and now he took the bold step and finally said it. My response was, "That's great, Dad. I knew you did." He died several weeks later.

In later years my mother wrote letters frequently. She would often remark, " I know it is hard to understand, but your father does love you. He just doesn't know how to say those words or show his love." Mom caught the meaning of our father-son relationship with those words. I wonder if there is some universal truth there that father's love their sons as best they know how, and with the gifts that they have. It seemed that way to me.

Six

High School Days

Sickness hung on to me like an old dirty sock. Dad suffered too: his head colds led to sinus infections. He spent hours under heat lamps for relief. No heat lamp worked for me. Mom smeared mentholatum on my chest, and then applied her standard prophylactic learned from Grandma Stanton. She bound one of my dirty socks around my neck. I never really got used to that strange treatment from out of frontier America.

After one cold too many, Mom drove me to see our doctor. With the examination came his prescription. He ordered an immediate tonsillectomy for me. On the fateful day, Mom drove me to a hospital in the hills above Sierra Madre. I was now 16, but I had to put on a silly hospital gown that exposed my butt and backside. Unrelenting pain waited for me at the close of surgery. The cool thing about surgery was the round of milkshakes that Mom bought for me. I lived on them for three days.

I was astounded by the outcome of surgery. The frequency of head colds receded, and my asthma disappeared! I had spent years coughing and sneezing, struggling to breathe. Dad's chain smoking of "Lucky Strike" cigarettes exacerbated the asthma. But that was no more. I could breathe normally after surgery.

Another wonderful side effect: my hay fever vanished. I couldn't believe it, yet it really happened. Ragweeds didn't affect me anymore. And additional good news. For years boils would break out on my body, usually on my back just above my belt line. On the day that they reached full size, I had to lower my pants, kneel on the floor and lay across my bed. Dad asked Mom for a sewing needle from her old Singer sewing machine. On a burner of our stove she heated it to red hot, and carefully handed it to Dad. He then lanced the boil.

That, however, was only the beginning. Then came the "squeeze". Dad took his thumb and forefinger and squeezed the base of the boil. At the moment that I screamed, the core emerged along with gooey pus. They gently wiped it away, applied Mercurochrome and a large bandage. I was then free to gently pull up my pants and cinch my belt as carefully as possible. Now after years of painful boils, I never had another one.

Adding to this litany of miracles, my nocturnal emissions and bed-wetting receded into the past. So did my earaches. I cannot explain this. I don't understand how this happened. But I witnessed a miracle. I moved into adolescence with a burst of new health. If I had been a wise person I would have gone to my knees and thanked God for this miracle of healing. However, I was lacking in that basic virtue of gratitude. But now I can publicly thank Him for all His gifts to me.

In May the Student Body Government at Alhambra High asked a trio to perform at our last assembly of the school year. They were "The Slim Gaillard Trio." We slowly filed in for another typical high school assembly. But this time we got an unforgettable surprise. Their black rhythm rang out totally different from the big band sounds of Tommy Dorsey and Glen Miller.

Soon we stood and cheered, clapping to the soul of their music. A new mood emerged. Their final piece brought our assembly to their feet: "Cement Mixer, Put-ti, Put-ti". They played and sang, and we stomped our feet and shouted. Never had we been entertained like this. It was a new wave of music, and we witnessed the takeoff. "More, more!" we shouted. Each man of the trio waved his instrument, gathered to whisper, then gave one more round of "Cement Mixer". We had felt the touch of soul music.

Several weeks later, my good buddy Mel and I brainstormed on our way home from the last day of school. We decided to hitchhike to old Mexico. *Why not? We were ready for anything.* We were now juniors, both of us 16 years old, and ready for adventure. We each bought an Army duffel bag from one of the numerous Army Surplus Stores that sprang up along Main Street. The war had ended and the Army had lots of surplus to sell. Mel packed his old 22-caliber bolt-action rifle, along with a box of ammunition. I put in shirts, pants, and blankets in no particular order.

Mom finally realized I was secretive, and checked to see what I was up to. Since I could not tell a lie, I blurted our plan to her. She reacted. She shouted at me to cease packing at once. I disregarded her. I finished packing, grabbed my old leather jacket, and headed for the front door, and started walking to Mel's house. Standing in the doorway mom cried out, "You come home this very minute! Do you hear me? Come home!" Her voice carried all the way down the street. I didn't dare look back. I kept walking. That was the first time I defied my mother so openly. This was new, and a bit scary, but I liked it. It was my personal Declaration of Independence. It felt as important to me as the one on the 4th of July.

Mel was packed and ready. We walked to Las Tunas Boulevard, stood at curbside, and motioned to passing cars with our thumbs. I wore a pair of Jim Pettit's Army Air Corps khakis, and that simplified our early pick up by motorists. Drivers thought I was a veteran. I told each driver quite honestly that I wore Jim's uniform out of respect for him. The drivers listened in silence. I'm sure they felt deceived by my maneuver. My naiveté was showing itself glaringly.

At each drop-off we knew what direction we were headed. We aimed for Highway 101 south which would take us past some beaches where we planned to camp, thence to San Diego. On the beach we ate a can of beans along with Coca Cola. We did some target practice, and took Kodak photos of each other holding the rifle. Our bed was simply two blankets; one above, and one below. Convinced that we were happy vagabonds, we endured all the privations of a campout, savoring our freedom from parental control. "Hey, Mel," I inquired; "Are you having fun?" "Yeah," he replied from under his blanket. "What about you?" Looking up at the stars while waves crashed on the beach, I said, "I've never had it so good."

A year earlier I had told Mom that I wanted to make a difference in the world. Now curled between my twin blankets I had time to think. It was so beautiful to be on the beach with Mel. Suddenly I felt like I was growing up. I had walked away from Mom and from home. *Maybe*, I thought, *I am on my way to becoming* a *man. I want to be somebody, but how?* Then I fell asleep, with the cadence of the waves making a sweet rhythm.

At San Diego we walked across the International Boundary and into Tijuana. We found a place to store our duffel bags, and then wandered through the city. On every corner locals sold tacos, Coca-Cola, and "dirty books." After food, I bought my first dirty book, hawked by a skinny teenager pronouncing "book" as "boook." My book was a series of cartoons of Pop Eye and Olive Oil having sex. Shock and fascination gripped me. Here were two cartoon characters cavorting behind closed doors in blatant sexual moves. I thought, *So this was what adults did behind closed doors.* Yet, this contradicted everything that I had learned from Sybil, and the denial of sexuality that I learned from Mom. Both of them would have blushed to turn these pages. Yet, I took it all in.

As I returned I was ashamed to take it home. I hid the thin book in the crack of a telephone pole two blocks from Milton Drive. When I went back to retrieve it days later, someone had taken it. *Oh well*, I thought. *I shouldn't have it*. I likened that first brush with pornography the same way as I did with my first kiss. I never forgot it.

I questioned myself. How could I explain such behavior? We had defied our parents, traveled to a third world country, put ourselves at risk, exposed ourselves to pornography, and returned home safely. One possible explanation: my Bohemian inheritance. Another: crazy teenagers insisting on their own way. But I had decided to know myself, and my world, even if it violated common sense. Later, Dad said, "You have angels watching over you." My response was "Yes."

High School Days

In July 1946, Dad offered me a treat. "Would you like to come with me to a place called Hearst Castle?" I had no idea what he meant, but he made it sound interesting and I loved to travel. My response followed swiftly, "Sure." I packed a small bag, then went to Mel's house and borrowed his 22-caliber rifle. Dad and I packed our things into his navy-blue, company 1937 Ford, and took off. He drove across Los Angeles, finally picking up State Highway One. Then we headed north along the coast, stopping for a meal in Santa Barbara. At my request, he drove by the Mission, the best preserved of all the California Missions. I saw it as a treasure in the afternoon sun.

By late afternoon we arrived at the front gate to the "Castle," and I was immediately impressed by what I saw. Looming before us was not a castle built in the style of my storybooks, but a grand mansion, its main turrets touching the clouds. Dad presented his Western Union credentials to the guard who then ushered us in to the grounds. We drove around to the side, and a security person showed Dad where to park, the entrance to the kitchen where workers' meals were served, and then upstairs to our separate bedrooms. When my bedroom door swung open, I could scarcely believe what I saw: a huge medieval looking room that seemed as big as our home. Large paintings provided the décor. A king-sized bed stood over against a wall, with a window offering a sweeping panorama of the estate. Dad got a similar room. We had never seen such opulence. After all, we were hoi polloi.

When we got past our surprise, we each unpacked and prepared for supper. Below, on the first floor, a staff of chefs prepared dinner for workers and servants. We formed a line and served ourselves from an array of meat and mashed potatoes, tossed green salads and breads, as much as we wanted. As I filled my tray with food I looked at Dad and grinned.

The next day Dad took his blue prints and went to the room where all of Mr. Hearst's teletype machines were located. Since Mr. Hearst owned newspapers around the world, his teletypes printed full copies daily of each newspaper he owned. Dad told me that "the old man" reviewed the papers. If he found editorials or news that did not reflect his philosophy of news, he would circle the item; make a comment to the editor, and teletype it back. This way, he stayed in touch with his editors and maintained a semblance of command and control. This particular summer, several machines malfunctioned, and since Hearst leased them from Western Union, Dad, as chief trouble-shooter, was point man to repair them.

I walked around the Castle, which I later found was called affectionately "the ranch" by Mr. Hearst. On the far side Mr. Hearst created a sanctuary for wild African animals. Zebras and giraffes in herds fed nearby. Their open range of dun colored hills stretched far away to the east to the horizon of the Coast Range. Strategically placed swimming pools graced the perimeter of "the ranch." Dad alerted me to bring swim trunks, and as the coastal sun warmed me, I took a swim in each pool. I wrote home that swimming in the gold-plated pool made me feel as though I was in a fantasyland. Gold plated tiles ringed the pool. I took my shoes off so my feet could experience a touch of gold.

But the pool I liked best of all featured Greek statues standing in a semi-circle on the perimeter of the pool. I swam in this pool every day for a week. The air and the grounds reflected a quiet calm. The silence was broken only by the splash of my swim strokes.

One afternoon as I swam in what I called the "Greek pool," Cary Grant and a lady friend took seats at the poolside. Mr. Hearst regularly invited Hollywood celebrities to come and share the ranch with him and his sweetheart/mistress, Marion Davies. He gave his guests rides to the ranch on his personally fitted Douglas DC-2. I recognized Cary Grant immediately. I had seen his photograph on theater marquees while growing up. He took some change from his pocket, took off his robe and sandals, and invited me to join him in diving for pennies. I don't know if he was a friendly kind of guy, or thought of me as the son of a notable. "Sure!" I blurted out as I accepted his offer.

His girlfriend sat in an easy chair at poolside, watching us. Her one-piece bathing suit fit her trim body perfectly. Coyly, she sat with one leg crossed over the other, looking sexy in her bathing suit. Did it occur to her to join us in the fun? Or was it her perception that she should sit and look pretty, and protect her carefully crafted hair-do, while we had fun? Whatever her thoughts, I felt as though she lacked the athleticism of my sister Sybil.

Cary threw a bright penny into the pool and invited me into a game of dive-for-it. I recovered it off the bottom of the pool, and splashed myself out of water so clear it looked like a high Sierra lake. Now it was my turn to throw the penny in. He dove in to retrieve it. As he emerged, the perfectly parted hair that announced Cary Grant appeared like a rag mop. We both spontaneously laughed as we realized what had happened.

In that moment the myth of Cary Grant disappeared. The real persona appeared. He was really Archibald Leach, of humble birth in England. I think that is who he wanted to be. The laughter signaled the moment of truth and we both could relax and simply have fun. A Hollywood studio created a myth, and Archibald was glad to be free of it, if only for a brief moment of time.

Then I parted and went to my room. What a memorable day! I swam with a star, and he with a "hoi polloi," and we had great fun. Funny isn't it, but now I felt like I was more than hoi polloi. *Was Dad trying to reduce my ego when he applied that phrase to me, or simply giving me a touch of reality training?* I wasn't sure, but I had much more to learn. How I liked this place!

Next morning after breakfast I looked out to the Pacific Ocean spread before me. I put the 22-caliber rifle in my bag, walked through the security gate, and down the long winding road to the beach. Sitting on the beach I could see numerous rocks offshore with sea gulls swooping and diving in their endless search for food. Some stood on rocks, quietly looking for food.

I took the bolt of the rifle, pulled it back, inserted a single round, and closed the bolt. I leveled the rifle, took aim, squeezed the trigger, and with a loud crack, a seagull simply fell lifeless into the surf, carried out to sea on the next wave. I shot another with same result. Then another. My aim was good, but my conscience was troubling me. A fog rolled in and spared any further killing.

Back up the hill I trudged until I emerged into sunlight. As the morning sun broke through the coastal fog, I had an epiphany. I realized that I had violated my sense of values. I felt guilty and ashamed for shooting seagulls. I was wrestling with my conscience, just as Jacob wrestled with an angel long ago on the banks of the River Jabbok. It was a God moment for him, and now for me. Have you ever felt as though God was personally speaking to you? He spoke to Jacob in that wrestling match and gave to him a new name that signified great things: Israel. God spoke to my conscience that morning. With the morning sun warming me, a tender spot in my soul stirred into life, I made a decision: I would never again shoot a living creature. If I used the 22 once more, it would be for target practice only. It was as if God spoke and I responded. I intended to keep that vow.

No one in my family had any use for guns. Perhaps this decision came out of that background. I had been learning a respect for life in my secret hiding place in the San Gabriel Mountains. And Mom, I believe, always wanted me to be a pastor. Thus, when the morning sun broke through the coastal fog, it broke through the fog in my mind and reminded me of the sacredness of life. It was another God moment.

Dad remained for a week until all the teletypes functioned properly. As we drove out the front gate, little did I know that within several years Mr. Hearst would leave his beloved ranch and seek medical care for his failing health, never to return. From this time on, I began to take an interest in his life. And, I would meet Cary Grant once again many years later.

Girls began to be of interest to me. A cluster of four girls sat on their front lawn in the shade right around the corner on Roses Road. They wore shorts, loose blouses, and sandals, or no shoes at all. I knew them as neighbors who said, "Hi, How ya doin?" and so forth. Now I decided to take it a step further and get acquainted. I sat on the front lawn with them and entered their conversation. They looked pretty as I came close. Their legs were shaved, toenails painted, and bobby pins held their hair in place. One had eyes that danced when I talked with her. I felt attracted to her, though a touch of shyness held me back from getting too close. I kept a respectful distance.

At that moment Mom drove by as she returned from shopping at the Market Basket. She glanced sidewise and saw me sitting in a circle with the four girls. I think the scene hit every panic button in her system. At the time I didn't understand her behavior. She slowed our Plymouth, kept her window closed, but gestured with her hands in the direction of home, and with her face glowering at me in unmistakable language, "You get home right now or else!"

I headed for our home, half way up Milton Drive, and received a tongue-lashing. "Why were you there? Who said you could go there? Why aren't you doing your chores? If I catch you over there again I'll ground you for a month! Do you hear me?" My dutiful response followed with, "Yes, Mom," though I didn't really understand her reaction. Awareness, however, was slowly taking shape in my mind; Mom was living her life through me, and seeking to control me. I think it began to explain why I had anxiety attacks. I began to dimly perceive why sex was a prohibited subject at our home. Yet, except for my Mexico excursion, I couldn't break free. I didn't go sit with the girls again.

Judging my mother for her behavior seemed easy. Yet, when I quietly thought about her past, I got a different perspective. The three sisters, abandoned by their father, were confronted by the death of their mother at the same time. Mom, I believe, was touched by her greatest fear: abandonment. I don't think she ever really trusted men, and never spoke to her father, William McFarland, again. Somehow that lack of trust spilled over into her relation with my father. Then, sickly as I was as a child, she overprotected me and put a dirty sock around my neck with each head cold. Now, she felt threatened as I began to live my life on my own.

However, soon after this incident, she took a new approach. She took a job as a clerk typist with the "San Gabriel Sun" newspaper. I didn't have to go straight home after school to be with her anymore. What a great transition that was for me!

Here was a conundrum that I could not resolve. I still needed my mother's love, in part because the relationship with my father was so tentative. But I also longed to be free to build my own life apart from her. The result was that I was conflicted and slow in growing up.

I still chafed when I looked at my skinny body. Charles Atlas placed ads in some of our magazines. His ads portrayed a "98 pound weakling" intimidated by bullies. Atlas' course of "Dynamic Tension" would build a body of bulging muscles that would end bullying. A newcomer named Joe Bonomo also promised the same thing. He advertised himself widely as a body builder who could do wonders for skinny and flabby bodies. I could work out at home with no special equipment needed.

I signed a coupon, and sent money to Joe Bonomo. He in turn mailed a program to me detailing how I could build my body at home. My goal, I wrote, was to build my biceps, pectorals, and abdomen. My legs were already the strongest part of me. With his illustrated set of exercises, I eagerly began working out. The bullies at school could pick on someone else for a change. My pectorals and biceps resisted change. My disappointment lingered since I wanted a bigger chest when I went to the gym or to the beach with my friends. But my abs blossomed. Soon I had a double train of ripples marching up my abdomen. Did I love to show off the one special thing I had created! Those ripples lasted for years. Dad noticed my zeal in exercising at home. Coming in from his chin-ups on the back yard clothesline pole, he would say, "Up and at 'em, my hearty!" I think that was a line from his favorite pirate story, "Four Bells." Or he began calling me "Joe Bonomo!" I took it in good humor because I knew I had made progress in shaping my body.

Then a searing incident happened at High School in the downstairs locker room in the fall. The hour was late afternoon, classes were over, and students headed home. I went downstairs to retrieve some books for homework. As I opened my locker, I looked over my shoulder and a dozen bullies moved quickly to surround me. They had trouble etched on their faces, and I looked like an easy victim. They harassed me with words, and threatened to take me down. Sizing up my situation, I knew deep trouble when I saw it. I slammed my locker shut and bolted for the exit. I ran swiftly, faster than them to the exit. Out the door I flew and over to a line of students who were ready to board Slim's bus. When the group realized I was within Slim's protective care, they broke off the chase and headed away.

My relief was temporary. All the way home an inner voice kept taunting me, *You're a coward. You should have stood to fight. I'm ashamed of you!* I couldn't still that voice. In fact, that voice haunted me for years afterward. To add to my distress, I couldn't talk to Dad. He had created a new nickname for me: "Silent Sam". Surely, I thought, he would agree with the charge of cowardice. Sybil was gone. I wouldn't tell Mom. She would throw her shoulders back, hold her head high and say with grit, "Be a man!" So I locked the secret in the attic of my mind and carried that voice for years. It never occurred to me that running away from those bullies was my best option.

But out of that incident I made a decision. If I couldn't cope with bullies by myself, I would take them on with friends. I developed a circle of buddies. Daily we sat on the west steps of the main high school building at noon and savored our sack lunches. We laughed, told jokes, and horsed around. Our group included John, Stan, Mel, Doug, Doug's girlfriend Leila, and a new guy named Norm who was big for his age, and now my buddy. With Norm on my side I got no more intimidation. Tommy Kaufman joined us occasionally, and our group was complete. Tommy was a golden glove boxer, the strong, silent type.

One Saturday while walking home from the El Rey Theater Tommy showed me a trick. We paused at a telephone booth, and he held the Los Angeles telephone directory in both hands. He manipulated it, and then gave a sudden twist and tore the directory in half. "Wow!" was all I could say. Later, in my back yard, we decided to put on the boxing gloves that Dad bought for sparing with me. I should have known better. Within minutes Tommy laid the leather to my chin and knocked me down. The pain was sharp and unforgettable. I did not put on gloves with him again, but we became fast friends. Such good friends that from now on I called him "Coffee." A funny thing happened after that. No bully wanted to take on Coffee, or his best friend. I was free of bullying after that.

Mel, Doug, and I formed a secret club. We called ourselves "The Boneheads." Suspended on a chain around our necks hung a small plastic skull. Into each eye socket we glued cheap, cosmetic diamonds. We wore our skulls every day under our shirts. We were now a brotherhood, bonded for life. I liked the sense of belonging. When I used to go roller-skating in Pasadena, or ice-skating in South Pasadena, I had carried a dim fear of abandonment. I had a fear that my friends would leave without me. But with my "brothers," I felt I was safe.

For fun I went to the Alhambra High School dances at Story Park every Thursday night. I took a bus into Alhambra for the dances. At the dance pavilion I laid my eyes on a young sophomore named Ruth. She was so sweet that I immediately felt an attraction to her. With hesitation I walked over to her and said, "Would you like to dance?" With a quick but shy response of, "Yes," we were on the floor, moving to the music of the jukebox. That night Doris Day sang her newest hit "Sentimental Journey." That song became ours.

Ruth's chin just fit on my right shoulder, and we snuggled up to dance to romantic music. I was 16 and quite sure I was in love. We held hands after the dance, and then parted at the bus stop on Main Street. Ruth was my first love. I was hesitant to kiss Ruth, being shy with girls. But I made up for it by holding her hand while my heart thumped and bumped.

In the meantime Sybil encouraged me with letters from Johns Hopkins School of Nursing in Baltimore. She asked me to consider entering the College Preparatory program at Alhambra High. In the spring of 1947, I went to my counselor at school and she put me on track for college when I finished High School. Sybil made it a point to watch out for me. If I successfully completed the plan I would be the first of our family to graduate from college. Sybil dropped out of her nursing program on February 28th, moved to Annapolis, and took an apartment there to be closer to Bill Yates. She wrote glowingly how Bill was selected by his classmates to welcome President Truman to the Naval Academy.

It was set to happen just before Navy's big game with Penn State. The President made a foreign policy speech on the increasing tensions with the Soviet Union. Sybil was proud of Bill as he sat on the stand with the President. She used every possible illustration as a way to encourage me to be "on purpose."

At home, Mom and Dad's relationship was tenuous. Highs and lows were followed by occasional flare-ups, which then shaded into quiet tolerance. Sometimes I didn't know what to expect.

My bedroom attached to the kitchen on one side, and our hallway on the other. The door that opened from my bedroom into the kitchen was a sheet of glass held in place by the doorframe. Over the glass was a shade that I kept in the down position for privacy. On this particular morning, the sounds in the kitchen had a certain predictability. While Dad shaved, Mom prepared breakfast. She knew the menu by heart: two eggs, sunny-side up with soft, gooey yolks, wheat toast, two strips of bacon, and coffee. She could do it blindfolded.

I could hear the sizzle of the bacon on the old, cast-iron skillet. Then came the crack of two eggs on the edge of the skillet. Now and then the fragrance of her cooking slipped through the seams of my bedroom door. Heavenly! Then came a pop as the toaster kicked out two pieces of browned bread. Finally the sound of fresh, hot coffee poured into two cups. Quiet, muted conversation usually followed.

However, the scripted action took a dramatic turn on that morning. Suddenly, murmuring sounds increased in intensity. Sharp words rang out, first from Dad, then the predictable response from Mom. With eyes wide open, I listened anxiously as accusations flew and tempers became red hot. I knew the sound of anger, and our kitchen was the source. As Dad's voice turned to an enraged shout, a kitchen chair crashed through my glass door, hit the shade, and shredded it.

The chair landed on my linoleum floor, badly damaged. I was out of bed by now, sensing fear deep down inside. I wanted to peek through the shattered door, but fearful of what I would see, held back. The back porch door slammed, and I heard Dad open, and then slam shut, the door of his Western Union Ford. The engine screamed, and rubber tires smoked as he backed out the driveway and sped away. I opened the door to check on my Mom, but already she had retreated to their bedroom and locked the door.

I picked up the shards of glass, and took down the ruined shade. I knocked on their bedroom door, but Mom would not talk. I got dressed, skipped breakfast, and walked to the bus stop where Slim's quiet stability and strength was a welcome presence.

I would have liked for Mom and Dad to explain to me what happened, and why. My anxiety led me to wonder if I was the cause of their fight. I waited for them to explain what happened and relieve my fears. Instead they never spoke of the incident again. The non-communication in our home was so loud I could feel it. But I had a part too. I failed to ask that they explain themselves. Thus, the puzzle pieces of our family lay scattered on the floor. I wanted to make sense of it all, but couldn't.

Seven

Adventures In Learning

My friend Doug attracted girls with a twinkle of his eye and a charming smile that revealed a mouth full of braces. No matter. He came on to girls, and they responded to his flirting. As with Coffee, he wore a surplus Navy Pea jacket, and with the collar pulled up he too created a macho appearance.

One day after school, Doug, his girlfriend, Leila, and I went to a café off of Main Street in Alhambra. Seated in a booth, Doug showed us his wallet collection of dirty pictures. What an unreal experience for me. First of all, Leila took an interest in the photos! That shocked my senses. I thought she would be embarrassed. Instead, Leila was curious and amused. Second, as I looked at them, I didn't believe what I saw. The photos lied. I thought the photos were fakes. Men and women were locked in passionate sexual acts. Thoughts raced across my mind as in a hundred yard dash. Women don't do things like that. Sybil and Mom had both taught me what girls like, so had my Presbyterian Sunday School, and surely, it wasn't this.

The cartoons at Tijuana were one thing, but photographs gave a new and jolting dimension of reality. I stared in disbelief as the photo images collided with the denial of sexuality that I had learned at home. This was a train wreck in my mind. The dirty sock around my neck prevailed in this titanic struggle, but just barely. I felt like Galileo looking at the moon and the stars for the first time with his telescope, trying to make sense of it all. I didn't make sense of it all, but a war was brewing.

It became clear that there were at least two sides simmering in Doug. On the one side, we were Bonehead Buddies, bonded for life. On the other side, lurked his darker self. Yet I have to admit that I needed Doug's dose of reality training. I couldn't go on being naïve forever. I had to come to terms with the ways of the world, and understand sex.

Once Doug tried to woo Ruth away from me. Another shade of his darker side happened out of town on a Friday night. We were in a drugstore with fellow Bonehead, Mel, checking out the magazine rack. Suddenly I looked up and they were gone. I walked outside and they were nowhere in sight. I panicked. We were in a strange town and I didn't know my way home. The archaic fear of abandonment gripped my gut as anxiety took over. Anger followed, then resentment.

I don't care, I thought, as I began to soothe myself. *I don't need you guys! I'll handle this myself.* But I really did care, and I needed them. This hurt. Twenty minutes later they showed up, laughing and making light of their absence. Friendship took a new meaning for me that night. Life-long friends may not be who they say they are. What a lesson!

When I wasn't with the guys there were always other things to do. On Saturdays, Dad took time to work with me on basic tennis strokes, teaching me as he once taught Sybil. He gave me one of his "woodies," an old wooden Wilson racket. When Dad wasn't there, I practiced on the backboards at Washington Elementary School. I liked the game. I wanted more.

He told me that once when he visited the Los Angeles Tennis Club, he got into a pick-up game with Pancho Gonzales, one of the era's tennis greats, and beat him. Dad wanted me to know of some of his credentials. He introduced me to his friends at Len's Tennis Shop at the Alhambra Courts. Then we practiced. He could always beat me, but that merely increased my incentive to get better.

I bought my first can of tennis balls. I loved the pop, and the hiss as I opened my can of balls. They were mine now, not Dad's, and I was going to play with them. I got a feel in my arm for follow-through as I stroked the ball to create lift and accuracy. Dad warned me, "Now, don't get any great expectations for your game. You should have begun ten years ago if you wanted to be a champion." Dad liked reality training. I heard him, but still wanted to be a winner.

I drew an imaginary line on the backboard where the net should be and practiced hitting over that line, first forehand, then backhand. There is a feeling of conquest when you make the ball go where it is aimed, and let down when you miss. Have you experienced that feeling? Tennis is a game where your worst enemy is you. What a realization! One weakness in our practice sessions was that Dad did not teach me strategy on the court. That proved to be a critical gap in my knowledge when I went away to the University of California at Davis.

Another activity on Saturdays was yard work. Dad had an old Philco radio that he plugged in on our service porch overlooking our back yard. He liked to putter to music. But the way he puttered made a lasting impression. He wore an old pair of tennis shoes for his feet. Then he stripped off his shirt to pick up some rays of sunshine. He wore a baggy, battered pair of faded khaki pants. Then he brought out his can of Heine's Blend tobacco and his pipe. His chest was average in size, and his chest hair, like a thin pine forest, grew in staccato fashion across his chest. Some of those pine trees curled in funny directions.

Out came his small box of matches as his finger tamped the tobacco down the barrel of his pipe. Striking a match, he would take a draw on his pipe, blow a smoke ring, and survey our yard. He always looked for jobs where he could putter, not on something that required major motion. I would go after weeds, pulling them up. Dad would edge the grass. We made the back yard blossom.

In April, we got some dramatic news from Annapolis, Maryland. Sybil and Bill announced their engagement. They would marry in the Naval Academy Chapel on June 7, 1947, the day after Bill would graduate and be commissioned an Ensign. We had joy in our hearts for them, even as silent regrets for Jim Pettit filtered through our minds. But we said nothing of that. Now we looked forward to June. Letters and phone calls flew between Annapolis and San Gabriel. The upshot was that Mom and Dad decided they could not attend the wedding. Then they posed a question to us, Would Carol and I go and stand in for them? Sybil wrote me a letter on May 2. She wrote, "Since you are a young man now, old enough to travel cross country, would you like to give your sister to the man she loves on her wedding day? You are so gentle and understanding, I really think it would be fun for both of us. The aisle is not very long and the chapel is cozy. It would be a moment I would never forget as long as we both shall live. As for a suit, you wear whatever you have. You are a handsome fellow, and always look well groomed in anything you wear."

Carol and I said "Yes!" and frantic preparations followed. Dad drove me to downtown Los Angeles to a men's clothier and bought me a fine herringbone sport coat, dress shirt and tie, and a pair of dark slacks. Wow! I was now dressed up as a young man. I liked the feel and the look. Mom hired a photographer to take my picture in my new outfit. Mom did the same for Carol. I went to my Principal at Alhambra High and requested a leave of absence. He granted it.

We boarded our train in Alhambra. Mom and Dad purchased seats on the coach. Tickets for the sleeper were too expensive. By now, Carol and I made peace. We ceased fighting. She had a full time job in downtown Los Angeles, and we saw less of each other. That was just fine. I wanted to see America, and this was my chance. We barely slept in our coach seats, and stirred awake in Ogden, Utah, the next morning. Wyoming seemed drab, and covered with sagebrush. But out in Iowa and Illinois saturated ground from torrential rains greeted us. Could the corn crop survive that? We walked to the diner, stretching as we walked. Then we came back to our seats for a look at more soaked crops.

Finally, we came to Chicago. Back home, Dad had taken me aside before we left. He wanted me to understand something about his mother Elizabeth. She was now a widow. I knew nothing of my grandfather except that Dad didn't like him. Grandma, however, was different. Dad and Grandma loved each other. She had tried to protect Dad from the harsh side of Grandpa.

Elizabeth, Dad explained, had a strange disease called goiter. The skin of her neck was not natural. It had a peculiar look, not smooth, but lumpy, as if the skin of her neck stretched over pebbles. He warned me that her neck swelled to almost twice its normal size. It would look unpleasant, but I shouldn't ask any questions, and was not to stare at it. Unknown to us in California, it was common in Illinois.

Sure enough, Elizabeth and members of her family greeted us at the station. Carol and I stepped on to the conductor's stool while members of her family grabbed our bags. Grandma wanted a hug and a kiss. It was our first time to meet. Around her neck she had bound a lace scarf tightly pulled to cover her goiter. I looked through the lace and her neck looked gruesome to me. I hardly knew how to hug and kiss her. I forced myself, and so did Carol. Laughing and talking all at once, they drove us to a downtown Czech restaurant. I had never seen such a thing in California. But there in Chicago such restaurants dotted the area where Bohemians clustered.

Dad had rejected his Bohemian heritage. He moved to California to get as far away as possible. Suddenly, Carol and I were supposed to get reacquainted with our heritage, and order dinner from a strange Czech menu. "Liza" spared us embarrassment by ordering a traditional favorite for all of us: chicken and dumplings. I found that I liked it. We stayed overnight with Grandma Liza, and then we went back the next morning to the station for the remainder of our trip to Baltimore. I was not supposed to look at Grandma's neck, but my eyes kept coming back to it, like a dog that returns to curiously sniff. We were glad to be back on track for Baltimore.

Sybil greeted us there and drove us to her apartment in Annapolis. She began to show us around. I liked the older downtown, and the Capital Building. History showed everywhere. I had bought a brand new pair of Levi's and wore them around Annapolis. It seemed to me that easterners would be interested in my western wear. But no one paid attention. I took a day to travel by train to Washington, D.C., wandered the city, and took in the Capitol Building.

Another day Sybil took Carol and me to walk around the Naval Academy grounds. Besides the chapel, which was a must-see, we walked to the bust of Chief Tecumseh. I took a picture of Sybil there. Plebes, as the cadets were called, liked to be photographed with their girl friends on the pedestal of the Chief. Tecumseh, the Plebes believed, showered good luck on those who gathered at his pedestal.

Bill regaled me with a special treat. Moored at the quay was a ship that Bill explained was a "YP," and weighed 60 tons. I got the impression it was a harbor workhorse. We climbed aboard and Bill powered it up. The diesel engines seemed immense to me. Once we were out on Chesapeake Bay with no other ships nearby, he turned the helm over to me. "Take the wheel," he said. I stepped into the helmsman's position and felt the pulsation of the engines and 60 tons of ship under my control. It was awesome to be shipmaster even if for ten minutes. The YP did as I ordered it; power up, power down, turn to starboard, turn to port. At Bill's word I did a 180-degree turn and headed her back toward the dock. Then Bill took over and brought her in. It was another day to remember.

The wedding took place on Saturday, June 7th, in St. Andrews Chapel. Feverish preparations continued between Sybil and her wedding attendants. I stood off to one side and out of the way. Saturday morning I put on my new sport coat and tie. The suit felt so different, but I liked dressing up. We drove to the chapel. Sybil looked beautiful in her white dress, her face covered by a lace veil. I escorted her from her car and held out my left arm so she could clasp it, and merge with me for the final approach to the chapel. I was doing what Dad had asked me to do: stand in for him and escort his daughter down the aisle of the chapel to be married. I felt so proud.

Her bridesmaids assembled into a formation ahead of us. As we approached the chapel a group of four midshipmen in dress white uniforms, Bill's best friends, stood at attention, two rows of two, facing each other. Each held up a ceremonial sword, the tips of swords touching so as to form a canopy for us. We walked through the archway slowly, pacing our steps. This was Sybil's moment, what she had lived for over the past three years. Here was joy, excitement, drama, and love. There were confident smiles as our awning of swords ushered us forward. The chapel was filled to overflowing, mostly cadets now having become Ensigns, but with civilian friends of Sybil's too.

The walk down the aisle became a fantasy. Time slowed down and then stopped. Each step seemed to take a minute. Faces were a blur. I felt my heart beating. The Chaplain and Bill were standing side by side at the altar and seemed so far away. The flowers on the altar highlighted a cross that beamed a message of joy. Was it five minutes later that we reached the altar? Bill stepped forward to receive Sybil's hand. White shoes and gloves accented his gleaming white dress uniform. Finally, he took her arm, and turned and faced the Chaplain. Now, I could step back and relax. I had played father to my sister and all went well. I breathed a sigh of relief.

The rest of the day was a flurry of activity. Bill had purchased a new 1947 blue Chevy coupe that they christened "the bluebird of happiness." They drove off later that day to Rehoboth Beach, Delaware, for their honeymoon. Carol and I packed and prepared for our return train trip home.

Somewhere that week I heard the Navy Hymn for the first time. It was so haunting that I have treasured it as a memento for all that happened that week. Titled "Eternal Father Strong to Save" it goes,

> *"Eternal Father, strong to save,*
> *Whose arm does bind the restless wave,*
> *Who bids the mighty ocean deep*
> *Its own appointed limits keep;*
> *O hear us when we cry to Thee,*
> *For those in peril on the sea."*

Only slowly did it occur to me that the music echoed in my soul because God was watching over me in a mysterious way. I was tiptoeing toward an understanding of His guiding light.

When Carol and I returned home, Dad and Mom wanted to take us to Yosemite before the summer crowds arrived. Mom purchased groceries and Dad prepped the car. Little did we know that this would be our last family vacation together. We took a housekeeping tent in Camp Curry and settled in. We hiked from there to the Fish Hatchery, then on to Vernal Falls. On a Friday night the Park Superintendent allowed a western band to set up a stage in the nearby meadow.

The band played foot-stomping music as crowds from around the Valley joined in. We had great fun. But the next day, as I walked beside the meadow, grass and flowers were destroyed, trampled down as if by a herd of buffalo. I was uncomfortable with the sight. I don't think the Park Superintendent allowed dancing in the meadow again.

By 9:00 o'clock at night, Camp Curry stilled into silence. We strained to hear a faint voice from Glacier Point calling from 3000 feet above to the valley below. "Firefall!" the voice came down as a whisper. The red-hot ashes falling toward the valley transfixed us. The first red ashes glowed in the darkness like a volcanic stream, then turned to yellow and slowly burned out. "Ooohs" and "aahs" followed. Then we sat by the fire and reminisced. Those were quality moments.

The morning before we left I got up at sunrise. The air was cool. Smoke from a dozen campfires created ribbons of haze over the camp. Something about the fragrance of burning pine powered my senses. For me it signified adventure and the joy of mountain life. I was addicted to it. I quickly dressed, put on my boots, and dragged a comb through my hair. The sights and fragrances of the woods signaled to me that this was a special day. Forget breakfast. I wanted a trail to take me to the tall mountains and let me test myself against them.

I walked to the Fish Hatchery, up and over Vernal Falls, then on to Nevada Falls. My legs were strong. They would carry me anywhere. *But wait. I had no breakfast and told no one of my whereabouts. Maybe*, I thought, *I should go back for both reasons.* I didn't.

I saw a trail marker pointing the way to Half Dome, several more miles ahead. *Go for it!* I thought. I kept hiking. I came upon the backside of Half Dome and looked up. It was past lunchtime and I felt starved. *It's OK. There's adventure ahead.*

On the sloping rock escarpment that is the backside of Half Dome, park rangers had hewn steps into the granite surface. Alongside, they placed a steel cable for climbers to steady themselves. That helped prevent some careless hiker from falling to his death. I climbed the stairwell while looking up. I didn't dare look down. At 3:00 pm I made it to the top. I wanted to yell to my family below that I was okay. But that would be futile. Instead I filled my senses with the grandeur of Yosemite laid out before me. To me it was the most beautiful place on earth. I sat and drank in the scene. One lonely pine tree stood nearby, bent low by the ceaseless winds that blew. But at that moment I didn't feel lonely. Rather, I seemed to be at one with all of creation. Granite domes, great waterfalls, and the Merced River meandering slowly through the valley below created an unforgettable scene.

Have you ever felt that you could touch the tops of the mountains? Have you had a vantage point from which you could gaze upon what seemed like all of creation? I was at that point on top of Half Dome. Here is where human beings are re-created. I saw God's creation and rejoiced. All the surrounding High Sierras stretched northward and southward from my vantage point, what John Muir called The Range of Light. Only reluctantly did I turn and get ready to return to the valley below.

When I staggered back to camp I was too exhausted and hungry to listen to Mom's geyser of angry words tinged with fear. Usually Mom had a quotable quote for all situations such as, "All's well that ends well," or, "Better late than never." That night her quote was unquotable. Dad's comment was laconic, "Moe came back all tired and sweat." I ate my meal late and crawled into bed for a deep sleep.

Not long after our return home Dad asked if I would go 50-50 with him on a new 78 rpm Philco record player. I agreed and he purchased it and brought it home. We could stack as many as six records on the spindle and the player would do the rest. Dad had his favorite songs. He took breaks from his tennis games on Saturdays or from our yard work to play his songs.

A scene began, taking a familiar pattern. After putting on his favorite records, Dad would invite Mom to dance. Her response was scripted, "No, Ed." His rejoinder came in automatic fashion, "C'mon, let's cut a rug!" or "Let's cut down the ole pine tree!"

Then, as if to make his appeal more attractive, he stood and began to move with the music. Mom's arthritis held her back, but her reluctance was more than that. Even when her health had been good, her response was the same. Dad then held his arms as if she, or some mysterious woman, was wrapped in his embrace. One arm hugged the mystery woman's shoulder. The other guided her free hand. A twirl followed, then a dip, then the imaginary woman would lean far back as Dad pressed her body into a backward arch. Holding that position for a moment, the mystery couple savored the delight of shared rhythm. Then back up into another twirl. They seemed to be on stage performing for all to see. But Mom and I were his audience. And so it was. The dance went on.

Emotions welled up in me. Here was my father, a true romantic under his tough Chicago shell, seeking a relationship that could fill his heart with love. But, imagination and rhythm was all he got. He danced alone. One of his favorite dance tunes was "Mexicali Rose." Sometimes I wondered if the mystery woman was a senorita that he met riding horseback along the Rio Grande River in Texas. Gene Kelley he was not, nor Fred Astaire, but he had a ballroom style of dance that was uniquely his. I felt sad for him. All I could do was watch this drama unfold.

Eight

Road Trips

I wanted to get out of the house. I had been saving for years to buy my first car. Now 17, I was eligible to drive. Both Mom and Dad gave me lessons in our Plymouth. I began searching for a car of my own in used car lots, even as America was buying new cars as fast as Detroit could make them. On Colorado Boulevard in Pasadena I spotted a green 1934 Ford coupe for sale. It was love at first sight. I wonder if girls know that where some guys are concerned his car is as important as his girl.

Since I did not ask Dad for help (as usual), I proceeded to talk to a slick salesman. He had a line that aroused my desire and made me an easy sell. His words dared me, "But you can't afford a fine car like this." Truth be told, he hooked me. As he knew, I wanted that Ford all the more. He insisted on a price of $400. Naïve as I was I did not bargain.

I went to my bank, withdrew $400 from my savings account, came back to his lot, and said I wanted the green Ford. He chomped his cigar, blew smoke, and fell silent as I counted out $400 cash. Amazement registered on his face. We both knew I was paying too much. But silence prevailed. My failure to ask for help when I needed it cost me dearly. I signed the bill of sale, took the keys, and drove away. Here was a proud moment, especially as I showed it to Dad. I showed my Ford to all who would look. I bought polish and hand-buffed it to a shiny green luster.

Summer was here. My wanderlust kicked in. I wanted to see California. No, I wanted to see the world. My "Green Hornet" and I would set out, like Don Quixote of old, and tame the world. Only I had no Sancho to ride with me. I went alone, devising plans as I traveled. Early in July 1947, I set out at 4 am. I was all of seventeen, and I had my folk's hesitant okay. It was hot. I had two blankets to sleep with, my boots, work shirts, some groceries, and a big jug of cool water.

I rounded the corner of Coolidge and on to San Marino Avenue. Immediately a police cruiser pulled me over. Eyeing me suspiciously, he checked my driver's license, and then asked, "What's in the bottle, Hooch?" "No, sir," I replied. "It's water for my trip over the Grape Vine." "Likely story!" he muttered. "You turn around right now and head for home and I won't bust you. Do you hear me?" "Yes, sir," I replied. I turned around, went around the block, and headed north again toward the Grape Vine. That officer was not going to thwart my plan.

Highway 99 took me over the mountains known as the Grape Vine, and into the San Joaquin Valley. The days were much hotter in the valley. But my Ford had an interesting feature – a windshield that I could crank open, and a rear window I could crank down. I had already installed a "necker knob" on the steering wheel. With it I could control my car with one hand on the necker knob while the other hand rested on the window. Later, I would put my right arm around my girlfriend while I steered with my left hand on the necker knob. (Hence its name.)

The temperature hovered at 100 degrees. I had no air conditioning, so I cranked open the windshield, lowered all windows and inhaled the hot air blowing over me. What a feeling of freedom that gave me. I stopped now and then at orange-shaped huts that sold only one thing: fresh orange juice. I found groves of trees where I could rest in the shade. But, I saw no "Help Wanted" signs. My plan was to find farm work and earn money to continue my travels.

Road Trips

Finally, north of Sacramento near Marysville, I saw a Help Wanted sign. I pulled in and headed down a dirt road to the farmhouse. The farmer was in the yard checking equipment. He wore a broad brimmed straw hat and a pair of overalls. He eyed me carefully, sized me up, and then offered me a job. He had a large plot dedicated to cling peaches. They needed spraying to control a leaf disease. "I'll drive the Caterpillar track layer," he said, "while you ride behind me on a spray rig, and throw a liquid mist on the peach trees." He didn't mention what kind of chemical solution I would be spraying. I knew it must be toxic, but I wanted a job and asked no questions.

We hitched the rig to his Caterpillar tractor. He showed me how to hold the spray wand, and how to keep the wand moving so as to cover the trees with the spray. Down the rows we went between fruit trees laden with peaches. He drove slowly while I kept the wand pointed upward and sideways to coat the trees. Droplets of spray fell from the trees and covered me. The mist soon filled my lungs. No matter, he kept moving. I kept spraying.

At the end of the day he asked me to report back to him at 8:00 a.m. the next day for more of the same. Now it was time to find something to eat and some place to sleep. I drove into town and bought a can of Campbell's pork and beans, a loaf of bread, and a bottle of Coca Cola. Each valley town had a park. I went to the park to savor my dinner. Not surprisingly, the beans got tiresome about halfway through the can. Ditto for the bread; it lacked butter and jam.

> *But*, I thought, *I am free of mom's control. This summer I will prove myself a man. I will shed the memory of my "cowardice" in the locker room at Alhambra High. I will stand up straight and return to San Gabriel victoriously.*

Those thoughts kept me going. I needed that goal. I was sweaty, had no shower or hope of one, and my bed would be the grass in the park. *But tough measures would produce a stronger me*, or so I thought.

I laid one blanket on the grass, and the other covered all my sweaty clothes and me. The only thing I took off was my boots. *I wonder, will someone attack me or rob me?* I was too tired to worry. I trusted my luck and the guardian angel that watched over me. I rolled over and went to sleep. About 2:00 am I awakened. The stars shone ever so brightly, and so silently. Then came an awareness. The evening dews and damps filtered through the bottom blanket and gave it a sticky, wet quality that soon made my Levi's squishy.

From that point on, I had a restless sleep. *I guess*, I thought, *this is all a part of what will make you a man.* It never occurred to me to go to a hardware store and buy a waterproof oilcloth to sleep on. Impetuous as usual, I failed to ask questions and get information. Remember the boyhood incident where I could not rig a sailboat alone? I did not ask for help. I then threw it to the ground. That was a life problem of mine, and it cost me dearly that summer. That was one of the ways that I learned about consequences in the refiner's fire. I survived those nights, and was not bothered by police or vagrants. But the cold, wet clothes bothered me a whole lot.

In the morning, I changed into fresh Levi's and shirt, draping yesterday's clothes over the passenger seat to dry them out. I found a faucet in the park and washed my face. Then, I finished the can of beans, had more bread and Coke, and drove to the farm for more spraying.

This time the farmer gave me a break; he offered to switch positions and take the spray rig. He gave me quick instructions on how to drive the "Cat." The throttle was in plain sight. Then, there were two brake pedals. The right pedal braked the right track; the other the left track. Thus, when I got to the end of a row of peach trees, I would press down on the left pedal. The left track slowed or stopped depending on the pressure I exerted, while the right track kept moving. I then swung a turn to the left and headed down another row of trees. This was so simple it gave me a great deal of pleasure to be in control. This powerful tractor did my bidding.

After two days we finished spraying his orchard. He paid me $20.00 in cash, and I was on my way. I kept traveling north looking for more work. I spotted another "Help Wanted" sign. When I turned in the driveway and met the farmer, he told me it was wheat harvest time for him. He had an old combine. He would drive it in straight lines through his field. My job would be to capture the threshed wheat in gunnysacks as it came down a chute. The chaff was scattered about the field to provide mulch for next year's crop.

He showed me where to sit next to him. On board were stacks of empty gunnysacks ready to be opened to receive threshed wheat. As a sack filled with grain, he taught me a quick stitch using heavy-duty thread attached to a monster needle. He gave me 10 seconds to stitch each gunnysack closed, push it aside, and open a new sack to receive more wheat as it poured out the chute.

This was hard work. My job was relentless. There could be no slip-ups. I lost all sense of time and place as I filled and sewed sacks. The combine clanked and roared noisily through the wheat field in straight lines as we cut a swath. The sun bore down on us. I began to learn why farmers' wore hats, and why city boys like me needed one.

As the wheat separated from the chaff we created a cloud of dust. It coated our nostrils and lungs, but we kept working. We couldn't let something like that stop us. An inner voice cried out, *Give me a break, something to drink, some fresh air, a shower, a change of clothes. Let me out of here!* Another voice responded, *You asked for it. Now you've got it. Live with it.* Was that a parent of mine shaping me up once again? I needed that voice at that moment. I listened and kept on sewing sacks.

When the field was harvested and the farmer had a year's income at his fingertips, he took out his wallet and gave me a grainy smile, a $20 bill, and a word of thanks. He went to his home to shower and change clothes. I went to the local Park, opened another can of pork and beans, more bread, and a Coke. What a dinner! I rapidly tired of this menu. My body screamed for a shower. But now I had two $20 bills along with left over cash I had brought with me from home. I made a plan; this would be my last time to search for "Help Wanted" signs. In the morning I would turn south to Sacramento, then head east into the Sierra Nevada Mountains.

Again that night the grass was as damp as before. The wetness slowly oozed through my blanket into my clothes. Breakfast was the same old, same old thing. But I had money in my pocket. I washed in the men's room, put on a dry pair of Levi's and a khaki shirt, rolled the blankets, loaded my Ford, and bid farewell to that little town.

With the exception of the farmer, no one knew I was there. I was a stranger in this valley in the sun. People like me came and went, and life went on. I had a sudden thought,

> *No one cared that I was there or whether I lived or died. I was like one of the vagrants that passed through all summer long. I was alone, and home looked ever so sweet.*

The drive into the Sierras proved daunting. Highway 80 in those days was a two-lane road. As I approached a curve, the sedan behind me suddenly bolted forward to pass. I thought everyone knew that you can't pass on a curve. Not this driver. As he pulled alongside of me, a Greyhound loomed around the bend heading straight at him. He panicked. He took the option to save his skin. He sideswiped me to miss the oncoming bus. My Ford coupe flew off the road and on to the shoulder.

He pulled over, parked his sedan, and walked to me. He had on a suit and tie with a fedora that gave him a gangster look. With no apology, he surveyed the damage to my running board and door. He quickly made an offer of $50.00 cash to repair the damage. Being a newbie driver, I figured $50.00 would cover it and accepted his offer. I walked back to his sedan while he reached into his glove compartment for cash. I looked in.

I shouldn't have been so curious. There on the back seat sat three ladies in skimpy dresses and heavy make-up. Red rouge and false eyelashes dominated their faces. I had never seen ladies like this in San Gabriel. They were different. One of them looked like the painted lady that I saw in the burlesque theater on Main Street in Los Angeles. The other two looked like she-wolves on the prowl. One of them winked at me. I wasn't used to this. I looked away.

The man in the fedora emerged with a $50.00 bill in his hand, and demanded assurance that I would not file an accident report. Once again, I nodded assent not knowing that state law required me to file such a report. My guardian angel had been busy for me that morning. Was it wishful thinking that saw my guardian angel as very real? I came to believe in my angel. It covered many, but not all, of my most grievous errors.

At Donner State Park near Lake Tahoe was a perfect place for a campout. Many years ago the Donner Party became trapped in snow drifts and some perished of cold, disease, or starvation. Mr. Shipman, my high school teacher of California History, spent time with us in our class detailing the winter tragedy for the Donner Party in 1846. Now I camped in the same place as they had. How different were the circumstances! A brisk summer evening along with an orange sunset glow made the Park look peaceful. The Donner Party starved and some died. But I stopped to buy a hamburger and fries outside the Park. What a contrast!

The sizzle of bacon, murmuring voices, and the sound of an axe laid to wood awakened me at sunrise. *Oh, how I wished someone would invite me to breakfast!* No one did. "Holy Toledo," I muttered as I opened another can of pork and beans. I began to hate the flavor. I rolled my blankets, packed my meager belongings, and took out my road map. I had a plan to continue east on Highway 80 to the point where it junctions Highway 395, then head south to Hoover Dam (Boulder Dam).

The craggy, snowcapped peaks of the Sierras were on my right; sagebrush, sand, and rolling dun colored hills of Nevada spread out on my left side. Occasionally I saw signs pointing off into the desert regarding "Diamond Lil's Ranch" or other such names. The signs reminded me that prostitution thrived in Nevada.

Bad news sounded. The flywheel on the engine began grinding against the crankcase. The noise set off alarms in my mind. The crankcase could split open and spill the engine oil on the roadway, leaving me stranded. I drove slowly to minimize any damage, and headed for Las Vegas and a repair shop.

I arrived on the outskirts of Las Vegas that evening. There wasn't much to see in those days, and I had no desire to see it. I grew up in a middle class home during the Great Depression, undergirded by the virtues of thrift and hard work. Mom and Dad left me with the impression that gambling was for people who wanted something for nothing. On his trips through Nevada Dad saved old silver dollars minted in Carson City and gave them to me. I became an amateur coin collector.

I looked for an auto repair shop still open. I found one and rolled in. The two mechanics looked like they had spent the day under the car hoist. Good, I wanted a mechanic like that. One of them listened to the grating sound in my crankcase. "Twenty dollars will do it," he said. I had two twenty-dollar bills in my pocket plus the $50 bill stashed safely away. This repair would cut my spending money in half. "Go ahead and fix it," I replied. "It has to be done." I watched him put it on the hoist, drain the oil, then slowly undo the screws that held the crankcase in place. Sure enough, the flywheel was loose and scraped the crankcase with every revolution. I bought a coke for five cents, watching and waiting.

Finally, I went to the men's bathroom. What a picture confronted me. A condom dispenser took a prominent place on one wall bearing a message of a thin skin of rubber for protection against disease. On the walls, someone scribbled names of local madams and their phone numbers. Lewd females, drawn by some doofus, filled the spaces between the names. The floor had not been mopped since Noah's great flood, and the toilet had dark brownish stains inside and out. I hurried so as not to linger there.

By 10:00 pm my Ford came down off the hoist and I parted with a precious twenty-dollar bill. But, oh the beauty of a V-8 engine that purred once again. I didn't bother to drive through town. In my mind Nevada had two claims to fame. One was gambling and the other, sex. Or was it sex and gambling? I drove to the edge of Las Vegas, parked, locked my doors, and drifted into a restless sleep in the driver's seat.

The next day I followed the road toward Kingman. God, it was hot. I cranked open the windshield again, but all that did was flood the cab with hot air. There was no relief. Outside of Kingman dark clouds appeared. Off to my right stood an airfield where WWII B-17 bombers were lined up in perfect rows as far as the eye could see, baking in the sun. I wondered how long it would be before they melted. It was too hot to stop, so I kept heading east toward some darkening clouds, and hopefully some cool air.

Road signs told me I was on Route 66. But what they didn't say was that this was the season for monsoon rains. I was heading into the eye of a major storm, and didn't know it.

The air cooled as the rain came down, gently at first; then in torrents. Now darkness took over. The rain drenched my windshield. I could not see. I slowed to 20 mph. But that compounded my problem. The salesman had not told me about the 1934 Ford electrical system. It was primitive, and useless in a storm like this. When I slowed down, the windshield wipers slowed accordingly, and my headlights dimmed. I was dammed by heavy rain if I sped up, and, by lack of vision if I slowed down. I drove slowly, unable to see the road. Suddenly, a much newer car headed toward me with headlights on high beam. His lights blinded me. In a moment, I skidded off the Highway, down a muddy slope, and came to rest sideways at the bottom of the embankment.

My Ford was up to its running boards in a reddish Arizona mud, tilted at a 45-degree angle. Racing my engine and kicking it into first gear, then reverse, accomplished nothing. My car would not move. The rain plummeted down. I held on to the steering wheel and leaned toward my side window, fearful my car would tip over if I didn't. *No sleep tonight*, I thought. *Just hang on tight*. At first light I could see that the Arizona engineers planned Route 66 carefully. The pavement was six feet above the floor of the desert to keep the roadway safe during monsoon rains. I was at the bottom of the six-foot slope.

Morning came. Above me, on the roadway, a grizzled rancher/cowboy appeared driving a battered Ford pickup truck. The rain stopped. He leaned out his window. I cranked my window open. Our eyes met, and the desperation on my face told him what he needed to know. "You need help, son?" he called. "Yes, sir," I responded. He turned off his engine, stepped out and looked more carefully at my dilemma. "I think I can help you," he said. "Sure could use it," I replied.

He stepped to the back of his pickup, lowered the gate, and pulled out a long piece of heavy-duty rope. He twirled it over his head like a cowboy about to lasso a steer on the loose. The rope landed in front of my bumper. "Good aim," I said. I slogged through the red mud, and with the help of his verbal commands, tied the rope around my front bumper to his satisfaction. Thank God for my boots. Mud was up to my calves.

We both clambered back into our cabs. He shouted, "Don't turn on your engine yet!" He inched forward, taking up the slack. When the line was taut, he began to pull with all the power of his pickup. The line groaned, but held. My car inched forward through the muck. Now he used raw power. To move me up ten feet, his engine began to scream. I held my breath. The line didn't snap. Inch by inch my car moved forward. I fought to hold the steering to the angle from which he pulled. The mud forced me into a tight grip. I held on. My bumper held. The line held.

In five minutes I was back on the pavement. I got out, heaving a sigh of relief. I unhitched my front bumper, and with a heart full of gratitude, shook his hand and thanked him. He didn't ask for money. That was good because I didn't have a significant amount to give him. After reloading his rope, he waved to me, and drove away. I became convinced the rancher/cowboy was my guardian angel in disguise. When Jacob wrestled with an angel long ago, he said, "God was in this place and I knew it not." *But who would believe that?* I did.

My car, with wheels caked in reddish mud, looked like a prehistoric monster. There were no car washes in those days, or I would have gone there immediately. I counted my last cash, did a U-turn on Route 66, and decided I had better head for home. I crossed the Colorado River and headed through the Mojave Desert for Cajon Pass, and San Gabriel Valley. Driving across Mojave I could hear chunks of mud break loose from my spoked wheels, hit the pavement and crumbled. *Good*, I thought, *the less mud, the better.*

But as I drove, my sense of accomplishment was muted by an inner voice. I had a strong feeling that someone else was living their life through me. I was vaguely aware that it was my mother. Sitting at her bedside after school for so many years, and wearing the dirty sock around my neck had left me with a sense of dependence on her. What a strange relationship it is to know that I needed my mother, yet had also arrived at a point where I wanted to live my own life. I was convicted that after two weeks of hard work, sightseeing, and adventure, I was still not my own man.

I hated that feeling. It clung like cloth to me, cloth that was laden with static electricity. I needed to discharge that static so the material would turn me loose, but I felt no such discharge. I was glad to get home to a warm bed and home cooking, but I felt myself slipping back into old dependencies and routines, a deeper sense of my dependence on Mom. When would I be free of that?

However, I had the rest of summer ahead of me. After I washed my car, Doug and Mel dropped by with an exciting plan. They had spotted an ad that offered an ancient 1923 Dodge open-touring sedan for sale. Who needed a top in sunny California? They bought it for $75. We took it down to our neighborhood 76 gas station and got permission to put it on the hoist. We changed the oil, replaced some hoses, serviced the tires, and cleaned the black paint so it shined. All the while the manager had his office radio on, listening to the news as he pumped gas and washed windshields. The newscaster kept a steady flow of details of a peaceful atomic bomb test at a far off island called Bikini. I listened as we worked. Willy-nilly, we were witnesses to history in the making as we buffed the black paint on the old Dodge.

We were ready for the opening day of school, now my senior year. Doug had a plan to create some fun. He put on his Pea jacket, a funny looking hat, and his secret Bonehead. We did the same, but with no hats. We headed down Main Street honking our horn whenever possible. The horn on the old Dodge got everyone's attention, a squawk like no other on the street. It brought back one of the sounds of the roaring 20's. People stopped to stare, and then laughed.

Doug pulled up directly in front of the school. As he slowed down, he turned the ignition key off, then back on. With each turn of the key, the engine backfired creating a loud "BANG!" Students milling on the front steps turned to look, then roared with laughter; some cheered. With the cheers, Doug doffed his hat and waved at the crowd. We laughed too and waved. What a fun way to begin my last semester. We repeated this many times that fall. Some students began waiting for us to appear, and then cheered.

NINE

Introduction To The Adult World

Days after my graduation from Alhambra High I began job hunting. I found an ad in the "Times" for help wanted at the Monrovia Nursery. I liked growing things, and drove to Monrovia to apply for one of the nursery openings. The Supervisor hired me on the spot and told me to report at 8:00 am the following day. I packed a lunch that night and rose early the next morning for my first fulltime job. The nursery was just east of Santa Anita, about five miles away from home.

At the nursery I was surrounded by Braceros, Mexicans issued green cards by the Immigration Service to help in the agriculture sector of the U.S. Few spoke English, but I did my best to listen to their conversations and translate them to English. Mr. Oleson, my Spanish teacher, taught us classic Castilian Spanish that was of little help to me. Those men spoke in clipped phrases that were a blend of rural Mexican idioms with some English mixed in. For instance, our word "lunch" became "lunche". (Pronounced lun-chay).

We were ordered into a large field where we were to transplant young shoots into long rows on raised furrows. The Braceros bent over, took a shoot and with one hand created in the furrow an indentation, and then with the other hand tamped a plant firmly into place. I tried that and found that my back hurt. So instead, I did all my work with my right hand while my left arm rested on my left knee to ease the strain on my back. I thought I had found a way to co-exist with backbreaking work.

My supervisor didn't agree. When he walked by he ordered me to use two hands, like the Braceros. But after he moved on, I reverted to using my right hand only. It didn't take long for the supervisor to see my ruse. By the end of my first week as I entered a shed to punch my time card, he told me to hand over my time card, gave me a paycheck, and told me not to return.

This firing shocked me. The shock felt like, *You are not wanted. Your work is not O.K. with us. Move on. Get lost!* I did self-talk all the way home trying to ease the pain of rejection. Slowly I began to recover, but it took a long time. I never wanted to go through that again.

Several miles down Hermosa Road from our home a local nursery named Hines Nursery did a thriving business. Here they had a great location to serve the needs of subdivisions springing up in the San Gabriel Valley. Thousands of veterans arrived here after the war and bought tract homes where they could raise their families.

The owner of the nursery, Mr. Hines, was busy when I arrived, but took a few minutes to interview me. I must have impressed him. He hired me to begin work the next day. Mr. Hines looked like a "strange duck." He was wall-eyed. He looked at you with one eye while the other eye wandered off in another direction. His shock of hair was loosely combed, and with one hand he tried to arrange his hair when he felt nervous. His speech seemed a little slurred, and his shirt, pants and shoes looked like leftover's from another era. He was not a people person. But he knew plants. And he knew how to turn a profit. He left the sales to his select staff while he ruled the roost from the background.

He put me to work on the lowliest duty, that is, watering the thousands of trees and plants in containers, pulling weeds, and carrying sacks of fertilizer to waiting cars. That was okay. I needed to start somewhere. I applied myself with diligence. Dad gave me a leadership manual authored by General Motors Corp. The lesson: give 100% of your best, be open to listen and learn, like people, and you will be in demand. I read it and I followed it. Mr. Hines watched me from a distance as he worked.

Spring crept up on us, and it was time for Mr. Hines to propagate camellias. Camellias were his specialty. He needed help and put me to work as his assistant. We made a team. I learned quickly what he wanted to teach me.

With his business skills, Mr. Hines leased land under the Southern California Edison power lines further east on Roses Road. He hired two Mexican laborers to make a crew of three, with me as supervisor. There was no increase in pay, of course. He spent several days teaching us how to build lath houses for the camellias. Slowly but surely the first lath house took shape. If Mr. Hines had ordered construction through union carpenters, he would have paid a pretty penny. As it was, my wage was $1.00 per hour, and I had no idea what he paid the other two in my crew, but it must have been less. This was Mr. Hines' way to huge profits.

As the work progressed we began transplanting camellias under our new lath houses. We got into a rhythm. We knew what had to be done and we did it. We transplanted young shoots into one-gallon containers. However, Jorge lagged at his shovel. It soon became obvious that he purposely balked at the workload. He began muttering a Spanish phrase loudly enough so we could hear what he said. His pet complaint became, "pinche cavrone." When I heard him I had a suspicion that the phrase would not be in my Spanish dictionary. So I went to several Mexicans that I knew well enough to ask them what it meant. Their response: "That is a very bad word, very bad." I responded, "So what does it mean?" Their response was the same, "That is a very bad word."

I later looked it up in my Spanish/English dictionary, but it was not there. All I knew was that Jorge didn't like his work. His mutterings became offensive as they mounted in frequency. I went to Mr. Hines to report on the matter. He fired Jorge and hired another worker, this time an elderly man. We then had a new trio to carry on.

Mr. Hines surprised me by hiring this older man. I think his name was Jim. He kept up with the workload and maintained a positive attitude.

Our lunchtime became a special treat for me. I pumped him for stories of his youth. He told me of growing up on the plains of the Dakota Territory. Early on, his father put him to work on their ranch. Jim took a buckboard and hitched it to one of their workhorses. He drove out on the plains daily to collect buffalo bones.

Frontiersmen, early settlers, and the U.S. Cavalry had shamelessly slaughtered the buffalo. The Cavalry did so to deny the Sioux Indians their most precious resource of food and hides. The settlers killed them to be rid of what they considered "pests." They were shot and left to rot on the prairie. What had originally been a vast herd was reduced by the 1890's to a scattered few. Jim was a witness to one of the world's greatest slaughters. He was living history. Jim found piles of bleached bones. He put on heavy leather gloves, stopped his buckboard at each pile, and loaded the bones on to his wagon. When fully loaded he drove back to the ranch, created a giant pile of bones, and went back for more.

His father sold the bones to dealers who took them and ground them into powder to be used as fertilizer. Thus the frontier closed, a fascinating era ended, and a different kind of American began to replace the frontiersmen. Now farmers and ranchers with barbed wire took over the territory. I listened intently as Jim shared stories of his youth, coming to maturity on the plains. Mr. Hines did me a great favor by hiring him.

I invited my other assistant, Eduardo, to teach me his brand of "Spanish." He helped me learn a host of expressions that Mexicans used for daily conversation. Since I had learned from Mr. Oleson the basics of classical Spanish, I simply added to my vocabulary with Eduardo and his everyday Mexican. As we worked he also taught me some lines from popular Mexican music: "La Cucaracha" and "El Rancho Grande." We sang or hummed as we worked and the day went faster.

Across the street from the nursery a new Methodist Church sprang up. The youth group there, called M.Y.F., or Methodist Youth Fellowship, attracted me. I left the Presbyterian Church and began activities with the Methodist youth, then joined the choir, and with that began singing for the Sunday services. The MYF took hayrides to Laguna Beach. We attended regional square dances in Long Beach, the only kind of dancing acceptable to the church. We went to youth conferences in Alhambra. I was socially immature in my relationships, and I had a tendency to be awkward in the conversations among youth.

    I substituted on the church's basketball team. But, where I found my comfort zone was in the bass section of choir. I loved to sing, and I learned to memorize my notes since I could not read music. I found that by listening to the other men in the bass section, I could create a unison with them so that my voice did not stand out, but telescoped into one beautiful tone. We sang an Introit each Sunday for Pastor Dick Dunlap's prayer, followed by a choral anthem. I came to love the Introit, and we sang the same one each Sunday. I began to grow and deepen into a prayer life of my own. The music became an invitation to me to learn to love God. I finally found a spiritual home. The words of our Introit were so beautiful:

> *"Spirit of God, descend upon my heart;*
> *Wean it from earth; through all its pulses move;*
> *Stoop to my weakness, mighty as thou art,*
> *And make me love thee as I ought to love."*

Sybil came home in February. My best friend was back. We spent hours talking. She urged me to get a plan for my life. She reminded me of my skill with growing things. "Why not go to the best agriculture college in the west?" she asked. "Where is that?" I responded. "Up in Davis. They have a great reputation. Why don't you write and request admission?" She soon convinced me. I wrote to the University of California at Davis and requested an admission form. Sybil reminded me again that no one in our family had completed college. If I went and finished the course of study, I would be the first. That gave me incentive.

    Within a month I was accepted to begin the fall semester in their two-year program of Agriculture. I had a plan. I had a goal. Suddenly, all the possibilities of a bright future opened to me. *Thank God for Sybil,*

I thought. She really is my best friend. She opened the doors of understanding for me by urging me to go to college. *Was not "understanding" the beginning of wisdom?* It was in one sense. But only later did I discover that the fear of the Lord is the beginning of wisdom.

Bill had been assigned to duty in Japan, leaving Sybil pregnant. We kept touching that big bulge in her midriff to feel the occasional kick from the newcomer inside. On the night of March 1st, while sharing a bed with Carol, Sybil cried out in sharp pain. Dad and Mom rushed her to the hospital and she delivered Steven in the morning of March 2nd. Mom and Dad were finally grandparents. Everything began to change at our house.

My life changed too. Aunt Laurine played bridge at a club in Whittier. Laurine was a skillful player and in demand as a partner. She, too, developed rheumatoid arthritis, and her outlet was to play bridge. One of her partners, Mrs. Bacon, was the wife of a wealthy farmer who owned a large acreage of orange trees in nearby Orange County. One day Mrs. Bacon told Laurine that her husband wanted to return to his birthplace in Ontario, Canada, but was too old to drive it. Laurine perked up her ears and told her about me. She said that I could act as the driver.

Laurine called me to inquire of my interest. "Are you interested?" she asked. "Yes, I am," I responded without hesitation. She gave me Mr. Bacon's telephone number, and I made a connection with him that week. He invited me to drive to his ranch in Orange County to get acquainted.

I easily found my way there. We met, shook hands, and before the day was over I was hired to be his chauffeur to Canada. Whereas with teenagers I was awkward, I felt no shyness with him. The plan he presented was simple. He purchased a new 1947 Buick sedan, oversized and layered with chrome. I would be his driver. He had a route picked out along Highway 40 to Chicago, then to Detroit, and from there we would proceed to his birthplace in Simcoe, Ontario. We would find lodging there for several weeks before returning. He would cover all of our expenses, but with no salary for me. He was one of the richest farmers in Orange

County, but he offered me no compensation. However, I was young and eager, and accepted his terms. When Dad heard of this, he remarked, "He's tighter than the bark on a tree!" That was his assessment of Mr. Bacon. Still, we would leave on July 1st.

I worked through June for Mr. Hines, giving him notice of my departure. On July 1, with an "Up and at 'em, my hearty," and "Get the lead out!" Dad drove me to Mr. Bacon's ranch where the old man was packed and ready to go. Dad then drove to work while I loaded our suitcases into the spacious trunk of his new Buick.

I headed east toward Cajon Pass, and over the mountains into the Mojave Desert. Since my trip the previous year, I knew what to expect of heat. Mr. Bacon, however, had purchased a new swamp air conditioner for his car, the best available at that time. It made our travels much more comfortable.

After viewing numerous cemeteries along the way, we arrived in Ft. Kearney, Nebraska. There I had intimations of trouble. After dinner I drove us to our motel. By the time I pulled in, I had chest pains. They became more severe. I panicked. I thought, *I'm too young to die. And I sure don't want to die in this place.* I said nothing to Mr. Bacon; I simply endured the pain, and thirty minutes later the pain passed. Then, after resting, it became clear to me that I not only had anxiety attacks, but now I thought I had become a hypochondriac. What a wakeup call. I still talked to no one about my fears and the threats to my well being. I didn't know anyone I could talk to. I didn't even know what anxiety or hypochondria were. How could I talk about them? I had more fears to tuck into the attic of my mind, and tried to keep the door to my attic shut. It still didn't work. The door burst open from time to time.

After we visited and toured Ontario, Mr. Bacon had a change of heart. At dinner one night he shared his thoughts with me. He wanted to stay in Simcoe, take up residence, and die there among his relatives. What he was going to do about Mrs. Bacon back in California was not mine to ask. He offered me three options for getting home. He would purchase either a plane flight out of Toronto, Canada, to Los Angeles, or a train ticket to L.A., or a Greyhound bus ticket. I chose Greyhound. I wanted to see America as up close as I could.

Mr. Bacon drove me to the station the next day. He gave me a packet of money for food and miscellany, then shook my hand and thanked me. I planned stops in Chicago to visit our relatives there, and a stop in Minneapolis to visit Mom's sister. I called Mom and asked her to telephone the relatives and alert them I was coming. She was glad to hear about me, and delighted that I would visit Dad's folks in Chicago, and hers outside Minneapolis. Always there were her insistent questions, "Are you taking good care of yourself? Are you getting enough sleep and enough to eat? Have you been a good driver?" I responded with "Yes" to each question. Any other response would have created fear in her. I learned not to touch her fear button. That could set off her worry syndrome. I learned to avoid that.

At the Chicago Station Dad's younger brother, Harry, born ten years after Dad, met me. Uncle Harry had a huge belly that announced his love of beer. He seemed proud of his ability to out-drink others in the family. He was brash. As we drove through downtown Chicago he pointed to a tall building on our right. "That's the biggest whorehouse in Chicago," he commented, as if I wanted to hear about that. Actually, I had never seen such a thing in San Gabriel. I feigned interest and a casual air as if that was common knowledge to me.

He drove us to Comiskey Park to watch a baseball game with the White Sox. He bought a pitcher of beer and was surprised to find that I did not drink. He brought two cups and poured some for me. I took a few cautious sips. Uncle Harry began to find that I was not a typical Bastear, and became wary of me.

To fit in I had to drink lots of beer, make runs to the men's room, cheer lustily for the White Sox, and talk baseball with the best of them. Harry was shocked to discover that this was my first professional baseball game. "Whatsa' matter with you people out on the west coast?" he muttered. "I told Eddie back in '29 not to move to L.A.! He didn't listen to me." Harry was bothered by my total lack of knowledge regarding

Introduction To The Adult World

professional baseball. Here I was a babe in the woods and he expected better from Eddie's boy. And so it went with Uncle Harry.

Another day in Chicago seeing sights in the Loop, meeting Dad's sister, Gladys, the baby of the three siblings, and I was ready to move on. This was my first experience at meeting aunts and uncles. I was surprised at how long it took to get an understanding of our family tree when I had been separated from them for a lifetime. Separation is what Dad wanted when he headed west to raise his family and build his career. He got it. I felt that sense of separation as I met my relatives. It was not easy to bond with them.

In Minneapolis, Uncle Horace and Aunt Minetta met me at the bus station. Minetta was Mom's older sister, and Horace was her husband. They met at the end of his Army service in 1918, borrowed money, and started a small farm in Kellogg, Minnesota. Minetta looked like my mother and was built like her. Both were solid, but not fat. Minetta gladly chose farm life, and fit in to be Horace's helper, serving three meals a day, and caring for their children while he worked sunrise to sunset on their farm. Both were friendly people, but Horace seemed driven to be a scientifically successful farmer.

They bought a 300 acre dairy farm in Roberts, Wisconsin, and had made good money in WWII selling their milk to the Army for conversion to powdered milk. The powdered milk supplied American troops on battlefields around the world. Their farm home was spacious, warm, and comfortable. The town of Roberts was a page out of one of my history books. The homes in Roberts were charming and well cared for, like a dream village where every home was surrounded by white picket fences covered with red roses.

Uncle Horace knew a city slicker when he saw one. He saw one in me, and determined then to make me into a farm boy. The next morning we were up at 5 a.m. Minetta sizzled bacon, brewed coffee, prepared toast and eggs, and we, along with their tomboy daughter, Laurine, sat at their table and devoured breakfast. Horace, with a gleam in his eyes, laid out his plan for the day. I was given a clean pair of overalls, a gleaming black pair of knee-high rubber boots, a straw hat, and given a huge, flat, wide-mouth shovel. While Horace and Laurine milked the cows in the barn, I went behind their herd of bovines and scooped the wet poop off of the concrete floor.

Cows were fastened into a stall to prevent their movement, and I freely moved in to clean the area. Then with my scoop shovel full of the wettest manure on earth, I walked to Horace's spreader and dumped it in. After several hours of this, the cows were milked and released to pasture, and the manure spreader was piled high with wet poop.

Now, Horace, happier than ever, showed me how to mount his green monster, a John Deer tractor. We connected the tractor to the spreader. Then Horace pointed to his 300 acres of Timothy Hay, the harvest of which nourished his dairy herd. "Begin spreading here," he said and pointed to his hay field. The John Deere coughed and sputtered, sounding like the cement mixers I had heard in San Gabriel. Once out to the field I pulled a lever on the spreader and mechanical devices in the spreader chopped the wet manure into bits and pieces and sent it flying out the back of the spreader in a 180 degree arc. The smell of the poop and the exhaust from the tractor combined to burn that odor into my nostrils. After eight hours of loading and reloading the spreader, and driving it up and down the gentle hills with the smell clinging to my nose, I gained a new appreciation for the milk sold at our local markets.

Uncle Horace was not finished with this city slicker yet. The next day he varied the routine. Laurine and I were sent to the barn to milk the cows. Every bit of the milking process had to meet rigid standards. We took clean wet rags and washed the udders of each cow. Then Laurine and Horace showed me how to use a stripping motion with my thumb and forefinger to get a teat to squirt milk. I learned to squirt some milk into the mouth of their cat that stood nearby. We sterilized their suction machines, and attached a rubber cup to each teat, then turned on the motor that created enough suction to empty the cow's bag of milk in a matter of minutes. The hand squeezing was a back-up procedure for the machine.

INTRODUCTION TO THE ADULT WORLD

If the machine failed to relieve the cow of all her milk, we followed with the stripping motion to complete the job. We used little footstools to sit alongside the cows and complete the milking. Of course, the big, fat cat got some too. Afterwards, when the barn was cleared of the herd, Horace pointed me to a power hose where I could wash the concrete floor free of urine, poop, and debris, and prepare for the next milking. What an education! Our schools didn't teach this kind of knowledge.

All this time of work together, shoulder-to-shoulder with Laurine and Horace, drew me closer to both of them. They asked me to stay for a week and I quickly agreed. Laurine was pretty. She had tomboy in her, all right. She also had quick hands when she milked cows. *"So what?"* I thought. *"She's pretty."*

Before I left they asked if I would like to meet my grandfather William McFarland. I nodded assent, not knowing what to expect. All I knew was that when William's wife, Mom's mother, died, on Mom's third birthday, William decided that raising three girls was too much for him. He took the girls to Mom's grandmother, Elizabeth Stanton, a widow, dropped them off, and high-tailed to a ranch in Montana. Grandma Stanton was a strong woman who took the girls and raised them to adulthood. When Mom raised us she told us that she never wanted to meet or talk to William again. Abandoning her and her sisters at such a critical time was unforgiveable.

Now I faced the prospect of meeting a scoundrel, yet a man who was my maternal grandfather. Minetta prepared a picnic lunch for us. As we gathered in their car, they told me we would drive to Red Wing, Minnesota. There was a "Poorhouse" there where William was a resident. We would picnic on the banks of the Mississippi River that flowed nearby, and I could get acquainted.

Meeting Grandpa was a strange moment in time. Dad's father died in Chicago in 1944. I never met him. William, my other grandfather, would soon stand before me. As we drove into the yard of his resident Poorhouse, he stood on the front porch waiting for us. *What is a poorhouse?* I wondered. *We don't have those in San Gabriel.* We pulled up as he stepped off the porch. He represented another era to me. He stood stooped in overalls and boots, a farmer to the core. He wore a straw hat. A long moustache gave his face a kindly, elderly look. He didn't look or act like an ogre. Horace stepped forward and introduced me. We politely shook hands. I shook hands with an ancestor, my mother's father. How strange! He stepped out of Major Elsie's history text, like a museum wax figure of old. *Was he real?* I had no anger or disgust with him. He seemed frail and harmless. I was back to overcoming all the years of separation again.

He got into the car and directed us to a grassy knoll along the Mississippi River. The grass was green and the river was wide. A cool breeze flowed down from the north. There was a quiet serenity here. I thought, *Maybe I can overcome the separation between Grandpa and myself.* But it was a maybe.

Minetta spread a gingham tablecloth on the ground, and placed mounds of tuna sandwiches, chips, and glasses of lemonade in front of us. The conversation flowed between Minetta and her dad. William came back from Montana and worked for Horace and Minetta on their farm. Minetta did not explain to me how or why William was now a county indigent. I should have asked, but didn't.

Yet my mind was full of questions.

> *Why do you live here? What is a poorhouse? Why did you abandon my mother when she needed you so much? Why didn't you write and apologize to her? You could have set it right if you had only tried! I hardly know how to understand you. The relation between father and daughter is so tender and so freighted with meaning; how could you tear it apart?*

These were the questions surging in my mind. But here I was, as always, full of questions at a pregnant moment, and not asking them. It was so like me. Curious to the uttermost, but then I fell silent when it came to follow-up. So I missed connecting with my grandfather, my questions unanswered. I never saw him again.

On Friday night Horace and Minetta had a special treat in store for us. The Ringling Brothers' Circus was playing in Minneapolis. We cleaned the kitchen after dinner, climbed into their new Dodge sedan, and headed into town. I had never been to a three-ring circus, and enjoyed the show. While inside, storm clouds gathered and we were treated to a deluge like the one in Arizona. The tent groaned under the force of the wind and rain, but held. This time I had no guardian angel, but I sat closer to Laurine and we held hands. Laurine and I took the back seat in the Dodge while Horace drove us through the storm back to Roberts. I surprised myself. I leaned over, looked into Laurine's sweet eyes and gave her a kiss. Her lips were red, warm, and soft.

I was in love again. I broke free of my shyness to reach out and kiss my cousin. She accepted my offer and responded to my kiss with open arms. How refreshing to lean into love. We promised to stay in touch. On Sunday, Horace, Minetta, and Laurine drove me back to Minneapolis and I continued my journey west on the Greyhound Bus.

The way west intrigued me. I know some of the story of the winning of the west, thanks to Major Elsie, my high school history teacher, and tried to imagine this country through the eyes of Mountain Men, herds of buffalo darkening the plains, or Sioux Indians confronting Lewis and Clark along the banks of the Missouri River. Then, at Little Big Horn, I could hear the bugles of the 7th Cavalry calling the men to circle up for their last stand. Over there stood the teepees of the proud Crow Indians, mortal enemies of the Sioux, who would send scouts to help General Custer find the Sioux camps and hopefully destroy them. The Crow scouts warned Custer that Sitting Bull was a strong warrior and bad medicine, but the commander would not listen. *Oh, to fly overhead and be able to watch the battle unfold. But, I could recreate it in my mind.* I wanted to step back in time and watch it happen, heroism everywhere and treachery, too.

Sometimes I wanted to become a frontiersman, pitting myself against this giant landscape and the Indians who proudly occupied it. I could put on beaded buckskin and take a place with the trappers at Jackson Hole, trading furs and whiskey with the Indians, howling far into the night around a campfire with a jug of whiskey. Around the campfires stories were exchanged, and when the Indians were drunk on "firewater," shrewd mountain men would offer a brave a jug of cheap whiskey in exchange for his squaw. Deals closed and the mountain man went to his teepee with his squaw.

I could ride with the Cavalry. How bold and daring I would be! *But then*, I thought, *I was born a century too late for all of this.* This big sky country was alive with history, and I was reliving it. *Thanks, Major Elsie!* I quietly murmured to myself. *You were an old fuddy-duddy, but a great teacher of the story of America, as you would say, 'to the contrary notwithstanding.'*

Finally, we arrived in Portland, Oregon, and the west coast. I called Mom and Dad and alerted them that I would be home in a matter of days. I weighed myself at the bus station. I had lost ten pounds. I knew, because my pants were slipping down. The rest of the way was a blur. I was too tired of sitting up sleepless for so long. I got off at the station in Pasadena, found a pay phone, and asked Mom if she would pick me up.

Home never looked so good! Forget the issues with Mom and her control needs. My bed looked so good, and I was ready to crawl in and sleep for a year. Mom's comment on the trip reflected the folk wisdom of Grandma Stanton: "All's well that ends well." The trip faded away. I went off to a deep sleep.

Ten

Joe College

The University of California at Davis was my destination, and I was eager to pack and get my "green hornet" Ford ready. Packing was easy. Washing and polishing my Ford was hard work. I applied chrome polish to the grill trying to coax a shine out of chrome grown dull. So too with the bumpers. After getting it into a body shop where all dents were removed and repainted, the body gleamed with polished wax. On September 1, I was prepared to roll northward.

Always ready to travel, I chose a new route to Davis. I decided to skip Highway 99, traveled the previous year, and Highway 101, which I had used to travel to Hearst Castle the year before that. I wanted new scenery. On the map a thin line marked State Highway 1, along the coast, and it beckoned to me. I chose it. Dad warned me that Highway 1 was a continuous series of curves all the way up the coast. "No problem," I thought. "I have all day." Dad's rebuttal was unclear to me. "Well, Joe College, you can see through a ladder." What did that mean?

I needed all day. I set out at 6 a.m. Mom was there to see me off: "The early bird catches the worm. Be sure to write," she said. I headed across Los Angeles as Dad and I had done the previous year. I picked up Highway 1 in Santa Monica. I filled my senses with the marvelous coastline, salty air, slow moving waves rolling to shore in succession, a blue summer sky, and I felt a deep satisfaction taking it in, beginning a new life for myself. My life was coming together now, and I had a new sense of purpose. The scenery grew in beauty and so did the day. Big Sur was enchanting. This was the "most beautiful meeting of land and sea in the world," or so said Mr. Shipman, our California History teacher, and it was all of that for me. I arrived in Davis at 9 pm exhausted. *It was worth it, but I don't think I'll go that way again.* Father knew best after all.

Davis was in a state of transition. Planned as the state agricultural college, it stood on 5000 acres of prime farmland with a small campus at its core. Suddenly, with the end of WWII, millions of veterans claimed their educational rights under the G.I. Bill, and clamored to build on the new opportunities that schools like Davis offered. Consequently we had a severe housing shortage on campus. The college brought in surplus Army barracks from military bases nearby, a home for us freshmen. They had no cooling system. We sweated profusely in the Valley heat of September, and showered often. Complaining was useless; the administrators were overwhelmed with a wonderful new problem – growth of the student population.

Because Davis was a Land Grant College, we freshmen were required to take a class every Tuesday afternoon called "Military Science". A first sergeant took our measurements, and then issued us surplus WWII Army uniforms. We also received an M-1 rifle, and soon began drills in handling our weapons and marching in formation. Our sergeant also had a lazy side. He liked to take us to the auditorium and show us WWII combat footage of battles with the Germans. He sat in back and dozed during these sessions. One such film etched on my memory was "The Battle of San Pietro." The combat footage took place near an Italian village by that name. The G.I.'s slogged through mud, supply trucks bogged down, infantrymen dug foxholes in the mud, and two armies slugged it out. How different war looked when seen through the eye of a combat camera rather than a Hollywood camera. Matthew Arnold, the English poet, had a great line for scenes like this,

"And we are here on a darkling plain, Swept with confused alarms of struggle and flight, Where ignorant armies clash by night."

I was fascinated by the terrible consequences of war.

We also had to fulfill an Aggie tradition laid on all freshmen at UC Davis. At the tiny bookstore that served the campus, we had to buy a blue and gold beanie as we purchased our books. The beanie served as a reminder of our lowly freshmen status, so upper classmen knew whom to tease. But this tradition took a hit that semester. Over half of the freshmen were veterans of WWII. Some of them had seen life and death in far off battlefields around the world.

As we formed a long line to get service in our book store, I could hear the vets scoffing, "What? You've got to be kidding! A beanie? You're crazy! I won't wear that damned thing. I'll refuse to pay for it. They can keep it and send it back where it came from." The Student Body Government faced an open revolt and could not contain it. Calls for loyalty to school and tradition were ignored. Something had to give. Student leaders conferred and saw the light. Times had changed. Tradition must yield to a new reality. The requirement to wear beanies was dropped. Of course, students could wear them if they chose. No one did.

Then, we had "rush week." Fraternities and sororities on campus had one week to select candidates to join elite houses to fill the void left by graduating seniors. Only the brightest and the best were selected for this honor. No fraternity men came to our newly installed army barracks now renamed Ash, Birch, or Cedar to look for candidates. As Dad had warned, we were hoi polloi, the common garden variety of students, unworthy of consideration. We silently endured our status.

But on Saturday evening at the end of rush week, a group of freshmen sat at long tables in the cafeteria eating dinner. We talked about the selectiveness of elitism, the chosen few versus the many. "Where's the fairness? Who do they think they are? Little Lord Fauntleroy? To hell with them!" Someone offered the idea of gathering tomatoes in a nearby experimental field. It was an idea whose time had come! A professor was hybridizing a bigger and better tomato for consumers. The tomatoes were the kind where the juice shimmers under the skin, so full of ripeness that it was ready to burst at any moment. At least a dozen of us walked to the field. We picked the ripest tomatoes we could find, the ones swelling with juice. If you were to cut one open, a wonderful concentration of seeds, juice, and flesh poured out. Those tomatoes were perfect. The professor had done well. Each one of us took all we could hold.

It was dusk. The sun had set leaving only a faint glow on the western horizon. We walked to fraternity row, a street lined with frat houses. We picked the house at the end of the row. At a signal we let fly with a barrage of tomatoes. We could watch our tomatoes soar through the air in a low arc. Suddenly they connected with the walls of the frat house and gave a terrific "SPLAT"! Juice and seeds oozed down the walls. Dozens of tomatoes hit their mark. The frat house was smothered with red tomato juice.

Doors and windows flew open. The members saw in a moment that they were under assault, and came rushing out like a swarm of hornets whose nest has been violated. We turned and ran in all directions. I ran down a side street. Speed was everything. Dusk had turned to dark and covered our tracks. My legs were always strong. I ran at top speed. No one got close to me. Several blocks away, I slowed and turned around. I was alone. I walked back to Birch Hall to an overheated room. The hot air felt overpowering. My heart still beat strongly, and I could not sleep. The next morning in the cafeteria we compared notes.

No one had been caught. And equally important, we sent a message about elitism on campus. What we didn't know was whether the message had been received as we had intended it. We felt justified in our action, yet on quiet reflection, I'm sure there were better ways to voice our concerns. It had not occurred to me that I was fortunate to be at Davis. I was a "C" student at Alhambra, had participated in no organized school sports, and had joined no school clubs. *Why had Davis even accepted me? This is my last time to throw tomatoes.*

An announcement caught my eye on the campus bulletin board. Tryouts for the U.C. Davis tennis team would commence on the following Monday. Practice was set for Monday and Wednesday afternoons. My antennae stood up. *Had not Dad taught me the basics over the previous two years? Of course*! On the following Monday afternoon, I took my old Wilson racket, a hand-me-down from Dad, and dressed in the locker room. I listened to the conversations. All of the tennis hopefuls had played for their high school teams. I was the only one with no team experience. At that, I felt a twinge of anxiety. *Was I biting off more than I could chew?*

We paired off and began warming up as doubles. I had no doubles experience, and I lacked the knowledge of coordination with my partner. Otherwise, I could serve, stroke and volley on a par with them. Dad recognized that I caught on quickly to what he taught me. "Get the lead out!" he shouted, and I chased the balls he hit to me. Trouble was, he had not taught me singles or doubles strategy.

The regular tennis coach was preoccupied in finishing the season with another sport and could not supervise us. After warm-ups, we newbies decided to play a game of doubles. The pair of players opposing us won the toss and served to us. I took the net while my partner took the serve. After a series of shots back and forth, my partner received a long shot and decided to lob a return. His lob went up in an arc, and then came down just over the net. The opponent opposite me saw it and was poised and ready for an easy kill. He raised one arm for aim and balance, and with his racket arm, slammed the ball at warp speed straight at me. If I had tennis skills I would have instantly backed away and had a slight chance of a return shot. But I did not know to do that.

I stood at my position, close to the net, my racket at the ready as he hit the ball into me. The ball struck me in the chest so hard that it knocked me backwards, off balance, and onto the ground. I got up, dazed, and realized that my lack of doubles experience was costing me dearly. There was no coach with a supervising hand, and it turned out under those circumstances, I was over my head. I found it hard to go back for more practice on Wednesday and stopped going. I turned my attention to my studies and let go of my dream of taking a place on the Davis Tennis Squad.

Reviewing my experience with coaches, the memories seemed largely negative. The absence of the coaching staff in the shower room at Alhambra was an open invitation for bullying, and we neophytes bore the brunt of it. Now, the absence of a tennis coach at such a critical time proved deadly for me. A tennis coach on duty would have put us through practice routines, evaluated us, and segregated us by skill level into practice teams. Such did not happen. The upshot was that I dropped out of my one opportunity to become part of a school squad. That hurt.

I also considered how I took risks. Many of my teachers spoke of our need for risk action, taking a measured look before leaping. My hitchhike to Tijuana, my lone hikes into the San Gabriel Mountains, and my trip to the Sacramento Valley to work on farms and sleep in public parks were all risks. I took them gladly. At Davis I dared, then took a risk to join the tennis squad. That risk exploded in my face. Perhaps that is the nature of "risk". As we jokingly said, "You win some and you lose some." I measured my risks more carefully after that. Dad's ex-post-facto remark, vintage Dad, was, "Moe, you should have begun tennis earlier."

Mom's favorite maxim of all was, "If at first you don't succeed, try, try again." There was wisdom in her words. Perhaps I should have explored other options, such as trying to find the coach. But I did not listen to what Mom said. Another bit of popular wisdom Mom used was, "Put on your thinking cap." I tended to treat it as an out of date saying from a faded generation. Yet thinking through my options could have been profitable for me. I could have learned through this refiner's fire, but did not.

There were other ways for a freshman to find a place on campus. I went to school dances on Saturday nights, and as I had done at the Pasadena Ball Room, I chose many girls to dance with, but got close to none of them. Not far from Birch Hall, across Russell Boulevard, was the Davis Community Church. I found that the choir needed members, and I joined the bass section. I immediately had a place. I sang with the choir every Sunday. The church had a program of outreach to the campus students called Cal Aggie Christian Association (CACA). We had "fireside" discussions on Sunday nights.

On campus there was an Aggie tradition to hold an Oktoberfest on the banks of Putah Creek, for male students only. Beer barrels were rolled out and placed on stands, paper cups passed out, and beer flowed freely. Give enough guys free beer, and action soon followed. Someone broke out singing a campus cheering song, followed by several Cal Aggie traditional songs, and then male bonding began in earnest. The more we sang, the louder we became, and more ribald became the tunes. Examples abounded: "Leprosy, my god, I've got leprosy." (to the tune "Jalousie"). Then we went on to the drinking songs: "On the Leland Stanford Junior Farm." Of course, no one wanted to miss singing, "Roll Me Over in the Clover." Then we went on to sing, "The Old Grey Mare Oomphed in Her Underwear."

Needless to say, as the evening proceeded, the men were reduced to their primal nature, a nature that is to be found in every man given enough beer and crazy songs. Far into the night the guys sang on. Then we slowly dragged ourselves back to campus, and some with help, to our dorms and fraternity bedrooms.

That month posters appeared around campus and in the community announcing that Gov. Thomas Dewey would make a whistle stop in Davis. Hundreds of Davis students turned out to the railroad station to greet him. His train pulled in with a roar and a cloud of steam. Gov. Dewey and his wife appeared on the platform of their rear car. He introduced himself as the next president of the United States. We cheered for him. But honestly, he looked like a slick politician to me, prim and proper in his fedora. I had recently heard President Truman's campaign slogan: "Give them hell, Harry!" I knew that if I could vote, it would be for a man like Harry Truman. So much for my first introduction to American politics.

Soon after, I received an ominous call from home. The Draft Board had sent me a "Dear John" letter. I was ordered to report to the Alhambra Board to register in person for the draft on October 10, 1948. I drove home only dimly perceiving the full implications of what I was about to do. I knew the Soviets had sealed off all entrances to Berlin; the city would be starved into submission by the Soviets. President Truman responded with a 24 hour-a-day airlift to supply the American sector of Berlin with all their needs. Tension filled the airwaves. I drove to Alhambra with some trepidation sensing that war was a remote possibility. I signed on willingly.

While there I checked with my Methodist Church and found that the choir had been invited to sing at the San Gabriel Civic Theater on Thanksgiving. "Will you come and join us?" they asked. "Sure," I responded, and took a hymnal back to Davis so I could practice there. Our director chose the hymn, "We Gather Together." The night before Thanksgiving I drove home. The next morning at 10:00 we gathered at the Civic Theater, near the old Mission, and practiced. Then the manager told us we would be broadcast around the world on the Armed Forces Radio Network. We sang with heart and soul all the stanzas to our troops in Berlin, Japan, and Korea.

> *"We gather together to ask the Lord's blessing;*
> *He chastens and hastens His will to make known;*
> *The wicked oppressing now cease from distressing;*
> *Sing praises to His name: He forgets not his own."*

Then we followed with the rest of the stanzas.

In just a few short weeks, I had gone from the ridiculous to the sublime. My life had become a roller coaster ride: highs and lows, risk and consequences, light and dark, dreams and failures. This was the story of my life, and I was on the brink of even more.

Unbeknownst to me, my sister, Sybil, met tragedy in San Diego even as our choir was singing for American troops around the globe. Only later was her husband Bill able to call Mom and Dad and give them the bad news. Sybil had moved to San Diego to be near Bill's deployment there. The two had a small apartment, and while Bill was on duty that morning, Sybil put on her new silken, hand-embroidered kimono that Bill had brought back for her from assignment to Japan.

She dressed a turkey, placed it in the oven, and lighted a match to ignite the burner. It was an old stove, a bit rusty, and slow to ignite. Suddenly, it blew up in a ball of fire. Sybil was thrown backward and her kimono caught fire. In seconds she was engulfed in flames. Steven, her only child, was nearby in his playpen. Fearing for his safety, she rushed alone out the back door into their small yard.

An ocean breeze fanned the flames to a new intensity. Sybil screamed, "HELP! HELP!" Her next-door neighbor heard her terrified cry and ran into his yard, saw her plight, and rushed to turn on his garden hose, spraying her with water until the flames were doused. Steven began to cry. Sybil went into shock, her body quivering uncontrollably. Her neighbor rushed back into his apartment to grab a blanket and wrap her in it. He also called the Navy Base to summon Bill. Bill ordered her sent to the U.S. Naval Hospital in downtown San Diego where a team of Navy doctors began around the clock care. Only then did he call our home to inform Mom and Dad.

When Mom was told the news she was terribly shaken. When we heard her response we knew something dreadful had happened. She handed the phone to Dad and began a collapse. That was the end of Thanksgiving. They wanted to drive to San Diego immediately, but Bill cautioned that Sybil was in intensive care and could have no visitors.

I drove back to Davis and awaited further news. A chill descended on campus. Gone was the heat. Now it was the season for cold north winds to blow. Finals were looming. My best friend, Sybil, was holding on precariously to life filled with drugs to stabilize her. I felt I should do something, but what? Internally I was a mess. I recalled the debacle on the tennis courts. I remembered how I ran from a group of bullies in the locker room at Alhambra High. There was my inability to get an adequate picture of what it means to be a person. My achievements with Mr. Rapelje, Mr. Hines and Mr. Bacon all faded from view. Bad memories dominated my mind. Now I added Sybil to my list.

On a cold weekend in December as I ate lunch in the cafeteria, three guys sat at another table and stared at me, shared some whispers, gestured, and laughed. Convinced that they knew all my secret failures, and had peered into the attic of my mind and read my memories, I wanted to simply disappear. I went to the football field, threw passes and punted the ball to whoever would join me. Then the three guys joined into the action. *Had they followed me?* I couldn't stand it.

I went to Birch Hall, found my Ford, and decided to drive to skid row in Sacramento. I was going to pick a fight with someone, anyone, and once for all, prove myself a man. I roamed skid row into the night acting belligerent. No one seemed interested in responding. *What?* I thought. *Here I am. Try me!* No one did.

Desperate, I took a room in a seedy flophouse. No sleep awaited me there. Other men were there sleeping off drinking binges. I lay awake and listened to the noise. In the morning I ate breakfast at a greasy spoon. Still, no one responded to my belligerence. They had seen it all many times before. The eggs were oily. The bacon was salty and hard. The coffee burned a hole in my gullet. I'd had enough. I went to my car and reluctantly drove back to campus.

As awareness settled in. Not only was I convinced that I was a coward and a hypochondriac, but now I faced a new reality. I didn't have a word for it, but I had become paranoid, and that on top of everything else. I sensed that the three guys in the cafeteria were mocking me, and yet I didn't really know that to be true. I had made a huge assumption. But, I had made it, and convinced myself it was so. My mind was ready to blow, and still I had no one I trusted enough to talk to.

Another awareness came much later. I had felt myself a coward at Alhambra High. I wanted to hit one of the derelicts on skid row. But, I did not. I would not do to them what bullies at Alhambra did to me. I was coming into my manhood, but could not believe it at that time. I picked myself up, threw back my shoulders, grimaced just as Mom had taught me, and prepared for finals.

Exhausted, I caught a cold, just as I had done in my youth. Added to it, a severe earache followed, and I would soon gain altitude on the Grape Vine going home for Christmas break. That aggravated the earache all the more. This was misery with no relief in sight. The hopeless feeling was not only physical, but spiritual. I had set off for Davis in September with all my flags flying, and now I headed for home with my tail between my legs. And Sybil needed me.

Snow covered the Grape Vine. A major storm broke over Southern California, and traffic slowed as many headed out for the holidays. Home was dark when I arrived. I headed for my bedroom, undressed, and climbed into bed even as Mom stuck her head into the doorway, welcomed me home, and offered me something to eat. She was so attentive in the way she took care of me. I demurred, pulled the covers over my head and wanted a year of sleep.

The next day as she listened to me talk, she sensed I was sick. She gave me the phone number of her doctor and urged me to call him. I did, and came home later with a bag full of pills. The snow melted, and the pills took effect. The earache lifted, and my cold symptoms eased. My body repaired itself, but my soul did not. I needed a doctor of the soul. But I knew of no one but Sybil who could be such a doctor, and now she needed that kind of doctor too. We talked about a day when we four could drive to San Diego to see her. We decided on the Saturday after New Year's Day.

Saturday loomed before us. Mom and Dad had already been to San Diego to see Sybil. Carol and I had not. On that Saturday morning, we dressed and ate breakfast in silence. I felt like those moments before a boxer steps into the ring. He must silence his fears and coax himself into readiness for battle. Ours too was a battle, and the battleground was of heart and mind. Here is a vignette that I wrote of that day:

Vignette - A Life Hanging in the Balance

To an observer we were on a casual Saturday drive down the coast. But inside our Plymouth, all of us were anxious. I was going to see my sister as a burn patient, for the first time, and I was nervous. I was 18 and had been reading the saga of Billy the Kid to pump myself up with some false courage.

When we got to the hospital it did not look inviting. There were manicured lawns edged with shrubs and trees and a structure probably designed by a Naval architect who had not the slightest idea of what fear feels like, or of the kind of reassurance that a family needs when they come here. It loomed before us like a fortress.

Dad parked the car. He did not get out. He lighted a Lucky Strike and then stepped out to begin drawing on it. He could not bring himself to go in and see Sybil, his beloved daughter and tennis partner in this crisis mode. Mom eased herself out of the passenger side, and my sister Carol and I emptied the back seat. We formed a threesome, each looking to the other for support. Mom led the way to the Information Desk on the first floor. We were politely told where the ICU Burn Unit was located and we walked there with hesitation-urgency. A nurse ushered us into her room.

Sybil lay under a canopy that was propped up by curved bars arched to fit to each side of her hospital bed. The canopy prevented the sheet from touching her burned body. Her face alone was visible for us to see. She was as beautiful and as gracious as ever. She smiled at us and beckoned us to come in and stand close by her side. Mom cried; Carol and I stood there speechless and unmoving. Mom bent over to kiss her then we followed her lead and kissed Sybil also. Here was my best friend, my athletic ideal, the only one who ever confided in me and gave me guidance, lying helpless and now needing my support.

Sybil told us she was in good hands. The Burn Unit doctors were doing everything they could to begin skin grafts on her body, and they had found compatible donors who were willing to donate their skin to her. Mom wanted to believe her, but Mom's faith was strained to the breaking point, and she simply nodded assent. I took a picture and everything looked just as Sybil had painted it.

"Would you like to see for yourselves?" she asked. We grunted and I nodded a "yes", but I knew I didn't really want to see her burned body. I feared being overwhelmed by the sight and smell. An odor of decaying flesh mingled with medicine, ointments, and urine combined to shock my senses like a child in a horror movie. She asked us to lift the sheet from its supports. I was not prepared for what I saw, nor were Mom and Carol. There was no skin on her body from her ankles to her neck. The sight was appalling. I gulped, held my breath, tried not to notice the odor or the sights, but I had to.

Her nakedness was more than I could stand. I wanted to run away, but could not. I was transfixed, as in a frightening movie. I didn't want to look at the scene but looked anyway because that is why I came. The colors of her flesh were outrageous – pinks, purples, black, orange, more pastel than primary colors.

All my senses were in shock. Do I cry out in despair, or bite my lower lip and hold back all my impulses? Mom and Carol cried. No one knew what to say. Finally, we replaced the sheet back on to its supports, and once again all that we saw was her face. She put on a gracious smile for us as if to say, "All is well." The sheet covered the sights, but the odors, and the shock remained etched on my memory.

We tried to cheer her, but really she cheered us. Strange how that works. Later, we found Dad walking the perimeter of the hospital, an ever-present Lucky Strike dangling from his lips, smoke drifting over his shoulder as he wandered a pathway. He had his nicotine fix. It helped him deal with the fact that he could not bear to see Sybil badly burned. Wasn't it Arthur Schlesinger who wrote that history is a tragedy? We were seeing the meaning of that up close. On the drive home no one spoke. No one even mentioned the idea of stopping for a bite to eat. We had lifted the veil; we had seen life and death, and it was too much for us. Life would never again be the same for our family.

Meanwhile, at the end of the first semester at Davis, I came home broke, and could not afford to return to Davis. My options were stark. I could go to Pasadena City College (P.C.C.) or go to work. Or I could enroll in a four-year degree program, complete two years at Pasadena, and then return to U.C. Davis for a bachelor's degree in Agriculture. Mom and Dad had given me advice the year before. They could not afford to help me with my tuition. "It is all up to you," they warned. I had confidence in my ability to pay my own way. I was a life-long saver, and I planned to work and save as I attended P.C.C.

Eleven

Highs and Lows

I looked forward to a new year. An urgency to find work pressed me forward. I gravitated to Mr. Hines, and he rehired me. Only now there would be a new order to things. No more supervising the construction of lath houses, or the backbreaking labor of transplanting camellias. Now he sent me to the sales lot on the corner of San Gabriel Boulevard. I spruced up my clothing. A new pair of Levi's, a pressed shirt, and clean boots was the order of the day. I was expected to help up front with sales.

I had lots to learn. I knew camellias. But our sales lot had hundreds of annuals and perennials, trees, and shrubs that I knew nothing about. For starters, I watered what seemed like 10,000 one and five-gallon containers, a never-ending job. I made deliveries to customers using our flatbed truck. I also kept learning and listening from the older salespersons so that I could become a salesperson too. I liked my work. I was outdoors in the sun. I was strong. This was my kind of work. Sybil was right all along.

In my English Composition class at Pasadena City College I found not only a subject that interested me, but a good friend named Guy Knight. He had just moved to Pasadena from New Hampshire and lived with his aunt and uncle. He had a New England twang in his voice that placed him geographically. We struck up an immediate friendship.

We found a common interest in music. Soon I drove to Pasadena every Wednesday night after dinner, picked up Guy, and drove him to the San Gabriel Methodist Church to practice with our choir.

Afterwards, I drove him back to Pasadena, and then returned home. The miles piled up on my odometer. No matter! Gas was only 25 cents per gallon, and it was worth it to share music with Guy and discuss our classes. On Sunday, I repeated the taxi service once again. Dad grumbled. "Can't you find friends closer to home?" "No," I replied. "I gladly do this to have a friend like Guy." In my mind he was a forever friend.

On a campus bulletin board I saw an announcement for a speech tournament. My imagination went to work. I could enter the tournament and in one fell swoop, overcome my low self-esteem, and my fear of public speaking. Several days later I walked to the Speech Department and boldly signed on as a participant in the tournament. I read the expectations for entry. I had to keep my presentation to five minutes and then be judged by a panel of speech faculty. Awards would be announced later.

At home I collected material on Alexander the Great, a prince of Macedonia, and perhaps the greatest general of all time. I had read several short biographies of Alexander. "National Geographic" sent out expeditions to trace his path of conquest through the Middle East. I read those carefully. I was fascinated with him because he was everything that I was not. I found it easy to prepare my speech, and if I was careful, I could also use it as a report for my English Composition class. I practiced in front of the mirror in my room, gestures and all. I created a simple outline on 3 x 5 cards that I could hold in the palm of my hand, a "cheat-sheet" as students refer to them.

The big day came and we in the tournament were ready. The campus looked casual that morning, but for me it had become another defining moment. There in the Speech Department room my chance to move from B.C. to A.D., from an immature teenager to a mature adult, awaited me. I took my place in the front row of seats. Other participants filed in and took their seats alongside me. I listened to the nervous small talk.

Just as at U.C. Davis with the tennis squad, all those present had previous tournament experience. Once again I was the only neophyte. My heart sank. I felt over my head again. I wanted to quietly get up and disappear out the door. Gone was the confidence I felt in front of my bedroom mirror. I was sure I would stumble and forget my opening lines. The outline that trembled in my hand was illegible to my eyes. The panel of judges was seated to one side, but clearly visible with their judging sheets in front of them.

The Master of Ceremonies began promptly at 11:00 with an introduction. She decided to present us in alphabetical order, so she called me forward to open the tournament. I felt like a criminal going forward to the scaffold for his execution. *If only someone would pull a lever opening a trapdoor, and I would drop out of sight.* No trap door opened. There in front of me sat my peers, the judges, and the audience.

In the panic of that moment, I did forget my opening lines. I glanced at my outline, but could not find the sentences I had prepared. I stumbled, grimaced, and lost eye contact with my audience. This was the worst five minutes ever. I slouched as I returned to my seat in shame. The Master of Ceremonies quickly took my place and explained that I was a novice with no previous experience. The judges nodded as they jotted notes on their sheets. The students beside me said nothing. The other contestants made their presentations, and by noon we were excused.

I bolted for the exit and headed straight for the parking lot. After I found my car, I drove through Pasadena, past California Institute of Technology, then down the avenue in front of the Huntington Library, then to San Marino Avenue and home. I shared with Mom my sense of failure, how my defining moment became a nightmare. Her response was a classic maxim, "If at first you don't succeed, try, try again." How I came to hate that quote.

But after days of skulking in my room I made a decision. There had to be a way out of defeat. I took the telephone directory and found the listing for San Gabriel Toastmasters. They met every Tuesday night and newcomers were welcome. Their meeting place was a restaurant near the corner of San Gabriel Boulevard and Las Tunas Drive. The following Tuesday night I hesitantly went to the Toastmasters meeting, held in the back room of the restaurant.

The men were taught to welcome visitors, and I was greeted and slapped on the back, then peppered with questions. The men were double, triple my age, in their 40's and 50's. At 19 I was their youngest member ever. Thank God, the chairman had a manual of protocol and knew how to use it. All of us who were newbies were formed into a group and given manuals to help us know procedures and expectations. We were introduced to the club members.

We started with simple exercises of introducing ourselves to the men on either side of us at our dinner table. Then we asked the men beside us for information about their lives. We took notes. After a month of this we were told to prepare a five minute introduction of ourselves to the club; nothing fancy, merely salient facts about ourselves. This was not easy. I felt uncomfortable introducing myself to men who were old enough to be my father. Then the members were asked to respond, avoiding any sharp criticism. That way we could maintain our self-confidence. We began to learn together.

In the months that followed, our assignments expanded. We learned to tell short stories, to give expository presentations, to share something humorous. Step by step we grew into public presentations. This was what I needed; mentoring that could guide me through the gauntlet of fear into a confident ability to share my story. I thought of the mentoring I needed in those days at Alhambra High when I was bullied, when I risked signing on to the Davis Tennis team, and when I volunteered for the speech tourney at Pasadena City College. *How much*, I thought, *every kid needs an adult he can lean on and learn from.*

Other than Sybil, our Toastmasters were the first such persons for me. Months later I used the material on Alexander the Great for a major speech at Toastmasters. All kinds of emotional baggage weighed me down. I remembered the debacle at the speech tourney. Besides, one of the men in the club was the father of a girl I was now dating. I sensed he was watching me carefully. I made it through the presentation and got some positive feedback from the men.

Such was the story of my life thus far: risk-failure-recovery. Sometimes it was even better: risk-success-growth. My life was a complex blend, and in each new situation I wondered what kind of outcome I would get. However, one thing stood out in my mind. I could study and get acceptable grades. I knew how to read, was learning to write, and improved my grades. Mine was a people problem. I had not learned to let go of the self-doubt about myself, nor my social skills.

One of the men in Toastmasters became a model of what I wanted to be, self-confident with quiet strength, and an ability to clearly state his case. One Tuesday night he made a major speech and told us of his recent trip to London. He shared his memory of visiting Westminster Abbey. He recounted his entrance into the Abbey. He looked up into the vaulted ceiling and saw why people found God in that place. The medieval stained glass windows, so vibrant with color, glowed with the story of faith. Then, he made his way to the Poet's Corner of the Abbey. There on the walls were busts of England's greatest writers and poets, going back all the way to Chaucer. Some of the poets were buried there. As he stepped around the engraved stones on the floor he felt as though he was standing on holy ground.

My imagination soared as I heard him speak. I could see the busts, the stained glass windows, the vaulted ceilings that reached up to the mystery of God, even as he described them. I made a decision that night: I determined that I too would visit Westminster Abbey. I wanted to experience it for myself. It was a simple, unmistakable decision.

Friday nights were special. Dancing still captivated me. I laid down my homework on Fridays, put on slacks and a dress shirt, and headed for the Pasadena Ballroom. The Ballroom always provided popular dance music, and good-looking girls who were well dressed. I forgot about any hesitancy, and walked up to single girls, or a girl in a group, and simply said, "Would you like to dance?" I got positive responses, and we stepped out on the floor.

Mom had sent me for ballroom dance lessons when we first moved to San Gabriel. I could do most any of the popular dances, and I had confidence in my abilities. I initiated conversation and found out who the girl was and what her interests were. When our interests blended, I would ask for another dance, and another. At times like that, I held her closer until her chin rested on my shoulder. With my right arm around her shoulder, I would press her body against mine, and I felt a tingle of painful desire. When she pressed her body to me, I was in ecstasy. I found that I had to switch from boxer shorts to jockey shorts to keep the bulge in the crotch of my pants from showing. It seemed to me that the girls knew nothing of how deeply I was aroused.

The dirty sock around my neck was still there. It represented a strong prohibition against intimacy and sex. After I had had one of these dances, I would move on to someone else, and begin the process over again. By closing time I walked out the ballroom door by myself and drove home. I did this most Friday nights, and I sought no long-term relationships.

Summer job opportunities appeared on our school bulletin board. One flyer announced a job opening at Emerald Bay, Lake Tahoe. I was immediately interested, even though I had a job with Mr. Hines. I loved the mountains. I placed a phone call to the number listed and the man who answered gave me his home address so I could stop by for an interview. I drove to his home after classes and answered his questions. He told me I was hired and was to report to a place called Vikingsholm, Lake Tahoe, as soon as classes were over.

When the semester ended in early June I drove straight to Emerald Bay, and was assigned to a single's tent behind the resort. I went to work in the kitchen as a cook's helper. All of the other new hires were from Oakland's Technical High School, a tightly knit group of friends. They worked at keeping the place clean. I was the only new hire assigned to the kitchen, and the chef put me to work cleaning and preparing vegetables for lunch and dinner. The job lasted three weeks. At the end of June I was let go with no explanation.

I did not feel good about being terminated. Except for my Monrovia Nursery job, I had not been let go. I thought I had done a good job. With more presence I should have asked why I was fired, but did not. None of the guys from Oakland said anything as I packed my gear and left. I knew I stood on the outside with them and did not fit into their circle.

Now as I packed my gear they watched from a distance. I drove away not having a plan for what I would do next.

Twelve

Lessons Learned on the Mountain

I was nineteen, but didn't feel mature. Nineteen is a great time for learning. I was too young to be cynical, but not old enough to be wise. I had a long way to go to learn wisdom.

I wanted to find some way to make the rest of summer profitable. I decided to head down from Tahoe on Hwy 50 to where it intersects Hwy 99 in Sacramento, then turn north. After several hours I saw a turnoff to a place called Weaverville, turned west into the coastal mountains, and got there at noon. It was blazing hot when I arrived and cruised through town. I drove past the old Chinese Joss House, one of the few still remaining from the days of the gold rush. The other building that interested me was the Forestry Service Headquarters for Trinity National Forest. I had wanted to be a ranger since my parents took us on summer outings to Yosemite. I parked, went in to ask about job openings. Soon a rugged looking ranger came to the front desk and told me there was an opening on a crew who were building a trail to the nearby Trinity Alps.

"Its hot, hard work," he said. "You will be working on the south side of the mountains with lots of exposure to the sun. It is a crew of seven men and they could use one more man. Interested?"

Without asking about wages I replied: "Yes, I'm very interested. That's my kind of work. I love the mountains. When do you want me to begin?"

The ranger replied, "Today is Saturday. On Monday a cowboy is taking a pack mule loaded with supplies up to their camp. Do you want to go with him?"

"Sure."

"OK, be here at 7:00 sharp on Monday morning. He will circle up in the corral behind this building. All the equipment you will need will be there in camp for you."

Nodding I said, "Thanks. I'll be there and ready to go."

I found a café, had lunch, and then wandered the town on foot. Not far away was a large store. Walking in created a lasting impression on me. Mounted on the wall behind the cash register, high enough so it caught my eye, was an old Winchester rifle, beautifully engraved in gold, with a hexagon shaped barrel. I had never seen anything like it before, even in the Buffalo Bill Museum not far from my home in San Gabriel. I stared at it while the clerk waited for my attention. Finally our eyes connected and I asked to see his pistol collection. He showed me a Colt 22. I fell in love with it and bought it along with a box of ammo, thanks to my severance wages from Vikingsholm. The salesperson gave me some equipment so I could clean it after each use.

Not far away was the Trinity River. I found an isolated bend in the River, loaded the ammo clip, then threw pieces of wood into the River and did target practice. The smell of the cordite smoke from each round fascinated me, but the crack and report took time to get used to.

I sometimes wondered why I bought it. While on the beach fronting Hearst's Castle, I shot seagulls three years earlier and the thought of killing birds for no purpose continued to haunt me. I had vowed never to shoot any wildlife again. Now, however, I had visions of bears or cougars that could threaten me. I wanted self-defense.

But another reason lurked in my mind. I continued to struggle with low self- esteem. I wanted to overcome that with a show of bravado. I still believed myself to be a coward. I still remembered the afternoon incident in the basement of Alhambra High. Dad had told me, "Never back down from a fight." Since I ran instead of fighting, I dared not tell anyone of my personal failure, especially not Dad. I was now carrying a secret load of self-doubt and cowardly shame in the attic of my mind. I felt alone. Then, I questioned why I had been let go at Vikingsholm Resort. I had a lot to prove in the Trinity Alps. It seemed as though I always had to prove myself, just like Dad.

Psychologists describe a phenomenon in personality development called "compensation." I knew nothing of the term that summer, but I now believe in perspective that I was compensating. I had developed a way to cope with my low self-esteem and the fears of my own personal cowardice. I became arrogant. I grew a beard. I now carried my new Colt 22 in my pack.

Soon after I arrived in camp with the cowboy and his mule, I unpacked, and created my own sleeping area. Then before dinner I took off for the woods and did target practice, acting like what I thought was a seasoned veteran of the mountains. But my arrogance also showed in some unexpected ways. I laughed too loudly at some of the mountain humor that the crew shared around the fire, laughter that sounded flippant to them, giving offense to one of them.

Then, needing recognition, I told how Mrs. Pettit, a family friend, had invited me the previous year to fly to Paris with her to recover her son, Jim's, body and bring it home. Being a new comer and sharing that story sounded haughty to them. They had spent their lives in these mountains and were not impressed with trips to Paris. I was off to a bad start.

Twin hopes opened for me, however. One was George, a man from Tennessee in his late 40's that enjoyed working with me on the trail. We had a six-foot long, two-man saw and George taught me how to notch a tree that stood in the way of the trail. He took a broad axe and created a large notch in the tree at a place that would force the tree to fall exactly where he wanted. Then we would work the two-man saw opposite the notch, he on one side of the saw and I on the other, sawing in a rhythm where I pushed and he pulled. When the saw reached the notch, sure enough the tree fell in the chosen direction. I loved this work. George had a fun sense of humor, regaling me with tall tales from the Tennessee Mountains and the girls that he had loved. He never told me why he had left. I should have asked him.

One day we were resting from a hot task of leveling a high spot in the trail with our shovels and adze. We took some shade under a tree and leaned into our shovels, like WPA men of the Great Depression. We smelled of sweat. Dust coated our Levi's. The dust was so bad that I began wrapping my Levi's with cord just above the ankles to keep the dust off my legs. Suddenly, George cried out and with gloved hand pointed behind me. I swiveled and saw a diamond back rattlesnake several feet behind me. It was not coiled to strike, but it sure had my attention.

It was over two feet long, and ugly as sin. It was its girth that caught my attention. It was two inches thick in its midriff. I had never seen a rattlesnake before. To me it looked like a monster from a horror movie. I reacted in fear. I brought my shovel from its leaning position on the pine tree, and slammed it down on his neck with all the force I could give it. Its head careened off its body. It lay in the dust for several minutes with the fangs snapping open and shut. The body writhed in the dust until its energy slowly faded into death. With my Boy Scout knife I cut off its rattlers as a souvenir to show in camp.

That night around the campfire I showed my trophy, passing it around to the circled men. The men were impressed and I became the center of attention. George corroborated my story. Soon the crew was sharing stories of their close encounters in the mountains. As we talked, smoke trailed up to the sky, the logs crackled as they burned, creating a fragrance that only a mountain fire can produce. A fellowship began as the night closed into darkness, and the stars appeared along with the Milky Way.

We were drawn closer to the fire and to each other. The stars bowed so low that night that they seemed to rest on the peaks of the Trinity

Alps. Happy faces were reflected in the glow of the fire. Somehow, in a way I cannot explain, there is magic created around a campfire. The fire drew us together against the black night. Male bonding took place and a unity was created that transcended all the issues of life. A deep satisfaction settled over me. Maybe, just maybe, I was becoming a man, a man among men.

When it came time to turn in I headed toward a large pine tree. Behind it I could pee one last time, and then slip off my boots and dusty Levi's, hang the Levi's with my shirt on a limb and burrow into my sleeping bag. But on this night it was different. With only the Milky Way to light my steps I went behind the tree. Suddenly, a rustling noise jolted every cautionary instinct in me. There in the darkness in front of me, raring on his two hind legs, was a bear standing as tall as I was. All I could see were his eyes and a dim outline of his body. It was enough to turn me into a tower of jello. He had been there in hiding waiting for us to fall asleep, and then he planned to enter camp and raid our food supplies. Little did he know that we cleaned our camp carefully after every meal, and hung our food in trees. He didn't know that. What he did know was that he smelled our sides of bacon on a high limb and meant to take them.

Now we were face to face. I don't know who was most traumatized, him or me. What I knew was that with one swipe of his forepaw he could rip off my face. I could smell his bad breath. In a split second I wheeled and dashed in the opposite direction at top speed. At the same instant he bolted and ran in the other direction. What a relief! I was spared the worst consequences of a bear encounter. I stopped and tried to catch my breath. My heart was pounding so hard I didn't know if I could recover. I did, and slowly found my way back to my sleeping bag. I called out to the men that I had seen a bear too close for comfort. I peeled, crawled in and warned the others to be on the lookout.

I liked to lay on my back in the sleeping bag and look at the stars. First I looked for "shooting stars". They traced across the sky and then burned out. I located the Big Dipper and from there it was easy to go around and find Polaris, the North Star. I would guess at the names of some of the larger stars and try to piece together constellations.

I wasn't much for God-things in those days, but the stars created in me a sense of wonder, a sense of my smallness in the universe, a sense that there must be a God, and just maybe He cares for me. God knows that I had prayed often when I was sick while growing up. I used to tell God that if He would make me well that I would be a good boy, and read the Bible regularly. Funny thing: I always got well, but then forgot about the gratitude and reading the Bible.

All those years in Sunday School at the Presbyterian Church, first in El Sereno and then in San Gabriel, and I knew practically nothing about God. I did have a sense that I believed in Him. I did know the old gospel songs that I heard around the house as Mom sang and hummed her way through daily chores, and some hymns that I learned in Sunday school. Sometimes, however, I wondered how I could be such a coward and believe that God could accept me. After all, I didn't think anyone would accept me if they knew this terrible truth about me, so why would God choose to love me? But I intended to make a comeback this summer and prove myself to these men. Then, I thought, perhaps I could find acceptance.

The other half of my twin hope was Charley, our straw boss. He was so unassuming that a person could easily misread his character. Most of the crew were in their 40's; Charley was in his 50's. Most of the men were locals, while Charley hailed from a little town down the road from Weaverville called Hayfork. He wore suspenders and an old slouch hat, spoke in a slow drawl, had an easy grin, and was never in a hurry. Outsiders might take him for a yokel, but he had a flair for knowing how to get work done in the mountains, and how to lead these men.

Respect for Charley radiated throughout the crew. They liked his practical wisdom and his knowledge of these mountains. The more I got to know him the more I realized what a natural leader he was. He welcomed me to camp when I arrived with the cowboy and his mule in tow.

The mule was attached to the cowboy's saddle with a 10-foot rope tether. I watched as the cowboy unpacked the mules. Charley could sense that I was a city boy, yet ready to learn.

Instruction number one from Charley, the first of many, was, never stand behind a mule. They are skittish when they can't see what is happening behind them, and they can get rid of a nuisance with one swift kick to the rear. I listened, not wanting a lifetime scar. I learned to stand in front or at their side to help unload. I observed the cowboy undoing the hitches that held the heavy canvas rectangular bags to the wooden pack racks, each rack equally weighted, one canvas bag on each side of the mule. Over the rest of July and August I helped load and unload the mules and learned the rope hitches that held everything together.

When the cowboy was ready to reload the mules, he always began by placing a heavy Indian blanket on the back of each mule. Attaching the wooden racks over the blankets, he then placed the canvas bags on the racks. By the end of summer and with Charley's patient instruction, I became an experienced muleteer. I felt proud.

Instruction number two soon followed. That first day, after I had been introduced to the crew, Charley showed me around the camp. Then, I went into the woods for target practice with my Colt, but the crew could hear the crack as each round went off. Some of the men went to Charley and complained about a stranger coming into camp with a loaded weapon. As soon as I reappeared Charley quietly took me off to one side. He did not speak loudly, just clearly. Since he chose his words carefully every word counted. He said, "Put the gun away and do not use it in or near this camp ever again. Understand?" "Yes", I understood. I took my new Colt and placed it in the bottom of my pack for the rest of summer.

There were plenty of duties around camp both morning and evening. Since I was the tenderfoot newcomer it became my job to dig a latrine for our camp. I was given a surplus WWII Army collapsible shovel and pointed to a direction outside of camp to dig the hole. It had to be sizeable enough for eight men for about two weeks, at which time we would move camp further up the mountain. Fortunately, except for some rocks, the soil was mixed with forest duff, which made it easier to dig. Alongside the pit I placed a stick on which I hung a roll of TP.

For the uninitiated, in order to use it you must learn to squat. There is nothing romantic about it. Squat in such a way that you don't fall in. Then, take the Army shovel, which I conveniently left by the pile of dirt, and scatter enough dirt on your deposit to do two things: 1) contain the odor. 2) Keep the pesky flies off. And, there is an added benefit: it makes squatting more pleasant for the next guy.

Other jobs in camp awaited. Charley was our chief cook. Every morning he got down one of our sides of bacon from its safe shelter high on the limb of a pine tree. Then he sliced plenty for us and re-hung the bacon. The crew had built a fireplace of stones with an iron grate on top to serve as our stove. As Charley fried the bacon in a large iron skillet over our camp fire, other men would start cooking eggs to order in another iron skillet: scrambled, sunny side up, or easy over.

George took our large coffee pot and filled it with cold stream water. Then came two careful steps: measuring coffee grounds to a strength where the majority of men would like the flavor, then counting the minutes the coffee pot boiled until the coffee was "just right." When brewed it was called cowboy coffee. Before serving it he would pour a dollop of cold water into the pot, causing the grounds to settle to the bottom. Now it was ready to pour. It usually tasted too strong, but woe to any complainer. George would scold him with some choice Tennessee curses. Cowboy coffee was not designed to be gourmet, but a waker-upper, and it was just right for that purpose. We each had aluminum cups, or iron cups coated with ceramic glaze. That summer on the mountain I learned to be a coffee drinker.

After breakfast we cleaned up. One kettle on the stove held hot water mixed with soap, another kettle held hot clear water for a rinse. We cleaned our own mess gear, rinsed it, then brushed our teeth, and waited for Charley's marching orders for the day.

We cleared rocks and trees along a pathway that Charley mapped for us. He had orders to build a trail that would take visitors as close to the tops of the Trinity Alps as possible.

Charley took me under his wing. We would go ahead of the crew and spot boulders and trees that stood in the way of our proposed trail. If a large boulder confronted us, Charley would assess the situation, then take out a bag that he carried around his shoulder. In it were sticks of dynamite and a small sack of fuses. Taking out his pocketknife, he would slit a stick of dynamite four times lengthwise: one slit for every quarter turn of the stick. Digging a small hole under the boulder, we would place the stick in the hole; sometimes two sticks if necessary. He attached a fuse in the end of the stick, and connected the fuse to two wires that were part of a cord. While walking away from the boulder a good 50 yards we reeled out the wire.

Behind a rock or tree we knelt down, and Charley carefully connected the other end of the wire to his magneto plunger. We scanned to make sure no one was in the area, and Charley cried out in a loud voice, "BLOW!" Then again, "BLOW", and again. Pushing the plunger down, a terrific blast shook the mountain. Rocks and debris flew in all directions. We crouched lower behind our shelter. After the air cleared we walked back to check the results. If the boulder could be cleared manually we left it for the crew. If not, we repeated the process. Then we went forward to spot trees that blocked our trail. Charley would call a two-man crew to come forward with our six-foot two-man saws, and take it down. Clearing the area, Charley and I would blast out the stump.

We worked like this ten days on and four days off. On one my four days off I hiked down to Weaverville, and drove to Eureka in my Ford coupe. On the docks I watched commercial fishermen bring in their catch of salmon. Then, I headed for the old whaling station at Trinidad, cooling off in the coastal fog.

On another four-day break, I learned a valuable lesson that I never forgot. I hiked to the Forest Service fire lookout on a nearby mountaintop and spent three days with a college student who was the resident observer. He was more than willing to share his space and food. He was lonely, stationed there by himself. We could look over the mountains and valleys, viewing the Trinity Forest where the mountains blended into hills, which undulated toward the western horizon. What a magnificent scene!

I was like an eagle that got a sweeping view of the northern coast of California. I spotted campers and their campfires by the thin wisps of smoke that curled skyward here and there. The forest created a carpet of green all the way to the Pacific Ocean. It humbled me to think that I was just one small part of creation, but never the less, a part. I wanted to thank God for his marvelous works.

At the end of the third day it was time for me to return to camp. I did not arrive back at our camp until dusk and then found that while I was gone they had moved the camp further up the mountain. It was now dark, and I was frightened by the prospect of a night alone in the woods. I did not know where the crew was, and had a sinking feeling that I was lost. I had no jacket and the nights were cold at this altitude.

One thing was in my favor. I had begun carrying matches whenever I went into the woods. I quickly gathered pinecones and twigs for kindling and started a small fire. Then I went further out into the woods to gather sizable chunks of wood for a blaze. I crept as close as I could to the fire for warmth, and to hold at bay the hobgoblins of fear in my mind.

In the blackness of night my imagination took over and I was sure that wolves, bears, or cougars lurked at the edge of darkness waiting to strike. I had no sleep that night. I was in a constant vigil. I was more lonely and afraid than I had ever been before. Who could help me? I shivered in the chilly mountain air. I looked up into the heavens looking for God. But all I saw was the Milky Way, like some gigantic merry-go-round in the sky, and a thousand million other stars, but they were cold, distant and silent. I really felt alone.

As a half-light of early morning muted the darkness, I could barely see that no creature was there to menace me. I waited patiently for the sun to rise over the eastern mountains. Then with my Colt still gripped in my hand I fired three rounds into the air. I hoped the sound would be interpreted as a signal of distress. It was. The guys were up and could hear the loud crack of my Colt echoing off the mountains. They began to yell and the sound of silence was dimly broken by their echoing voices. Friends. I found them. I followed their echoes and as they got louder, found their camp an hour later located near a small lake.

They were preparing breakfast, and I was just in time to enjoy it with them. Charley said nothing about the gunfire. He understood. I put the Colt back into the bottom of my pack, so glad for it, for the matches, and for some one up there who delivered me safely from danger.

I learned two other skills that summer. One was to play a harmonica that I bought in Weaverville. Embossed on it were the words, "Made in Germany by M. Hohner." I toyed with it all summer and finally taught myself the song "Oh Susanna." Sometimes I would play it around the campfire. I wasn't sure the crew really enjoyed my amateurish sounds. But I was young and eager to learn, so I kept on practicing.

The other skill came from watching the guys roll their own cigarettes as they sat around the campfire. They smoked handmade Bull Durham cigarettes. I was alone in that I did not smoke and had grown up having a terrible time with Dad's Lucky Strike cigarette smoke irritating my lungs. Asthma was a constant problem for me in my youth. I tried to avoid being around smoke. But, my curiosity and my desire to be one of the guys finally overcame my hesitation.

I watched them take their sack of Bull Durham, their pack of Riz La papers, then roll a cigarette with one hand. Mind you, most men require two hands for this maneuver. One night I could watch no longer. The next mule train arrived within days. I helped the cowboy unload the mule packs, and asked the favor of returning with him to Weaverville. I was going to buy my first bag of Bull Durham.

On the way down the mountain I smelled the odor of horse sweat and road apples. I liked it. *What a great life these men have in the mountains.* I wanted this kind of life for myself. The cowboy drove the mule into its corral, and I headed into town to the nearest store and bought a bag of Bull Durham and Riz La papers.

A quick drive to Eureka took the rest of the weekend. I watched the fishing fleet bring in their catch of salmon. I slept in the driver's seat of my Ford coupe each night. Sunday was my day to head back to camp. Placing my precious goods in my pack I headed back. That night around the fire I surprised the crew by pulling out my supply of cigarette materials. They laughed and challenged me to roll my first one, watching carefully to see how I would manage it.

Holding the paper between my index finger and the middle finger of my left hand, I carefully poured Bull Durham into it with my right hand. The trick was not to spill any tobacco while pouring. Then setting the bag down and holding the paper with the fingers of both hands, I folded and rolled until I had a lumpy-dumpy cigarette. As I tried to light it, it fell apart, spilling tobacco on my boots. The guys laughed and urged me to try again: "It's easy," they said, "like this," and they proceeded to show me their technique.

Now I took more paper and more tobacco. This time I licked the leading edge of the paper and then sealed it shut. It was still lumpy-dumpy, but it held as I lit up. I took a draw, coughed, and exhaled. There were more hoots and laughter. I practiced my new skill each night around the campfire with the guys. By the end of August I was an accomplished Bull Durham smoker.

Now the air was getting chilly as fall approached. It was time for me to return to Pasadena City College and my studies. Part of me wanted to stay, but I knew that in a short time snow would fly and these men would scatter to their homes. I took a last lingering look at our camp, and the guys, and thought:

> *I had learned to bond with these men, to call them friends. I had learned lessons from both Charley and George. I felt indebted to them. I now knew I could take care of myself in the woods. I knew I was accepted in the fellowship around the fire and this gave an awakening to my*

self-esteem. I was forming a "God concept" in my mind. God is present in ways we do not always understand. He was at work in my life. I was becoming a man, with a little less that I had to prove.

I said goodbye to the men. One last time I put my things in my pack, cleaning my equipment as I did so. I waved again and headed down the trail. As for the Bull Durham, my fingers and my tongue were yellowed, my lips blistered, and my mouth reeked of nicotine. I rounded a bend in the trail, took out the sack of Bull Durham, tossed it into bushes, and never smoked again.

Thirteen

In And Out Of Love

There were still a few weeks of summer weather left when I got home. My friend Jay Stevens and I decided to drive to Lake Arrowhead for a fun weekend. We saw some Alhambra buddies, and then we went to the lake for a swim. Not far away we saw a bulletin board with a flyer announcing a community dance that night several miles away in Crestline. After a hamburger and fries Jay and I decided to drive to the dance hall. We got there shortly before the 7:00 pm start.

As I stood looking at the empty bandstand the pianist came out alone, sat at the grand piano, and played "Claire de Lune." It was so beautiful that I stood there mesmerized by the Debussy classic. All too soon the band emerged and began tuning their instruments for the evening, breaking the spell. The dance hall began to fill with young people moving to popular music.

I spotted a girl with long shapely legs, short hair, a winning smile, and asked her for a dance. The way she looked at me as she said, "Yes," touched my heart. We bonded in that moment of time. She came close and put her chin on my shoulder. She held me as tenderly as I held her. I felt giddy as I held her closely in my arms. Something special was happening here. Dance after dance kept us on the dance floor, neither of us wanting to break the magic we had created. Her interests became my interests.

Later she asked if we could go for a drive. (She was bolder than I). We walked to my Ford as the moon poured light through the pine trees while creating romantic shadows. I drove only a short distance on a nearby logging road and parked. I didn't need the necker knob on my steering wheel. She was in my arms as we kissed again and again. I had never done this at the Pasadena Ballroom.

Kisses like this startled me; her lips were warm and beckoned for more. Back at the dance hall we exchanged phone numbers and addresses. She lived in South Gate, quite a distance from San Gabriel. When we finally split at midnight she wanted to make sure I would come and visit her in South Gate. Her name was Janelle. I was smitten with her.

Once home, she called and asked if I could come with her and her South Gate High School buddies for an evening on the beach roasting wienies, followed by some grunion hunting. I had heard of grunion, a small silvery fish about six inches long that would come ashore as late as September to spawn. It sounded like fun and I picked her up on a Friday night at her home, and then we drove to the beach to meet her friends. Roasting wienies over a campfire on the beach brought out the fun side of our group of 20.

After dinner we sauntered to the shoreline. It was dark now. Small waves came rolling in. The waves brought with them tiny grunion that paused in the wet sand, wriggling and splashing as they laid their eggs. We reached down to take some with our hands, the girls screaming as they actually caught one. I had never seen such a sight. I captured one and cupped my hand gently around her so I could see her form.

She looked like a silver dart. The grunion, however, squirmed wildly in my hand, squeezed through my fingers, and landed on the wet beach, determined to complete her cycle of life. I watched for her eggs to appear, but they were hard to see. I believe her mission was fulfilled, for she went out to sea on the next wave.

Back around the campfire someone stoked the fire with more wood. The bright flames pulled us together in mysterious ways, just as the campfire in the Trinity Alps had created a bond of fellowship. We stood in a circle, some holding hands, and some cuddling up to one another. Each person seemed to be in a reflective mood, perhaps wondering if evenings like this could go on forever.

Janelle brought two beach towels and I laid them on the sand as close to the fire as possible. Her bathing suit was splashed with salt water, as was mine. As she lay down on her towel facing the fire, I laid beside her, facing her. We embraced; I could feel the soft warmth of her body pressing into mine. Droplets of water on her thighs blended with those on my thighs. We came together so closely that I felt as though I was one with her.

Powerful new sensations coursed through my body. I wanted more. My body strained to hold my sexual arousal under control. She turned her face to mine and opened her lips for a kiss. Her lips were warm, soft, and passionate, seeking ever-greater intimacy. I responded to her invitation.

So this was what my mother wanted to hide from me. Such intimacy was what she feared. That was why she demanded that I come home when I sat on the grass talking to the girls around the corner from our home. That is why she tied a dirty sock around my neck. She would ward off germs and dangerous feelings of arousal that could lead to the prohibited knowledge of sex. She wanted to protect me from a dangerous world. Indeed, I found sex was a powerful reality, but as I held Janelle in my arms I knew I would not turn back. From this point on my life would be a balancing act between deep sensual desire and my need for restraint.

The moans of passionate kissing stirred the air around our campfire. Slowly, the fire turned to hot, bright embers, and then faded into ashes. 11:00 pm arrived and couples began to stir, arise, and fold their towels. Janelle and I released our embrace. We helped clean up our area, and then walked across the sand holding hands. I felt more romantic and passionate than at any other time in my life. Driving back to South Gate I used my necker knob so I could hold her close, and she did the shifting of gears. We had more passionate kisses in front of her home. She taught me how to French kiss, igniting more passion inside of me. She was a good teacher. Reluctantly, I headed back to San Gabriel.

Weekends for the rest of fall became a division of activities. Friday nights I spent with Janelle. Saturdays were a balancing act between visits to San Diego to see Sybil, and my work as a salesman for Hines Nursery. Sundays were for Guy and me to sing in the Methodist Church Choir.

Sybil did not improve. Her husband, Bill, offered himself as a source of skin to graft on her body. The grafts did not take, and the Navy doctors were stymied. Mom and Dad were too old to be skin graft candidates. The doctors weren't interested in Carol and me. Burn therapy seemed to be emerging out of the dark ages. Sybil's forearms were an ugly purple with sores where nurses placed intravenous feeding tubes, often unsuccessfully. Her arms were covered with bruises.

We bought her a small record player and a 78rpm single of her favorite comfort music, Brahms Lullaby. She played it often. Bill brought Steve to see his Mom. I took a picture of Steve on his rocking horse at her bedside. Sybil looked on with a faint smile, unable to hold her baby.

Mom sought comfort music also. Her favorite song was from a Broadway musical called "Carousel," "You'll Never Walk Alone." Mom played it frequently to ease her sadness. Sometimes she would sing along or hum with the music. I got to know it by singing along with her. It gave us a sense of peace in a threatening storm:

> *When you walk through a storm,*
> *hold your head up high*
> *And don't be afraid of the dark*
> *At the end of the storm, there's a golden sky*
> *And the sweet silver song of a lark.*
> *Walk on through the wind*
> *Walk on through the rain though your dreams be tossed and blown…*
> *And you'll never walk alone…*

That song and those words resonated with her character and mine and gave us hope. It was a terrible burden for us to see Sybil immobilized, making no progress at growing new skin. Mom prayed often and read her Bible.

For New Year's Eve Janelle invited me to her home to watch the New Year arrive as we watched TV with her mom and dad. TV was new. We were fascinated with it, and with the rabbit ears that sat on top of the set. About 11:00 p.m. her parents said, "Good night," and retired from the front room to their bedroom.

It didn't take long for us to begin hugging and kissing. By midnight our passions had peaked. Janelle turned the lights down low. She lifted her skirt and smiled at me seductively. Her legs were shapely, long, and inviting. Suddenly, I was standing on the south rim of the Grand Canyon and looked out at one of the most beautiful scenes in the world. There was color, depth, and fascination converging at the same moment. For the first time in my life I saw the mystery of her femininity. That was a region forbidden to me. I had been taught that sex did not exist, but now I was being invited into her inner sanctum where I could let my libido run free. Janelle lay back on the couch and beckoned me to come to her to taste and touch a whole new dimension of intimacy.

My mind suddenly became a cacophony of clashing images. I was like the grunion that I found on the seashore weeks earlier. It must finally fulfill its destiny and come ashore to spawn, to deliver its eggs and then return to the sea. My urge to go to Janelle and lie with her was an instinct that roared like a lion. But other images intruded. First was that of my sister Sybil. We had gone to see her the weekend before. She lay on her hospital bed, stripped of her flesh, struggling for survival. Her smile and her words of encouragement to us broke into my consciousness. Then another image emerged. All that I had learned as a choir member singing praises to God Sunday by Sunday. Also there was the dirty sock around my neck that warded off germs as well as the sins of the flesh. I became a civil war.

One dominant image prevailed in my mind. Sybil in her hospital bed was praying for deliverance and healing. How could I lie with Janelle, satisfying my desires and myself, when my sister was in such pain? I could not do it. Like Joseph with Potiphar's wife when she pleaded with Joseph to come into her bed, Joseph turned away. I told Janelle that I had to go. Stunned, she looked at me and said nothing. I put on my jacket and headed for the door. The next morning was January first, and I told my Mom that I would not see Janelle anymore. I did not call her, and she did not call me.

However, I was left with a peculiar feeling, as though there was unfinished business between us. I owed her an explanation of my behavior. We both needed time to explore what had so suddenly happened to our relationship. I wondered how our friendship could have turned out if we had both given it another try. I chose to move on and not look back. But was it the right thing to do? I wasn't sure.

Fourteen

Life Against Death

Palm Sunday was coming, and Pastor Dick announced that he would baptize those who were ready to commit to Christ. I was growing in my Christian faith, singing in the choir each Sunday, active in the Methodist Youth Fellowship, and now I was ready for more. After the service I told the pastor that I wanted to be baptized. He gave me literature to read, and invited me to a class where I would learn the significance of baptism. Mom told me that she had purposely skipped infant baptism so that it could be my decision when I came of age. Now I was twenty, and I was ready to take this step.

On Palm Sunday, 1950, I sat in the congregation rather than the choir loft. Pastor Dick preached on the Great Commission of Christ to go forth into the world with the gospel of good news. The highlight of his sermon came with an illustration of the cost of discipleship. He told us that he wanted to rent an airplane, fly over Russia, bail out, be prepared to tell the people of Russia of our aim of peace, and share the good news with them. Then, he asked our congregation, "How many of you will go with me? How many of you love God so much that you take his word seriously? It is one thing to say you are a Christian; it is something else to obey His commands." Without hesitation I was ready to raise my hand and say "Count me in. I'll go!"

Relations with the Soviet Union were at a historic low. Winston Churchill announced that an "Iron Curtain" had been put in place by the Soviets from Stettin on the Baltic to Trieste on the Adriatic. Our world was bifurcated, and the Cold War had begun. But, Pastor Dick was young and bold. We would seek reconciliation with the Russian people by being faithful to God's good news and go to them in peace.

When he called us forward for baptism, I walked to the altar rail and knelt there in a high and holy moment. Pastor Dick baptized each of us by sprinkling us where we knelt. When we were all baptized he then sent us out to be the salt of the earth. It was my first time to realize that I wanted to be a Christian, and make a difference in the world. I reached a new stage in my development as a person. Perhaps the refiner's fire was purging the dross from my soul. It was a great time to be alive.

Dad continued to play tennis with me. First he played his buddies at the Alhambra Tennis Club, and then later he and I worked on my strokes. One Saturday he reminded me (again) that he played Pancho Gonzales at the Los Angeles Tennis Club. Pancho was one of the top players in the world. Dad beat him in a pick-up game, and felt proud while telling me. Dad was only able to play on weekends, yet his innate athletic skills enabled him to play and win with the best.

One class at P.C.C. caught my eye that spring: Biology 52. I don't remember the instructor's name, but he and his textbook held my interest. His text was a large book, 15" x 20", and full of photos of life forms. The author enjoyed showing photos of the unusual forms of life. One photo showed a newborn baby with a tail growing from his spine. The doctor clipped off the tail and no one knew the difference. The author went out of his way to demonstrate the reality of evolution. His photos of the growth of a fetus, for instance, were designed to show us how the fetus replicates the development of a single cell to complex life forms by way of evolution.

He kept my mind in a lively debate as to how to reconcile my faith in God with the theory of evolution. I couldn't resolve the question. But I was determined to not surrender my faith in God, nor would I deny the power of science to spell out how the creation evolved. I decided to live with both realities held in a tension in my mind. *Someday*, I hoped, *it will all become clear to me.*

In June my buddy Stan Henry invited me to join him for a trip to the Central Valley for a job interview. He was interested in a job as a camp counselor with Kenyon Cattle Company in Springville. They had opened a boys' ranch there and needed young men to supervise the boys.

As we drove north the heat of the valley blasted us. There was no air conditioning available so we opened the windows and the hot air evaporated our sweat. Stan turned on the car radio and we heard a newscaster report that North Korea had invaded South Korea. President Truman called an emergency meeting of the Security Council of the United Nations to respond to this act of aggression. It was June 25th. Stan and I glanced at each other, both of us wondering the same thing: would we be drafted soon? The news was ominous, yet the fighting seemed so far away in that summer heat.

September brought shocking news. Sybil committed suicide! Bill called early on the morning of September 10 to tell Dad, and Dad relayed the news to Mom. It was like a bomb went off in our home. All of Mom's worst fears came to pass. We were ready to immediately jump into the car and drive to San Diego. Bill cautioned us not to do that; there was nothing we could do.

The internment was set for September 13. Bill had her cremated and the urn containing her ashes was placed in the wall of the sanctuary of St. Paul's Episcopal Church in San Diego. The hole in the wall was sealed by a brass plate that gave her name, birth date, and date of death. A part of me was in that brass urn behind her nameplate.

We went to the committal service at St. Paul's Church. Grief erupted everywhere. We had all lost a person too young, too beautiful, and too brave to die. After grief subsided insistent questions emerged in my mind. *How did Sybil take her life?* She must have planned her death well in advance, for she waited until past midnight when the nursing shifts changed, and all was quiet. She then slit her wrists with a razor blade and slowly bled to death alone in her room.

It is hard for me to write about this after all these years. That was a dark night of the soul. My mind tried to grasp the enormity of what had happened. I thought:

> *I would have held your hand Sis, if only you had told me how desperate you were. I would have talked you out of this if it were in my power to do so. The thought of you slowly bleeding to death by yourself in that lonely room with no one to comfort you or pray with you is more than I can bear. If you had told me I would have come to hold your hand and die with you, and comfort you all the way to heaven. But you were determined to quit this awful scenario of hopelessness. There was no skin on your body and no hope of growing any. How did you endure that for 22 months?*
>
> *A part of me understood why you did it. We have to cling to hope. Without hope we die. So I understood even though I could not accept what you did. I believe you were ushered into God's loving arms even though some friends said that suicide was a terrible sin against God. They said you could not go to heaven. I didn't listen to them. I didn't believe them.*

Mom and Dad began asking questions. How did Sybil get a razor blade? She had no place on her body to shave. Would one of the nurses in good faith give her a razor? Shame. We should have called for an investigation by an outside review board. But neither Mom nor Dad was willing to take that step.

That was my first funeral. I had missed the deaths of our relative's back east. I did not know them and could not relate to their deaths. But Sybil's death hit me hard, as though I had been hit in the solar plexus. At the same time I found that grief was new to me. In reality, I did not know how to grieve. So I wept only in part. "How do guys express their emotions?" My hero, John Wayne, said that feeling sad was a sign of weakness. Dad held his emotions in check. Mom wept openly. Only years later did I learn how to grieve, and be unashamed to show my tears. But that took time.

Back at Pasadena City College I no longer had Guy Knight in any of my classes. I found some new friends and we had lunch together in the quad where the school had a temporary building, and they served simple lunches. I bought a Mexican burrito and a coke, and had a hearty meal at a cheap price. A girl joined us one day and remarked to me, "You have the smile of a Cheshire cat." I didn't know what a Cheshire cat was, or how it smiled. There must have been some reality to the comment. I let no one know of the struggles in my mind. A student would ask, "How are you doing?" My response was a smile and the words, "FINE." I felt like a duck on a pond. To a casual observer I was placidly gliding along the surface of the water. But a hidden camera under the water would have showed my feet paddling furiously to keep my head above water.

I needed to sustain some kind of inner peace. I got up early, and after breakfast headed out to my car. I drove along Huntington Drive eastward toward San Dimas where groves of orange trees were planted on rolling hills. Surrounded by quiet orange trees, I practiced blocking out issues that troubled me and soaked up the peacefulness of the place. I was now a Christian. I had to face the issues of suffering and death. Still, answers were hard to come by.

At the Rose Parade that year I took time to drive to the end of the parade where all the floats were parked for public display. The multitudes that gathered along Colorado Boulevard were gone now. Here were curiosity seekers who had come to see the floats up close. The bands departed, and the horses were trucked away. Gone were the beautiful people who mounted the floats and waved to the crowds. Here was spent energy; a year's worth of work had come to a climax and ended.

The flowers wilted. The floats sat like proud queens whose glory was faded, leaving only memories. *Perhaps*, I thought, *this is the image of the year that is behind me.* Sybil was dead. Mom and Dad struggled with their grief. Dad kept his feelings under tight control. "Men don't cry," he believed. Mom was not restricted that way. Her sadness rose to the surface, like cream that rose to the top in a milk bottle. She wept frequently. I felt the loss of my best friend. Singing in the Choir on Sunday mornings helped me cope, as did my baptism the previous spring. When I sang the choral Introit for our worship services I allowed the words and the music to course through me, "Spirit of God descend upon my heart." Mom loved to say, "Hope springs eternal." Maybe there was hope.

Fifteen

Peaches

"California is the fruit bowl of the nation." That happens to be a great slogan for the California Chamber of Commerce, but for those who harvest the fruit bowl it is a hot and thankless job. Now I was centered in the fruit bowl again during the summer of 1951. Residents of California love to brag about our fruit and vegetable production, but none of them would ever stoop to work in our fields, even if they were starving. Harvesting is left to the rag-tag of society, and to a multitude of brown hands that come north out of Mexico to bear the burden of stoop labor in the valley of the sun.

I contacted the Student Employment Office at U.C. Davis and asked if they could help me find a summer job. "Dear Sirs," I wrote, "I am an Ag major who will be returning in the fall semester to continue my studies. I need work that will help me in my major field of Agronomy and Irrigation Science. Can you help me?" Their response was to offer me an opening at a ranch north of Davis in a town called Yuba City. I applied, got the job, and the ranch manager asked me to report in at the end of the spring semester.

I skipped commencement at PCC, packed my duffel bag, and headed north again. The 300-acre Del Monte peach ranch on the outskirts of Yuba City made an impressive sight. The ranch headquarters were painted white and well maintained. The manager and his staff were responsible for producing cling peaches in the intense summer heat of the northern Sacramento valley. Since I had worked this valley during the summer of 1947 I knew what to expect. This time, however, instead of being freelance and looking for farm work, I would have a room in a bunkhouse, a shower facility, and a large mess hall serving hungry ranch hands.

Each small room slept two men, and my roommate turned out to be the boss' son. He kept to himself and spent a lot of time with his father. A single light bulb hung in the ceiling, and one window provided some air, hot during the day and cool at night. A washbasin stood beside a small closet, and the boss' son got the bunk closest to the window. He also got free run of the ranch.

I still carried attitude problems. These attitudes wouldn't go away. Sometimes I acted arrogant, one of my typical coping mechanisms for my lack of self-confidence. Some days I affected an attitude with the crew boss. He gathered us together after breakfast each morning to give us our orders for the day. After he told his crew where to thin peaches he said to me, "Bastear, continue from where you left off." My response: "More of the same, right?" only with an attitude. I wanted to be accepted by the crew as one of them, and not as a college student with a peach of a job. Maybe he saw my response as a request for clarification. Mercifully he didn't challenge me when I said that.

My job analysis was simple: equipped with a soil augur I was to map the hard pan under the surface for the entire 300 acres. I was to dig down to the hard pan with the augur, then measure the depth to the hard pan. With a map of the orchard attached to a clipboard, and noting on the map exactly where I drilled and the depth, the underground features of the hardpan slowly emerged. I carried a jug of water, the clipboard and pencil, the augur, and a hat for protection from the intense summer sun. If there was sun block available, I never heard of it. We were exposed to the worst damage the sun could inflict. Now, many years later, I pay for it by making an annual trip to a dermatologist to have pre-cancerous sunspots burned off my face and arms. I also supervised Mexican crews when it came time for harvest. The plan called for me to be finished by the end of the peach harvest in early September.

With the map, the boss showed his tractor crews where to throw up the irrigation checks to more efficiently flood irrigate the orchard. I worked alone, joining the rest of the crew for lunch and dinner, and finally for the harvest.

The rest of the crew consisted of restless Anglo drifters who followed the harvest up and down the Sacramento Valley. Poorly educated school dropouts, farm work became a last resort for them. During the months of June and July they moved through the orchard using 10-foot and 12-foot bamboo poles. They looked for thick clusters of peaches, and when they found one they hit it hard with the end of the pole to knock off excess green peaches. With fewer peaches on the cluster, those that remained grew larger and fetched a better price at the cannery.

There was an onerous side effect to thinning peaches. Cling peaches have a coating of fuzz. I found out by working with the crew some days that hitting the peaches brought down a shower of fuzz and it drifted into your hair, eyes, and down your neck. As the heat in the orchard intensified the fuzz acted like tiny fleabites causing itching and scratching. The fuzz pooled in your sweat and ran down your front and back. My body screamed for relief from the itching. When the boss gave the signal to quit for the day, the crew rushed for the showers. There were shouts of: "Make way, I'm first." Or, "Who stole my soap?" The men quickly stripped, entered a shower stall, and felt the baptism of fresh water on a ranch mixture of fuzz/dust/sweat. When we finished washing we put on fresh underwear, and dumped sweaty clothes into the washing machine.

The cookhouse prepared hearty meals: corn bread, veggies, and mashed potatoes, alternating with ham, beef, or meat loaf. The men sat at long tables and ate until they were filled. After dinner was relaxation time as twilight settled over the valley. Sometimes the air cooled, but more often it simply dropped a degree or two and remained sticky. Men gathered in small circles and shared stories of places they had worked and of women they had known and loved. One man spoke for others when he said: "There's a sheriff down in Tulare who's lookin' for me. I ain't goin' back there again." Bedtime came early; lights went out at 10:00 pm. Wake up was 6:00 am. The air was cool then.

Weekends provided a change of pace. The men looked forward to Friday. Clean pants and fresh shirts suddenly appeared. After dinner the crew headed into Yuba City. It wasn't much to see; bars, liquor stores, card rooms, and sidewalks littered with empty bottles of Thunderbird wine. Many bottles were still tightly wrapped in the paper bags in which they were sold. It was a strange attempt at secrecy, for it was no secret as to what was inside. Thunderbird wine carried a certain cachet. It became the cheapest way to drink and escape the burdens of rootlessness.

Some sat at curbside while others slid into nooks and crannies along the storefronts. Heat arose off the streets and sidewalks intensifying the miasma. Poker bets rang out from inside and echoed on the streets. Women moved about in the bars and card rooms selling drinks. This was like a picture out of the Old West, only less romantic. There was a sickly sweet odor of new and old liquor in the air. These men were lonely, rootless drifters taking pleasure where they found it.

Growing up in San Gabriel had provided me with a secure cocoon. I was protected from the harsh realities of the mean streets of Chicago or Los Angeles. Our suburban neighborhood was clean and neat. But now I was being exposed to a dimension of life such as I had never seen. Here were alcoholics, prostitutes, and gambling, and now I was getting a wakeup call to a new reality. Mom and I had formed a web where I was Mom's precious darling. I came to believe that the world should treat me as she did, and of course the world did not. Now I awoke to a new kind of world. I was slowly learning to deal with a new reality that was at once scary, educational, and truthful all at the same time. *Isn't this why I wanted to get away for the summer?* I kept reminding myself of that.

The behavior of these restless men was not the kind of behavior that my Mom would accept. Her stern Presbyterian virtues would judge these men for stooping to the lowest level of humanity. Her ethics were imbedded in me. Yet I would never be able to see or hear these men if I continued with a judgmental attitude. I would have to break free of her in order to be my own person. These men were thus the means to a new self-awareness on my part.

Sunday mornings on the ranch were quiet. The men slept late, snoozing off their hangovers or their gambling losses. The boss' son lay on his back in a pair of boxer shorts, sleeping off his late night too. I quickly put on clean pants and shirt and headed for the cookhouse. Pancakes, bacon and eggs, juice and coffee were ready. After breakfast I walked to the Yuba City Methodist Church, while it was still cool. The church folks were not used to men walking to their church from the ranch.

I didn't have good social skills, and I failed to walk up to the members to introduce myself. I should have said, "Good morning. My name is Dick and I am here to work on the Del Monte ranch. Thought I would join you for this fine Sunday morning." But at that point in my life I lacked those essential social skills that lubricate human affairs. They too on their part seemed hesitant with their social skills, and no one greeted me. They were busy talking to friends. Perhaps theirs was the greater fault.

I took a seat in the sanctuary and read the bulletin. It announced that choir met on Wednesdays at 7:00. I walked over on Wednesday evening after dinner, and unannounced, joined the choir for practice. For a stranger to walk over from the ranch must have seemed strange to them. Again, I quietly took a seat and sang with the bass section. I continued in that isolated position for the rest of summer. For some reason the choir and I remained in a polite Mexican standoff. As a Christian fellowship, the church was a spiritual vacuum for me. It dawned on me: this was a failure of fellowship.

Part of my job analysis was to supervise a crew of 20 Braceros when the harvest began. Braceros are Mexicans legally invited to come to the U.S. to help harvest fruits and vegetables. They are also called campesinos because they came from poor rural areas of Mexico, had minimal education, and worked hard. The Bracero Program began during WWII to provide help in the agricultural sector as Americans went off to war by the millions.

I could speak limited Spanish with them. My Spanish was formal Castilian, learned in classroom books with my teacher, Mr. Oleson. Their Mexican speech was rural, informal, and down to earth. But we managed to communicate. Actually, I enjoyed practicing with them, and they responded to my attempts to cross the boundary of our cultures. Some of the campesinos referred to me simply as "Gringo," quietly from a distance. Others, obsequious to the rigid traditional ways of rural Mexico, called me "El Patron." I wasn't their boss, but they viewed me that way. A precious few dared to cross the boundary between us and call me, "Ricardo."

I liked crossing the boundary, and responded by asking them: "What state in Mexico are you from, and what is your name?" By listening to them I learned a host of Mexican idioms that I stored in a notebook in my room. For instance, in Castilian I was taught to ask: "Cómo está usted?" (How are you?). In the campesino idiom it became less formal: "Cómo le va?" (How is it going?) I liked the informality so much that I wrote the phrases as I heard them talk, and it became a dictionary that I referred to frequently. The boss handled the cultural divide in typical fashion. He housed the Braceros separately from the Anglo workers.

The Braceros were the "invisible ones." No one noticed them, and they were told to leave when their work was done. Somehow as I worked with these men their invisibility became visible, at least to me. I thought: *What a loss that our cultures are so separate and apart. These Mexican men were far from home for long periods of time. We can't learn about them this way.* They clustered, staying together, since there existed little exchange of conversation with the Anglos. The crew boss and I were the only ones to communicate with them.

But on Friday and Saturday nights, like our drifters, they had ways to entertain themselves. On weekend nights women driving vans or pickup trucks with covered tops arrived, parking on the other side of the orchard, away from the ranch offices. They were referred to as "putahs" by the campesinos, and an immediate change took place amongst the men as the putahs parked their vehicles.

The word putah, or whore, rippled through the men as when a breeze blows across a lake. Some broke into giggles, others into laughter, and some lifted their heads to the sky and howled like wolves that have caught a scent of prey. These men anticipated some lusty pleasure, a touch of home, and talking with someone who understood them so well. The communication seemed to be a part of the drama. They needed the female, not only for sex, but also for a reminder of home. These invisible people were really lonely.

Octavio Paz in his book "The Labyrinth of Solitude" tells of the loneliness in which a Mexican man lives. One of the ways that the Mexican male breaks out of his solitude is with a woman, and the male tends to see women as universal channels for his sexual gratification. Now with a putah he could find an end to his solitude, even though it would only be temporary.

Did these women know what power they had over these men? The putah could bring the campesino out of his loneliness and leave him with laughter in his heart. The workers changed from passive day laborers to active seekers. Now they came alive. Fresh shirts appeared, they washed hands and faces, combed their hair and adjusted their sombreros. Hands dipped into pockets to make sure they had cash. They started walking across the peach orchard, through the evening shadows, in the direction of the trucks.

The scene has been burned in my memory like a French Impressionist painting. The evening shadows lengthened across the orchard, the heat of the day now moderating. The peaches slung from branches like golden orbs, as the men quietly moved toward the vans. A fascinating dance began. The putah would make money, and break out of the rigid expectations placed on a Mexican woman: to be barefoot and pregnant at home. She would make money and be independent of cultural expectations. She could be free. But she had to bear the opprobrium of her profession. After all, she was a putah. She could never be accepted as a member of polite society.

The Bracero, on the other hand, would gratify himself with her. It was a meeting freighted with meaning. The men queued up by the trucks and bargaining began. The ritual would be repeated on Saturday night. Afterwards the men slowly filed back to their bunkhouse with quiet talk among them. The changed, peaceful look on their faces appeared palpable. Now it was time for lights out. Hard work began early tomorrow.

On the ranch I saw once again how wide was the gulf between us. My middle class virtues were little help in trying to grasp this new cultural phenomenon. Truly, they were separate and unequal. How slow I was to see this reality, but I was learning.

When the harvest began, the campesinos went to the warehouse to pick up tall tripod ladders. These ladders allowed them to go to the treetops to harvest peaches. Around their shoulder draped a basket that held their peaches. When it was full they clambered down and walked to where I had a check stand. I examined their baskets to make sure they had harvested no green peaches. Then I weighed their baskets, emptied them into a wooden bin, and kept track of each man's harvest. Anglo workers placed the loaded bins on to flatbed trucks, and when the truck was full, the driver took his load to the nearest cannery. The ranch lived in a frenzy of activity as we reached the climax of a year's work.

By the end of August the burst of activity eased. The harvest gathered in, the campesinos moved on to their next location. They were no longer wanted or needed at this ranch. Some of them went on to Oregon and Washington, following the harvest. Many sent home money orders to support their families or their parents. The ranch also released the Anglo workers. Now a core group remained to tend the ranch. I completed my hardpan survey and turned in my updated maps to the boss. I got a "Thanks," and a final paycheck, and a letter of recommendation for my file at UC Davis.

It was quiet now. A stillness hung in the air as September began. U.C. Davis beckoned. It was time to drive to Davis and re-open my studies there. Pausing, I recalled that I had learned something that summer not taught in books: I came to be more accepting of my fellow man; I became less judgmental of them. I reached out to the Mexican men in my crew. I liked them. The strengths and weaknesses of my Victorian, middle class virtues now shone more clearly in my mind. I was a gringo, but I liked understanding and accepting the Mexican crew. We began to build a bridge across the cultural divide between us. We took the first steps toward understanding each other.

I was a slow learner, but learned never the less. Life became more interesting as I slowly emerged from my cocoon. I was left with a lingering desire and curiosity to see more of the world, and understand more of human nature.

Sometimes when I go shopping at a super market I would like to ask one of the ladies examining the cans of fruit, "Do you know what goes in to making a can of peaches?" Then I think better of it. I forget my question for it is time to move on.

Sixteen

Planes

Returning to Davis gave me a sense of unity in the learning process. Combining work on the ranch with my course of studies was wiser than I knew at the time. I now transferred into a four-year course of study of Irrigation Science. I re-joined the Cal Aggie Christian Association (CACA). Dave Burnight was still the director, hired by the Davis Community Church for an outreach to the students. He brought intensity and focus to the Association.

We met on Tuesdays for a brown bag lunch, sang praise songs, found out who among us was facing difficult issues, and turned to intercessory prayer for one another. I learned new songs, made new friends, and started becoming interested in Christianity as a way of life. I sang in the Community Church choir and participated in study groups with Pastor Dave.

Dave looked to be in his late 30's, had a kid smile, was balding, and had an encouraging, attractive personality. Our group grew in numbers.

I had always been interested in airplanes. Now, in our meetings I found that several of our CACA members were preparing to become missionaries in far off places, some to South America. Stan Moore became a friend and he had already decided to go to Chilean Indians with his new agricultural skills and open a school amongst them. Soon I was dreaming intensely. I decided to join our Davis flying club, the Cal Aggie Flying Farmers, and become a missionary pilot who would supply the missionaries in the remotest parts of South America with medicine, Bibles, and food. I sensed adventure as well as a life purpose, for I had always been attracted to both.

Somewhere in my Bohemian heritage lurked a Gypsy mystique and I used it to buoy my newfound Christian faith. I rode my clunker of a bicycle several miles north of campus to the Davis Community Airport. There I found a World War II Navy combat pilot, Russell Robinson, who agreed to give me flight lessons. He rented a Cessna 170 for my instruction. I learned how to file a flight plan, to read pilot maps, understand the weather, the principles of flight, and so forth. I learned the inherent dangers of flight as well as the safety features of the Cessna. After weeks of preliminaries, I was itching to go up.

Finally, we went out on the tarmac and inspected the plane. Russell showed me how to do visual checks of the aircraft such as the wings, the trim tabs, the tail assembly, and all controls. I discovered there is much more to flight than simply going up into the air. The day came when he deemed that I was ready for flight. He took the pilot's seat and I took the passenger seat. We buckled up and he showed me how to check all instruments, especially the gas gauge. "Hear my warning," he said, "never leave without double checking your gas gauge." Then, "Are you ready to go up?" I gave him an excited "thumbs up," but inwardly felt fear.

I had dreamed of being a Spitfire pilot in my callow youth, and wanted to shoot down German planes in the Battle of Britain. But now I had to ask, *Am I ready*? I wondered. Russell checked once again that all controls were functional, pressed the start button and the engine came to life. He revved the engine and we taxied out to the runway. He gave me an order: "Check above us for any incoming flights." When I signaled him with an all clear he pulled the throttle all the way out and we roared down the runway. It was amazing how quickly we were airborne.

A sensation seized my belly as the plane left the ground. We were airborne, and it was at once both thrilling and scary. I had been nailed to earth for a lifetime, with all of the failures and successes that I had experienced. Suddenly, I was lifted high above my life. What a new sensation! Old issues of self-esteem melted away. I was far above school, home and routine. Now I was liberated into a new sense of self and my place in the world. All my life I had built model airplanes, collected airplane photos, and dreamed of flight. Now I was soaring. My youthful Spitfire pilot was in the air, finally.

Russell took us up to 10,000 feet and leveled off as we headed toward Sacramento. When we were over open country I got a warning from Russell, "Watch carefully. I am going to take us into a stall." Then he reassured me, "Don't worry, the Cessna is designed to recover itself from a stall." *Thanks for the warning, Russell*. He pulled back on the controls and the nose of the Cessna angled into a 45-degree climb. He continued to increase the angle until we suddenly stalled. The thrill of takeoff was erased, and a sickening lurch took hold of my stomach. The nose of the plane dropped abruptly and my knuckles turned white as I grabbed the edge of my bucket seat and hung on. I thought we would spin all the way to earth.

True enough, the plane automatically recovered itself and continued with level flight. Russell repeated the stall many times that morning. He gave me a verbal criticism for not relaxing during the exercise. At one point he said, "Pay close attention." Soon after he followed with, "Relax!" I wasn't sure which was uppermost, and I sure couldn't do both at the same time.

Russell didn't smile much. I guess that as a Navy combat pilot he had to learn to kill or be killed in aerial combat with Japanese fighter planes. He wanted me to learn the wartime pilot's survival skills, and learn them immediately. I wonder if he had ever completely unwound from aerial combat. Dad had another favorite quote from Alfred Lord Tennyson that Russell would have liked, "Yours is not to reason why; yours is but to do or die."

It was taking me time just to learn that we wouldn't fall out of the sky on one of our stalls. We practiced all the way to Sacramento, circled over the Capital Building and headed back to Davis. I got more instruction on the flight back, but mercifully, no more stalls. As he brought it in for a landing I had a deep sigh of relief that I didn't get airsick. I had completed my first flight lesson, and could still stand up. I wasn't the combat pilot that I dreamed myself to be during WWII, but, with some pride welling up, I had made a beginning. Now it was time to thank Russell, get on my rickety bicycle, and head back to campus.

We continued the lessons each week through October and November. He taught me how to bank the Cessna to the left, then to the right, how to start a dive and then pull out, and how to set up a cross-country flight plan. As winter approached a north wind began to blow. I left Birch Hall, headed my old bike into the wind, and barely made it to the airport on those days. By November 21st, I had completed my learner's lessons. The Civil Aeronautics Board awarded me a temporary pilot's license. Russell told me I would be ready to solo in December. I thrilled at the prospect of having mastered an important new skill.

Little did I remember that in October 1948 I had gone home for the weekend to register for the draft with the Alhambra Draft Board. In early December of 1951 I received by registered mail my draft notice into the Army of the United States. The Draft Board ordered me to report to the Los Angeles Induction Center on February 5, 1952. My heart sank. The plans I had so carefully made were unraveling. My dream of becoming a missionary pilot was now indefinitely postponed. Also out the window was my hope of graduating in the next two years. It took days for the shock to wear off. I now realized that the poor grades I received at Pasadena City College had probably led to this, and would now haunt me.

Headlines blared of the war in Korea, the tragedies of the American retreats, first from the North Koreans, then from the Communist Chinese. Now I was next in line to enter the war.

I was slow in coming to terms with these new realities. One way I coped was to imagine myself becoming a good soldier and fighting bravely in combat. Then I could return home with a new sense of self-esteem. Another coping mechanism came by way of an important decision I made. I would complete my course of studies, and take all the final exams before I went home. I postponed my solo flight until after I was discharged in two years. I prepared for finals in Bacteriology, Botany, Organic Chemistry, Irrigation Science, and Pomology.

At the same time I was growing in my Christian faith. I began Bible studies in earnest with CACA. At the campus bookstore I bought St. Augustine's classic "Confessions." It intrigued me even though "Confessions" had no steamy revelations about the sins of a saint. But a phrase jumped out at me and I held on to it. "O Lord, Thou hast made us for thyself, and our hearts are restless until they rest in thee." Thus, I might not be able to fly as a missionary to South America, at least not now, but I could hold on to those words for the rest of my life.

I grew academically too. My final exams revealed a new trend emerging. The more I studied the better my grades became. I ended the fall semester with three "B's" and three "C's." In High School I was a "C" student. At Pasadena I raised my grade average to a "C+" level. Now at Davis I was improving even more. The more I learned to focus, to clarify my goals, to sharpen my study skills, the better my grades became. I found that I was capable of becoming a better student. That was a revelation. My grades validated the progress I was making.

Seventeen

Army, 1952-1954

Sometimes you find that you are a small part of some historic event, picked up like a leaf on a river and carried downstream against your will, toward an uncertain end. Such was the Korean War, and I was now caught into it with a draft notice. I was part of a major world crisis, but felt as though I was such a small, insignificant part of it.

I was drafted into the Army at the Los Angeles Induction Center on February 5, 1952. Processing took place at Fort Ord, near Monterey. From there a group of us were sent to Camp Roberts for basic training. My Drill Instructor (DI), Sergeant Carey, turned out to be one of the Army's best. He was probably in his 30's, and as firm and fair as he was demanding. He drilled us, shouted at us, and made us clean latrines until they shone like newborn babies. He was dressed and ready when he called us to reveille at 5:30 am, (4:00 am during rifle training), flipping on the lights and giving us 30 seconds to hit the deck. He led us on forced marches in intense heat, leading the way while calling cadence. We marched to the songs and cadence that he shouted to us, and echoed it right back to him.

Slowly but surely a bunch of kids from down the street and around the corner morphed from gangly teen-agers and cool young men into a wonder to see: soldiers who could manage a rifle and bayonet, throw a grenade, bivouac in good and bad weather, and take orders without question. We became one part of the US Army.

Respect for Sergeant Carey grew the more we learned to become professional warriors. What added to the dynamic was his color. He was a black man. Only four years before, President Truman ordered an end to segregation in the armed services, amidst deep grumbling from the brass and enlisted men that integration would never work. Well, this is the army, and orders were orders. Sergeant Carey was one of the first in this social/military experiment.

I admired him because I believe that he had to work twice as hard as his white counterparts just to prove himself worthy. There were older soldiers who said a black man couldn't stand and fight in combat. There were those who, while proud of our army, said a black man was not worthy to wear the uniform of a non-commissioned officer. Sergeant Carey proved them all wrong. We in our platoon were living witnesses that Sgt. Carey could lead, and he taught us how to make America proud.

We finished 16 weeks of basic training in June. Several of us signed on for Leadership School that began in July. We were taught how to lead men into combat, how to handle fear, and how to set an example in dress and in character. All of this happened in the blazing heat of summer. Some days I was not sure I would make it.

October 18 signaled our graduation ceremony for Class 66 of Leadership School. Our school printed programs for the occasion and I stood proud. Our Class had 39 still standing out of an original 70 soldiers. I graduated in the top ten of our class. I received a promotion to PFC. I groaned, "All that work for a lowly stripe!" But I was proud of it, and immediately hired a camp seamstress to sew on my first stripe. My decision, made in February to be the best soldier I could be, had paid off.

The last two weeks of October we anxiously awaited orders. I thought for sure we would be sent to Korea to fight. That is what I had emotionally prepared myself to do. My orders came on October 25. Imagine my shocked surprise when six of my buddies from Basic

Training, including Toy, Caron and Bartel, were selected for duty in the Free Territory of Trieste. With a unanimous response we blurted out: "Where's Trieste?" We scrambled for maps. We looked. We could not imagine why we had been selected for duty there. But we were men under orders.

Trieste stood at the north end of the Adriatic Sea, where Italy and Yugoslavia meet. It anchored the southern end of what Churchill had called, "The Iron Curtain." The Iron Curtain stretched from Stettin on the Baltic to Trieste on the Adriatic and the Iron Curtain became the focus of the Cold War between NATO and Soviet Communism. We were excited to be sent to one of the world's "hot spots." And we were relieved to know that we were not being deployed to Korea. Oh what a relief that was. But the dramas of history were pulling us along even deeper into a moving river, and we were but one small part of the drama. We packed our duffel bags and each headed home for leaves with our families. "I'll see you in Camp Kilmer. Have a great time at home," I shouted. We rejoined at Camp Kilmer, New Jersey, in November.

I can hardly remember leave time at home. I could think only of my deployment to Trieste. Now, a mixture of opposites stirred in my gut. I had anxiety with the unknowns, but I was excited as I considered the new life in Italy that shimmered in my imagination. A "hoi polloi" from the little town of San Gabriel would now enter into a much larger world, into a greater moment of history. Now I didn't feel so much like a leaf in the water. I had an assignment and I would fulfill it.

Dad often reminded us that we were not like the wealthy people who lived two miles north of us in San Marino. We were "hoi polloi." Yet now I felt lifted out of my station in life by being sent to a history-making post. "Imagine that, Dad. I'm going to Trieste. Isn't that exciting?" "You had better wait and see what it is like when you get there," came his considered reply.

The evening of November 7th, 1952, became a defining moment for me. Dad drove Mom and me to the Los Angeles International Airport. We stood in the waiting room listening for the announcement to board my flight to New York City. The Army was paying the fare for my first commercial flight. But that was negligible compared to the push-pull I felt.

Now I would truly break out from Mom's control.

Now I would be free, or so I thought. Yet was I ready to face the unknown of Trieste? Wouldn't it be easier to be at home in the cocoon that had always nourished me? Why the anxiety in my stomach? Why the awareness that things would never be the same? I stood on the precipice of a new life, 9,000 miles from home, with a ten-hour difference between us. Was I ready? Had the Army done everything they could to prepare me for this assignment?

A TWA clerk announced my flight was ready to board. On the tarmac a bright aluminum TWA Lockheed Constellation stood ready for us. Scheduled arrival time in New York City was set for 11:00 a.m. the next day. I turned to Mom. I hugged her more intimately than ever before. I kissed her. It was hard to give my mother a farewell kiss, and say goodbye to 22 years of nurture, care, and control. But, I reached out and hugged her closely. Then Dad turned to me. I wanted to hug him, but he was not ready for a hug, so we shook hands and patted each other on the back. Dad was not comfortable with close, nor was I the athlete that he had hoped I would be.

One of Dad's favorite quotes was William Henley's closing line from "Invictus:" "I am the master of my fate: I am the captain of my soul." Dad needed that line for reassurance at Western Union. Engineers from USC and UCLA surrounded him, a high school dropout. But now at this moment I needed his reassurance and protective arms around me as I faced a whole new world. I was hungry for a hug from my father, but in this tender father-son moment, he did not know how to give that to me. I suddenly saw the lie in Henley's line. Those words did not ring true in my father. He was not the captain of his soul. If he was in charge of himself he would have broken out of his cage and given me a hug.

Years later I solved the dilemma of my letdown feelings. When I came home, I gave him a hug and told him, "Dad, I love you." I meant it.

I learned how to reverse the energy flow back to him. He never learned how to return my hugs nor my words

I turned and walked to the exit for my flight. The other passengers and I walked across 30 yards of tarmac to the Constellation. Those 30 yards seemed like 1,000 yards. I took a step forward, but felt a pull to turn around and go back to the cocoon of home. I turned and saw Mom and Dad at the window waving to me. Mom blew me a kiss and I returned that sentiment by blowing one to her. But a feeling in the pit of my stomach told me that I was leaving behind everything familiar of the last 22 years. I moved to the ramp and climbed up and into the plane.

As the Constellation surged for height the great city of Los Angeles appeared below sparkling with lights. With a grand sweep over the city the lights disappeared. Alone with my thoughts, I had a sense that both my feet were planted in midair, and that this was a simile for my life. I was heading into a vast unknown. *Good Lord*, I thought, *Be with me now*.

We landed at La Guardia Airport at 11:20 am the next morning. I collected my duffel bag and hoped that everyone noticed my brand new Private First Class stripe. They didn't notice such things. Having several more days before I had to report to Camp Kilmer, I headed for a bank of telephones. I placed a call to New London, Connecticut, where Bill Yates was stationed with the submarine service. His wife, Bea, answered the phone. She invited me to catch a train that morning, and she and my sister Sybil's 4-year old son, Steven, would greet me at the station. I demurred and told her I wanted to stay in the city for the first day and see the sights. I would plan to catch the commuter train to New London the next morning. We agreed to that plan.

I made an exciting day by visiting tourist sites in the city. That night however, became the best part. I bought a ticket to Radio City Music Hall and the Rockettes. The Rockettes' precision dancing mesmerized me. Afterward, to top it, I walked across the street to a classy restaurant for dinner. After placing my request with the maître d' I stood and waited, and waited. Those who came after me were seated and I alone was left unseated. After a half hour of this I had an awful awareness. Korean War be damned! PFC stripes be damned! He was not going to seat a lowly PFC! I had been shunned. Now I experienced the pain of being silently rejected. Dad had warned me that I was common hoi polloi. Now I felt the full brunt of that message. I left and walked to a café for a hamburger. Maybe I should have given a vocal protest. At that moment however, the sting of rejection hurt so much I couldn't talk.

The next morning I went to Grand Central Station and caught a commuter train to New London. Bea and Steven were at the station to greet me and drove me to their home. They had a beautiful home, built in 1853, overlooking the ocean. Steven played games in his room while Bea and I talked. She was firm with him and spanked him once, telling him what he could and could not do. Kindergarten would begin the next day.

Bill came home early so that he could join us. Always a commanding presence when he walked into a room, our eyes turned to him. He fit the picture of a naval officer who was on his way to the top. He was strong, vocal, handsome, and debonair. He was a role model to me of an officer and a gentleman. I could see why Sybil hesitated with her first love, Jim, and turned to Bill instead. She could not continue to love two men at the same time, and now I could understand why.

All these thoughts came to mind as we sat in their front room sipping coffee and munching cookies. How different was the picture now. In Annapolis it had been Sybil with Bill. In New London it was now Bea with Bill. I had to make an adjustment to this new reality, even though Mom and Dad could not or would not relate to them.

When I arrived in Camp Kilmer the air chilled me to the bone. I was issued a woolen army overcoat. Frost turned the leaves brown. The smell of coal-fired stoves was brand new to me. All day that odor hung in the air. The coal smoke was a constant reminder that I was in a new and different place. We were now in a holding pattern. There was no more training. Instead, we waited for our orders to set sail from New York City. Rumors flew as to when we would sail.

The time for departure from Camp Kilmer arrived. My buddy Bartel and I took a train to Jersey City on November 17, then boarded the

Staten Island Ferry, which took us to Pier 10 in New York Harbor. That afternoon we boarded our troopship, the General R.E. Callan.

The Callan sailed at 8:00 the next morning for a 22-day voyage to Trieste. We were assigned bunks in the hold. Bunks were made of durable canvas in a foldable steel frame, and were stacked four high. Two-foot aisles separated us from the next stack of four bunks. We stuffed our duffel bags under the bunks.

I was seasick the first three days until all I could manage were dry heaves. A sailor in the galley gave me some important information. He said, "Eat nothing but saltine crackers and dill pickles for one day. You've got nothing to lose. Try it." Amazing! It worked. I had no more seasickness.

Our 22 day voyage was marked by stops at Casablanca, Naples, Athen's port city of Piraeus, Izmir, Turkey, and Istanbul. I have always been interested in history, but these stops impressed a kind of culture shock along with history. We were bussed to the ruins of Pompeii on the outskirts of Naples. It is the best preserved of all Roman ruins. In many buildings lay bodies encrusted in volcanic ash exactly where they fell, overcome by the toxic gasses from Mt. Vesuvius in 79 A.D.. Volcanic ash preserved their bodies for 1900 years. We were in a time warp where 1900 years peeled away before our eyes.

Our guide took us to a temple of Aphrodite where temple prostitutes met their customers. My deepest Presbyterian beliefs and my Victorian virtues were now colliding with a new awareness. On the walls an artist had painted scenes of men and women copulating. Those scenes shocked me into a new reality. The invisible now was plainly visible. The secret so long hidden from me became very real. I was face-to-face with the sexual secrets that Mom wanted to keep hidden. I wasn't easily resolving this clash of opposites.

The ancient bazaars in Casablanca and Istanbul combined sights, sounds and smells of thousands of years. The fragrance was unforgettable. The freshly tanned leather, handmade rugs, and brewing Arabic coffee filled the bazaar.

The coffee, prepared in strange looking urns, was served in common coffee cups that were too dirty to drink from. In Istanbul I tried an espresso anyway, and it was so thick and powerful that I felt a jolt through my body as I sipped it. I said to Bartel, "You could serve this to an army and create a formidable fighting force." We both laughed at my attempt to bridge the cultural divide in Istanbul, the city with a history of east meeting west.

Our guide took us to the ancient church of Hagia Sophia, built in the 5th century by the Emperor Justinian. This was the oldest church I had ever seen. The Greek architecture, the mosaics in the floor, the absence of pews, the high pulpit, led my imagination back to the 5th century where worshippers dropped to their knees to worship God.

But it seemed to me that such churches are built at a great price, and much time and effort is spent to maintain them. Sometimes they get in the way of a personal relationship with God. I thought, *we get distracted by the pomp of the church and miss God.*

Finally we arrived at the port of Trieste on the morning of December 9th. "Welcome to Trieste", the ship's loudspeaker announced. This time we had our duffel bags packed and ready to go. The remnant on board was Army personnel destined for this last stop. Queuing up, each soldier was debriefed by a major who gave out assignments. When I stood before him and saluted, he informed me that because of my Surveying 71 Class at Pasadena City College, he would send me first to Camp Sistiana for two weeks of orientation, then onto "H" company of the 2nd Battalion. "H" Company was the 81mm mortar unit at Banne, at the top of the hill above Trieste.

Thanking him, I felt relief that I had been spared from the infantry. I hadn't done well in surveying, but the class had paid off for me. I was now assigned to the artillery. Bartel was assigned to K Company, an infantry company in the 3rd Battalion. We met on weekends for meals and shows downtown.

An icy cold wind called the "Bora" swept over us as we boarded Army trucks. Our overcoats and long johns barely held back the chill. I threw my duffel bag aboard, and someone reached down to give me a lift on board. When we filled the truck the driver drove us to Camp Sistiana where we would be oriented until December 24th.

On Christmas Day we were trucked up the 26% grade toward the hilltop town of Banne, overlooking Trieste. All of us were in our dress Eisenhower winter clothes with wool overcoats and garrison caps. My first Christmas 9000 miles away from home was strangely different. I missed the tradition of sitting around our Christmas tree and opening gifts with my family. Now I was with a group of soldiers I had never met before. It was hard to celebrate.

I jumped down from the truck as the Master Sergeant greeted us and directed us to the office of our Company Commander, Captain Saletto. He was imposing. He stood well over 6 feet tall with tanned features and a practiced scowl on his face like that which General George Patton used so effectively with his troops in WWII. The men feared Patton and that is exactly the effect Patton wanted. I surmised that Captain Saletto was leaning on the same strategy of leadership from fear. We felt the aloof welcome, and were escorted to our barracks.

The guys in our 81mm. mortar unit had a Franklin stove filled with glowing coals that warmed our end of the barracks. After Camp Kilmer the smell of burning coal became familiar. For me it was a pungent fragrance, but it meant warmth. The barracks were cold except for the area around the stove. As we gathered in that circle of warmth, questions popped-up quickly: "Who are you? Where are you from? Where were you trained?" Introductions began. Since I was new, I got the unpleasant task of going out into the cold for a bucket of coal. These were the guys I would live with for the next 14 months.

The barracks were old buildings. The Austrian army, and the Italian army had at one time used it in WWI. In 1943, the German Wehrmacht occupied the barracks. Hitler ordered Trieste be seized and made a part of the Third Reich when the Fascist Grand Council surrendered to the Allies in 1943.

The Nazis created a prison downtown at San Saba, now a tourist site. Seven hundred Jews were rounded up, tortured and killed, then cremated in that place. The Italians quietly hated the Nazis. The resentment showed in a nearby German army graveyard. Black crosses bearing soldiers names filled the area. Many of the crosses tilted precipitously from neglect, but no one seemed to care. There was no one to take care of the place.

The hills around the city were pockmarked with slit trenches left over from WWI. I was not a historian, but the sense of history showed everywhere in Trieste. I slowly became connected to the place.

Our 81mm mortar unit, Company H, supported the 2nd Battalion of the 351st Infantry. We were all part of the 351st Combat Infantry Regiment. The 351st had been sent here by Allied powers at the end of WWII to take control of the city from Marshall Tito's partisan fighters..

Marshall Tito organized guerilla fighters in the mountains of Yugoslavia to fight the occupying army of the German Wehrmacht. Tito was the *de facto* leader of Yugoslavia when the war ended. Tito's men swept into Trieste as the German Wehrmacht retreated in May, 1945. Marshall Tito was warned by General Eisenhower to back off or face military consequences. He backed out of Trieste, but with belligerence and threats to come back.

An area called the Free Territory of Trieste was created by the Allies, and divided into two parts: Zone A included the city of Trieste, occupied by 5,000 Americans of the 351st, and by 5,000 British soldiers of the Lancashire Division. Zone A was designated "TRUST" (Trieste U.S. Troops). Zone B, included the hinterland around Trieste, mostly Slavic rural villages, and was occupied by Marshall Tito's Army.

For many years there were threats from the Italian government demanding Trieste be "redeemed" by a return to Italy. Marshall Tito maintained a drumbeat of war-like speeches demanding that the Allies leave Trieste to him lest he take military action to retrieve it by force. And so it was that the 351st was there to keep the peace until a United Nations plebiscite could be held, and a free and open vote of the people would decide the matter.

Trieste exuded an Italian character and longed to return to Italy. However, complicating that desire lay the fact that as our Intelligence Officers alerted us, one in six Triestini was a card carrying communist,

Army, 1952-1954

and even more were sympathizers. Their sympathies lay with Marshall Tito. The communist party had a headquarters downtown in Piazza Unita. We kept a constant presence in the city. We were peacekeepers.

Our "*caserna*", or base for the 2nd Battalion, was in the city of Banne. One mile east was the city of Opacina, the end of the line for streetcars that sloped up and down the hill into Trieste and back.

Jan Morris wrote a book called "Trieste and the Meaning of Nowhere." She sketched what the Austro-Hungarian monarchs did in the 19th century to make Trieste into a major port. Trieste became one of Austria's imperial outlets to the sea. Austria built a rail line to connect the city to Vienna. It is true that Trieste is off the well-known path that travelers take over the Alps to Italy. We were 90 miles east of Venice. But I became fascinated with the city and took in all the sights I could and did make it someplace special to me.

"Eaves, are you going to sign up for conversational Italian," I asked our squad leader. His reply was affirmative: "You bet. Let's do it together." We signed on for a correspondence course given by the University of Maryland. I liked the class so much that I later signed on for part two of a follow-up class. Before long, with my new language skills, I made Trieste my home away from home. I also began to consider changing my major at U.C. Davis from Agriculture to International Relations, or Political Science.

One Saturday I went downtown to try my new Italian speaking skills. Before entering a barbershop, I practiced how to ask for a haircut and a shave in Italian. I wanted to impress the barber, and I recited my memorized words; "*Voglio farmi tagliare i capelli, corti intorno il lati.*" He was so excited to hear an American soldier speak Italian that he poured forth a torrent of Italian praises and questions that overwhelmed me. I decided to ask simple questions from that point on, like, "Where's the bathroom?"

Besides Eaves and myself, there were 24 others that served in our heavy mortar unit providing support to the 2nd Battalion of infantry. The infantry guys who bunked at the other end of our barracks jealously called us "the sewing circle." That was a jibe to remind us of the prerogatives that we had as artillery, and tease us regarding our privileges.

Since a 81mm mortar weighs 300 pounds, we rode to our maneuvers in Jeeps and trucks, whereas the infantry marched. Hence the jibe. We practiced our field maneuvers together, but our mortars were always situated behind the infantry in order to provide fire support for them. Our Fire Direction Center (FDC) became the nerve center of the 2nd Battalion when we were on maneuvers.

I was trained by Joachim, a long time member of FDC, to be a Horizontal Control Operator (HCO), a part of the Fire Direction Center. My job was to take information from our Forward Observer (FO) who was placed ahead of the infantry. The FO spotted enemy gun positions, troops, or targets, and the FO would call in to FDC the target's approximate position on our map. I would then make calculations and call to the mortar firing crew to crank the barrel so many turns to the right or left so as to be "on target". Then the vertical control operator would order so many turns of the crank up or down to be on target. We would "bracket" the target by firing a round over the target, then a round short of the target, and then split the difference to be on target.

In March our motor pool loaded Company H into their trucks and drove us to Valbruno in the Italian Dolomite Alps for snow maneuvers. Frankly, I enjoyed this close-up of the snow-clad Alps in winter. We were issued skis, snowshoes and parkas and taught how to use them. We broke the mortars into parts and packed them on sleds, pulling them through the snow into a valley ahead. There we set up our mortars into firing positions, selected targets, and fired live rounds at our targets. Only years later did I discover that the loud BANG of a round going off had damaged my hearing, and I needed hearing aids to make up the difference.

We lived in five man tents pitched in snow, cooked our own rations on our own stove, had clear weather, and after daily maneuvers, took delight in talking far into the night. Eaves, Kosaka, Joachim, Jones and I were together in one tent. We bonded in friendship.

Strangers from across America, we were now a fighting unit who connected high in the Italian Alps. I never dreamed that the army could be like this. These became the guys that I was closest to for 14 months. The tent became our home away from home. The weather outside was frigid, but inside the tent we were family and that meant warmth. I know it may sound crazy, but I enjoyed our maneuvers in the snow. I began to feel less of a need for my father and mother. These buddies were making the difference.

Back at our *caserna* we began each day with reveille. Sergeant Swindle bellowed, "Fall in with a rebel yell!" After roll call we had our Army daily dozen calisthenics, followed by 30 minutes for breakfast, then cleaned up the barracks.

Our time was spent cleaning equipment, punctuated with days spent out in the fields practicing maneuvers with our mortars. When we returned to base all of our equipment had to be cleaned again. We made forced marches of 10 miles, always a challenge. Every soldier had to complete the march with a pack and helmet liner, or try until he did. We performed the Army "daily dozen" every morning to stay in shape. Then there were classes, and much time spent trying to look busy.

Spring slowed down the Bora, the infamous wind of Trieste, and the days warmed. Preparing for Saturday inspection by Lieutenant Durst and First Sergeant Swindle was our regular assignment. Anyone who failed inspection was denied a pass for the weekend. Severe consequences awaited anyone who failed inspection. It meant a trip to Captain Saletto's office to face his scowl and a tongue-lashing. The captain would order a denial of privileges for two weeks and extra KP duty.

The men had long ago nicknamed Captain Saletto. They quietly referred to him as "the blade." We obeyed him out of fear. I don't admire that kind of leadership, but some officers and non-commissioned officers depended on it. One of the responses among the men was a German phrase "machts nicht" –i.e. it doesn't matter, or, this is the Army.

Apparently Captain Saletto checked my background report and found that I had graduated from Leadership School. He called me to his office and appointed me Company H "Guidon." My job, he explained, would be to carry the Company H banner, attached to the top of a six-foot standard, in all Battalion and Regimental parades.

I learned to march with precision holding the guidon in an upright position above my head with the company H banner snapping in the wind. As I approached the place where Captain Saletto stood at attention, I halted exactly six feet behind and smartly snapped the standard from a vertical to a horizontal position at armpit level. The company fell in behind me. I loved this duty and I was proud to do it. I was serving my country here in Trieste.

To instill pride TRUST Command ordered the men of the 351st to wear sky blue silken braided bands, attached to the epaulets on our right shoulders. Lt. Durst pumped us up by telling us that we were "The queen of battle." During Regimental parades all 5,000 soldiers marched in cadence, with sky blue braids on their right shoulders. We made an exciting scene of pomp and circumstance, and reminded ourselves of who we were.

We had some glorious Saturday parades; the drums were drumming, and the Army Band provided our marching music. We marched around the parade ground, and then formed in front of the regimental commander, General McFadyen. At regimental parades, battalion commanders marched in front of our company commanders. Each of the battalion commanders would lead our company commanders into pre-selected positions in front of the General. They halted, saluting the General while standing at attention. Then 16 guidons marched in unison and took our positions behind our captains. At a regimental command, we saluted our general in unison by a lively movement, whipping our standards parallel to the ground.

At one regimental parade, I stopped several inches off my mark. As I snapped my standard down, the tip grazed the glinting chrome helmet of Captain Saletto standing in front of me. A metallic clang echoed across the parade ground. I could have crawled into a hole and hid, I felt so embarrassed. I stood at attention as did Captain Saletto and faked that all was well. Of course, after the parade, I received a summons to the captain's office. Anxiously awaiting my fate, I gave my, "No excuse, Sir!" as a memorized response. I received extra KP duty and a denial of privileges for two weeks.

I believe the Captain also slowed my promotion to corporal. I continued as company guidon, but was well aware there could be no further errors in judgment. Jones, ever alert for some fun, reminded me of the regimental five P's: "Prior Planning Prevents Piss Poor Performance." I got the message.

At Company H headquarters we took turns checking each man's pass on Saturdays. The men were required to report to headquarters when they returned to the post. Midnight was the deadline to return. However, if we overlooked one man's tardiness in returning and covered for him, he would do the same for us when we were late checking in.

Each Saturday afternoon Captain Saletto came to the headquarters office. With flair he went to the desk where our company kept a large box of condoms available to all of the men. He reached into the box and grabbed a fistful, and in that maneuver, several condoms squeezed through his fingers. His fist looked like a porcupine of condoms. He jammed them into his front pocket and his scowl vanished, replaced by a grin. His closing words were "I'm heading downtown!" Now he commanded with bravado. We responded "Yes Sir!"

We rotated for guard duty. An eight-foot high wall surrounded our barracks and battalion headquarters. When the Bora winds blew, we went to the guardhouse to be issued fur-lined parkas, woolen caps and mittens. In the mortar unit we were armed with carbines loaded with a full clip of bullets. We slung the carbine over our right shoulder, and walked the inside perimeter all night, two hours on guard, then four hours of rest in the guardhouse. The Officer of the Guard checked us in and out.

On Friday and Saturday night we kept a conspiracy of silence regarding a black market trade between soldiers on the inside and Italians on the outside. American cigarettes were available by the carton at our canteen. They were highly prized by the Italians, who looked down on their own brand of cheap cigarettes.

It was illegal to resell to them, but some enterprising G.I.'s saw an opportunity for profit. With low whistles after dark, an Italian on the outside of the wall would toss over the wall a wad of prearranged cash held together by a rubber band. Then a carton of American cigarettes flew over the wall to him. The soldiers demanded and got a higher price than they paid for them at the PX. The Italians would return to downtown Trieste with their cartons and sell packs of cigarettes on the street for an even higher price. This black market trade was common knowledge and those on guard duty made no report of it.

I offered my services to our chaplain, Herman Davis. I helped by setting up chairs and passing out hymnals to the men who worshipped on Sundays. The chaplain not only provided Sunday services for us, but also gave frequent lectures on morality. He wasn't an inspiring speaker, but his earnestness carried conviction. He did not address the black market trade, but gave us warnings to avoid the prostitutes in Banne and in downtown Trieste. Not only were there sexually transmitted diseases (STD's), but some prostitutes had criminal records of theft and assault.

He also cautioned us regarding the local girls who came to our dances at the Hangar Club downtown, or to our dance parties on base. Many were interested in gaining passage to the United States. The quickest way to accomplish this was to have an affair with a soldier, then hope it would lead to marriage. Once in the U.S. such women got citizenship, then a divorce, and went their own way. Chaplain Davis discouraged these relationships.

Downtown one of our favorite places was the Hangar Club. It had a library, gym, snack bar, and dance floor. Our favorite eatery was Mario's, on the Piazza del' Unita, the civic heart of Trieste. As spring warmed the days, local cafes set up tables along the sidewalk where families came on weekends and evenings to eat and drink and savor their favorite Chianti wine. We would take a table and enjoy the scene as families came together for an evening out.

On Friday and Saturday nights the Birra Dreher beer hall was a popular place to be. Families, single women and G.I.'s came to drink beer and listen to the band play mostly American music, and German polkas. The soldiers and the single women flirted with each other. The Italian families came often with their extended families and children. They looked stoic on the streets, but once inside they laughed and sang songs with the five-piece band. We had fun watching the Italians, and then singing along with them, and sometimes catching a dance with one of their daughters.

Our most common entertainment centered on bowling alleys and movie theaters. We had a theatre at our *caserna* in Banne. The British Army operated a theater in Opacina, which they called "The Cinema." The Americans also had a theater down the hill in Trieste called the TRUST Theater. Most of the movies were grade B or C. Only a few were worth remembering: "High Noon", "African Queen", "Viva Zapata", "Quo Vadis", "The Quiet Man" and "Cyrano de Bergerac."

Triestini took pride in their Giuseppe Verdi Opera House or "teatro". On Sunday's their concert orchestra played classical music. One Sunday we heard a Tchaikovsky concert. Another Sunday was devoted to George Gershwin's music. One Sunday after church some buddies and I went to see "The Barber of Seville." I couldn't relate to this kind of music, but I was glad I experienced at least one opera.

Ninety miles to the west of Trieste lay Venice. We could get there *subito* (quickly) on a *rapido* train. We must have gone six times that year. A highlight was a canal trip through the ancient city. As our gondolier reached an intersection of canals he cried out with a loud voice, *Ay Oooh! Ay Oooh!* That cry helped prevent collisions. Such were the traffic signals in Venice. Once this was a great city. Now it was merely a tourist site. We returned to our base refreshed with the change of scenery.

American music became my identity with home, especially as we were 9,000 miles away from home. All of the latest records were played at our dances and parties. One song created a lasting place in my heart; Jo Stafford singing "You Belong to Me." I played it over and over again on the jukebox in our Enlisted Men's Club. Along with the music I ordered my favorite comfort food: a fried egg sandwich. Now, I had both a food "fix" and a music fix at the same time.

Why do certain songs and foods tie us to home, or to someone far away and special? Music has always played a significant part in my life. Now, it was even more so. This song flooded me with memories of home. If I hear Jo Stafford today I am immediately back in Trieste hearing and seeing the city once again.

That spring, Jochim told Kosaka and me that he planned a trip to Rome in May. "Would you like to apply for leave and join me?" he asked. Our answer: a unanimous, "Yes." Then *Subito!* do it. We applied, were accepted, and purchased our tickets at the train depot. We then packed and left on May 11. The weather was glorious. I tracked the cities we passed through as our *rapido* headed south: Venice, Padua, Bologna and Florence. We arrived in Rome that evening at 10:00 p.m. Grabbing our bags we headed out of the modernistic station looking for a taxi to take us to our hotel.

Along the street numerous prostitutes boldly approached us, seeing we were single American males, (viewed as having more money). Sensually, they offered sex at our place or theirs. They were dressed in tight outfits that accentuated their boobs and butts. Their blouses revealed remarkable cleavage, and their short skirts grabbed our attention. Their English was broken, but understandable. Most of them traveled in pairs, with rakish make-up. I had culture shock again. I had never been approached and offered sex. Such a thing was unknown in San Gabriel. The three of us maintained a chorus of "No thanks" all the while trying to hail a taxi. We finally found a taxi that dropped us off at our hotel.

In the next few days we saw many of the important tourist sites, traveling by foot, bus and trolleys around the city. Jochim was Catholic and told us he was going to the Catholic Youth Organization to get a pass for an audience with the pope. "Would you each like a pass?" he asked. Again we said, "Yes." I was curious. I had heard of the Pope and wanted to know more about him. On May 13 we took a bus to St. Peter's and walked into the huge church.

Crowds surged into the sanctuary. Many were there in groups, and held up signs identifying their hometown. Nuns in their unique habits passed their prayer beads through their fingers. Curious people created a noise that echoed off the walls of the marble sanctuary and startled me. Swiss Guards in their purple and yellow uniforms kept a watchful eye.

Pope Pius XII was ushered in on a great chair mounted on a platform and carried by young priests at each of the four corners. Swiss Guards marched front and rear. Other altar boys flanked the pope. They walked with hands clasped in an attitude of piety and prayer. The pope was dressed in robes that were so white they dazzled my eye. He held up his hand and gave a papal blessing to all who caught his eye. He blessed rosary beads that were handed up to him. Others handed caps to him, which he quickly placed on his head, blessed them, and gave them back.

With a loud *"Viva!"* he took a chair on the altar and blessed the people, while surrounded by cardinals of the Church. He then read greetings to the congregation in twelve languages, including English. He spoke with a light, keen tone, which carried well and did not vary much in pitch, a monotone.

After the audience, insistent questions filled my mind. Pius XII was Pope during WWII. He knew as well as Roosevelt and Churchill that the Jews were being exterminated in concentration camps. Roosevelt and Churchill remained silent. Pius XII also decided to keep silent. Yet he was the one leader in Europe who had the power to present the conscience of the Church to Adolph Hitler. To do so would have made him a spokesman for Christ. It seemed to me to refuse to speak was a moral failure eroding the influence for good that the church possessed.

Later, however, a friend told me that Pius authorized several bishops in Holland to speak to the Gestapo there about the inhumane treatment of the Jews. All were summarily arrested by the Gestapo and never seen again. Also, the German Army could surround the Vatican with tanks and destroy it with one word from Adolf Hitler. Hitler brooked no opposition to his absolute authority. *Perhaps there was more to understand about the Pope's silence.*

In Rome we also paid a visit to a place called "St. Paul's Outside the Walls." It was reported to be the place where the Romans executed St. Paul after his trial before Caesar. The contrast between Paul and Pius was to me obvious.

We left Rome on May 21st by train and traveled north to Paris by way of Milan and Geneva, arriving at 9:00 am the next day. We had extended our vacation request for another week. Paris in May was so beautiful that I had no words to describe it. My eyes and heart were dazzled. But Paris was also a mix of profiteering in the midst of beauty and culture. Several men had approached us and offered to give us a grand tour for a hefty price. We declined, traveling by busses and subway instead.

We went to a bistro for a beer while making our tour of the city. As we sat at the bar, three pretty ladies appeared dressed to attract our attention. They got our attention and we bought them drinks; this went on for several hours. Only after we left did we discover that the girls were "shills" who worked for the bartender. When the bartender saw likely tourists walk in, he would buzz his girls to come in and sit beside them. Their job was to flirt with us and encourage us to buy them drinks. The bartender would later split the profits with the girls. Welcome to Paris, the city of love.

The Louvre had too much to see in such a short time. Two works of art are fastened in my memory, the Mona Lisa and the classic Greek Statue, Winged Victory of Samothrace. I stood quietly gawking at both for a long time. Then, Versailles beckoned.

Meals in Paris were overpriced. We turned instead to meals at the American Embassy that were tasty and inexpensive. We took an evening at Les Follies Bergere, Paris' famed cabaret. The Follies had peaked in the 1920's, but we went anyway for bawdy, bold music, Can-Can dancing, and shows. Nothing at home matched this performance. But if you wanted grace and finesse this was not the place.

As we returned to our hotel rooms, prostitutes traveled in pairs, looking for unattached males. When they spotted us, they called out, "*soixant neuf* (69), and again, "*soixant neuf*." To really get our attention they raised the decibel level to, "*SOIXANT NEUF!*" and looked directly into our eyes, seductively. These ladies knew how to fascinate men. One of the guys went with a pair to their place. We continued back toward our hotel.

But the drumbeat of human sexuality appeared again and now my own sexuality began to emerge. What had been reclusive now came to life. This produced a conflict within me. One part of me was grounded in the teachings of my parents, my church, and my Base Chaplain. The other part sensed the attractive power of women and their femininity. I wanted to know more about women. The openly flouted sexual allures of Paris were tugging at me. A ditty we sang at Cal Aggie Christian Association came back to me: "How do you keep them down on the farm after they've been to Paree?"

How does a guy who has been raised in the neutered atmosphere of the unreality of sex deal with that reality when it floods in on him? My response was to hold on what I had been taught, keep the faith, and remember who I am. It wasn't easy, but I did so as long as I could.

We purchased return tickets on the Orient Express, which connected to Istanbul via Trieste. It showed its age, but was elegantly painted and upholstered. On board we were tempted to imagine princes or dukes riding somewhere on the train, as well as spies and secret agents traveling back and forth between east and west. It was fun to speculate, but the passengers looked like regular travelers. The Orient Express made regular stops in Trieste. We arrived back on May 28th. Now, it was a return to the routine of training, and finally a promotion. I got an upgrade to Corporal.

Headquarters alerted Company H that we would be assigned our first black soldier in July, 1953. Never mind that President Truman signed an Executive Order ending segregation in the military in 1948. Now five years later the Army began carrying out the order in the 351st. Rumors abounded in our barracks. Some men boasted that they would "rough him up" so badly he would transfer out at once. Others threatened to teach this "N—" a lesson. Some of the racist comments from our barracks were so crude that they cannot be repeated here. Talk in the barracks reached a threatening level.

Finally, the day arrived and the front door to the barracks swung open. In walked a young black trooper. He dropped his duffel bag off his shoulder, looked up at us and said, "Hi guys!" A limp response followed. The men found something to do to look away and feign "busy." They did not want to be first at shaking hands with a black soldier. He found a bunk, unpacked his duffel bag, and began engaging the white soldiers around him. "Hi," was his opener. Then he asked, "What's your name? Where are you from?" A thaw began. Slowly the men fell into conversation with him. The racist threats ended, and we began a token integration of Company H.

On July 25 a busload of our men signed on for a trip into the previously forbidden territory of Yugoslavia. Charters and I went together. The bus took us across the Istrian Peninsula to a town called Abbazia. The officer in charge turned us loose for the day. Abbazia is the Miami Beach of the Dalmatian Coast. Unlike Italy, the streets were clean. The public toilets were clean and comfortable whereas in Italy the typical men's toilet was a hole in the concrete where you either stood or squatted.

The girls at the beach were good looking, especially in their bikinis, and although most were brunettes, some had blonde hair. The food was excellent; the restaurants had more to offer than pasta. We had a meal of Slavic stew, steaks done medium well, fried potatoes, tomato and lettuce salad, a glass of port and some rye bread. The total cost for both of us: $10.00. The tart I had for desert simply melted in my mouth. I thought *Yugoslavia has been our enemy? Something is wrong with what we had been told by our officers.* I think this trip reflected a new era in our relationship with Marshall Tito.

In the early fall eight of us from FDC earned weekend passes. We hailed an Italian bus to a town north of Zone A, on the border with Yugoslavia, called Gorizia. We did the usual sidewalk cafes, visited a bar, and walked the avenues downtown. "What next?" we began to ask. "Where to?" another said. Jones responded, "I know where a local madam has girls." "Where?" we asked. He led us to a building off the main street. We looked at each other, waiting to see who would take the first step in. Pfisterer opened the door and much to my surprise the waiting room was crowded with blue-shirted politzia, (police) hats off, patiently reading newspapers as they waited their turn with one of the girls. Some politzia stood impatiently waiting their turn, arms akimbo.

The madam kept control of this potential chaos by keeping a careful eye on who was next in line, and then calling them forward to one of the girls. Madam knew by our apparel that we were Americans. Americans were known to pay better than others. The madam ushered us into a back room while she temporarily exited. She returned quickly with eight scantily clad girls. I knew in a moment that I was in the wrong place. A war broke out in my mind. Should I follow the lead of my friends, or go where my conscience led me? My conscience won the battle, but only reluctantly. I left the room even as the Pfisterer called out "C'mon Bass, grab a girl."

This was another defining moment for me. All my years at home with Mom, Sybil, and my local church tugged at me. I had been taught the ethic of a Christian youth and had learned Victorian virtues both from my mother and my church. I was baptized on Palm Sunday three years earlier. Pastor Dunlap preached and asked who would fly with him to Russia and bail out with him in order to proclaim the Gospel to the Communists. I had assisted our base chaplain Sunday by Sunday and made a commitment to be the best soldier I could be. Was this to be the collapse of that decision? Now I faced the prospect of denying it all for a crossover to the wild side. I wouldn't do it.

Yet I felt like odd-man out. The guys were celebrating lustily, and I refused to participate.

Was there something wrong with me? Was I some sort of a self-righteous prig? Must I walk alone? Maybe, I was still a mama's boy, unable to live my own life and make my own decisions.

A full-scale civil war broke out inside me. The fracture split my soul down the middle.

There is a Dionysian element in us that we are not aware of until times like this. Suddenly my cocoon split open. Dionysius, the Greek god of wine and sexual revelries, emerged within me and I experienced the power of that myth.

The following weekend Bartel and I went downtown to a waterfront bar. We ordered Birra Dreher, and noticed that a woman sitting a few tables across from us would wink at me whenever I looked up. Once she knew she had my attention she began signaling me with her lips. Sitting across from her was a man encouraging her, obviously her pimp. Bartel and I laughed heartily at the invitation and drank more beer. She signaled with her hand toward the door. Bartel grinned and said, "Why don't you go?" I responded, "I'm not sure." Bartel encouraged, "Oh, go ahead!" I finally nodded to the big grin on his face and rose to walk to the door. She soon followed. Out front she pointed toward a dark side street where her apartment was located.

> *I'm scared, and I wonder if this prostitute knows that I am a 23 year-old virgin? I don't know what I am doing, but I am determined to find out about carnal knowledge. I'm sorry Mom, but I have to learn about this now this way. My dirty sock is coming off.*

My heart was thumping at the prospect of a massive about face in my life. I would finally touch and experience feminine sexuality. All that had been denied and forbidden, taught to me as a sin and beneath a man of Christian virtue, was there. A drumbeat, like a Gene Krupa drum solo, one of his new and exotic rhythms, played insistently on my mind. We went up to her room.

From that point on she did a gigantic switch. All charm vanished. With a sharp business eye, she demanded to see my money, and looked me over suspiciously. I suddenly realized this woman was hard. There was not a marshmallow in her. *What had I gotten myself into?*

Her pimp had ordered her to go with me. But who was using whom? She appeared to be a puppet in a game of sex for sale. But perhaps she used him too. Sex is so easily manipulated to become a weapon or a strategy. She was tough, and it began to show. Here I was a trembling virgin and she appeared to be angry. Her attitude was suddenly stripped bare. It was as if she was saying: *"This is business. C'mon now, get this over with."* Sex in a situation like this was a meaningless gesture.

An awful awareness dawned: *Is this all there is?* What a letdown. Disappointment surged through me along with a deep sense of regret that I had fallen for her deceitful charms and cheap invitation. For years I had been denied the truth about human sexuality and longed to know about such things for myself. Now at this defining moment, sex became meaningless, a non-event. *Never again*, I thought.

Little, however, did I know that this affair became like a shot of heroin in me. This was forbidden fruit and I tasted of it that night. I was repulsed by my behavior, but at the same time I found myself drawn to sex like a moth to a flame. That affair, so barren to all appearances, was like a drug, and I was hooked on illicit sex, but didn't know it.

Once the Dionysian motif was turned loose inside, I had a tiger by the tail and couldn't let go. I now encountered the dark side. This woman was a femme fatale. Many weekends from then until I left Italy for home, I found women who caught my attention, made their signals, usually a wink, and gave me their sensuous invitation. (The good women of Trieste never looked you in the eye).

There was never any intimacy. This was purely a business transaction. They meant it to make money. I, on the other hand, wanted to resolve my lifelong curiosity about sex. Instead, I got a vacuum of meaning and tenderness. I experienced regular disappointment, and yet I kept going back for more. Freud would call this a neurosis.

Every sexually transmitted disease (STD) infected me in the process, and I used all the preventative medications available to us at headquarters. Alongside the box of condoms in the front office was a box of antiseptic crèmes. None of them worked. I had to go to our Army doctors for relief.

I discovered my own sexual impulses, and they were powerful. Once that Pandora's box was opened I could not close the lid. But what I didn't know was even more important. I didn't have a clue about what went on inside the women I had grown up with. *What does such a woman really want? What is truly important to her? What does she like in a man? What is intimacy?* I had a lot more learning to do before I ever found out. That came later.

We entered the chill of fall. Bora winds off the Julian Alps from the east and north scoured Trieste. On September 16,[th] 1953, headquarters cancelled all leaves, but we were not told why. We had been alerted to a possible regimental move to Austria.

Lloyd Triestini ran a shipping line, headquartered in Trieste. I had purchased a ticket on one of his ships to Haifa, Israel, sailing in November, to walk in the land of my dreams. It may seem strange that I longed to walk the places where Jesus walked, including the Via Dolorosa in Jerusalem. The Holy Land beckoned me to come even as I pursued women of the night. I was a study in contradictions, and I was not sure I could explain it. *Would the real me please stand up?* But, when headquarters cancelled all leaves I cancelled my ticket to Israel. Now, U.S. destroyers and cruisers were deployed to Trieste as a show of force and sailors became a major presence in Trieste.

Company H was ordered to break into three eight-hour shifts and began moving furniture out of bachelor officer quarters (BOQ), and married quarters. We trucked furniture to a large downtown warehouse. My shift began at 5:00 p.m. and ended at 1:00 a.m. By the end of the year we had emptied 635 officers' apartments, and then loaded the furniture on 156 boxcars. With a sigh of relief from us, another company took over Company H duties and finished the job.

Back on base I received an assignment to guard duty once again. I was issued a fur-lined parka, mittens, and carried a loaded carbine slung over my right shoulder. On this particular night I had an early shift from 8:00 pm until 10:00 pm.

As I rounded a bend on the interior perimeter of our *caserna*, a trooper nicknamed "Red" and his buddies, stood drinking beer and carousing. Evidently they were waiting for me. Red taunted me. When that didn't stop me he yelled, " Put down your weapon and c'mon over here!" He wanted a fight and his lackeys egged him on. I faced a precarious situation. I don't like to fight, and I especially don't like to fight with a bully and his coterie of drinking buddies.

I recalled a similar situation at Alhambra High. In the basement lockers a bully and his friends surrounded me. I ran at top speed to get away, and all those years since I considered myself a coward for scampering away. Now I faced déjà vu: history repeating itself. However, if I laid down my carbine I would be derelict in my duty, subject to severe military penalties, and a court martial. I would be sentenced to detention and perhaps miss my ship home, sailing on December 30th. But if I carried on with my duties I would be considered a coward. I faced a terrible dilemma. I continued my round of guard duty, but hated myself for doing so. When I completed my next round, Red and his buddies were gone.

Only later did I take time to reflect that bullies are cowards. They can't face you alone, but only when surrounded and pumped up with beer and their rowdy friends. In the meantime I suffered doubts once again about my courage, and my manhood. Growing up a mama's boy was no help in situations like this.

In October the alert to our regiment heightened. Trouble loomed, but we were not given details. A war of words between the Italian government and Marshall Tito's Yugoslav government had broken out again over Trieste. Both sides threatened military action to seize Trieste.

None of our officers took time to explain this and no training was given to us on crowd control. In WWI Italy had lost 650,000 men fighting Austria for control of North Italy. The feeling of Italians ran deep for Trieste. Trieste, they believed, was Italian, always had been Italian, and the WWI deaths reminded Italians each Armistice Day of the price they paid to win it. Italians feared that the U.S. and Britain would renege on their promise to return Trieste to Italy.

On Italian Armistice Day, November 4, scores of thousands gathered at Redipuglia, 20 miles northwest of Trieste, where 100,000 Italian war dead were buried. The crowd listened to Premier Guiseppe Pella make a patriotic speech where he demanded that Trieste be "redeemed" to Italy. Then the crowd heard an open air mass, and sang patriotic songs. After the memorial, some 12,000 civilians marched back to Trieste. They sang, shouted slogans, and headed for Piazza del 'Unita. Our officers kept us informed of the dangers of communism, but they failed to warn us of the dangers of Italian nationalism. Nationalism broke out in full force, and we were completely unprepared for it.

Crowds of students joined the protestors when they entered the city. Trieste's Special Police arrived in jeeps, and trouble erupted as the crowd jeered at them. What happened next comes partly out of my experience, and partly from "Time" and "Life" magazine reports for November, 1953. Their correspondents gave on-the-spot accounts of what happened next.

Trieste's Special Police were recruited in Trieste and trained by the British command. Britain's Major General Sir Thomas John Willoughby Winterton, commander of the British and American troops in Trieste, controlled and paid the Special Police. Triestini disliked the Special Police because they were paid double what regular Police were paid, and Special Police were suspected of trying to maintain the status quo. Scuffles broke out. Special Police used rifle butts and truncheons to hit civilians who jeered them. Triestini responded by heaving paving stones at the Special Police. By midnight 15 rioters were hurt, scores arrested.

On Thursday November 5, another confrontation took place, this time in front of the old Church of San Antonio. In violation of the right of sanctuary, Special Police followed student rioters into the church and clubbed them. The Bishop of Trieste reconsecrated the church afterwards, which set off more rioting. This time the police fired over the head of the crowd. However, one student was killed. Now, 50,000 Triestini took to the streets around the piazza.

On Friday November 6 rioters broke into Independista headquarters, and threw furniture, draperies, and records out the windows. As rioters surged into the piazza, the Special Police fired their carbines into the crowd, clearing the piazza, but killing rioters.

General Winterton called the American commander and requested American troops come downtown immediately and restore order. Winterton then ordered the Special Police to withdraw. That night Captain Saletto ordered us to be ready for action in minutes. Down the line came the command, "Lock and load!" We loaded clips of 30-caliber bullets into our M-1's and carbines. Another order soon followed, "Fix bayonets!"

There was no doubt in anyone's mind that this was the real thing. All the barrack banter halted. Kids from around the U.S. realized that they really were an army and that we would follow orders. Our presence in Trieste was threatened and we would respond, with deadly force if necessary. I felt a sense of anxiety and excitement as we faced the unknown.

We loaded into our trucks, just as we had practiced many times on maneuvers. The roar of our engines echoed off of the silent buildings as we raced along the city streets. Our driver pulled up on a side street just off the piazza. Anxiously, we waited in the darkness on the side street. We could hear the yelling and screams of the rioters as they hurled pavement stones and bottles at the Special Police, who were now ready to withdraw. It seemed to me to be a noise created straight out of hell. The sound sent tremors through us.

All of us felt a dread of our situation. *Lord, spare us from facing this mob*, I prayed. No one explained to us any plan. We were trained simply to take orders when given. We assumed that our officers knew what to do. I am not sure they did know.

The only other time that I heard the sound of a mob was in San Gabriel on VJ Day in August 1945. But they were a crowd ecstatic with the joy of the Japanese surrender. Here was a crowd that was in a rage against the Special Police. Their anger boiled over into threats, curses, shouts and screams as they aimed rocks and bottles at the police. Mobs have long been shapers of events. Now they were trying once again, creating a sound and fury I cannot forget.

In my mind a paramount question loomed. *If ordered, would I shoot a civilian?* We were trained to kill enemy soldiers, not civilians. *If ordered to charge the mob would I use my bayonet on a civilian as I had on straw dummies in basic training?* Those thoughts revolted me. But we were men under orders, and we would follow orders. The idea of facing a mob throwing stones intimidated us.

Here we were far from home and expected to do a soldier's duty and put down a riot for which we were never trained. Our commanders really let us down by failing to train us in crowd control. General Patton feared a bullet obliterating his nose. I feared a pavement stone crushing my face or chest.

The company of U.S. infantry who were in line ahead of us was ordered into the piazza. As that company took up positions in the piazza and displayed their bayonets, they were cheered by the mob! An American presence was what the mob wanted to see, and peace was restored. But two British platoons received curses as they cleared City Hall of Italian flags. Our company was relieved to find that we were not needed.

Order was restored in a matter of hours. Officers sent us back into our trucks and we headed for Banne, relieved at how this had worked out peacefully for the Americans. But the toll of three days of rioting stood thus: six dead rioters. (Life magazine reported 10 dead), and 56 wounded or injured; 100 arrested, and for the police, 72 wounded.

After the riot, one reporter, James Whitmore, reported seeing shards of flesh scattered about on the paving stones of the piazza. Bullets fired by the Special Police had ricocheted off of granite and marble surfaces of piazza buildings, and tore into the bodies of the mob; bloodstains were everywhere. (Life, 11/16/1953)

Within weeks the TRUST Command ended the high alert. We returned to routine duties. Now, however, all our FDC equipment and mortars were packed in boxes for shipment by truck to Linz, Austria, our next duty station. Those of us to be rotated home on December 30 would not go to Austria. Captain Saletto gave us more time for recreation. Leaves were again approved as well as three day passes.

Bartel and I applied for a one-week pass. Our plan was to get tickets on the Orient Express and be in Paris, December15-22. I took time to write the Registrar at U.C Davis and request admission to the spring semester opening on February 4, 1954. I followed up with a letter requesting a change of major from Agriculture to Political Science. The riots confirmed in me that I had a desire to know more about world affairs.

On December 15th we caught the Orient Express to Paris. But when we arrived the sky was overcast and the weather was cold. Gone were the balmy days of May. Jackets and gloves now became necessary. We ordered espresso along Champs Élysée, and did Christmas shopping. Christmas in Paris was so different from Christmas at home. The lights and the Santas all looked different, and strangely unfamiliar. It was hard to get into a Christmas spirit where the Santas looked so strange. I missed the friendliness of my hometown. Christmas wasn't the same so far from home. Even the Christmas Carols were different. We were ready to return one week later

We arrived back on December 22. Our troop ship was to sail on December 30. We had eight days to get ready. We counted off each day. On December 29 we boarded a train in Trieste bound for Livorno (Leghorn) on the west coast of Italy. We traveled all night. Bartel and I jointed two others and played pinochle until we arrived the next morning in Livorno. Sitting at the back of our coach alone and sullen was "Red." He appeared to be pouting. He had none of his drinking buddies with him. He looked like a lonely kid. The bully in him was quiet now. I knew I had unfinished business with him, but I said nothing, nor did he.

What little we got to see of Livorno etched a place in my memory. The pine trees along the hills gave a touch of beauty to the city. We exited the train at the docks. Bartel and I had sequential boarding passes, just as we did on Staten Island. The Captain of the troop ship took us out of the harbor that afternoon after we finished loading.

Once past the Tyrrhenian Sea and into the Mediterranean Sea, the weather became violent. Black clouds descended and blotted out the sun. Winds of 40 miles an hour careened our ship. The high waves rocked us up and down, back and forth, and the ship yawed in the heavy sea. But, I had no seasickness this time. I had no idea the Mediterranean Sea could be so dangerous. I thought of St. Paul and the bad weather that drove his Roman ship onto the rocks of Malta. Now I understood why. His ship was so vulnerable, while ours was so safe. I watched carefully as the storm blew over to catch a glimpse of the Rock of Gibraltar. I could barely see it in the distance.

Out in the Atlantic the ocean settled down, and again dolphins played alongside our ship. Our ship arrived in New York just before sunrise on January 12. The weather chilled down to freezing, but not cold enough to prevent us from a topside view of the harbor. Millions of lights shimmered along the shore. Already ships were on the move. A huge tugboat came alongside to guide us into our dock.

But the best sight of all was the Statue of Liberty, her flame of freedom burning bright in the early morning shadows. She was like a beacon of hope welcoming us back home. Who could not be inspired to be an American while seeing this? I welled up at the sight. Joy emerged among us as we stood transfixed by her majesty. Never before had the Statue of Liberty meant so much to me. This was America. The old world of Europe was behind us. The new world beckoned.

The Statue of Liberty had other meanings too. I discovered that the invisible elephant in our front room at home was visible and real. The dirty sock around my neck came off. Like Adam and Eve in the Garden of Eden I had tasted the forbidden fruit of sex. I emerged from my cocoon of innocence into the garden of good and evil. I fell from grace by contradicting all that I had been taught. But at the same time I took hold of my humanity. I too was a part of the fall of humanity,

We boarded trains in New Jersey. Many of us were bound for California and we boarded our train together. That night as we passed through Pittsburgh the rain pelted our train. Could this be the beginning of a cleansing I needed? One flaw remained, however. I still carried all my STD's and would have to treat them when I got back to San Gabriel. We arrived in Antioch, California three days later, at the dock of Camp Stoneman. We picked up our duffel bags and were bused to our barracks.

The next day the "separation" process began. All our military records were updated. We were issued a D.D. 214 record to keep in safe storage for the rest of our lives. We would use these records to receive veteran benefits, buy a home, go back to school, and so forth. I received $280.00 final wages, and $300.00 mustering out pay. This was a generous sum to me, and would set me up for my return to school.

I used the mustering out pay to buy my first investment in a mutual fund, a practice that paid off for me in later years. Once completely discharged, four of us hired a taxi that took us to the Oakland Airport. United Air Lines sold us one-way tickets to Los Angeles for $10.00.

Dad picked me up at the airport. We had our usual handshake and pat on the back. I still wanted a big bear hug from him, but did not know how to ask him for it. Years later, I learned to simply give him a hug and not ask anything of him. He never knew how to hug me in return, even to his dying day. What a lonely state of existence that must have been!

Home was a series of misperceptions. Mom opened her arms and loved me just as she did the day I left home. She thought I was still the same boy. But I was not. I had changed, but she could not see the change that was inside me. I was not going to risk telling her. Knowing there was no way I could explain my life to her, I simply played along with her that everything was still the same. How could I ever tell her, for instance, about my STD? How could I explain why I needed to see our family doctor? How could I explain to her my entry into carnal knowledge? She simply could not or would not understand.

A year later I asked for a one-on-one with her. I tried to explain the estrangement that I felt with her. She burst into tears and sobbed, "Oh, what did I ever do wrong? Oh God, I do not understand." I never again tried to explain these things to her. The gulf was too wide. As one of her homespun maxims went, "Let sleeping dogs lie." She wanted to live in the past where I was her boy, and when illness threatened, care for me, and put a dirty sock around my neck. Her folk wisdom was her strength, along with her faith in God.

I took heart when we turned the calendar to February 1. I packed my things into our old 1941 Plymouth sedan. Dad gave it to me for $1.00, the price of a transfer of ownership. This time I drove Highway 99 due north. I had several days to pass through registration lines, and then began classes on February 4.

Registration was bittersweet. I was glad to be back, but my original goal eluded me. I had planned to return with a chest full of medals, a record that would prove beyond a doubt that I was a good soldier and a brave man. My self-esteem would be buoyed, and I could begin college with a fresh start. This was not to be. I had not been the best soldier I could be. All of us experienced fear when we were about to face an out-of-control mob in Trieste. I had not become a hero. In fact I had become just the opposite.

My dalliance with prostitutes and my resulting STD dragged my sense of right and wrong into the mud. How could I face my friends and God with the sense of guilt and shame that I carried? All of these things blotted out the good I had done.

Yet I had done good. I learned to speak conversational Italian. I was Company H guidon. I was promoted to corporal. I led the men on our Saturday morning parade reviews. I assisted the Chaplain on Sunday mornings. I had helped protect our national interest by being a peacekeeper in Trieste. The following year the United Nations held a plebiscite in Trieste and the people voted to reunite with Italy. Our mission was accomplished in a peaceful transfer of power.

Added to that were the trips I had taken on the way from New York City to Trieste. There were travels to Rome, Venice, Paris, and Yugoslavia. All of that made me a world traveler, and was a glorious learning chapter in my life. But it was now drowned out by the knowledge of the STD that I carried.

When the Army drafted me I became aware that I now entered into one of the dramas of modern history, swept along like a leaf in a stream. Then, I found even more drama. When our commander ordered us to the piazza on November 6 with 30 caliber bullets and fixed bayonets, I faced a deep moral dilemma: that of using deadly force against civilians. There could be no concept of right and wrong, only obedience to orders.

And some day, somewhere, history would judge us. Fortunately, we were spared that terrible dilemma of judgment. But other dilemmas were ahead. Where was the concept of the ethical right? I lacked an answer. I had doubts about my future. I had lost my way. The question now for me was whether I could find it once again. The refiner's fire was at work. The dross of the molten silver emerged and rose to the top. There it remained to haunt me.

Dick waiting for a movie outside the Cinema in Opacina, Free Territory of Trieste, May 1953.

Mom and Dad in our back yard in San Gabriel, California, July 4, 1947.

Dad, center, demonstrating his 3-point football stance with his buddies, Zanesville, Ohio, 1922.

Mom's mother, Grace McFarland, and grandmother,
Phoebe Ann Stanton, circa 1900, in Chicago.

Dad's Mother and Father on their wedding day, August 6, 1901, in Chicago.

Dick and his high school buddies, Tommy (far left) and Norm. They kept the bullies away.

Break time while building a trail to the Trinity Alps for the Forestry Service in Northern California.

Dick's sister, Sybil, holding one of her tennis trophies at Alhambra High School, Alhambra, California, 1942.

Bart Clyde married Carol, Dick's younger sister, on June 17, 1950.

Rosemary, Suzanne and Dick outside Kerman Methodist Church, his first full-time appointment, Spring 1959, Kerman, California.

A family cabin for Mexican migrant laborers at the Weedpatch Camp just south of Lamont, CA. Dick visited here often during his ministry to the Lamont church. John Steinbeck visited here while writing *The Grapes of Wrath*.

Saturday night in the courtyard of Chicago's Ecumenical Institute preparing a giant BBQ to bring black and white together in fellowship.

Ecumenical Institute members building a children's playground in West Side Chicago.

Steve and his dog, Eddie, on the left with his friend Clint Krueger and me on the right holding a string of trout we caught where Cold Creek empties into Lake Edison, California, June 1974.

Steve and Dick entered the La Kahuna Tennis Tournament, 1974.

Suzanne's Stagg High School junior year photo, Stockton, California, June 1974.

Wedding photo of Dick and Gayle and their children. Rear, from left, is Mike Dorville, Steve Bastear, and Gary Dorville. Center left is Jim Dorville, Dick and Gayle, and Suzanne Bastear. In front is Lynette Dorville, August 18, 1979, Stockton, California.

With Suzanne in Woodstock, Illinois before we returned to West Side Chicago to see if anything remained of what we had built in 1967. There was nothing we could find.

Family members gather for what turned out to be Gayle's last Christmas.

Gayle Louise Bastear. This photo was taken in 2008 and was chosen by the family as her memorial photo.

Dick and Marilyn's wedding on February 12, 2011. On far left is Jim Dorville, holding brother Mike's photo, Gary Dorville, Suzanne Bastear, Marilyn and Dick, Lynette Frontera, Ken Duren (Marilyn's son), and Steve Bastear.

Dick and Marilyn's wedding with grandkids. In back row, left of Marilyn is Shaylin Duren, Jessica Bastear, Allison Aber, Jenna Bastear. In back row, right of Dick is Jason Dorville, Andy Dorville, Ben Duren. Front row, left of Marilyn is Amanda Frontera, Robyn Glover, Nichole Dorville. Front row, right of Dick is Austin Dorville and Tim Frontera.

Marilyn and Dick at their reception the day before their wedding.

Eighteen

A New Beginning

Davis was a beacon of hope to me. It held out the possibilities for change. I wasn't the decorated war veteran as I had dreamed I would be. That was not to be. But with an honorable discharge from the Army and a new major in Political Science, I started off with a closer look at the world and my part in it. *Perhaps I can go to work for the State Department when I graduate.* With my counselor's advice I signed up for Economics, Recent U.S. History, Comparative Government, American Political Theory, and International Organizations.

I was welcomed back to the Cal Aggie Christian Association (CACA) by Pastor Dave Burnight. He was as friendly as ever, and wanted to hear about my Army experience. What I shared with him were the highlights. I told him nothing of my fall from grace in Trieste. Trieste became a testing ground for me. I rose to the heights of my best service for my country while there, and ended with sexual escapades that shamed me. Jan Morris titled her book about Trieste "the meaning of nowhere," and that is about how I ended my time there. Now, however, I was among Christian friends once again, moving forward with them.

CACA members came together for lunch on Tuesdays and sang hymns and prayed. We interceded for those who asked for prayer. We formed a close knit fellowship and stood by each other in times of need. This was just what I needed to make a transition back to civilian life.

We also continued with our Sunday night discussions led by Pastor Dave. Sometimes we met at his home, and sometimes we met at the Davis Community Church. We played games, drank lots of hot chocolate, and got into some God talk. The group elected me to the Board of Directors of CACA as Publicity Chairman. I had never had any such experience, but I found that I could cut out Jello ads from Life magazine and use them to create posters inviting students to our activities.

The Jello ads showed colorful cartoon characters made of Jello that invited readers to take a bite. My message was simple. "Why not take a bite of the Christian way and find a whole new life?" It was pure guesswork for me, but I liked doing it. Our group did grow. I also rejoined the chancel choir and sang with them most Sundays.

The CACA Board planned a retreat at Camp Cazadero in the woods not far from Jenner. Volleyball was on our minds and we played the game with joyful abandon. When I stood behind the front row of players I trained myself to set them up for a killer shot. When I played at the net, if someone set me up, I took a leap in the air and slammed it over the net at the opponents. I liked to play for "keeps." Other than tennis, volleyball was my favorite sport.

In the camp conference room we placed logs on andirons in a large fireplace, lighting them to create an ambience for our morning and evening discussions. We preceded each discussion with a round of camp songs, ending with our favorite spirituals such as: "Swing Low, Sweet Chariot," and "Lord, I Want To Be A Christian."

At mealtimes we created fun with, "the loyal order of forkers." Those who were seen to eat the most food were named to the club. Dave said, "Induct Dick. Look at how that guy eats." I was soon made a member. We also practiced the art of serving others by reaching our forks, laden with delicious morsels, to feed the person opposite us. We learned to serve them first.

At the same time my transition to civilian life was bumpy. Part of me felt a little ahead of the others in CACA because I was the only one there with military experience. Many of the students were still pampered. They knew nothing of the hard life of forced marches, bayonet training, bivouacs in the hill country, guard duty on cold or wet nights when we stood alone in the elements. Now I was told to put down my carbine and return to civilian life. It was really not that easy.

However, the other part of me felt hypocritical because of my experience with ladies of the night in Trieste. I was troubled by the tension created within me by my new carnal knowledge. As usual I shared that burden with no one. I thought I would be unacceptable to them if they knew the truth about me. There was no peace for me when I kept secrets like that. It was like sitting on a volcano.

America was near the midpoint of the 50's and Eisenhower was president. I had cast my first vote for him by absentee ballot. America had defeated two of the world's most terrible tyrannies: Hitler's Third Reich in Europe, and the Japanese Empire in the Pacific. We could all stand tall as we considered that. Had not Henry Luce declared this to be "The American Century?" It bothered me, however, to watch Sen. McCarthy on TV go on a witch-hunt for communists in the Army, and then try to embarrass the Secretary of the Army with false charges. It appeared so ridiculous that we mocked McCarthy's fear tactics at our school assemblies. We playfully looked under rugs to find communists.

That spring the Student Body Association sponsored a beard-growing contest. We who signed on had six weeks to grow a beard, and then be prepared to appear before an assembly of students with judges who would choose the best beards. When the judging was held I won the category for the beard with the most "yolk." I failed to ask what that meant, but blithely accepted the award. Afterwards, the student body president asked all winners if we would consider participating in the "Burro Express," a stunt to advertise Picnic Day coming in May. Most of us agreed to be a part of the promotion.

I was paired with a character named Jack Wilms. We promptly gave him the nickname, "Cactus Jack." We agreed on "Sourdough Dick" for me. We were given a mule named "Marilyn". We hung a sandwich board on her loudly proclaiming, "Picnic Day, May 10. All are invited. UC Davis." Jack and I were to be trucked to San Francisco where we would have a photo op with Mayor Robinson. Then we would walk 78 miles back to Davis, walking the main street of every town along the highway on the way back. It was spring vacation so we didn't have to worry about missing classes. Two others went to Stockton, two to Placerville, and two to Yuba City. Each group walked with a mule displaying the same sideboards that Marilyn carried.

On April 2nd we were trucked to the San Francisco City Plaza where Mayor Robinson was to meet and greet us. Newspapers sent photographers to capture the moment. However, Mayor Robinson was indisposed, so he sent a trusted aide to the photo shoot in the Civic Plaza. Then we began our trek down Market Street.

The local residents saw us and honked their greetings to us, or irritation with us, because of our invasion. We had neglected to bring a shovel to pick up any "road apples." No matter: no one had seen mules in San Francisco since the gold rush of 1849, and most enjoyed the novelty of our appearance. At the foot of the Bay Bridge a UC Davis truck picked us up and transported us across the bay. Apparently it was illegal to walk a mule across the bridge.

Once across, we dismounted the truck and began our pre-arranged walk to Mills College, an all-girls school in the heart of Oakland. Once again the cars honked, and pedestrians waved at us with an amazed look on their faces. We were having fun. Some thought we were prospectors who had lost their way. We simply pointed to our sandwich boards and shouted an invitation to them. The girls at Mills College were waiting for us by the front gate. They escorted us to the dining hall where we were free to order as we pleased.

Female students, curious about us, surrounded our table. We were dressed like prospectors, and that piqued their interest. Cactus Jack was in his element, speaking in a drawl, and showing a smile to all the girls. This should have been bliss for me, but it was not. I felt strangely out-of-place in an all-girls college. They offered us a separate room

A New Beginning

for the night and helped us tether Marilyn the mule near some green grass.

The next morning we headed up Telegraph Avenue with Marilyn. A gentleman, slightly inebriated, offered us $100 on the spot for Marilyn; "No sale," we responded. Later, an elderly woman, thinking we were prospectors, invited us to her gem and mineral show. We showed her the sideboards and she then understood. We arrived at the Campanile on the UC Berkeley campus in a four o' clock drizzle. A campus police officer came to check us out.

At the same time, several girls from the Alpha Omicron Pi sorority stopped by and asked us to their house for dinner. We checked with the officer and asked if it would be OK to tether Marilyn to a "No Parking" sign nearby. He not only agreed, but also said he would keep an eye on her as he patrolled! We slept that night at the foot of the Campanile in sleeping bags since the girls at the sorority had no room for us. Fortunately, the rain stopped.

The next morning some girls from the Theta Upsilon sorority hosted us for breakfast. Meanwhile, a scribe from the campus newspaper reported that, "Marilyn planed the grass around the Campanile to an all time low." We untied Marilyn from the No Parking sign. It was time for us to leave Berkeley.

We walked through East Bay communities until we reached Vallejo. Once there it began to rain again. We spotted a barn off the side of the road, and located an old, creaky gate to let Marilyn inside. Marilyn helped herself to the hay inside the barn, while we rolled out our sleeping bags on the hay. The farmer must have been at home keeping warm. He never saw us using his barn. We were too young and tired to worry about the legalities of our right to use his barn. We had no dinner that night, but at least we were warm and dry. The next several days we walked through Fairfield and Vacaville on our way back.

On April 8 the "California Aggie" newspaper carried news articles and photos of our progress. The reporter described our whereabouts, "When last seen they were reported… entering a winery, ostensibly to post a Picnic Day placard." We were welcomed back on campus by the student body president and his officers. We put Marilyn out to pasture and thanked her for her services. We had a great turnout for Picnic Day.

Back on campus Pastor Dave wanted to begin a study of a YMCA/YWCA booklet titled "Where Are You?" I was a resident of North Hall and he asked me if I would organize a study group in my dormitory. I responded clearly that I thought he had the wrong man. He had no idea of the depth of my hypocrisy. How could I teach others the way to God when I had acted so unethically in Trieste? I said "no" to Dave, but he would not take "no" for an answer. His persistence changed my mind. I took a handful of the booklets, and later asked Don Bell, my roommate, if he would join my study group. He agreed, as did several other guys in the dorm. Now all I had to do was get ready to teach the material.

The first chapter was the reprint of a sermon from Paul Tillich's new book, "The Shaking of the Foundations." One of his sermons titled "You Are Accepted" opened the study guide. Immediately, I was interested. That spoke intimately to the condition of my soul. I set aside Saturday night to dig into the chapter so I understood it well enough to teach it.

That evening I was alone in my room, looking out at the sunset. It was quiet. Most of the guys were out having Saturday night fun. I sat down on the edge of my bed and read what Tillich had to say. He set out to make clear to modern minds the meaning of the Biblical words, "sin" and "grace," the two most important and misunderstood words in the Christian lexicon.

He defined sin as "separation." Then he broke the concept of sin into three parts: 1) separation from self, 2) separation from others, and 3) separation from God. The concept of separation spoke to my spiritual self. I knew of a certainty that I had experienced a split inside myself ever since the sexual escapades in Gorizia and Trieste. I felt a separation so deep that I knew I was out of touch with myself, or what Tillich called "the essential self." I was lost and couldn't get in touch with the real me.

When the young ladies at Mills College invited Cactus Jack and me to dinner I felt a deep discomfort in their presence. Somehow, after my experience with women in Trieste I felt alienated in the presence of "good girls." The same was true with the girls at the Berkeley sororities who invited us to share meals with them. What could have been a fun time turned instead into a time of anxiety for me.

I already felt like a hypocrite at CACA; the cleft in my nature was invisible to others, but the anxiety I experienced because of it was a heavy burden to bear alone. The co-ed at Pasadena City College spoke insightfully when she said "You have the smile of a Cheshire cat." She and Paul Tillich were speaking to me.

As to "separation from others," that addressed my condition also. I didn't know our family in Chicago, nor, except for my mother, did I experience closeness to my parents. I lost all contact with my friends at Alhambra High and with my Army buddies like Eaves and Bartel. I had no girlfriend. I was slow to create friends on campus. I experienced myself as a "loner" at Davis. I had retreated deep inside myself because of my fears that others would find out who I really was and reject me. I regularly pretended to be someone else.

"Separation from God" was clear to me. Even though I attended church all my life I did not experience God as my guide nor as a presence in my life. And now to add to it all, I felt a sense of guilt and shame because of my behavior with prostitutes in Trieste. The awareness that I had sunk that low, had violated every instinct of my conscience, knowing no one to whom I could talk, drove me to the edge of despair.

Tillich went on to explain the concept of grace. Grace comes when we least expect it. We cannot command it. It is a gift over which we have no control. "Often," Tillich explained, "grace comes when we are in deepest separation from ourselves and from others." The text Tillich used for this sermon came from Paul's letter to the Church at Rome, 5:19, "Where sin abounds, grace abounds all the more."

Tillich wanted to avoid using a hackneyed concept of sin, so instead he used terms like "alienation" and "separation" to describe what he was talking about. "Grace," he explained, "was simply the healing and reconciliation that can come to us in the midst of our despair." I was in despair, and was deeply in need of the experience of grace. He continued,

> *"Grace strikes us when we are in great pain and restlessness. It strikes us when we walk through the valley of a meaningless and empty life… Sometimes at that moment a wave of light breaks into our darkness, and it is as though a voice were saying: 'You are accepted, accepted by that which is greater than you, and the name of which you do not know…Do not seek for anything; do not perform anything; do not intend anything. Simply accept the fact that you are accepted!'"*

On that Saturday night in North Hall, alone in my room, I read that sermon, and I knew without a doubt that God was talking to me. Suddenly, a light shone through to my soul and into my despair. I felt forgiven by God of the terrible burden of guilt and shame that I carried. "You are accepted." That is exactly what I needed. A heavy rock of loneliness, despair, guilt and shame dropped off my back. *"Free, Free!"* I kept saying to myself. I felt 50 pounds lighter; the fresh air of freedom coursed through me. I felt freedom from fear, freedom from guilt, freedom from shame, and freedom from the split in my mind. I had a wonderful sensation of peace, a peace that I hadn't experienced since leaving Italy.

> *So this is what Paul meant when he wrote to the Church at Rome. No wonder that Paul labored year after year in difficult circumstances to proclaim this gospel, the good news of peace and reconciliation with God.*

Grace touched my whole being that night, and I knew the healing of my soul had begun.

St. Paul had his epiphany while on the way to Damascus to persecute the Christians there. *Was this my "road to Damascus?"* Paul heard the Lord speaking to him. I did not. But there was a heavenly light in my soul that cleansed me. I was certain of that. If ever there was a turning point in my life, this was it. That night was a defining moment for me. I went from B.C. to A.D., and from that moment on I wanted to learn more about God.

The next morning I dressed, skipped the cafeteria breakfast, grabbed my clunker bike off its rack in front of North Hall, and pedaled furiously across campus. The old bike picked up speed. All 5200 acres of the Davis campus stood in front of me, or so it seemed. I pumped my bike through to Russell Boulevard, the boundary of our university. Across the street Dave Burnight's home stood quietly in the early morning cool. I jumped off my bike and double-timed to his front door, and pounded on it with my fist. Dave opened the door, dressed casually and unprepared for visitors. I blurted out the events of the previous night. Dave listened intently. He grinned when I told him of finding God's grace while reading the study guide. We rejoiced together while I danced a jig on his front porch. When my joy mellowed, I said goodbye and pedaled back across campus to the cafeteria and a hearty breakfast.

Soon after I began teaching in my room from the YMCA study book "Where Are You?" We were a small group, but we started learning together. Unbeknownst to me, I was baptized into teaching.

The tide had now turned in my favor. I likened it to the victory at Midway in June of 1942 when American dive-bombers sank four Japanese aircraft carriers. Out of that fight came the awareness that the Americans held the advantage and could win the war. There were so many struggles ahead for me, but now I knew I was a more confident person who could take responsibility for my life from this point on. I had begun the defeat of the enemy within.

It was no doubt the most significant turning point in my life. But it was a beginning and not a conclusion. For I soon found that I was unwilling to risk letting others find out about my behavior in Trieste with women of the night. I believed I would be rejected if others knew this part of my past. So I kept that as a secret from all. I should have trusted my new Christian friends to accept me as God had done. Keeping that secret was a heavy burden to bear. But I did not take that risk—yet.

I met a girl on campus named Mary. Of Armenian descent, she hailed from Parlier, south of Fresno. Somewhere I read that guys unconsciously search for their mothers when they look for a girl friend. Mary was built like my mother, solid but not fat, had a laugh like hers, a soft voice, and a sweet smile. We started sharing lunches together. I was smitten with her.

I began writing love poetry to her. One day on campus we walked through a blossoming fruit orchard covered with fragrant pink blooms, and I proposed to her. She did not say yes nor did she say no. I strung along hoping for an unequivocal response, but none came. Mary was not ready to make such a decision with me.

Soon after, Pastor Dave posted an announcement on our bulletin board. The headline read that the International YMCA/YWCA would hold a summer project in downtown Los Angeles starting June 17th called "Students in Industry." It was located on the campus of USC at a fraternity house. I registered for the summer project as did 29 other college students from around the country

God must have had his hand in my choice of "Students In Industry" for my 1954 summer project. I didn't realize it at the time, but it had the earmarks of a divine appointment, for it was here that I met, and fell in love with Rosemary, the girl whom I would marry.

Our group had dinner in Los Angeles with the Advisory Committee of the YMCA on June 17. We followed up with a party where we all got acquainted. That was my first time to meet Rosemary, and I knew immediately that I was interested in her. Isn't it amazing how quickly we make such decisions? We quickly sort out the people we would like to meet.

She too was like my mother, but it took my mother a while to warm to her. After all, what girl was good enough for mama's boy? I edged alongside of Rosemary at the hors d'oeuvres table. (We pronounced it, "horse-duvers"). I tried to be sly about my introduction, but my intentions were probably showing. The closer I got, the more I wanted to know about her. I spent the rest of the summer in my spare time with her.

The next day the Los Angeles Chamber of Commerce rented a bus and showed us around Los Angeles. Paul and Louise Pfuetze, our directors, concluded the day by telling us their goals for the summer project. They wanted us to learn what industrial life was like, and then to see what could be done to make it more humane.

We organized ourselves, and then the group elected me chairman. I was both surprised and unready for such a task. Being chairperson was not a skill of mine. Several weeks later the members recognized that and elected a co-chairman to help in leadership. We began studying the "Los Angeles Times" for help wanted ads. We took to the streets to find industrial work, for that was our main purpose. Fortunately, most of the jobs called for unskilled labor (and paid minimum wages). Rosemary got a job sorting used IBM cards, which were then turned into toilet tissue. We had fun in the evenings with that one. We joked about what kind of card was used to make our toilet paper.

I found work at a paint factory. It too was menial work, and required a strong back to lift and stack paint cans. After two weeks I was let go. No reason was given. I then found work at a factory making searchlights for the Navy. My job was to operate a machine that took square sheets of aluminum and cut them into circles. Those circles would then become aluminum reflectors at the back of the searchlight. I stood at that machine all day long cutting circles, and passing them down the assembly line.

All of us became aware that working in the industrial sector of a metropolitan center was noisy labor, dull and boring to the maximum. The work was repetitious, and monotonous. The workers watched the clock for breaks, and for the time when they could go home. They took little pleasure in the product they were making, and became robots on American assembly lines. This is exactly what Karl Marx charged in his critique of capitalism "Das Kapital."

I suspect that is the very reason Dr. Pfuetze brought us together to work in the industrial system, and find out what could be done to make the free enterprise system more worker friendly. But the United States was in a head-on collision with communism, proclaiming the evils of communism, and confronting it in hot spots around the world.

Our leaders railed against the evils of communism. Yet our workers had become cogs in an industrial machine, lost in the rhetoric.

Rosemary asked a question in one of our discussions, "How do people spend a lifetime in such monotonous work?" Isaiah, the Old Testament prophet heard God say, "Come, let us reason together, says the Lord." (Isa. 1:18) Reasoning together between capitalism and communism was impossible at that time. In the project we were so bored with our jobs that all of us agreed the only way out of the dull monotony was to continue our college education and graduate into something better. But what about those left behind on the fetid streets of the city?

To help answer that question, the Pfuetze's invited industrial leaders to our fraternity house on the USC campus. We heard prominent economists, labor union leaders, businessmen, and clergy offer solutions to our industrial maze. The heart of Los Angeles was a perfect place for this. Here were cheap apartments, numerous factories, and a lack of nearby cultural amenities. If the capitalistic system could be improved here it could be made better anywhere. At the end of the day our group of 29 students grappled with what we had learned and tried to create a vision of a more dynamic America.

We proposed more free time for workers, paid maternity leaves for women, a guaranteed annual wage, and councils where labor and management could work together to improve conditions and production. But who was listening? Weren't we mere college students?

One thing I especially liked about being chairperson was that I took part in all the discussion groups that met at night in the attic of our fraternity house. Many nights small groups met and discussed the issues we confronted during the day. Eventually we turned to the question of our faith in God, or our search for God.

"I am hungry to know God better," I said. All of us were in some way participating in that search, and the others responded, "So am I." Often we stayed up until midnight talking about our faith, or our questions about faith in God. Then we had to get up early the next day and get ready for work. Rosemary and I were always there in the attic and found that we had much in common. We both knew that we were Christians, and yet trying to explain the nature of our faith was always up for discussion.

To keep ourselves fresh, we planned outings for our group: Griffith Park Zoo and Planetarium, Hollywood Bowl concerts, the L.A. Philharmonic, prominent churches, Olvera street, and several trips to nearby beaches. On each occasion Rosemary and I spent quality time together. I splashed her when we swam, and she doused me right back. "Take that!" I said playfully. "I'll get you," she shouted back. Love was in the air.

On August 13 we got on a bus taking us south to the mountain community of Idylwild. We got to see the unusual formation of Mt. Tahquitz, and then found a campground not far from Mt. San Jacinto. We built a large fire, arranged our sleeping bags around it, and after dinner gathered around the fire and sang songs. Later, after the stars began to twinkle, Rosemary and I went to a prominence on Mt. San Jacinto and looked down 10,000 ft. on the lights of Palm Springs, and saw the Coachella Valley stretched out to the south. The lights were magical. I took the opportunity to kiss her and hold her tight. With romance gripping us, my words flowed hesitantly, but clearly, "I love you." Her words of response held the same intensity. How can anyone forget a moment like that? We embraced tenderly, for we had fallen in love.

On August 28, the day before we were to shut down our community, I invited Rosemary to drive with me to the top of Mt. Wilson. We left in the late afternoon after work and got to the top around sunset. Once again we were looking down on a sea of lights, only this time the glow of lights was the City of Los Angeles spread out like an illuminated magic carpet. From such a vantage point all things looked possible. I held her hand and proposed to her, "Will you marry me?" and she accepted. We stayed for quite a while savoring the moment, basking in the light of love. I was in a daze of joy as we drove back to our fraternity house.

Rosemary received news from her parents that her brother Jim, serving in the Navy at San Diego, had been arrested and taken to the brig on charges of homosexuality. She asked if I would drive her to San Diego and meet her brother. My answer was, "Yes." Our group of 29 seasoned veterans of industrial work packed our things. We had so little we were soon ready to go. We hugged each other, and as we did so all of us promised to stay in touch. We especially thanked Paul and Louise Pfuetze for their patience and leadership. Without them we could not have completed our summer of learning. One by one we got into our cars and headed for home or to school.

Rosemary and I drove to San Diego. When we got to the Navy Base we were told that only family members were allowed in to see Jim. I waited outside while Rosemary was ushered in. It must have been an hour's wait. She looked sad when she came out. We sat and talked while she poured out the story of Jim's life, such as the frequent uproars between Jim and his dad, Floyd. Floyd realized early on that Jim was "different" and sometimes tried to beat it out of him, but never with success. Rosemary cringed as she recalled these incidents. Jim suffered psychological damage as a result, and never fully recovered his self-confidence. When Jim came of age he joined the Navy, but that was not the solution he needed. He was found out, court-martialed, and dishonorably discharged from the Navy.

We had lunch, and since Rosemary had no car and needed to return to Denver University, I drove her to the Greyhound Bus Station and waited with her until her bus was scheduled to depart. We promised to write to each other, and let our families and friends know of our engagement. She was to graduate from Denver University in the spring of 1955 and wanted to come to Davis to find work, and fulfill our marriage plans.

She had majored in both education and religion. She wanted to qualify for a California Teaching Credential and go to work as a teacher. She boarded her bus, and I drove up Highway 101 to San Gabriel, spent a few days with Mom and Dad, and headed back to U.C. Davis.

I signed up for some interesting political science classes that fall. I dug into my studies with zeal. So many great issues in America were now politicized, and discussion of "loyalty oaths" became a part of our class dialogues. Fear of a spreading communism gripped America and some leaders demanded that those who wanted jobs had to sign loyalty oaths. My classes were part of the discussion. I didn't like loyalty oaths for they implied that we were disloyal if we didn't sign. Of course, then you could starve without a job.

But, I began to see other problems at work in me. In Mr. Puryear's Foreign Policy class I could see red spots appearing on his face. I had never experienced anything like this before. I knew I was in trouble because the spots existed only in my mind. I went to a school counselor, a major first for me, and I asked for a an off-campus counselor with whom I could talk. I had never before asked for help for myself. Now I did, and my epiphany with Paul Tillich's, "You Are Accepted," put me over the top. And it gave me strength to seek help.

All my life I had struggled with critical decisions alone, not trusting others to understand my fears. For the first time I was now reaching out for help. The counselor gave me the name of a psychologist in Sacramento named Dr. Herb. (first name only). When I first drove to Sacramento, I knocked on his office door hesitantly, not knowing what to expect, not believing that I could be truthful with him and still be accepted by him.

He sat relaxed in his easy chair with a pen and legal sized pad in his hand in order to take notes. He asked numerous questions. As I answered his questions I am sure it became clear that my low self-esteem was an ongoing issue, as was my sexual identity, and the triangular relationship that existed between Mom, Dad, and me.

He talked to me in regular tones and gave me the impression that I was an important person to him. I responded in kind and became more and more transparent to him. "Dick," he said, "I want you to feel free to talk openly of your relationships with ladies of the night in Gorizia, Udine, and Trieste." That opened a door to me to talk freely of my heaviest burden.

Being invited to air my past in the light of day and be accepted, not criticized, felt good. I had found God's love and acceptance in my room that night of the previous spring with Tillich's sermon. Now, I was finding human acceptance with Herb. It was what I always wanted from my father, but found it now with him.

I often went to him during the fall semester. I grew closer and closer to him. Eventually, I realized that a whole new relationship was emerging. It was as if he became my new father. He slowly became the father I had always longed for. We hugged at the close of each session. Sometimes I welled up when we hugged. I felt his strength and compassion flowing through me. I walked tall when I left his office.

Here I was, a veteran of the Korean War. Congress enacted Public Law 550, and it declared those who served in the armed forces between June 27, 1950 and February 1, 1955, were Korean War vets, and eligible for benefits. When I was inducted in 1952 I was disillusioned with my prospects in the Army. Now, however, I was able to pay Herb using my veterans benefits. I whispered a prayer *"Thank you Lord for my Army service."* I had come full circle.

I applied for veterans' education benefits and received monthly checks to continue with college. It was those checks that enabled me to pay for tuition and books at U.C. Davis, but also to pay Herb. I could not have paid the price without help from Uncle Sam.

Herb loved to share his library books with me. I became an eager reader. One of the first books had a title like, "We Walk Alone". A former prostitute wrote the book, and she simply told her story in straightforward fashion, of lonely nights walking the streets of her city; beatings by her pimp, and attacks by some of the more hostile male clients. It was not a pretty picture. I changed my mind about prostitutes. When I brought the book back to him he said to me, "You were burned when you were a child." I didn't know the precise meaning of what he said, but those words meant to me that the prohibition against sex and sexual knowledge, the prohibition against girl friends, and the unusual relationship with my Mom left an open wound on my sexual identity.

Herb invited me to read another of his library books, Soren Kierkegaard's, "Either/Or." Lights went on in my mind as I sought to understand this complex Danish philosopher.

Then he urged me to buy my next book, Rollo May's "Man's Search For Himself." I bought it, carried it with me wherever I went, and read it so thoroughly that it became a second Bible to me. Whenever I read it I felt a sense of wholeness within me. It was as though I was being put back together as the human being I was intended to be. Dr. May spoke often of the structure of personality. It was a new concept to me. He meant that each individual builds such a structure. Since the individual built it, he can change it. That was good news.

Then Herb invited me to buy a truly difficult book to read, Karen Horney's "The Neurotic Personality Of Our Time." He warned me in advance that reading it would be like, "Walking through a slaughterhouse." It turned out to be just that. Page after page recounted neurotic personalities, their patterns and behavior, and I realized that Dr. Horney was talking about me. She pinpointed me so accurately that I had nowhere to hide. I felt defeated just as I was beginning to heal.

Sometime later I read Harry Emerson Fosdick's "On Being A Real Person" Somewhere in this marvelous book Fosdick called psychology "The language of defeat." It had become just that for me. Now I found a way to soften the blows given by Karen Horney.

I also bought and read the latest popular psychology of Erich Fromm, "Escape From Freedom." He had such a clear way of showing the cultural dangers that led us away from our destiny to freedom. For instance, his definition of a free person is one who has "spontaneity." But we are tempted to surrender spontaneity and thus our freedom in the presence of authoritarian persons or systems. The people of Germany, said Fromm, had given their freedom to Hitler and then lost everything. We must learn to reject authoritarian systems in order to retain our freedom. I began carrying a book with me wherever I went and would snatch several minutes of reading in each day. Whenever I stood in line or took public transportation, I read a book. Books and Herb became my new friends.

Herb kept feeding me information that I could build into the new concept of self that was emerging, such as "You are your own best long term investment," and, "Build on that investment." I soaked up whatever he taught me, like a son who loves his father. I was ready to learn from him. As we continued our sessions, I learned a psychological term that helped me understand our relationship: "transference." In counseling where positive relationships have been established along with trust, the patient begins to take on the characteristics of the therapist. I could see that it was happening to me. I began to feel Herb's strength and confidence building within myself.

Sometimes I wanted to grow faster, and lamented the lost time of my youth. Herb asked me a question, "How long does it take for an acorn to become an oak tree?" I knew what he was saying. I had begun a quest. I was taking my first steps forward, and it would take time. But I was in a hurry; I wanted to make up for lost time. That acorn was just beginning to send up shoots. He added this bit of wisdom, "It is better to strive than to arrive." When I struggled in my relationships with fellow students or with faculty, he gave me this philosophy, "There are people who are half-pint sized. There are those who are pint-sized. Some are quart-sized. Finally, there are a precious few who are gallon-sized." In other words, "Don't expect gallon-sized relationships from pint-sized people."

A humorous exchange took place between us one day. Herb knew of the Victorian thinking I had picked up from Mom and the priggishness it sometimes caused in me. Herb said, "Sometimes the best part of the day is when you take a good, healthy shit." We both roared with laughter at the spontaneity of what he said. There was truth in that statement and the fresh way he said it.

He also shared his thought of a well-balanced life. Such a life consisted of four ingredients: Work, Love, Worship, and Play. Those were words to live by.

An unspoken thing happened in me as we talked. Previously, it seemed as though no one understood me. With all the reading I had done I was ahead of my peers. When I spoke out of my knowledge, I could tell by the response I got when the other person didn't really understand me. I really needed to be understood. Sometimes I felt strange when no one seemed to know where I was coming from. Now, with Herb I was understood. I wanted more of this. The lesson I learned is that to get it, I had to give it, and I could do that. In America intellectuals are suspect. I began to learn to carry my knowledge lightly, and not proclaim my educational credentials. I was also glad to find out that the spots on Dr. Puryear's face disappeared.

The school declared a holiday for Christmas (what they called "Winter Break"). Rosemary and I talked on the phone and shared letters. She invited me to come to Denver by Greyhound Bus for Christmas. She promised to meet me at the Greyhound station and take me to the home of the campus Chaplain, Rev. Ralph Odom.

Denver was covered with snow when I got there, and I was not prepared for the icy blasts of wind coming down from the Rocky Mountains. *Didn't I have some long johns somewhere?* We visited Denver University, where Rosemary majored in Religion and Education. She invited Ralph Odom to have coffee with us.

orte I shared with him my experience in the Army, and my deliverance from guilt and despair when I returned to U.C. Davis. Rosemary and I talked of our experience with "Students In Industry." Ralph was interested in all that we had done. When we finished with our coffee, he asked me "Have you ever considered the ministry?" When he heard my hesitant "No," he asked me to pray and consider the ministry. I knew that Mom had quietly wanted me to enter into the service of God, but this was my first time to confront such a question. I responded by telling him, "I will pray about it, and talk to Rosemary for her opinion."

Rosemary and I went for some long drives. One was into the nearby mountains to visit the famous Buffalo Bill monument that looked out over the Great Plains below. We talked about the ministry. Rosemary told me that she was interested in ministry because of her religious studies.

Back at Davis I spent January in final exams. In Mr. Puryear's class on Foreign Policy I got an A. In Philosophy 6, and Mr. Jacob's class on the Constitution, I received B's. All my other classes were C's. There was a certain pleasure in getting an A and two B's. Again, my grades were showing an upward trend. I was becoming a better student with each semester.

The spring of 1955 would be my final semester at U.C. Davis. I stood on the edge of a major decision each graduating student must ask, "What will I choose as my career?" I had already chosen my life's mate. I began to feel pressure and excitement building inside myself.

Rosemary graduated from Denver University in March and had decided to take a Greyhound bus to Sacramento after receiving her degree. I met her in Sacramento and drove her to a home with a room for rent just three blocks from campus. She soon got a job at the university library while I completed my final semester. I introduced her to my friends at CACA, and we attended Sunday night sessions at Pastor Dave's house, and Sunday morning services at the Davis Community Church.

In April Rosemary and I went to see a new Hollywood film "A Man Called Peter." Peter Marshall's ministry spoke to me. Something deeply personal stirred within me. I was a young Christian, and I knew nothing of the Holy Spirit, but I experienced a tug on my heart, and in that attractive pull were the words, *You should consider the ministry*. It was clear to me and I spoke to Rosemary about it as we left the theater. She drew close to me as we talked. She had just received her degree in Religion, and was eager to use her knowledge in practical service. I was drawn to Rev. Peter Marshall, and wanted to serve where I too could make a difference in the world.

Soon I talked to other members of CACA, some of whom were also considering the ministry. Stan Moore was preparing himself to go as an agricultural missionary to the Indians of the Atacama Desert in Chile. Don Appleton, son of the Presbyterian minister in San Gabriel, was ready to follow in his father's footsteps. Dick Ramsey, and Gaynl Stouffer also pondered calls to ministry.

One seminary leapt out as the best in our area. My fellow students called it, "Holy Hill," or Pacific School of Religion in Berkeley. I talked to Pastor Dave and applied for entrance. I got my formal acceptance several weeks later. I was amazed. "Dave," I called out, "They accepted me for the fall semester!"

Did they know what they were doing? I wondered. But I kept in the back of my mind that this would be a trial balloon. I would go for a quarter and see if ministry was truly my calling. Could I handle the challenge of theological studies? I wasn't sure. Would I prepare myself to become a minister, or instead teach classes in religion? I had a bag full of unknowns.

Then came a notice of bad news for me. My college advisor called me to his office two weeks before graduation and announced, "You are two units short of the required amount of units for graduation. The upshot is you cannot graduate with the rest of your class." I was devastated and angry. He was my advisor and he planned my semester's classes with me. It was his job to know the total units required and see that I met the requirement. If I were better informed I would have appealed the decision. But I did not know of such appeals. He said, "I am so sorry for this mistake." My response, "Me more than you."

I left his office discouraged. Rosemary and I discussed my options, and I began to see some alternatives. I wrote to the University of California in Berkeley for a list of their correspondence courses. I found a correspondence course titled "The Bible as English Literature." I was surprised to find that a prestigious public university taught a class like this, but I paid my fee and gladly signed up. It's funny how God "causes all things to work together for good for those who love Him."

That was one of the best Bible studies I have ever taken. It was actually a close-up look at the patriarchs in the book of Genesis. Each time I finished a lesson I mailed it to my professor in Berkeley and he graded my responses and sent my next lesson. I worked harder on this class than any other I had taken at Davis. I worked on lessons all summer so I could be ready for Pacific School of Religion in the fall with all my requirements completed.

Rosemary and I began to talk about that big word WEDDING. Suddenly this new reality intruded. I needed money and had none. As we planned our wedding the list of friends grew. The bills grew along with our expanded list.

I got a job at the Sacramento Nursery that helped pay those bills. In the blazing hot sun I kept all of their stock supplied with water. It was an all day job every day to keep their plants from dehydrating in the summer heat. I was the one who got dehydrated.

West Sacramento had a large cluster of immigrants in an enclave called Bryte. One home featured a For Rent sign in its front yard. We stopped to look at the rental. The owners had converted their garage into a small unit with a bedroom, bath and kitchen. It was clean and neat. The landlords were Russian immigrants who spoke little English. They had the look of peasants, honest and hard working. They told us they had fled from the Russian Revolution and came to America. They charged $35.00 a month for their rental unit. We took the apartment, and began moving our things there. We found out that we liked them, and they returned our affection with their own. They were named Loozin, but we simply called them "Mama and Papa."

Each time we drove into the driveway and moved something in, if it was mealtime, they offered us some Russian soup called borscht. Mama also made a platter of meat pastry called pirozhki, baked and filled with chunks of beef and vegetables. She brought some of those too. In her booming voice and deep Russian accent she would say, "You come. You eat now. This make you strong." Mama and Papa may have been what the world calls hoi polloi, or Russian peasants, but to us they were the salt of the earth, and we loved them.

Rosemary found a teaching job in West Sacramento at Westmore Oaks Elementary School. But she had to sign a one-year contract in order to get the job. That meant that when I went to Pacific School of Religion for the fall quarter I would travel alone and get a room on campus in Benton Hall, the dorm for single men. Each weekend I traveled home to be with my sweetheart.

When Herb found out about our wedding plans he gave me more words of wisdom as we waited for the big day. He said, "Don't be afraid of the pollywogs!" I took his advice and Rosemary and I met each other passionately whenever we could, in our rental. In those days that was a no-no, but we let tradition fall away. We set our wedding for October 18th.

We were married in the sanctuary of the Davis Community Church. We had a simple meal in the Fellowship Hall with our CACA friends. Then Rosemary and I tried to make a quiet getaway. But it was not to be. Our friends dashed to their cars and followed us along Highway 80 honking all the way to West Sacramento. As we drove up to our rental unit, they surrounded us again, honking their horns, and making loud noises with their yelling. The neighbors became curious and looked out their front doors to see the event. We were now in the glare of headlights and neighbors. We made a dash for our rental unit, and locked the door. Our friends slowly dispersed back to Davis.

We enjoyed some humor on weekends. We pulled the blinds shut for times of intimacy. Mama and Papa might bring some borscht out from their kitchen to our unit, but if the blinds were shut they took the soup back to their kitchen. Later, when we raised the blinds, they would bring us our soup and have a good laugh about how often the blinds were drawn. We were poor by worldly standards yet full of joie de vivre (joy of living) at the life we now had. Between her beginner's salary as a teacher and my income from veterans benefits, (PL 550), we paid all our bills, and I was ready to begin graduate education.

With hesitancy and excitement I now began the biggest step of my life. I was a newly wed, and about to begin seminary education at PSR in Berkeley. I didn't know where all of this would lead, but as I drove quietly to Berkeley, I was filled with apprehension and excitement. I was amazed to consider that in the short time since my service in Trieste I had come so far. In one year I had resolved three great issues facing a young man: *I have found a wife, I have found a career, and I have found God, (or God's grace found me).*

> But, my inner voice asked, *Are you really ready for ministry? Are you up to such a high calling?* And an insistent question emerged again,

What if the seminary finds out about my sins of the flesh in Trieste? Wouldn't they expel me as unworthy of ministry? Can a guy who had fallen so far be redeemed for Christian ministry? Perhaps, I sighed, *I should consider entering religious education as a teacher.*

Those thoughts simmered in my mind. I sat up straight, intent as I drove to Berkeley, to begin a course of studies that would change my life forever.

Nineteen

The Indelible Footprint

One hundred students gathered at the Pacific School of Religion (PSR) in Berkeley, California, in September, 1955. We were the largest class in school history. We stood for a class portrait. Then, we were invited to a school picnic in the hills above Berkeley. We played a game of tag football and got acquainted with one another. The weather was balmy, and San Francisco Bay spread out below like a beautiful panorama. I never tired of the view.

On Saturdays the sounds from Cal's football field in Strawberry Canyon reverberated through Berkeley: crowds cheering, bands playing football music, and a roar whenever a touchdown was scored. Berkeley was a great learning environment. I fell in love with it. Rosemary and I were separated each week, but I went back to Bryte in West Sacramento on weekends to be with her.

When I arrived on campus at PSR I didn't know what to expect. *What is Holy Hill? Is it a place where choirboys learn the basics of Christianity?* If so I was going to be sorely tested, for I knew I did not fit that mold. I had scraped bottom in Trieste, but at Davis God touched my soul, and He forgave me. Inwardly, however, I felt like a hypocrite. I didn't believe I was acceptable to the school or my classmates if they knew of my past. I kept that part of my past a deep secret. I hated keeping secrets.

Early in the quarter a group of freshmen were entering Benton Hall after class. Upper classmen stood on the stairwell and began hooting and laughing at us. "So what's going on?" we asked. They responded, "Wait until you guys find out that everything you learned in Sunday school was dead wrong, some kind of joke. Wait until you take Dr. Otwell's class in Old Testament and find out who really wrote the books of the Old Testament. Just wait till you take Dr. Finegan's class in New Testament and find out that many of the books of the New Testament weren't written by Apostles after all. You are babes in the woods. You are in for it." Then we got more mocking and finger pointing.

What an introduction to life at seminary! We were in for the ride of our lives. These were not choirboys, but adults with powerful new information in their minds. I resented those upper classmen at first. But time was to prove them right. My Sunday school faith seemed useless in this different learning environment.

I didn't know it at the time, but this school was under the influence of modernism. German theology was in the ascendance. This was a theology that challenged everything in Christianity that had been received from the past. Every book of the Bible was researched and subjected to rigorous scrutiny. We read the books of foremost theologians like Reinhold Niehbur, and Paul Tillich. We dealt with ultimate topics like "the nature and destiny of man." The creeds of the church were given intense scrutiny. This was heavy theological questioning.

The Scopes Monkey Trial was in the past. It determined that Fundamentalism was fatally flawed, and liberalism now flourished. At least that was the point of view. My school fell into line and changed its name from Pacific Theological Seminary to the more prosaic Pacific School of Religion. My Bishop, who later ordained me, used to quietly remind us at our Conference meetings: "I am an unreconstructed liberal." We students willingly aligned ourselves to be on the right side of history. We would break down doors of ignorance. We would challenge old assumptions of fundamentalism and over–zealous evangelicals.

Could Christianity stand up to the onslaught of modernism? The Dead Sea Scrolls had been found by a Bedouin and revealed to the world. Archeology was uncovering old tombs and treasures thought lost. Was Christianity able to survive debates about the credibility of faith in a world recovering from a disastrous World War? Our answer was "yes" if we applied the new theology to the preaching of the gospel. But in my haste to learn the new theology I almost lost the simple faith that brought me here in the first place.

Here we were at mid-century, riding on the crest of a religious revival, with people returning to church, and affirming their faith in God. New churches were built to accommodate them. We were preparing ourselves to go forth and help build a new Christianity. We had a refrain that we liked to quote to one another: "Reform thy church beginning with me."

I was preparing myself to be a shepherd of the sheep plus a leader in the church. But little did I know that the United Methodist Conference wanted more than that. They wanted CEOs who could raise money, build churches, bring in members, pay bills and preach a good sermon. I wasn't prepared to become a CEO. Nor did the seminary prepare us for that. The meeting of our seminarians with the expectations of denominational leaders was a train wreck waiting to happen.

I applied myself eagerly to the classes in theology, Old Testament and New Testament. In Dr. Otwell's class on Old Testament he taught that Moses did not write the first five books of the Bible. Instead Dr. Otwell applied the Graff-Wellhausen Theory that identified the various sources used to create the first five books. (called the Pentateuch). We went through the book of Genesis and underlined in color, sentence by sentence, depending on the source: red was for the "J" source from Judea, green for the 'E" source from northern Israel, blue for the "D" or Deuteronomist source, and black for the priestly "P" source. Soon my Bible looked like a Christmas tree. It was exciting to learn this source theory and many others.

However, what was left unsaid was as important as what was taught. We were slowly but surely undermining the accepted version of the Bible, that it was the pure Word of God, handed down to earth from God by inspired prophets and holy men. For two thousand years the Bible had been preached as such. Now, we students were standing on a new planet out in space. We were learning how much of scripture was the work of human hands, inspired or otherwise. In my zeal to learn these new theories I was ready to pass on this learning to my future congregations. Little did I know that such information was considered heresy outside of seminary.

I found that a time bomb was planted in me with these new theories. On the one hand I trusted my professors to transmit the truth to me. The other side of me wondered how I would preach to a congregation as if scripture was infallible when in reality I had been taught differently? What about my own faith? How could the Bible retain any sense of authority with me when I now knew how it came to be put together? My professors could take the Bible apart, but I now found that it was up to me to reconstruct scripture so it was believable to me and to others. I needed to give back to the Bible its authority. I didn't know it at the time, but I would spend a huge chunk of my life trying to resolve that issue.

Then there were the classes in New Testament. We learned that the Apostles did not write the Apostles' Creed. Some of Paul's letters were not written by Paul at all, Ephesians, I & II Timothy, for instance. Peter's letters were not by the Apostle Peter. The synoptic gospels of "Matthew," and "Luke" each copied from Mark, and Mark used as his source a mysterious document called "Q." (Q in German stands for Quelle or Source). German theologians had pinpointed that the ultimate source of the gospels was "Q." But who was he? Who knew? Furthermore, scholars couldn't discern who wrote the Gospel of John. Everywhere there were more questions than answers. It is no wonder that the upper classmen hooted at the freshmen. Those who survived this "higher criticism" could laugh at us who had to digest it now and take our turn trying to make sense of it all.

Dr. White, our professor of Theology, tried something to help out. He broke us into what he called "theological bull sessions." Groups of six would find a quiet niche on campus and hash out what we had been taught. We were all over the map trying to solve the riddle of the new theology. We not only had to make sense of it, but we also had to figure out how to apply it in congregations who considered this new learning a dangerous subversion. And, how were we going to prepare sermons that remained true to Christ, but also to our new learning? It was a precarious balancing act. Could we apply this to our Sunday school curriculum? We had a tiger by the tail. Seminary education was not for the faint of heart.

And there I was, a callow youth, tainted by my fall from grace, seeking to apply God's saving grace to this demanding environment. Surrounding me were preacher kids (PKs) that I was sure were smarter than me, or at least more ready for this than me. They had no ethical stain on them as I did. I looked up to them because they had been born in parsonages, and raised by ministers. Only later did I realize that I was a Christian too, and that if I had shared the story of my conversion it would have deepened our discussions. At that time, however, I was hesitant to believe in myself.

There were some programs to help us along. After lunch each day we organized a game of volleyball outside the library. We quickly divided into two teams and went at it with all the skill we could muster. I loved the intensity, and played with gusto. Dr. White, our professor of theology, commented that we learned more theology on the volleyball court than we did in the classroom.

PSR insisted that each student be assigned to a local church. The plan was that these local pastors would take us under their wings and teach us how to minister to a congregation. The congregations weren't interested in our theology. They wanted to know if we had the grace and gifts to lead families in worship and in Christian education.

Because I went home to Bryte in West Sacramento each weekend, I was assigned to the First Methodist Church in Sacramento. Dr. Panzer, their pastor, gave me the Junior High class to supervise and teach. I soon found out why teachers consider Junior Highs tough nuts to crack. My classes in seminary were little help with them. They sensed that I was new and put me to the test. At the end of that year I knew I did not want to be a Junior High leader. Dr. Panzer gave me a check for $50 the following June, and with a blessing, sent me on my way. Thank God I had veterans benefits continuing to fund me. I could not have gotten through school without Uncle Sam's support.

The summer of 1956 I had another opportunity to expand my horizons. Bill Miller, one of my seminary friends, offered Rosemary and me the leadership of a program called Christian Youth Fruit Camp. No pay came with the offer, as usual, but plenty of challenge to serve high school Christian youth from northern California. Our friends teased us that we were serving "Christian fruits," which we took in good fun, and learned to live with the jibes. We accepted the leadership.

We spent the summer at a peach ranch on the outskirts of Hughson, a small town outside of Modesto. At the back of the ranch were hastily built cabins for the 25 youth we would host. There was a separate cabin for the leaders, and a larger cabin that served as a kitchen/dining room.

Not far away the Tuolumne River meandered its way westward toward the Delta. The camp was primitive, but livable, built by local farmers at the end of WWII to help feed a hungry world, recovering from a disastrous World War. With the abundance of peaches that grew on farms in the area, we were going to help feed that world.

Local ranchers gave us permission to glean fallen cling peaches that lay on the ground in their orchards. They loaned us a flatbed truck to go from orchard to orchard collecting peaches. We brought the fruit back to our camp. Evenings, in the dusky heat of a valley sunset, we created a production line. We sliced peaches into halves, pitted them, and put them onto racks, sunny side up. All the while the kids broke out into fun songs followed by some favorite hymns. We filled the peach orchard with our music.

Trays of split peaches went into smokehouses. At the end of each day Stan, my assistant, and I lit sulfur pots, located on the floor of each smokehouse. In the morning, after the peaches had been exposed to sulfur fumes all night, the trays were ready for a two-day sunbath to dry. We produced over four tons of dried peaches that summer. All of it went to Hong Kong to feed refugees fleeing from Mao Tse Tung's Red Army and the rigid system imposed by the communists.

Rosemary, Stan Moore, and I took turns leading the youth in worship each morning. The Tuolumne River was one boundary to our camp and a beautiful place to gather in God's presence. The River flowed slowly at this point in the valley. Lined with trees and green shrubbery, it lay before us like a graceful deep blue lifeline watering the valley. Sometimes it looked like the trees and the river in the Garden of Eden, so idyllically perfect.

There was silence on the bluff overlooking the river as we meditated and then prayed to God. I read scripture and said a few words. It was very simple, surrounded as we were by soft, cool morning light. I took the Psalms and read the verse, "This is the day the Lord has made, let us rejoice in it and be glad." Each prayed. Then someone else would quote their favorite verse of scripture. Then another and another until we swelled into a chorus of praise to our Creator and Redeemer.

This was a breakthrough for both the campers and me. They were gaining in their self-esteem and in their love for God. I was learning that beyond the walls of seminary was a dynamic faith that stood the test of time, regardless of the latest theology. Seminary proved to be a buffeting experience. But here were youth reaching out in praise to God and wanting to serve Him. I found that to be refreshing to my faith.

Now Rosemary, Stan and I had a Christianity that was alive, spiritual and vibrant with faith in God. We were on a roller coaster ride that circled this planet. We were exhilarated, taken to the edge of our mental capacities by this ride. Where would it end?

Meanwhile, at the end of a month of labor and fellowship, the parents came to pick up their teen-agers. But they were not the same kids that they dropped off. The campers had grown in stature and faith. We formed a circle, held hands and sang, "Blest be the tie that binds." There were tears of sweet sorrow as we prepared to say goodbye. Hugs followed. Then we reluctantly went our separate ways. Faith was alive and well outside the walls of seminary. What a learning-serving experience this was.

I asked myself a thousand times,

> *Why did I choose PSR? Why did I choose the most liberal seminary on the west coast? Wouldn't it have been easier to go to a good old-fashioned conservative school that accepted the traditional story of how the Bible came to be? Then I could skip higher criticism about the Bible. Wouldn't it be better to simply accept the message once and for all handed down by the saints, and preach it and teach it?*

An answer came the following year. In 1957 some fellow students and I went to Stern Grove in San Francisco to hear Billy Graham preach a Crusade. He was zealous to preach to us. He shared how he struggled as a young man to accept the Bible as the Word of God. Part of him denied many of the stories in the Bible. He shared that he was troubled and distressed by his doubts. Finally, he reported, he fell to his knees and asked God to show him the truth about the Bible. When he arose from his prayer, he reported that all his doubts about the Bible melted away.

In his zeal to transmit the Gospel to us he then held up his Bible, thumped on it, and told us that we had to take it on faith that every word was true from Genesis to Revelation. "Don't doubt a word of it," he said, "It is all God's word." But, we had been to our Bible classes, and Graham's story was to us, a kind of blind faith. We were learning a different approach to the Bible. I respected Billy Graham as America's greatest evangelist. But I could not accept his idea that every word of scripture was infallible, and that we had to accept it as such.

My response to Graham was: it is better to know the truth about how scripture came to be, and the struggle to understand it, than not to know. Even though it was difficult to take the Bible apart, I needed to understand how the Bible came to be. Jesus said, "You shall know the truth and the truth shall set you free." It took time to put it together again, but it became for me an indispensible part of life with God.

Sometimes I felt the dilemma that Marilyn Monroe faced. A reporter asked her who she would like to be if she could come back and start over again. Her mother was in a mental institution, and her father was unknown. Placed in foster care, she was raped at age 11. She thought for a moment and said, "I would come back as Marilyn Monroe." What a profound answer. We are given just this one life to live. We have to make a decision to pick up our life and live it, as it is given to us. In the same way we take the Bible as scholars, using higher criticism, research it, and then learn its message to our generation. What an exciting time to be alive.

I know what the mainstream Bible scholars teach, but I find spiritual meaning in scripture when I study it carefully. Sometimes the words leap off the page and grab my attention. The message is still compelling, and even more so with the knowledge of how it was formed. The years have flown by and I am convinced that I have a deepening respect and love for scripture because I know its origins. Then it becomes a treasure trove pointing us to Christ. We have not served our churches well when we refuse to teach our congregations how the Bible came to be.

Weekends in Bryte were special. I got to reconnect with my new father, Herb. He was my north star. It was so refreshing to sit and talk with him and be myself. I let go of my pretense when I was with Herb. Every youth needs an adult like that in their life, someone you can lean on and talk to about all the questions bubbling up inside. Also there was Rosemary at home and we cherished our weekends together. At times like that I believed I was going to survive the rigors of seminary education.

In June of 1956 my District Superintendent of the Methodist Church appointed me as an Associate to a small struggling church in Point Richmond, not far from Berkeley. It was known as a "student church" because seminarians could go there and make their mistakes, and do the least amount of damage. The full-time minister was a layman, Pastor Ray, and he struggled to find his way with this small congregation that was locked in the past and languishing as members dropped out to go elsewhere.

One of the hard lessons that I had to learn is that older churches like this don't change, they just keep chugging along as best they can. Pt. Richmond Church "down by the gas station" was doomed to be a student church. Yet I wanted to give it my all.

Back at PSR I took a class from Dr. Hogue called Homiletics, or the art of preaching. He did our class a service when he invited us one by one to come to his office and take a speaking test. He invited me to pick up my Bible and read a selected passage into a tape recorder. Then he replayed the tape so I could hear my voice. I was shocked when I heard my voice. I had the driest, most boring monotone I have ever heard. The paramount question was why would anyone want to listen to that voice? Dr. Hogue then recommended a retired speech teacher in Berkeley who could help me.

I went to that teacher immediately and he diagnosed my problem. I had learned a host of poor speaking habits. I didn't enunciate. He had a cure for that. In his office was a tall stack of children's books: "The Three Little Pigs," "The Little Engine That Could," "Billy Goat Gruff," "Cinderella," "Little Red Riding Hood," "Goldilocks and the Three Bears" and many more. He handed me one of the books off of the top of his stack and told me to begin reading out loud to him. When I got to a passage showing fear, I had to color my voice with fear, making it palpable. When a character showed exuberance I had to put life into my voice and make the passage come alive. When someone was in the doldrums my voice had to reflect dismay.

We did this for an hour each week, and he sent stories home with me to practice reading out loud, in front of a mirror. I laughed at myself, but it worked. All year I put life and enunciation into those children's stories. I learned to squeeze every ounce of emotion out of them. When my two children Suzanne and Stephen were growing up I loved to read storybooks to them, especially at bedtime. Reading those stories was a goldmine for us. I gave emphasis to the verbs and adjectives, and it was fun. My kids loved it and asked for more.

This wonderful old retired speech teacher also gave me short sentences to pronounce clearly: "She sells seashells by the seashore." And "Rugged rubber baby buggy bumpers." Then I had to say them faster and faster. As my children came of age they giggled as they listened to me practice at home. My voice was a flat tire, but I was determined to fix it. However, just as soon as I fixed one tire, another went flat. At least now I recognized when I needed help, and searched until I found it. Truly my conversion experience at Davis was the beginning of a life adventure, not a conclusion.

Rosemary and I moved into the campus housing of PSR for married students in 1956. There we joined with other married couples and made new friends. We drove into San Francisco on weekends to see a movie and then went for hamburgers. Hollywood released Cecil B. DeMille's new blockbuster, "The Ten Commandments." While it was intensely popular with the public, we, on the other hand, took it apart and criticized it based on what we learned in our Old Testament classes. From now on everything we did was subjected to what we were learning at school. We panned this movie as pure sensationalism.

I took classes in Pastoral Psychology, Church History, Christian Ethics, Christian Education, Methodist Heritage and Polity, World Religion, and Personal Devotional Life. Each class offered new vistas on how to understand God, people, the church, and the religions of the world. It was an intense ride. I hung on to the saddle and tried to keep my horse steady. All the while I had one hand on my hat so it would not blow away.

By 1957 we students had to take "Comprehensives," a test that would determine if we had really learned what the professors were teaching. If we passed the test we went on for the last two years of seminary. If we failed the test we had to go back and start over again, or drop out. Most were able to pass the comprehensive exam. With a sigh of relief, I did too.

In June I met the qualifications to become a Deacon in the Northern California Conference of the Methodist Church. Twelve candidates drove to Stockton, California, to the campus of The College of the Pacific.

We went to the chapel and were examined once again by Elders of the Methodist Church. We were shown the vows that we were to take. One vow in particular grabbed my attention: Will you refrain from all alcoholic beverages, and practice total abstinence in your ministry? Even though Dad had two highballs every night I willingly said, "Yes" to that vow and kept it. I felt satisfied. It was not as difficult to keep as I imagined.

That June morning was glorious. To me the chapel of the College of the Pacific (now a University) is the most beautiful on the west coast. Stained glass windows showing patriarchs, apostles, and saints gleamed in the sunshine. Over the altar was a huge stained glass figure of Christ filling the chapel with his presence.

Bishop Tippett entered, prayed and then called us forward. One by one the Bishop and the Elders laid hands on us, ordaining us as Deacons into that endless line of splendor called the Disciples of Christ. We reached all the way back to Jesus, who commissioned the twelve disciples to come and follow Him. I was humbled to be a part of such a calling.

At Annual Conference that week Bishop Tippett appointed me pastor of the Point Richmond Methodist Church. The previous year Pastor Ray was the senior pastor, and I was his associate. Now I was to be senior pastor. Even though the small congregation was a backwater in a conference of hundreds of churches, I felt the burden on my shoulders. I was now the responsible one. When Harry Truman was told of President Roosevelt's death he said he felt the weight of the world now fell on him. I resonated with that feeling.

Along with a full load of classes I now had to prepare a weekly sermon, and call on all the members. When it came to preaching I was an empty well. All I knew was that God touched my life at Davis. Other than that and my classes I was a greenhorn trying to find his way. I gobbled up books on preaching and sermons. I stuffed myself full. But in solid preaching you have to deliver your soul. I didn't know how to do that yet. I had put a hedge around my soul. I had secrets to hide. The congregation had to deal with yet another student minister.

I bought a pulpit robe and colorful stoles to adorn it in hopes of adding some gravitas to my presence. Sometimes I simply copied some famous preacher's sermon. There is a danger in that, however. It is easy to develop a "pulpit tone" where you try to sound more righteous, more "holy" than you really are. That is an ever-present danger. You still have to be yourself in the pulpit, and doing that required a certain degree of honesty that I lacked at that time. My past in Trieste continued to cloud my desire to be open about myself. Having something important to hide was a ball and chain around my preaching.

An incident happened at school that added to my struggle. The wife of the president of our seminary liked to stay close to events on campus and be the eyes and ears for her husband. One evening after dinner she helped out in the kitchen clean up while I cleared the dining room tables. Everyone else had left d'Autremont Hall, except for a student who helped the president's wife, and myself.

Something then happened that was no accident. I could hear the two women talking in the kitchen. I'm sure they knew that their voices carried out to the dining room. I heard her ask the student, "What about Dick Bastear? Is he ready for ministry?" There was a long pause as the student gave a thoughtful response. She finally replied, "No." I was devastated when I heard that. I felt that she set up that discussion so that I would hear it and reconsider the ministry. I already carried doubts about my readiness. Transitioning to Point Richmond Church was difficult. Now I carried that word into my mind and I felt the sting of what seemed like rejection, the thing I feared most.

Who was she that she made herself judge and jury over my fate in school? She was not one of my teachers. How did she know me? Was she like Cassandra at Troy prophesying the doom of that city? I was both hurt and angry at the same time. But I look back on it now, and time has given me a better perspective. She was right. I was not yet equipped for ministry. I had a lot I needed to learn about myself and other people. I needed a closer walk with Christ. I needed to work with a seasoned pastor and shadow him in his work. I needed to learn how to be a fundraiser so the church could pay its bills.

There was something else that I needed to learn, but was only dimly aware of. Thus far I had learned an intellectual faith buoyed by my new theology. Everything was now cast in theological terms. I was awakened by the knowledge of what I was taught, and I became an eager student.

But I was to soon find out, however, that the greatest journey was yet to come. It was the journey from my head to my heart. I had a grasp of what the Christian faith was all about, an intellectual faith in my head. But I was not grounded in a personal relationship with God, or with Christ. That is an affair of the heart. I could only get there through an act of self-surrender, and that was yet to come.

A wonderful thing happened in November. Rosemary, who by now was pregnant, started having contractions. I rushed her to Kaiser Hospital in Oakland. I waited into the night for her to deliver, and finally, on a nurses recommendation, went home to Pt. Richmond. Then came a hurried call to return to the hospital. By the time I arrived our daughter was born, and we named her Suzanne. I was now a father and that knowledge gave a whole new dimension to my concept of ministry. God's love became more real to me as I held my tiny daughter in my arms and felt her warmth and softness close to my face. *This*, I thought, *is how God loves us.*

Rosemary and I painted an upstairs room sky blue in our cavernous, 1890 parsonage, just for Suzanne. I learned to change her diapers, and feed her. I took a class in childcare with Rosemary. I loved being a father.

I came to a realization. Any man can produce children. But it is a humbling experience to become a father to your children. Consider this: we don't create life. Rather, we transmit the mystery and miracle of life. I decided to sit down and write a letter to Suzanne, to be opened in ten years. In that letter I pledged myself to love her to the best of my ability, and care for her as a gift of God.

I kept taking more classes. I registered for a class at Napa State Hospital. *"Perhaps,"* I thought, *"if I learn more psychology I will learn more about myself."* I became the Chaplain's Assistant. I was deeply surprised to find how much like us were the people inside the hospital.

I had Hollywood visions of bizarre behavior inside a mental institution. Instead many were struggling with what Henry David Thoreau described as "quiet desperation." The Chaplain counseled me with these words: "If you can't love these people with an unconditional love you are no use to me." I had to get rid of some prejudices about "crazy" people in order to do that. At the same time I needed to learn to accept these people as human beings.

The Chaplain also asked me to help bring patients to a room where electro-shock therapy was administered. We helped strap the patient to a gurney, and then the attending physician attached electrodes to the patient. When the Doctor threw a switch a charge of electricity surged through the patient. The patient writhed as the voltage reverberated in his body. His face contorted as if it was too much for him, and his eyes looked as through they would pop out of his head. His body shuddered violently. Suddenly, the Doctor cut the power and the patient lay like a dead man on the gurney. The Chaplain and I helped the patient into a wheelchair and back to a recovery center.

I know that it all sounds very gross. And I can understand why the State Legislature stopped such procedures. Yet when we went to the Doctor's office to discuss the patient, he shared with us that in some mysterious way the electric current helped re-organize the patient's brain and thus speeded his recovery. Patients were getting better under this treatment. At the same time my brain was being re-organized. I was growing in in my confidence at being able to work with all kinds of people in this institution.

I also took a class at Herrick Hospital in Berkeley where we learned hospital ministry under Dr. Leslie, PSR's teacher of Pastoral Psychology. I wanted to understand human behavior, and especially my own, so I took every one of his classes. But mostly we learned Freud, Jung, Harry Stack Sullivan, and a system called non-directive counseling developed by Carl Rogers.

The hospital gave us lists of patients to call on. We practiced the new skills we were learning with the patients. We made verbatim notes of each bedside conversation. We were to listen with what Dr. Leslie called our third ear, to hear the meaning behind the words, and respond to those meanings. We gave our notes of these bedside conversations to Dr. Leslie so he could see if we were learning non-directive therapy. I learned, yet I came away with questions.

For instance, people in a hospital are usually worried and fearful. Often, it seemed to me, when a person is hospitalized there is a spiritual crisis going on. Patients have questions about the goodness of God. They ask themselves, where is God? Does He care about me? My Mom used to think she got sick because she had committed some sin and was being punished by God. Dr. Leslie, however, taught us to wait and see if the patient wanted to go to this level of deep conversation.

I found that as a young pastor with numerous responsibilities, time became a critical factor. Non-directive therapy takes time. I didn't have an indefinite amount of time. So I began to use my awareness of the human condition and apply it to the patient, or to one of my members out at Pt. Richmond. I brought God into the conversation to see if they wanted to go there. Most did.

Somewhere I read a quote from Jung that adults don't really get well until they come to terms with God. I found that to be true. There is a God-dimension in dealing with people who are ill, and sometimes it is up to the pastor to take the conversation to that level and explore it with them, if they are willing to go there. Thus I ended by moving beyond non-directive therapy.

In my ministry I found that calling on members was my favorite thing to do. I was not yet effective, however, in becoming the business manager of the congregation, or in my preaching. I failed to insure that apportionments were paid, and I found the consequences were swift. My minister's pension fund was debited by that amount. That result pushed me to resolve to lead in fund raising so that did not happen again. Thus, I had to become a business manager.

Preaching was a different matter. With the help of Dr. George Buttrick, our guest professor of Homiletics, I learned how to create sermon outlines, and coordinate them with scripture and illustrations to help the sermon drive home my point. But preaching was not my forté. I learned to preach the gospel, but my low self-esteem kept me from being as effective as I could have been.

Why was I so afraid to tell people who I am? I felt so much like the real person God created me to be when I shared with Herb and Rosemary. I did good ministering at Herrick Hospital and at Napa State Hospital. Why not be bold with at least some of the church members, as with those who had a welcoming presence?

The short answer is that I feared rejection. I believed no one could accept me if they knew about my past. Those demons in my mind had a life of their own and died slowly. I felt like the Wizard of Oz as he hid behind a smokescreen of bluffs that kept Dorothy and her three companions from knowing the truth. The truth for me was that God loved me, but could other people do the same? I doubted that others could love me unconditionally. Could I take a calculated risk to find out? At this time I was unwilling to take that risk.

Thus I pretended to be all right when in reality I didn't feel that way. It took me a long time before I realized that many people are great pretenders just like me. How much anxiety I could have been spared if I had known that sooner. Then we could have dropped our pretenses and dialogued together to become real with one another.

I took several classes in 1959, my 4th and last year in seminary, that really spoke to me. One was Personal Devotional Life by Dr. Albert Edward Day. We read devotional selections from the lives of the saints over the past 2000 years. It was amazing to me to discover what depth of humanity the saints possessed, and how they struggled with their own faith in God. We tend to put "saints" on pedestals, and fail to see them as real persons. Now I found how they struggled to find their faith in God. I strengthened my devotional life and maintained it for the rest of my life.

Another class of special interest to me was called Theology of the Lay Mind. Professor Georgia Harkness taught us how to view the Christian faith as laymen see it. The Civil Rights campaign was in full swing across the south. Dr. Martin Luther King and his Southern Christian Leadership Conference faced massive resistance both north and south as they marched to end Jim Crow. Dr. Harkness invited us to read King's new book "Stride Toward Freedom."

Have you ever had an "Ah-ha" experience? Reading his book was an awakener for me. Prior to this I conceived the minister's work to be that of leading the flock into green pastures and helping them cope with the storms of life. Suddenly I realized the meaning of God's justice. It is a full partner in the proclamation of the gospel. We must have justice if we are to have peace. From this point on I had a deep desire to reinforce the concept of God's love with His justice wherever possible. Never before had one book made such an indelible impression on me. I later contributed to Dr. King's cause, and also marched for him. That was a quantum leap forward for me.

The other class I took with an impact on my thinking was a course in New Testament Greek. There were only ten of us in the class. Our texts were a Greek-English lexicon, and a Greek New Testament. The professor taught us the Greek alphabet, and how Greek verbs are declined. I just about dropped out at that point. Pardon me, but it was "all Greek" to me! I couldn't grasp a language with a completely different alphabet. I told Rosemary that I was going to drop the class. It was too difficult. She encouraged me to stay the course, and try again.

What happened next was inexplicable to me. The professor asked us to open to the Gospel of John and begin reading it in the original Greek. It took me an hour or more to translate the first two sentences of John. But I tried again the next day, and the next. Soon I read two more sentences in one half hour, then two more in 15 minutes. At that time a miracle of learning took place. A light came on in my mind. It was a sense of confidence that I could master Greek. With that light I felt a sense of certainty. My awareness enlarged and expanded. I now understood English as never before. Why the light in my mind opened not only to Greek but also to English at the same time was a mystery to me. English in High School was a bore. All grammar and sentence construction. But now, English was my language, and I owned it, as though it was mine to master. English became the means by which my deepest thoughts can be expressed. Our longings and love can be shared through this marvelous thing called language. I could break through the barriers imposed by the self and use language to reach out to others. *Wasn't language God's gift to all of us to help in creating community?* This was the thrill of learning and I decided to become a life-long student.

I read the Gospel of John in Greek and it was as though I was reading the gospel message for the first time. I got a whole new look at Jesus, and a new awareness about Him, his healing miracles, and the drama of his life. Greek was the original language of the gospel and it enabled me to step back into the first century. Now was my time to become a disciple of Jesus.

I could see nuances in the language that our translations often miss, or over-simplify. I can see why there are so many translations of the New Testament. The words and meanings can be translated in so many ways. That class was an epiphany for me.

Things were now coming to a head. On February 15, 1959 the Bishop told me that I was being transferred to a small church west of Fresno called Kerman. We said our farewells to Pt. Richmond, bundled up Suzanne and our few belongings, rented a trailer and drove to Kerman.

In June at Annual Conference in Stockton the Bishop and Elders ordained me an Elder (Minister) of the Church. This time, instead of a ceremony in the chapel at College of the Pacific, we moved downtown to the Civic Center. The heat was oppressive and the crowds immense as we probationary members came on stage to be ordained. Then I was formally appointed to Kerman Methodist Church. Finally I could begin my career.

Twenty

A Full Time Ministry

How wonderful to be driving in the warm sun of the San Joaquin Valley as we headed south toward Fresno! We were now out of the fog zone of the East Bay. We hauled a trailer filled with our few belongings, and sang and talked excitedly about our new appointment to Kerman. Suzanne sat in her baby seat behind us, pointing out all the interesting things to see along the way.

I was 29 years old in the spring of 1959, and finally ready for my first full time appointment as a Methodist minister, the beginning of the rest of my life. It was a time to dream a dream of what I could accomplish as a young minister. Optimism bubbled in my heart and I felt that I was driving to my destiny in Kerman. I even dreamed of becoming bishop some day, elected by the acclamation of my peers in ministry. They would see my leadership qualities and bow to the inevitable. Such a grandiose fantasy was soon washed away in the gauntlet at Kerman.

At Madera we turned southwest off of Highway 99 and took a short cut into Kerman. It was a small town with a typical main street of businesses surrounded by middle class homes, not new, but not old either. Vineyards stretched toward the horizon, along with fields of alfalfa and cotton, starting at the edge of town. Along each road that radiated out from Kerman were farmhouses centered along the roads, or built on the center of their farmland.

Life was different here. American farmers scattered themselves over the land and traveled into town for business and socializing. When I was in Italy, however, the farmers clustered into villages, and surrounded themselves with family and friends. Then in the morning the Italian farmers would travel to their plots of land, do their work, and return home in the evening when their work was done. Their villages provided their community life and their spiritual life, since the churches were at the heart of each community.

Farming in Europe was communal, while here in the U.S. farmers were isolated from the town's people, and from one another. The sense of community was lacking. I didn't know it at that time, but this would affect Kerman's image of the church's purpose. The picture in my mind of the church's mission came out of my classes at PSR and was far different from theirs. There was going to be a collision of understandings.

Kerman was a real test for me, though I didn't know it at the time. I likened it to a gauntlet, with the people of the church on one side, and the District Superintendent on the other. I was alone in the middle.

The people came to church on Sunday mornings to socialize as well as to worship. They closed the gap on their isolation. Their previous minister was a local supply pastor who was folksy and one of their own, but with no seminary training. He left the church to begin ministerial studies. Sunday services were informal. So were the "Jitney dinners" on Wednesday nights where the members brought potluck to share as they talked.

When I arrived I was brimming with ideas for worship right out of Dr. George Hedley's class at PSR. Dr. Hedley taught us that worship was a high and holy time to come before the Lord of the universe and humbly seek His face, and enter into reconciliation with Him. When I entered the pulpit I got out of the way so that the Holy Spirit could enter our midst and renew us. Thus, I knelt behind the pulpit when I prayed. I minimized announcements, and then began to preach.

That style was highly irregular to the congregation. I should have consulted with the leaders before I began that structure, but did not. I was sure that what I was doing was the true form of worship and needed no examination. But underneath the outward form of worship I was nervous about being the shepherd of the sheep. It was a solemn responsibility and I wondered if I was ready for such service. Deep inside myself I felt insufficient for the task. To cover my hesitation I fell back on an old habit of mine: acting confident so as to cover my fears. Thus what happened on Sunday mornings were a collision of expectations, and a resultant sense of dissatisfaction in the congregation. They felt that this was not what they wanted on Sunday morning.

Rosemary, Suzanne and I moved into the parsonage, situated next door to the church. It was old, cheaply built, too hot in the summer and cold in the winter. The kitchen floor sagged and creaked when we walked on it, and tilted toward the east. A day room had been added to the back of the parsonage, and must have been built by volunteer labor. Mildew appeared on the walls and windows throughout the year. An old swamp cooler that was ready for burial cooled the house on hot summer days. Everyone knew that the parsonage needed to be replaced, but the Official Board of the church took no action. I did not push for replacement housing because I was so new. Thus, there was impasse on the need for a new parsonage.

The first Official Board meeting was a disaster. Rosemary and I had talked of a dream trip to Denver that summer. It was Rosemary's home and her parents and all her relatives lived in the area. I purchased tickets on the Vista Dome train that ran through the High Sierra and across the desert to the Rocky Mountains, while all the way we could sit in the Vista Dome car and watch unmatched scenery roll by.

I was proud of being able to afford such a trip. The Official Board meeting brought together the leaders of the church. I presented my plan for the trip and requested time off in June. They appeared to be nonchalant in their response, part of the reason being that they wanted to hear of any plans that I had for the church, and not about my vacation.

Unbeknownst to me they also were unhappy with how Sunday services were being conducted. They reluctantly granted vacation time. The non-communication of the real feelings among the Board members was loud enough to be felt by everyone. It was a huge mistake on my part to present my request for vacation time as the first item of business.

The youth group had planned a retreat with their previous pastor before I arrived. We drove in our cars to the Sierras east of Fresno. The youth were cliquish as are teenagers everywhere. They held together in tight circles, and I was hesitant at how to break through to them. In theory I was responsible for the weekend, but I needed their support in order to make things happen. When I gathered them together for discussion and planning most withheld their comments, or were non-committal. Our retreat fell flat.

When we returned to Kerman I began to have doubts about my calling as a minister. Nothing seemed to be going right. I was off to a bad start and I knew it. But I didn't know what to do to begin fresh again. Was the president's wife right that night at PSR when she said I was not ready for ministry? Herb had asked me a probing question in one of our sessions in his office: "Are you sure you want to be a pastor?" At that time I blurted out a forceful "Yes!" But now I wasn't so sure.

Within two months my District Superintendent, Bob Boswell, informed me that the Official Board had sent him a letter and requested that I be assigned to another church. They wanted a new pastor appointed to Kerman. Our Methodist Annual Conference was scheduled for June and they wanted the change to be granted by the Bishop at that conference.

I was devastated at the news. My heart sank. Here I was in my first full time appointment, ready for ordination as an Elder in the Conference, and the congregation rejected my leadership. I felt my inner world collapsing. What a start for a new minister! To add to the stress I had a talk with Rev. Boswell and he informed me that I was not good material for the ministry.

He recommended that I request a leave of absence at Conference. Bad news kept multiplying. I was now running a gauntlet between the church on one side and my District Superintendent on the other. How much more alone could I get? Was I now experiencing the Refiner's fire of which Isaiah had prophesied to Israel? Isaiah proclaimed that God's people would be subjected to a crucible of fire in order to purify them of their sins. It was as if I was in that crucible now. (Isa. 48:10)

Another incident that spring highlighted the broken relationship between the District Superintendent (DS) and myself. He called for a district meeting of our Fresno District pastors to be held in Porterville at the local Methodist Church. I was several minutes late getting there, and arrived without lunch. I stopped and bought a candy bar and took a bite as I entered the sanctuary and sat down at the rear in the last pew. The DS saw me encumbered with a candy bar and suddenly opened the meeting and asked me in a loud voice to open the meeting with prayer. Can I paint a more graphic picture? Bob magnified every stupid mistake I made.

During the meeting Bob called for reports on new church construction going on in our district. Bob's image of a dynamic pastor was that of a money-manager who could build larger churches (and parsonages), serve a growing congregation, and build the Kingdom of God one church at a time. We were to be administrators, fund-raisers, and businessmen as we preached the gospel.

The image in my mind of pastoral leadership was far to the opposite pole. I believed my calling was to be a shepherd of the sheep by offering the good news of Christ, and add converts to the congregation. Bob and I differed on every aspect of ministry. And of course, Bob called on me for my report. I had no report. The Kerman church had a flat tire, and a pastor on his way out. I thought I retrieved the situation by reporting that we had put in new curbs and gutters around the church that spring. The assembled older ministers chuckled at that news. Humiliated, I sat down.

When I returned to Kerman I was depressed. I came to Kerman pretending to have a grasp on leadership. My attempts to lead failed again and again. I had a long talk with Rosemary. I poured out my heart to her. She was the one person I could lean on in a situation like this.

She then shared with me how lonely she was as a pastor's wife. Pregnant with Stephen she was in the depths of depression. There were no young mothers of her age in the congregation. She desperately needed some young mothers to talk to. We poured out our combined sorrows to each other. In deep need we prayed together.

Some time later I made one of the most important decisions of my career.

T.S. Eliot's line came to mind: "The world will not end with a bang, but with a whimper."

Was I going to allow my years of preparation for ministry to end with a whimper? Was I going to quit without a fight? No way! I could sure do an about face and start over again.

I picked up the telephone and dialed our resident bishop, Bishop Tippett, at his home in Berkeley. When he picked up the phone and answered, my whole future was on the line. I told him who I was and requested a consultation with him. He agreed, and we set a mutually convenient date for me to drive to his home.

When I drove to my date with destiny, comfort was elusive. I shifted in my driver's seat as I thought of what I needed to say to the bishop. *Would he listen to me? Would he be judgmental of me? Would I be chastised?* I felt certain that Bob Boswell had reported to the bishop what was happening at Kerman. But, I put my hesitation aside. This was my last chance to redeem my calling as a pastor.

The Bishop invited me to sit down in the spacious front room of his beautiful home. We sat so that both of us could see out a large window overlooking San Francisco Bay. The Bay waters were calm that day, unlike the storm that I felt inside. Mrs. Tippet served us coffee and invited me to feel at home. I got to the point quickly. This was not a mere social call, but a time to plead my case before the leader of our California-Nevada Annual Conference. Bishop Tippett was responsible for hundreds of Methodist pastors who served churches all the way to the Oregon border, as far south as Tehachapi, and eastward to Elko, Nevada. Seven or eight DS served under him to supervise pastors at the local level.

My mea culpa (acknowledgement of my errors) came first. I owned my part in the mistakes I had made. They were serious errors in judgment, and I took full responsibility for them. Then, I placed before the Bishop a request. If he would reappoint me to Kerman I was prepared to change my attitude, change my approach to worship, and work more closely with the Official Board to help move the church forward. Bishop Tippett graciously accepted my offer with the clear understanding of the changes I would make. I think I must have been there for at least an hour, but the time went swiftly as we shared such important issues. At the conclusion Bishop Tippett offered to close with a prayer that God would bless both the Kerman church and me as we sought God's will in the coming year. As I drove back to Kerman I was exultant. I felt like the man that I had always longed to be: strong, responsible, and committed. I had taken charge of my life by going to the Bishop and I felt good, and clear inside myself that I had done the right thing. I knew I would change my attitude and learn how to work with this congregation, person to person. I sang songs all the way home as I had done after my conversion experience at Davis. I could hardly wait to share with Rosemary all that had happened. I took her out to dinner that night to celebrate our new beginning.

At Annual Conference in June the bishop re-appointed me to Kerman. At the closing Sunday service at the Civic Center, on a blazing hot afternoon in Stockton, the bishop and elders laid hands on our group of candidates, and ordained us Elders of the church. They voted to grant us full membership in the Conference. The massed choir sang "The Battle Hymn of the Republic." I had goose bumps up and down my entire body. God was present that afternoon and He called me to be His servant. I was ready to go forth to the challenge. The bishop also appointed me to a board called, Board of Ministry, but I will speak more about that later.

The Kerman Board wasn't happy with the bishop's decision. But I had made a commitment to begin again with a fresh attitude. The church sensed my changed approach without my having to say a word about it. I began by teaching myself how to administer a church. I bought a large three ring binder and with tabs, divided it into sections for activities in the congregation for which I was responsible: Finances, Evangelism, Christian Education, Official Board, etc. I made a decision to make five pastoral visits daily, and keep records of those on whom I called. I bought a large accordion envelope where I could file 3X5 cards with information on each family.

I could no longer be philosophical about dues to the conference, which were called "Apportionments." I made sure that our church treasurer paid our apportionment to headquarters in San Francisco on time. I began work with the Chairman of the Finance Committee to plan for what Methodists call an "Every Member Canvass," to seek tithes and pledges from the congregation. I finally learned how to be the CEO, the function I had to master if I was to be their pastor. I didn't like it, but I did it out of necessity.

Our budget for the year was all of $7,000! My salary was $4400 and was the biggest part of the budget. Rosemary and I barely subsisted on that salary, but we were in no position to ask for more. Many months we only survived economically when Mom generously sent me a $10 bill from her meager Social Security check. It looked miniscule, but it carried us over to the next payday. Mom was still watching out for me.

I registered for a speed-reading class at Fresno City College. The professor showed us numerous skills to increase both our comprehension and speed. Step one was to broaden our vocabulary. I made a decision to read a book per week. I shopped at a bookstore in Fresno and at the College. Reading books was always one of my hobbies. Now I read faster and better. Along with speed-reading I also kept doing exercises to strengthen my diction. I took phrases like "She sells seashells by the seashore," and repeated them as quickly as possible. Sometimes I practiced as I drove our 1952 Dodge sedan. Suzanne giggled when I practiced with her.

Rosemary and I took Mondays off. Since Suzanne was not in school she got to be a part of our Mondays too. We were as poor as the proverbial church mouse, but we could afford to drive to Roeding Park in Fresno, walk through the park, and then visit the geese. One day Suzanne got too close to a flock of geese, and one goose charged and quacked at her. She ran screaming into our arms.

We took picnic lunches with us. We were too poor to buy a lunch. Actually, I don't know if the federal government had established a poverty income, but if they had I am confident that my salary of $4400/year placed us at poverty level. Yet we adapted wherever we could and kept our heads above water.

We loved Mondays together and had wonderful times doing the simple things of life. I took on the task of cooking breakfast for us. Suzanne tried to help by bringing her cup and plate to the table while I fried bacon. We took trips to parks, drives into the Sierras, and fished along local rivers. We were poor, but we did not let that fact depress us.

A paradox emerged. Though we could barely meet our bills, Rosemary and I grew in our love for one another. The closer we grew in our relationship and our caring for one another, the deeper was our fellowship with our Lord. Our struggle to survive caused us to pull together in order to stay afloat. I likened it to the Cross, where in the central act of God's offer of redemption, Christ turned evil into good. Thus, our poverty became a blessing. But please don't tell our deacons that, lest they use such information as an excuse to continue paying minimum wages! However, I did have to terminate my Army life insurance policy, purchased when I separated from the Army in 1954. I could not keep up with the low premiums, and that troubled me. It reminded me that we were one step away from poverty.

Another thing I did was to learn politics and good will with the Official Board. I started stroking the ego of the chairman of the Board. I gave him recognition in front of the other members. I thought that he and some of the other members wanted to be big fish in a little pond. So I recognized them as "big fish." They warmed right up. I kept it up for the rest of my service in Kerman. Who would have believed that ego building could play such an important role in the church? But, that is part of the contradiction of the local church. I ministered to saints and sinners in the church. We had our share of Philistines and Pharisees out in the pews. Some of them were difficult to love unconditionally, but I did the best I could.

Another decision followed while I attended Annual Conference. I met a young pastor named Fred Wilken, who served a Methodist Church in Fresno. He and I bonded quickly. He told me where the local YMCA was located, and I started going there for exercise, and an occasional massage. He also told me that he was beginning a group counseling session for young pastors in the Fresno area. He asked a local psychologist who taught at Fresno State College, Dr. Stan Lindquist, to come to his church every Tuesday morning at 6:00 am and meet with us. I accepted Fred's offer and started attending right away.

Stan appeared to be in his late 40's, tall and dignified, but not a stuffed shirt. He came across as a real person. He was a WWII vet, and had one glass eye as a result of a war wound. He was wounded in the Battle of the Hurtgen Forest in Germany, in the fall of 1944.

With our approval Stan decided to administer the Minnesota Multiphasic Personality Inventory, or MMPI. It consisted of 530 questions and took several hours to complete. I could tell that the questions were so constructed that a client could not "game" his answers so as to get a desired result. I found out that the Department of Defense, the CIA, and the Federal Aviation Administration, used the MMPI to clear new employees.

Now it was our turn. I did it willingly because of the promise I had made to our bishop to program in a new attitude. I was finding out that my conversion experience at UC Davis was not a conclusion of my spiritual search, but was truly a beginning. Now I was taking my life to the next level.

At our breakfast meeting Stan handed out ten slips of paper to each of the ten young pastors in attendance. Each slip of paper gave an assessment of one aspect of our personality that needed our attention. We read the slips carefully, for each contained a potential personality problem.

One slip reported to me that I tried to do too much, and consequently the tasks that I completed suffered as a result. Another slip of paper told me that I did not pay enough attention to social mores and expectations, and thus I did not always fit in well with others. I swallowed hard, for none of this was easy for me or for the others.

We became a fellowship of believers. All of us were serving local churches and found ourselves struggling with the expectations and frustrations of those churches. To a casual observer a church looks like a haven from the crushing blows of life. The church can be a first aid station for those with spiritual wounds. But it is also a place where there are Christians who like to have power and control, and show the pastor how to direct the life of the church. I found out that my fellow pastors had experienced the same frustrations as me. We bonded in our common struggle. We made a commitment that "what was shared in group stayed in group." Privacy was a primal need in order to foster openness.

Stan invited us to talk openly about what the slips of paper meant to us. I had been aware that I tried to do too much. That much was not new. But what I now learned was that the over-scheduling in my personal life as well as my ministry kept me from being more effective, and some of my projects suffered as a result.

Picture a juggler with a cluster of balls flying constantly from one hand to the other. I was that juggler. Those balls represented my various commitments: personal devotions, Sunday school, finances, evangelism, and family. However, in my case I was juggling one ball too many, and it would fall to the ground.

That information caused me to consider how I could be more deliberate in the tasks I chose. I found it very hard to change. I would slow down one day only to speed up the next day. I learned Heraclitus' dictum: change was the only constant. But when it came to changing myself, progress came slowly.

Watching and listening to the other guys, I found that they struggled too. That was the beauty of our group sessions. We struggled together and learned together. I found that most of the problems that I encountered were of my own making. I was my own enemy. What a revelation! I was shocked to learn how many of the pastors had given serious consideration to leaving the ministry, either for themselves, or for their unhappy wives. I found that Monday mornings I awakened and wondered if I had accomplished anything useful in the Sunday sermon.

Even though many people thanked me for my sermons, I didn't see any change taking place in the congregation. Monday mornings I evaluated myself. I questioned my effectiveness as a preacher. Some Monday mornings I considered quitting the ministry. The other young pastors reported that Mondays were the worst day of the week for them also. They too considered leaving the ministry.

The antidote for me was to go to our rickety kitchen and make breakfast for us. I poured Suzanne's plastic drinking cup with orange juice and she would bang it on the table and gleefully cry out, "Duce! Duce!" After breakfast, our family talked about what we could do together that day. Slowly, Monday mornings became our family time. Rosemary, Suzanne and I created a bond to carry us through the day. I was blessed with a loving family, and that brought me out of any discouragement that I felt.

Stan guided us each Tuesday morning. We confronted ourselves and one another, using what we learned in our feedback slips. We were invited to be candid as we shared our frustrations with the local churches that we served, and equally candid about ourselves. When I felt a lack of confidence in leading the Kerman church, I was learning to face it openly and find ways to be more honest with the members.

Another feedback slip showed me that I needed to be more regular as a person and as a pastor. I needed to be more personable with the people. I stopped kneeling behind the pulpit to pray. I gave careful time to presenting announcements to the congregation. I crafted my sermons to be more direct and Bible based.

At our Jitney dinners on Wednesday nights I began circulating among the tables so I could discuss local events with the people. I invited the young people from the United Brethren Church to join our youth for Sunday night dialogues on questions of faith. We took time for fun and singing also. I liked the young pastor there, Bob Keller. I sought his friendship, and Rosemary reached out to his wife. We tried to get together with them for coffee, but our efforts were seldom successful. Slowly we came to realize that our esteem for them was not returned to us.

Loneliness in the midst of an active schedule is part of the pastor's life. Finding a couple or a pastor with whom we could talk was a deeply felt need. We learned at PSR that getting confidential with laymen in the church could easily backfire. So we sought friendship outside the congregation. The Tuesday morning breakfast meetings helped meet the need for friendship, at least for me. Rosemary found a young mother in the neighborhood with whom she could relate.

Being more regular and aware of social expectations had other implications for me. Sometimes in social settings I felt like odd man out. Thus, I was often out of touch where others were coming from. Stan invited me to be aware of that and get into the other person's point of view.

During the spring of 1959 I got an invitation from the Conference Camping Committee to direct a Junior High Camp at Lake Sequoia. Called Camp Redwood, it was located on the boundary with Sequoia National Park. I assembled a staff of Fresno district pastors, a Sunday school superintendent, Mona Dyer, and a young man named Jerry Baba. Jerry and I were to become life-long friends. I asked all of them to come to our campground two days early so we could prepare ourselves to lead Junior High young people into a deeper understanding of themselves, our world, and God's will. There were 75 campers, all from local churches in our conference. I continued this for two summers.

What I liked best was leading them in singing around a campfire each night. I also had a group of seven that I took out into the woods after breakfast and morning worship. We found a comfortable spot to sit, gathered in a circle, and talked about our stewardship of the natural world. That conversation led ultimately to the nature of God who gave us all of this. "How can we come to know Him better? How can we be better stewards of His creation?" I asked. We got closer to each other as we sought God's will. This was a deeply satisfying experience for me. It was what I trained for.

A week later it was time to leave. We gathered into a huge circle where we held hands and sang, "Blest Be the Tie That Binds." Spontaneous prayers were offered to God, and then the kids formed into small clusters where they hugged one another and wept openly for the friends they were leaving behind. Seeing the young people so emotional and tender brought out deep feelings within me of love for them. I said to as many as I could, "I love you and hope we will meet again." They responded in kind. I found it hard to say goodbye.

That fall I got a letter from the bishop's office to come to San Francisco headquarters for a Board of Ordained Ministry meeting. Now I was going to find out what my assignment involved. I bought a round trip ticket in Fresno on Howard Hughes' airline. Because his planes were painted yellow I called them "Flying Bananas." During the flight one of the hostesses gave out free sample packets of Marlboro cigarettes. Only later did I learn that the handsome Marlboro man died of cancer. I said to the stewardess, "Thanks but no thanks. I don't want any." I was glad that in the Trinity Alps I threw away my Bull Durham, and any further flirtation with cigarettes.

At headquarters I met with a dozen pastors who had the same assignment. We were called, "The Joint Review Committee." Complaints lodged against pastors were referred to our committee. Recall that before ordination each candidate took vows to do nothing that would embarrass or bring disrespect on the ministry. Now we had letters that brought serious charges against certain pastors. Noted in each letter were accusations of how the pastor in question had broken his vows in very specific ways.

Our procedure was to read the letter and make sure the charges carried validity and warranted our attention. The bishop's secretary had already called each accused pastor, and told him that charges had been filed against him. He was told to come to headquarters and tell his side of the story. We gave him 30 minutes for that. Then we called in the person bringing charges. We gave him 30 minutes to present his complaint. After both were ushered out of the room, we began deliberations.

Depending on the seriousness of the charge we could choose from any number of options given to us by "The Book of Discipline of the

Methodist Church." If the charge involved inappropriate relations between the church secretary or some other woman and the pastor, and it appeared to be a once-only situation, we often recommended that the pastor be assigned to another church. If the failure involved chronic unpaid personal debts, we could recommend counseling. If the pastor was charged with serious defects in his pastoral leadership, we could recommend that he be given a leave of absence, sent for counseling, and not return to the pulpit until we were satisfied that he resolved his problems. Sometimes we recommended that the pastor in question surrender his ordination. We sent our recommendations in writing to the bishop and he gave the final ruling on the matter.

I often wondered who recommended me to a committee like this. If I was supposed to learn lessons about ministry, I was learning them quickly. I saw for the first time that pastors were subject to all the frailties of human nature. They (we) were subject to sins of the spirit and sins of the flesh like everyone else. I felt a strong sense that I needed to be disciplined in my calling, and faithful to my Lord.

When I took Dr. Day's course in the Spiritual Life at PSR he urged us to make every day "an affair with God." Now I saw the necessity for that more than before. It was painful to see how quickly a pastor could fall from grace and bring ill repute on himself and his ministry. Could it happen to me? My answer was yes. I was so human and still under construction.

Christmas was coming and Rosemary was pregnant again. She was close to delivery time, but still our Christmas shopping had to be done. We left Suzanne with a baby sitter while we went to JC Penney in Fresno. As we walked up the stairs to the second floor, Rosemary stopped and doubled over in pain. Both of us had taken a class on natal care and knew what that sudden pain meant. Slowly, I walked her out to our Dodge and sat her on the back seat where she could stretch out. She cried out in pain as I drove her to the local hospital where she had received pre-natal care. The nurses quickly took over and rushed her to a room. Early the next morning, December 12, 1959, Stephen Eugene was born.

Exhausted, I drove back to Kerman alone, and began preparation of a sermon based on the book of Isaiah (Isaiah 42:14). Isaiah spoke of God crying out in anguish over the condition of His people. Just as a woman does in childbirth, so God cried out for us. I had heard that cry from Rosemary, and it made an indelible impression on my senses. Now I saw that God had that kind of sorrow over us, His lost and rebellious people. My message was that all humans cry out to God when we are in trouble. Deep calls unto deep. God responds with a cry of love for us.

In January I went to Bob Keller and proposed to him that we invite "The Bishop's Players," a Christian drama group from Santa Barbara, to come to Kerman and perform Alan Paton's "Cry, The Beloved Country." We agreed to that and invited other pastors to join us. We sold tickets for $5.00 each, and were able to fill the auditorium of the Kerman Elementary School.

I worked hard to sell my quota of tickets. I had seen the Players perform at Annual Conference and I was impressed with their acting. I had already experienced the power of drama from college days and knew it would change lives in Kerman.

On February 13, 1960, we were ready with a full house at the school. The Players darkened the stage and opened the drama. What followed was sensational. Laid out before us was the ugliness of racism in South Africa. Yet Paton was balanced in his approach to racism. He looked at the collision between black and white in South Africa from both sides.

Arthur Jarvis, his son murdered by a Black native, represented the white point-of-view. The role of Absalom Kumalo and his sister Gertrude, a prostitute, clearly revealed the disintegration of Black tribal culture and the evil that it brought. All sides were deeply wounded by the sin of racism. The narrator's voice carried like a bugle across the audience.

Our audience was transfixed by the drama. We felt compassion for those caught up in such a system. Their wounds were ours, if only for an evening. When the curtain closed the audience stood and gave the Players a standing ovation. I had never before seen such a demonstration of passionate emotions like this in Kerman. What a night to remember!

I felt ever so strongly that taking time to bring that play to Kerman was the highlight of my service there.

I got a call from someone in the Fresno County courthouse asking for my help. The county morgue had responsibility for indigents who died in the countryside, or on the city streets. The clerk asked if I would be a chaplain for the dead indigents, and provide a decent funeral service for them. He offered to pay me $15.00 for each service. I was desperate to supplement my cash flow, but I also felt compassion for men who died a derelict's death, and had no one who cared for them. I agreed to come to the morgue as often as he called me, and conduct a simple funeral service for what he called "John Doe."

The morning for my first service I parked in the morgue's lot, and proceeded to the chapel. I carried with me the "Ritual of the United Methodist Church," a manual containing every conceivable service that a minister could conduct. A technician wheeled into the small chapel a simple pine box mounted on a gurney. On top were the words, "John Doe." I was left alone to do my duty.

It was eerie to provide a service for someone known only to God. Every part of me questioned this experience. I began a soliloquy with the corpse in the pine box.

> *Who are you? Were you a derelict? A drunkard? A drug addict? What kind of life did you live? Did anyone love you or care for you? Was anyone there to hold your hand as you died? What a terrible way to die. There were no friends to weep at your funeral.*

I knew he would be buried in a potter's field on the edge of town, with an "Unknown" to mark the spot. That must be the worst kind of death.

The Pharisees in my congregation were certain that a derelict like this was a sure candidate for hell. But when I read my New Testament I noticed that Jesus kept company with winebibbers, gluttons, and tax collectors. That was the shocking scandal of the Kingdom of God.

I opened my Ritual to "The Order for the Burial of the Dead," and read selected scripture readings of Jesus as He promised a resurrection to His followers in their death. John Wesley, the founder of Methodism, designed this service for the funeral of church members. Now I was using it for someone who was alienated from the church. *Was this unknown pauper ready for a meeting with God?* I wondered. Yet I believed the Lord was ready for him. I was facing another of faith's contradictions; offering a resurrection prayer for one whom society had cast away. I closed with a prayer for the soul of the departed, and read the 23rd Psalm. I reached out to touch his pine box, and left. I thought, *There, but for the grace of God go I.*

In the spring Rosemary, Suzanne and I decided that Suzanne was ready for baptism. I wanted to baptize her myself, but we decided to invite our DS, Bob Boswell, to come and perform the service. Our thinking was that I had created another breach with Bob by going over his head in order to speak to the bishop. In doing so I had violated the "chain of command." I knew it and he knew it, and it left another wound in our relationship. So we asked Bob if he would come to our church and perform this service with high hopes that we could get off to a better start.

He came all right, but nothing had changed. Rosemary dressed Suzanne in a pretty new dress, and a jacket that she made for the occasion. During the service I presented her to Bob and he baptized her by sprinkling, our usual Methodist procedure. Rosemary and I were both so proud and blessed with Suzanne.

Now we stood even taller as we walked with her out to the patio after the service. Bob and I sat in lounge chairs while Suzanne played and Rosemary prepared treats for us. My practice with Suzanne was to give her permission to play freely and to say "Yes" to her as often as I could. Bob took that as a symptom of laxity on my part. In his view I did not exercise enough discipline with her. He believed that I should put more limits on her behavior. We were at cross-purposes again. I don't think we ever really communicated.

Finding ways to connect with this rural congregation was an ongoing issue. I had been trained in the teachings of world famous theologians. Names like Reinhold Niebuhr, Paul Tillich, Emil Brunner, Dietrich Bonhoeffer were familiar to me, along with the works of mainstream biblical scholars from around the world. I read volumes of sermons by

Harry Emerson Fosdick. Yet their theology did not resonate with these people. Week after week I struggled to craft relevant sermons, but my thralldom to those theologians and scholars got in the way.

Slowly, by a process of self-criticism and evaluation, I had to learn to go to scripture and lay it open so the people could understand it. With that in the forefront of my thinking, I then learned to lean on the theologians as a backup. It was not an easy process. I tried again and again to preach like Dr. Fosdick and found that I could not do it. Only with hesitation did I learn to trust my own instincts and let the scripture speak to me.

Like a diamond cutter in Amsterdam, if he hit a raw diamond in the right place with his hammer, it fell open into its natural parts. So too, if I slept with the scripture verse and meditated on it, eventually it fell open into a sermon. When that finally happened, I wrote like a man possessed until it was completed.

I bought a small pocket three-ring binder and carried it everywhere. Walking, shopping, or driving, if a scripture verse spoke to me out of my morning devotions, I stopped where I was and wrote it down in my notebook. Soon I accumulated several notebooks full of such sermon "seeds," a few of which later became sermons. I never reached the heights of preaching to which I aspired, but could present an acceptable message. Preaching was not my forté.

June was approaching, and it was time to consider appointments by the bishop. We had a new Chairman of the Official Board, and I believe his name was Bill Sebastian. I had already learned the art of ego stroking with him, giving recognition and complements for work well done. But still it came as a pleasant surprise when Bill told me that he had written to the bishop and requested my return appointment at Annual Conference in June. Wow! I had made good with my promise to the bishop of a change of attitude along with a fresh start. Later, Bill was elected Mayor of Kerman, and I started calling him "Mr. Mayor." I had a deep sense of relief that I had accomplished my goals.

I turned to pastoral visitation. I called on all 150 members in their homes. About 35 to 50 attended on a given Sunday. Dr. Buttrick, in his class on preaching, urged us to try for five calls a day. I made that my goal. Calling in their homes was a pleasure to me. I enjoyed that more than preaching. In their homes is where a pastor can learn to fine-tune his sermons as he listens to what is happening in the lives of his people.

Wayne and June Gentry were my favorites to call on. We liked each other. But we were warned at seminary never to show favorites in the congregation. We were asked to treat everyone equally. So when Wayne and I got together it was always in private. That is part of the burden of the ministry. I needed friendship as do other human beings, but I had to proceed with caution.

Another issue in pastoral calling was what I called, "The Affluence Differential." When I saw how well most of the members lived, and the newer cars they were driving, I felt a pang that Rosemary and I were reduced to poverty. I knew the ministry was not a calling to get rich, but neither should I have to live in such a shabby parsonage, barely able to pay my bills. Something was wrong.

We younger pastors in our Tuesday group talked about it, but found few answers. The older pastors had bigger, more affluent churches, and good salaries. Added to that, their kids were grown up and gone, while we were just beginning our families. It is a situation that still troubles many pastors and their congregations. The answer for young pastors was to seek a better appointment to a more affluent church. But that was a denial of our decision to serve where God called us. This was another conundrum confronting ministers.

Later, Rosemary and I agreed that I had done what I could at Kerman, and that it was time to ask for a new appointment. In the spring of 1961 I wrote a letter to the DS with a copy to the Bishop explaining our wishes. I went to Annual Conference in June in great expectancy, not knowing what the bishop and his cabinet of DS would decide. Midweek of conference I was told by Bob Boswell of my new appointment. He assigned us to Lamont, just outside Bakersfield. We began to pack. It was time to say farewell to Kerman.

Twenty-One

Rip Tides and Cross Currents

The call to ministry is intoxicating. It is like a multi-faceted diamond glinting in the sunlight, or a Holy Grail on the altar that draws you into Christ's service. You know in your heart that it is life's highest calling. *Where else can a person have more opportunities to impact their world than here? Where else are there such opportunities to make a difference in the lives of people?* Herb told me, "The pastor is the most important person in the community." I was now driving to my second full-time ministry. I was excited and ready to begin.

Lamont was different from Kerman. Kerman was a middle class farming community. Lamont on the other hand, was a mix of Anglo farmers along with a large contingent of Mexican farm laborers, plus refugees from the Dust Bowl of Oklahoma. The city was larger than Kerman because of that mix, but the churches were about the same size.

The ministry puts your personal faith in God to the test on a regular basis. Are you ready to accept the cross as part of your service? Are you ready to see few results from your earnest sowing of seeds? Sometimes what you get are thistles instead of wheat. Are you prepared to have your plans blocked by those in power? Are you willing to live on the edge of poverty? These are some of the realities of ministry that are not taught in seminary, but are part of the service to smaller, rural churches.

You also soon learn that the Official Board is the nerve center of the local church. All decisions that affect the local church are made at the Board. At its best the Board processes all the activities of the church, from finances, to education, evangelism, worship and hopefully the spiritual life. But the development of the spiritual life of the congregation often takes last place in their concerns. The "Discipline of the Methodist Church" makes it quite clear that the pastor is in charge, but the reality can be different. Though it is not stated anywhere, the Board can become a power forum where visions clash and egos collide. That is where some of the bruises begin for the pastor.

At Lamont the Chairman of the Board was Ralph, an old cotton farmer. He had been chairman forever, even though the Discipline called for regular elections to rotate leadership. He had worked his way into farming, beginning as a "roughneck" in the oil fields of Kern County. He was crusty, tough, and liked things his way. The members of the Board were afraid of him, or of opposing him, so they kept voting him in as chairman. His vision for the Lamont church was to keep all our spending local. My work as pastor was to minister to the people of Lamont, but always under the guidance of programs from the Conference Headquarters in San Francisco. The Chairman and I clashed immediately. His vision, and my calling, were like two trains on the same track headed toward each other. There was trouble ahead.

When the Conference asked me to begin a new program I would take it to the Board for their consideration. Their response was Ralph's. If it didn't have a genesis in Lamont, or use Lamont thinking, Ralph said, "Vote it down, and keep our focus on Lamont." I ran into frustration bringing Conference items to the table, only to find that each time I did so those items were summarily cast aside. I was consistently outvoted. I went home after Board meetings feeling blocked, frustrated, and unable to move the church into Methodist programs. They did, however, support the bare bones requirements of Apportionments. Those payments enabled the church to stay in touch with the Conference and secure the appointment of young pastors.

The pastor is in an anomalous position. He is in charge of the local church, but the Board has the option to outvote him, especially if he is new or not trusted. Consequently, there is formal power meeting informal power, and it can be a fascinating dance.

Money was always an issue. It is not supposed to be that way for a minister. He more than other mortals should be able to rise above such mundane details. But, truth be told, you have to provide for your family like every other man. You have to provide transportation, housing, gas and insurance. At poverty level you need to learn survival skills, and then lean on the grace of God to see you through.

Lamont is like a prune on a branch laden with plump, ripe plums. That is not a criticism. Lamont simply lacks beauty. It is a functional town, serving a farm community. There are no stately churches, no fine public buildings, and no plaza that invites citizens to come and reason together. There is no higher vision of what a community can become where it seeks to help people be the best they can be. Lamont is a utilitarian place that serves white farmers, and tolerates the Mexican-Americans who plant and harvest their crops. Lamont also made allowance for the sons of Oklahoma who fled the Dust Bowl and ended their odyssey in Lamont. The business of Lamont is business.

Ralph Crawford, the pastor of Lamont was moving out, as we were moving in. A veteran of serving small churches, he had seen them at their worst and at their best. His parting words to me were, "Dick, I want to challenge you to read a book that will tell you what you need to know about Lamont. It was written by John Steinbeck and is called "The Grapes of Wrath." Read it."

I took his advice and as soon as we were moved into our parsonage I bought the book through a mail order catalogue. Its message rocked me off my safe perch as a preacher of the gospel. Steinbeck wrote parts of the book while in Lamont, and at the Weedpatch Farm Labor Camp. That only added to the power of his words. My feelings as I read the book were like riding an elevator in the Empire State Building. I could go from the ground floor to the 100th floor in minutes, and then down again. I alternated between tears, laughter, anger and sadness. This was a book for the ages.

What an introduction to Lamont! No wonder that when I tried to talk about it to locals the response was predictable, "That book is a lie. Don't believe a word of it. In fact, burn it." Some others retorted, "Steinbeck is a damned commie." Many folks summed it up with, "Don't read it." "The Grapes of Wrath" was banned in Salinas, Steinbeck's hometown. Steinbeck was unwanted in his birthplace.

The city fathers of Bakersfield banned it also. For all practical purposes it was unmentionable in Lamont. Well, I already had read it, and now it was part of my vocabulary. The only problem was, there was no one I could talk to about it. Did Ralph do me a favor by recommending it to me? Not in the short term. In the long haul, however, I always treasure it. I wondered what Bob Boswell's expectations were in sending me here.

There was a flip side to this rude introduction to Lamont. One member of the congregation was an older man named "John." Everyone knew John. He was a gadfly into everything. As in other small towns, he knew the choicest gossip about the pillars of the church, and he knew who were the saints. He had coke-bottle lenses for glasses, a great big kid grin, and a sense of humor honed over his lifetime. His favorite phrase was, "I'm not always asleep when my eyes are closed." He could tell good stories in a funny way.

He introduced himself to me as he walked through the greeting line at the end of my first sermon. "Pastor," he said, "I think I can help you get started in Lamont." I took his invitation and called him and asked for his help finding my way to the homes of our members. There were 150 of them, and many were scattered through the rural countryside. Only 35-50 attended Sunday services. He offered to show me the way to each home. He knew them all.

Day by day we would meet after lunch and he would park his gangly frame into my 1962 Volkswagen "Bug," the best I could afford. I had already decided to make five calls a day. I continued with that practice, only now with John riding shotgun. We developed sweaty shirts in the cab of my Bug. There was no air conditioner in my car, and the valley heat was intense. Our laughter made it easier as we went from farmhouse to farmhouse. John knew how to find them. In his homespun way he introduced me to hardworking farm families, and we invited them to start coming back to church. His introductions paved the way for my ministry to them. Thus, with John's help, I got off to a good start with the congregation.

Lamont was to be my challenge. I was ready to give to the church the best that I had, and continued to improve my skills of ministry. In fact, I was ready to burn the candle at both ends if need be. Lamont's location told something about its character. It is the last church at the southern end of our conference. Consequently, the people felt neglected by Methodism. Over the years Lamont heard what they called, "The Tennessee Waltz" from the Conference: sending pastors to Lamont, and then sending them elsewhere if they proved to be effective. The Official Board made sure that our local church did only the bare minimum to stay connected to the Conference. In fact they didn't really care about the Conference. They only cared about securing pastors when they needed them. Calling it "Community Methodist Church" was a misnomer. The actual title should have been, "Community Church."

Lamont is a fractured community. Without precise numbers at my fingertips, about one third of the people were Anglo farmers, many of whom had pioneered to come here and begin cotton and grape culture at the end of World War I. Another third were Mexican-Americans who worked the fields, and the rest were refugees from the Dust Bowl. Those who fled the Dust Bowl arrived in their tin lizzies and Model A's in the 1930's, and coasted down the last mountain barrier into Bakersfield and Lamont.

Instead of using polite words to describe these strangers from the Dust Bowl, the locals referred to them as "Okies." That was a misleading name because many of them came from other mid-western states and some southern states. It was originally a pejorative word meant to put the newcomers in their place and keep them there. But by the time

I arrived in the summer of 1961 the second generation used it as a general descriptive word for the whole group. So I learned to use the word the same way as did the second generation. I use the term here without malice.

Lamont formed a three-tiered triangle. At the base was the Mexican-American farm workers. They were supposed to be served by the local Catholic Church, but it was my impression that most of them attended no church at all. They were Catholic in name only. The second tier from the bottom was the "Okies." Many of the second generation had now grown up. Those that stayed in Lamont went into business. The rest left town to find greener pastures elsewhere. The top tier was the Anglo pioneer farmers and their children, who were now growing up in Lamont. Some of the children left and moved to the city. Those that remained often went into farming. The Lamont Community Methodist Church was made up of the Anglo farm families, and those that were working in tandem with the farm economy, such as teachers and mechanics.

At the rear of the church were dilapidated cabins populated by Mexican-American farm workers, not a single one of which came to church. None of their children came to our Sunday school. That bothered me. I knew that they had a heritage of Catholicism. But the Catholic Church was not serving them. Also it seemed to me we were not fulfilling our mission to proclaim the gospel to the entire community. Rather, our church reflected the segregation in the community.

Lamont had a small town mentality. Segregation was obvious, but most people chose not to see it. The Mexican-American families took their children into the fields to increase the family take home pay. The law said that they must send their children to school, but many paid no heed to the law. After the work was done the Hispanics were reminded to remain invisible in their side of town. The Okies had their own social network, their own holiness churches, and their own sense of community. They had a unique, peculiar place in town.

Gossip in Lamont was endemic. Privacy was at a minimum. We knew who was in trouble and who was not. When groups remained so isolated from one another, exaggerated stories emerged to fill the gap caused by ignorance. Sometimes young people bragged of throwing rocks or bottles at the cabins of the ethnic poor as they drove through their section of town.

There was another side to this small town mentality. Our family physician was a man named Dr. DeSmet. He cared for our family through all of our health crises for six years. We were so poor we could not pay him for his services. But he spared us any embarrassment regarding his fees. He never charged us for his services. He considered his work a "professional courtesy" to me in my ministry. How could I ever repay him? I owed him my deepest thanks for his sense of professionalism.

Another plus side to Lamont was the fact that we had several second-generation Okie families in our congregation. They were the spearhead of more who were to come and build a place in our church and community. An elderly Okie couple named Smith provided our childcare when we took a trip out of town. They were kind and gentle with our kids, and they never charged us for their services. They were the salt of the earth to us. They also refused welfare payments when they were fully entitled to such checks. They too were part of the mix that was called Lamont.

Many of the church members were kind and helpful to us. There were several saintly couples in the church that everyone respected. Calling on our farm families was my greatest pleasure at the Lamont church. After I had called on all of our families I began calling on the families in shantytown. All I had to do to reach them was walk through the back yard of the church and I stood in front of the nearest cabins.

Usually the lady of the house answered the door. She would be dressed in faded clothes, and as she stood at the door, children eager to catch a glimpse of a gringo pastor surrounded her. They peeked at me from behind her skirt. I reached out my hand to greet them. They sheepishly grinned, and then hesitantly placed their hand in mine. Most were in bare feet. I gave them my best Spanish, though I was limited in how much conversation I could carry. I think my attempt at communication gave them a hint of my friendly intentions.

I was dressed in my parson's best, a cheap seersucker suit purchased at JC Penney for $35. It was what I could afford, and the only suit in my wardrobe. That is how Dr. Hogue suggested we dress when he taught Homiletics at PSR. But, I was meeting families in the barrio who didn't even have a suit. Their homes were bare bones subsistence living, revealing their origins from rural Mexico. We faced a cultural divide as we stood on the doorstep. I knew that these people had a deep respect for pastors and they treated me kindly. But though I worked hard on my Spanish, we could barely communicate. Is it any wonder that they didn't know what to say to this stranger, this gringo in their midst?

Those that invited me in were timid and embarrassed. The lady of the house treated me with considerable deference. She seemed embarrassed wearing such shabby clothes. She did not look me in the eye. Their custom was to offer such a "padre" something to drink. But most had nothing to offer me. However, I had no expectations.

Once inside I was aware that the shanties were always hot in the summer. They had only a simple framework for their cabin, with no insulation, and there were cracks showing in the frame where hot air crept in. Most of the cabins had no air conditioning. In the winter months they had a single electric heater to warm the cabin, and kept it on all day long. The same cracks in the frame now let in the chilly north wind. Hence, they left the heater on.

On a mantle over the heater the lady of the house created a grotto. To the left was a black and white photo of president John F. Kennedy. To the right was a colorful print of the Virgin of Guadalupe. In between them sat a votive candle mounted in a glass jar. So, I surmised, they did not go to church, but they carried their church with them all the way from Mexico for all in the house to see. I was looking at a portable altar. The Virgin is the patron saint of Mexico, and of these farm workers. To her they offered up their prayers. The family also announced their democratic faith with the photo of the president. Mama appeared to be the culture carrier in these poor families, transmitting the cultural values of the older generation to the younger generation.

I closed my visit by inviting all to come to our church. That was not going to happen. With my functional Spanish I asked of each child, "*Como se llama?*" (What is your name?) Each answered in barely a whisper. I asked mama her name, and shook hands with all of them. I was trying to cross a cultural divide and finding that it was like trying to shake hands across the Grand Canyon. "My husband," she explained in broken English, "is out in the fields." Was she asking me to come back when her husband was there? Later, when I came back for another visit, I asked the lady of the house if her children could come to our Sunday school. "We will teach them about Jesus and the Bible," I said. She would smile and respond, *Tal vez*, (Perhaps.) But they never came.

Just south of Lamont was a farm labor camp. Locals told me it was the oldest farm labor camp in Kern County. Built by President Franklin Roosevelt's Farm Security Administration in 1935-36 for the oncoming Okies, it was now populated by Mexican-Americans and Braceros. The units were a simple one-room frame built on a concrete slab, covered with plywood, and painted an atrocious green. There was a foul odor to the place as if too many poor people had lived there for too long a time. There was a commons where all the residents could bathe, wash clothes, and use toilet facilities. Many called it 'The Weedpatch Camp," for the community of Weedpatch was a little further down the road. The name itself suggests the nature of the camp.

I watched as a mother took a large metal washtub, filled it with water, and then put her children into it one at a time and gave them a sponge bath. The children giggled and laughed during this process. As the senora lifted each child out of the tub to dry them, their nude little bodies shimmered in the sun. This scene held a fascination for me, a stranger to this kind of innocence. There was a peculiar beauty about this picture set in the midst of such poverty. This area was to be my ministry for the next six years. Nothing in my training at PSR ever prepared me for a community like this. I needed a mentor to show me the way, but at the south end of the conference and the San Joaquin Valley, I was on my own.

Rosemary and I were eager to fulfill our calling here. Suzanne and Stephen fit right in. As PK's, (Preacher Kids), they were accepted into the community, and pampered by some of our members. Rosemary did yeoman service. She drove Steve to DiGiorgio for childcare. Later, she decided to start a childcare center at our church. It took a year of planning, but eventually we met all the federal, state and local requirements, and opened for business. Faye Gribble, our local school superintendent, suggested that we make it into a Compensatory Education school. So Rosemary and her staff used it as a childcare facility in the morning, and for Compensatory Education in the afternoons. Thus, we began serving not only the Church, but also the larger community.

There was only one pastor in town with whom I could relate. That was Russell, the pastor of the local Lutheran Church. He and I were the same age and of similar theology. But there was a fly in the ointment: we were both trying to reach the same people, the farm families of Lamont. Hence there was some subtle, unspoken competition between us.

All the other pastors in town were what we called "Holiness" pastors. They had no formal ministerial training, and pastored small churches that looked like cracker boxes with a cross perched on top. They reached out to the first and second generation Okies, and preached that if you were not born again of the Holy Spirit you were no Christian in their sight. Most were self-appointed pastors who said they had heard the call of the Lord and responded to Him.

The local pastors had little in common with us, but we did manage to form a group called The Lamont Ministerial Association. We met occasionally and sent letters to the Kern County Fair requesting that they end the sales of beer and alcoholic beverages. The pastors elected me to be president.

However, what it meant was that I took responsibility to give out baskets of food to our resident poor when they came for help. The outflow of baskets was especially heavy at Thanksgiving and Christmas. Later, a group of leading citizens came to me and asked if I would go to the local theater owner and ask that he play only Walt Disney films at his theater.

I refused this specious request. How could he make a profit showing only Disney films? On the surface it looked like parental concern for their kids, but deeper down bore all the marks of censorship, and I did not want to participate in that.

Russell and I were both invited to become members of our Lions Club. In a fascinating way the club subtlety revealed the silent cracks and divisions in the community. Some of the members were Hispanics who had become successful storeowners. Others were second generation Okies who were emerging into the community. The rest were members of the agri-business community. The telltale divisions among them were made evident as the meetings opened. Russell or myself would be asked to pray. Then the group would be seated and the waitresses brought in garden salads. The men would pick out an olive, or a pickle slice, and as they cloaked their action, threw an olive at someone across the room. Pretty soon olives and pickles flew in all directions, followed by great peels of laughter. This lasted until the waitresses brought out the entrée.

On the surface, and to a casual observer, it looked like fun and general horseplay. Perhaps it was. But it seemed to me that there was hostility behind behavior such as this. Rather than face their differences openly and deal with them by frank discussion, they chose to cloak their mistrust under the guise of horseplay. Thus, the fractures in the Lamont community were continually papered over.

I continued to make five pastoral visits each afternoon. These people honored the office of "pastor," and they trusted me to be true to Christ. I may have been blocked at the Official Board meetings, and come home frustrated. But out on call those frustrations melted away. In their homes these people were generous and kind. It was a pleasure to meet them and hear the problems and joys that were theirs.

It's been said among pastors that, "There is a broken heart in every pew." I found it to be true. Sometimes I wondered, *"What is holding this community together?"* St. Paul wrote to the church at Galatia, "Weep with those who weep, rejoice with those who rejoice, and so fulfill the law of Christ." Each family was coping with burdens. Listening and praying with each family, or with the lady of the house, gave me insight on what to preach.

Finally, after all the years of preparation and training, I was finding my stride in the ministry. The Official Board asked me to lead our church's Methodist Youth Fellowship on Sunday nights. I did so with hesitation. A gifted layman should lead the youth, but such were hard to find in Lamont. I took it for a year or two and found their fellowship to be fun. The youth president said to me, "I like you. You listen to what we have to say. My parents don't know how to listen to me." We sang at the homes of shut-ins, and trick or treated on Halloween for UNICEF. We sang Christmas carols throughout the community on Christmas Eve. I loved working with the youth.

I formed a choir. On some Sunday nights I held healing services for those who were sick. I became a member of "The International Order of St. Luke the Physician." A handful of our church members would come and pray with me, and I laid hands on those who requested it. We also began holding retreats at Breckenridge in the nearby mountains. I turned these retreats into times when we could lay plans for the new church year.

I flew to San Francisco to fulfill my appointment to the Board of Ministry. We continued to meet whenever charges were brought against a Methodist minister. There were the usual charges of infidelity, unpaid bills, failed ministries, and a host of issues common to mankind. Sometimes we on the Board would gather and ask, "What next?" "How," I asked, "can preachers fall from grace so quickly?"

Yet, truth be told, I faced temptation on a regular basis. When I called at isolated farmhouses out in the countryside, there was often no one home but the wife. Some wives were quite beautiful, warm and friendly. Usually I could count on a hot cup of coffee and some homemade cookies to help jumpstart the visit. I knew it was lonely for them on their isolated farms, and some of them were having marital problems. I also knew that there were cases of infidelity out in the fields and farms.

There was an interplay of emotions between us, but I never crossed the line to inappropriate behavior. I thank God for that. I listened and prayed with them as with the other farm families. As a pastor I needed to stay focused on Christ. I became less judgmental of my fellow pastors that fell from grace as I reflected on my own temptations.

By 1965 danger signs began to appear. A cloud on the horizon, no bigger than a man's fist, came into view and it signaled a storm approaching. Congress terminated the Bracero program in 1964. That meant the legal, unlimited flow of Mexican farm workers into the U.S. ended. The significance of this change, however, showed later. It gave labor organizers like Larry Itliong, of the Filipino community, a real chance at organizing farm workers into a union. He began a farm labor organization.

In Kern County a man named Caesar Chavez along with Delores Huerta and Larry Itliong formed "The United Farm Workers" in the town of Delano, just north of us. It was September 20, 1965. The small dark cloud on the horizon drew closer and a storm was brewing. The formation of a farm labor union that couldn't be broken by farmers using imported Braceros signaled a big change in the Valley. The cracks in the social pyramid now appeared for all to see.

When I was a teenager I used to go swimming at Huntington Beach on hot summer days. Those were glorious days of fun for us guys. But one day I headed out toward deeper water and suddenly found myself in a rip tide. I had heard of them, but this was my only time to experience one. First I was pulled sharply one way, and just as quickly was then pulled another. Once, I was pulled under. In a moment I knew I was in deep trouble. A pang of fear swept over me. I could not guide myself back to shore. The rip tide out-powered me. I was being swept out to sea. When I saw the shoreline receding I panicked. I swam furiously with no success. There was a feeling of terror, "*This is it. My life is over.*" Somehow, in ways I did not understand, God was with me once again. The rip tide closed in on itself and ended, allowing me to swim to shore. I sensed that now a rip tide was forming in our great valley. Some of us were going to get caught up in it, and swept out to sea. The question begged for an answer, who would that be?

The call went out through the farm fields of the valley, "Huelga!" "Strike." Here and there small bands of farm workers rallied to Chavez' call and walked out of the fields. Farmers up and down the valley soon galvanized into resistance. There were confrontations in the fields. I was soon caught up in the crosscurrents. A part of me was pulled toward sympathy for the farm workers. I had visited their cabins for the previous four years. I knew the degradation of poverty. I knew that a Christmas basket of food was not the answer to their dilemma. What they needed was a living wage, and a union that could bargain for them and provide a decent living.

To find out more for myself, I let my imagination be my guide. Curiosity is part of my nature. I located the place where Mexican farm workers met their labor contractors. I chose a day to join the farm workers for work in the fields. Pick-up was at 5:00 am. I dressed as humbly as I could: old faded jeans and a T-shirt, plus a pair of boots, and of course, a "sombrero." A rickety old bus picked us up on time, driven by the contractor. Clutching my sack lunch we lurched out to a field where a farmer had just turned over the sod in his field to lay open his harvest of ripe yellow onions. The onions lay glistening in the first rays of dawn, like giant beads lying in a row, ready for harvesting.

The contractor shouted at us, "Vamanos, pronto!" (Get going, quickly) He handed each of us a big leather belt and when I buckled it, two ominous, sharp, steel prongs, pointing straight up, appeared. I walked over to where the contractor had a pile of burlap sacks. "Tomelo!" (Take one!) he barked. With a thrusting motion I brought one side of a burlap sack down on the two steel prongs. Now I watched the workers. They knew what to do. First, I learned to bend over, and with both hands, start picking up onions and place them in the gunnysack quickly, and keep moving. There were men, women and children on board. All joined in the harvest.

Soon I found out why the workers call the contractors "coyotes." The coyote charged a fee to drink out of his water tank. He charged for the trip to the fields. He was supposed to provide port-a-pots for our use and did not. Women were forced to find a patch of tall Johnson grass and squat in order to relieve themselves. I also found out why the workers often bring their families with them. They could harvest more and add to the family income. The law said that children must be in school. But the law did not seem to apply out here in the fields.

I wanted to pull my old Monrovia Nursery maneuver and support my back with my left elbow on my left knee. I tried unsuccessfully to keep up with the workers and see how much I could bring in for a day's work. I harvested with my right hand only. My back was screaming by noon. We stopped for lunch and sat in the shade of the coyote's bus. We did not get charged for that. We brought each sack of onions to the coyote and he weighed our production, and wrote it down on his record. I was so thankful that the coyote called a halt to harvesting at 3:30. I could barely stand up straight.

I walked over to the coyote, as did the others, and he tallied my harvest. He paid me $13.00 cash. He drove us back to the pick-up point, calling out: "Adios. Hasta la mañana." (Until tomorrow) There would be no mañana for me. One day was all I could take. But the rest of the farm workers made their living this way. They would be there mañana, for the rest of their lives.

It occurred to me *that we gringos are spoiled. Brown hands, whose labor is sure and whose pay is small, harvest our crops.* They are up against not only the farmers, but also the coyotes that exploit them, and all the power of corporate farms in the valley. When the strikes began they were also up against the police power, for the sheriff sided with the growers. To me it looked like David versus Goliath. I thought these people deserved better. Thus I chose to support Chavez and the United Farm Workers as they now called for a strike.

Is there anyone who cannot see that this valley's lifeblood is agriculture? Because it is the absolute base of the valley economy, it follows that the valley churches are linked to the productivity of the farmers and agri-business. I knew I was on tenuous ground. Farmers are the backbone of our church's budget. If my farmers knew of the empathy I was developing toward farm workers and their new union, there would be a volcanic eruption. But a question lingered in my mind. *Where is the church's ministry to the poor?*

Several times I went to Delano to hear Chavez speak. I was on tiptoe as I listened. He had a soft voice, and those listening might be deceived into thinking that he was a meek leader. The local grape growers certainly underestimated him. They had confronted numerous labor leaders before and won their case, and they were convinced that they would do it again, or so they thought. Chavez had a limp handshake and wore humble farm worker clothing. But look at his eyes. There was something about his piercing look that grabbed my attention. Miriam Pawel in her book, "The Crusades of Cesar Chavez," pointed out that behind the scenes Chavez was a fierce strategist who believed he could win and set out to do it.

Chavez, a Catholic layman, did not quote the Bible, but he certainly could have added weight to his argument if he had. There are numerous times that the Biblical prophets demanded justice for the disinherited of the land. Amos cried out to Israel:

> "Hear this word you cows of Bashan…who oppress the poor, who crush the needy…" And, "You sell the needy for a pair of shoes."(Amos 4:1, 2:6).

Instead, to his supporters in the audience Chavez listed the outrages that workers suffered in the fields. He laid out a plan for what the union could do for the workers, and for California agriculture. The workers responded with great shouts of approval, "Viva la causa! Viva la huelga! Viva Chavez!"

I also went to Delano when Robert Kennedy arrived in the spring of 1966. He was the only politician with the courage to come. He spoke in support of the farm workers. Kennedy, as the U.S. Attorney General, confronted the sheriff, who had sided with the growers, and forced him to admit that he had arrested farm workers on suspicion that they "might" strike. As Attorney General, Kennedy had the power and the courage to confront the sheriff on such activities. The sheriff's policies were a clear violation of the Constitution. The farm workers were thrilled to see someone in power confront the sheriff. Kennedy was the only politician to speak up on behalf of the workers. I felt a deep sense of pride that he had the conscience and the courage to speak up at a time like that.

I was on shaky ground when I went to Delano. The farmers in my congregation hated Chavez and if they knew of my activities, I would be told to pack up and leave town. I supported Chavez out of respect for the man and his movement, and because of my reading of the Biblical prophets. I also read Martin Luther King's "Stride Toward Freedom," and I saw Chavez as a Hispanic Moses leading his people out of poverty in farm labor and into a new sense of dignity. I quietly joined a new group of young pastors who called themselves The Valley Ministers Association. We raised money and forwarded it to the United Farm Workers. I told no one but Rosemary of my activities.

Crosscurrents developed quickly. Our Farm Bureau held agitated meetings. I decided that as pastor I needed to be even handed and give the farmers an equal hearing. Besides, I had been reading Paul's letter to the Corinthians and he called on Christians there to be, "Ministers of reconciliation."(II Cor. 5:18). I felt that was my calling. I wanted to be a reconciler between our farmers and the farm laborers. I attended several Farm Bureau meetings, but the tobacco smoke was so thick I could not cut through it. There was an animus among the farmers against Chavez. There were ominous voices in the Farm Bureau meetings. The chairman said, "We will fight this union. The farm workers union will not dictate wages to us. We are angry and we stand united in opposition." The roar of approval was overwhelming. This was a declaration of war. I decided that reconciliation was out of the question.

I had come to love our farmers of Lamont. I was their pastor, and their confidant. How could I support the union while ministering to the farm families at the same time? I found no easy answer. If I was not careful there would be a riptide and a crosscurrent, leaving me as the casualty who would be swept away. I was dangerously close to losing the balance between ministering to the church versus ministering to the valley.

Other issues emerged at the same time. I spent more time at the church meeting with committees, and working in the community. Our local cemetery, for instance, was for Anglos only. When a Hispanic died the family had to pay to have the body shipped back to Mexico. I decided to right a wrong. With the Ministerial Association giving me verbal support, I went to the Kern County Local Agency Formation Commission and asked them to expand the Arvin Cemetery District to include Lamont. It took a year of meetings, but eventually Lamont put it to a vote. The vote in favor of annexation of Lamont carried, and from that day forward Mexican-Americans could be buried in our local cemetery. I felt it was a signal victory. Politicians have told me, however, that if you do good, no one thanks you. But make a mistake and a multitude will let you know. It was true in this case: Not one word of thanks was given for the year of labor I gave to this issue.

I also spent time with a local gadfly named John King. Together we passed out flyers across Lamont warning everyone of the danger of swimming in the irrigation canals. Several Mexican children drowned each summer in the canals. The number of drowning's dropped when we passed out flyers.

As I spent more time with the church and in the community, I spent less time with my family. I did some mental justification and told myself that I was doing God's work. *"Why slow down?"* I asked myself. Rosemary came to me several times with tears in her eyes telling me that she could not raise the children by herself. "Please help me," she cried out. I held her, and promised to re-arrange my schedule so I could help with the kids. Her tears subsided and I took her out to dinner. But the next day I kept the same busy schedule. I didn't start out my ministry as a workaholic. But I slowly became one.

I did reserve Friday nights and Saturdays as a family time. We watched our favorite television programs, such as "Flipper," "Candid Camera," and "Mission Impossible." I loved to cook breakfast for all of us on Saturday morning. When I prepared waffles Suzanne and Steve jokingly called them "manhole covers." One of our favorite trips was to drive to Shark Tooth Mountain and explore for fossilized shark's teeth. We made a collection of those teeth, and then ran down the mountain together. As we drove through the countryside the kids would stand on the back seat of my VW Bug, roll back the sunroof, stick their heads out, and enjoy the view. They loved the feel of the air stream brushing the sweat from their faces. Was that illegal? We were too carefree to wonder. We also enjoyed cookouts in the nearby Tehachapi Mountains.

The kids and Rosemary meant so much to me. When I was with them I forgot my work schedule and simply had fun. I needed those respites and so did they. What would I do without them? But I did not give them enough of those quality times.

I did not pay attention to my own limits, and I tried to do too much. In my personal devotions God would nudge me to slow down, but His still, small voice was soon drowned out by my self-imposed work schedule. Years later I would pay a price for my stubbornness, for Rosemary requested a divorce. That event forced me to learn to balance home and church, along with home and community. For now the crack in our relationship was just beginning to show.

The John Birch Society was active in Kern County, and some were members of our congregation. I stood in line at the close of Sunday services to greet the people. The Birch Society members would press into my hands some reading material from their headquarters. They saw themselves as super patriots who guarded America against labor organizers, communist sympathizers, and pastors with so-called liberal tendencies. I was angered that they saw themselves as the grand inquisitors of American patriotism and American faith. *"Didn't they know I was a patriot at heart? Didn't they know I was a Christian? Didn't they know that I preached Christ and not some jingoistic nationalism?"*

Several men on the Official Board must have been members. Curt was one of them. I liked this big hulk of a man, but he insisted that I read the alarmist book written by J. Edgar Hoover titled "Masters of Deceit." The more I read it the more I knew that Hoover and I were polar opposites. When I found out about Hoover's snooping on Dr. Martin Luther King and other civil rights leaders I felt someone should expose his duplicity. But Washington D.C. was afraid of him. No one spoke up and Hoover continued intimidating loyal Americans. Did these John Birch members have the right to put a pastor's sermons to their acid test? My loyalty was to Christ and his Kingdom, not to them.

An item in our budget irked them. One part of our apportionments was designated for "World Service." The conference treasurer then allocated about 1% of that to the National Council of Churches. That inflamed the Birch Society. "Didn't we know that the National Council was infiltrated with communists?" they asked. Of course, proof of their charges were never offered. Attempt after attempt was made by Chairman Ralph to cut our World Service apportionment as a protest. Gladly, our conference treasurer informed the Board that such maneuvers were illegal. It was comforting to have the conference back me up on this issue.

I got a letter from Rev. Cecil Williams, the pastor of the Glide Methodist Church in San Francisco inviting me and other conference pastors to a Saturday workshop at Glide. The topic was, Human Sexuality. Curious as always, I decided to find out what was going on at Glide. Our Conference had been debating Cecil's unorthodox style of evangelism in San Francisco. I decided to fly to San Francisco on one of Howard Hughes' "Flying bananas," and find out for myself what the ministry at Glide was about.

There must have been 20 other young pastors who came to the church. Two staff members from the Glide Foundation oriented us. One was Rev. Don Kuhn, and the other was Rev. Ted McIlevenna. We got coffee and donuts, and they shared their passion for their work in what is called "The Tenderloin" of San Francisco. They explained the people on the streets to us, and many were now members of their church. Most of them were gay, lesbian, or transvestites, and on drugs. They tried to help us understand them, and Glide's ministry to them.

After lunch was served in the church we were invited upstairs to meet the denizens of the Tenderloin and let them speak for themselves. We were seated in a large circle with an empty chair beside each one of us. Ted then welcomed 20 members who were active in the church, and had them sit in any of the empty chairs in the circle. A transvestite sat down beside me.

Here I was, a straight arrow from middle class, suburban San Gabriel, sitting next to a cross-dresser. Two hours earlier I did not know such people existed. "He" looked to be in his early 30's. But he was dressed like a "she." His dress did not fit well and looked funny to me with his hairy legs, and a partially shaven face. His shoes were not feminine. He wore a little lipstick and some rouge on his face. I was not sure if the hair on his head was his or a wig. "She" lacked any resemblance to anything I knew as feminine. I was sitting beside a conundrum personified.

Two worlds were now colliding and we were supposed to converse. We stumbled along talking about what we did, and where we came from: typical banalities. He kept his identity closely guarded and so did I. I think he wanted to ask me the same questions I wanted to ask him, *Who are you? Why do you dress that way? How did you come to be like you are? Help me to understand you."* But we danced around the edges of real dialogue because we were afraid of each other.

On the other hand, when I read of Jesus' ministry he was always crossing human boundaries. He spent time with untouchables, lepers, prostitutes, and tax collectors. Why did I hesitate to cross the obvious boundary between "Sue" the transvestite and myself? Why was he afraid to tell me who he was? Isn't it fear that shuts down our curiosity to understand another human being? It is what keeps us from creating understanding with those who are sexually different. We cloak our fears with theology or with Bible quotes, and miss the healing power of dialogue. Thus we miss the Christ. At least Don and Ted were the opening salvo at beginning a new dialogue in the church about homosexuality. It was a day of new awareness for me.

Today homosexuality has become a defining issue among Christians. Should churches have a role in welcoming such people into our fellowship? Should gays who experience a call to ministry be admitted into the pastorate? After this experience at Glide Church I slowly became convinced that those who seek fellowship in Christ ought to be admitted. It was fear that created so much mistrust in us about Glide Church. We mount our theological cannons and keep at bay those who disagree with us. In so doing we miss what Reuel Howe called "The Miracle of Dialogue." The early church at Jerusalem was aghast when Paul took the Good News to the gentiles. Now we face a similar dilemma. We can resolve it by keeping the channels of communication open. Fear and contemporary legalistic attitudes are the real enemy.

Our fall retreat in 1966 was held at Mt. Breckinridge again. This time I invited a Methodist layman with experience in Viet Nam to come be our resource person. The Methodist Church is a historic peace church. President Johnson had ordered a surge in American troop involvement in Viet Nam to stop the communist Viet Cong. Some parts of our church were raising questions about America's reason for being there. After dinner on a Saturday night our resource person showed us photos of American troops torturing Viet Cong captives. The captives were bound hand and foot. Then a rope was connected to an Armored Personnel Carrier (APC). The soldier driving the APC then put his heavy machine into gear and as the rope became taut, the Viet Cong captive was dragged through the jungle feet first until he died. I had never seen photos like this before, nor behaviors like this from American soldiers.

John Wesley, our Methodist founder, said it long before General Sherman: "War is all hell." But seeing it photographed was new to us. This was one of those times when I felt squeamish about my patriotism. Never again could I be as blindly patriotic as I was in my childhood and youth. I was still a patriot, but from this point on I began to raise questions about American foreign policy. *Could we believe what our leaders were telling us about our involvement in Viet Nam? I doubted it.*

Rosemary and I attended a conference in San Francisco led by the Ecumenical Institute in Chicago. We heard amazing stories of what they were doing in West Side Chicago. The Ecumenical Institute was bringing whites and blacks together in a transforming relationship and creating change in the black ghetto of Chicago. The style of the leaders was remarkably different. Long after the conference we discussed if we should accept an invitation from the Institute to spend part of the summer of 1967 in Chicago with the Ecumenical Institute. Our decision had momentous implications, which at the time we could not see. Once we both agreed to save dollars and attend, other decisions fell into place. After 6 years at Lamont, we decided to ask our DS, Bob Boswell, for a new appointment. Thus, with a sigh of relief, we would say farewell to Lamont. After six years it really was time to move on.

With us wrapping up our ministry in Lamont the relationship to our church changed. In some personal conversations I let slip that I was a part of the Valley Ministerial Association, and that I had supported the United Farm Workers attempts to unionize. My relationship to the church began to change. Some friendships hardened. Some farmers stopped coming, and some stopped giving to the church. Farmers began treating me as an enemy even though my pastoral concern for them remained the same. It was as though I had crossed the Rubicon and war was declared.

I told my District Superintendent that I wanted to invite all our district ministers to Lamont for our next meeting. When they were gathered, I requested time to read a letter from Dr. Harry Emerson Fosdick. I had written to him and told him of our work on behalf of the farm workers to organize for a living wage. His response, even though a retiree, was very supportive, "Continue your work, let nothing stop you. God bless you in your endeavors." I was proud to be in touch with a great pastor like him. But our local church relationships continued to harden.

I invited Rev. Gaxiola of our Hispanic Methodist church in Bakersfield to exchange pulpits several times. He preached to my white farmers and I to his Hispanic faithful. I invited his Ladies Fellowship to come on the same weekend as Rev. Gaxiola and teach our ladies how to prepare Mexican tacos, frijoles, and treats. When the ladies met in the kitchen both sides went through the motions, but there were no real breakthroughs. It was like the meeting I had with the "Sue" at Glide: banalities in a sauce of deep caution. Fear lurked under the surface.

The same result happened when I got one farm worker family to come to church. They looked, they saw, and did not come back. I felt like Jesus when he gazed out on Jerusalem and wept over the city: "O

Jerusalem, Jerusalem! Slaying the prophets and stoning those who have been sent to you! How often I would fain have gathered your children as a fowl gathers her brood under her wings! But you would not have it!"(Mt.23:37)

In June after conference, we had the services of a moving van, for the first time, courtesy of the conference. They packed us and moved our things to Martinez. But there were no farewell parties to see us off.

Several years later we learned that the Lamont church shut its doors. It's 50 years of ministry closed, I immediately began to wonder why. Was it because the church never really had an effective outreach to the community? Was it because of my support for the Valley Ministerial Association? Or was it because of my quiet support for Chavez? I really don't know, but I felt sadness that the church shut down.

Hopefully, I learned a lesson about maintaining balance in myself and in my ministry, for my family, with my God, and with the wider community. Someday I will stand before Christ. It is he who judges, and not men. I leave that to Him.

Twenty-Two

On the Edge of a Volcano

Flying to Chicago exhilarated us. It was June and we felt as though we were off to see the wonderful wizard of Oz, only in this case Oz was the Ecumenical Institute (EI). We were on a yellow brick road to a date with destiny and we could only imagine what lay ahead. My aunts and uncles met us at the O'Hare airport and drove us out to the home of my Aunt Gladys. Invited to stay for a few days, we settled in while she made preparations for a family BBQ and a welcome party with the Bastear clan.

I never knew I had so many relatives. We were isolated in San Gabriel. But now, our Chicago relatives surrounded us, and we were trying hard to learn their names and faces. On Saturday we had a party. Food and drink were in abundance. We did some fun singing of old familiar songs. Then came the inevitable question, "Why are you here?" We told them in brief about the Ecumenical Institute. But when I told them where it was located, on the west side beginning at the corner of 5th and Kedzie, there was a gasp of horror. When they heard that, it was like a lightening strike in our midst. After the thunder came disbelief, and a cacophony of incredulous jibes.

"Why," they asked, "are you going there? You can't be serious. Only a fool would go there." Then began a torrent of racist slurs such as I had never heard before. Here was my family, the ones I had longed to meet all these years, casting awful caricatures of the people I had come to serve. What a twist! At first I could hardly believe this was my family that was speaking. The most printable thing they could call the black west side was, "Congoland." Otherwise, the "N" word was in abundance. The behavior of the black males who "refused to work," and of black females who "bore children simply to collect welfare," poured forth in a torrent of animus. That night I discovered that racism was very much alive in America, and especially in my own family. Chicago was a witches' brew of racial hostility and the witches were crying out, "Fie, Fie, Fie!" What an introduction to our summer service. We were distressed as we left the BBQ that night.

All spring I had been reading Dietrich Bonhoeffer's book, "Letters and Papers From Prison." E.I. let us know that Bonhoeffer's thinking was seminal for what they were doing in Chicago. I read it cover to cover and highlighted his main thoughts. Bonhoeffer spoke out against Hitler and the policies of Nazism, and thus was cast in prison as an enemy of the state. I also read his book, "Life Together" as a devotional guide for both Rosemary and myself. We prepared ourselves for a unique commitment to social change with a theological context.

Mom and Dad worried about us. Watts exploded into race riots in 1965 with ominous warnings of how badly America was split into two nations: one white and one black. Race riots in New York City and Rochester became national news. Martin Luther King led non-violent protests across the south and created tremors that all of us could feel.

Some of my colleagues in ministry went to Mississippi to help in voter registration for blacks. Some reported being shot at by rednecks or the KKK. The war in Viet Nam escalated, and protests broke out in colleges and universities. Back in the central valley Caesar Chavez conducted a grape boycott, and his United Farm Workers sent men into the fields crying, "Huelga!" (strike). Americans asked, "Was America coming apart at the seams? What could hold us together?"

Our family was walking right into the eye of a storm where rip tides and crosscurrents could wash us out to sea. I pondered,

Are we biting off more than we can chew? Am I endangering my family? Am I an idealist? Do I have a need to see the world through my own lenses without giving credence to the community's concept of reality?

Yet Rosemary and I carried a sense of divine mission. We were not going to read about history, or watch race riots on TV. We were going to make history in Chicago. We believed that we were going to turn things around in our corner of the world. We were going to diligently study Bohhoeffer and modern theologians and apply their wisdom to the racial sickness of America, especially here in Chicago. We were warned that Ecumenical Institute was located in the worst ghetto in America. But if change could be brought here it could be brought anywhere in the United States. That knowledge spurred us onward.

One wakeup call occurred when we heard the racism of my family. Another shock soon followed. On Sunday morning we took the subway out to the West Side where EI headquarters was located. The subway proceeded into a heart of darkness the further west we went. At our station we stepped off the subway and walked one block to an abandoned protestant seminary that was to be our home for the month of July. Once upon a time it was home to young men studying for the ministry. But a black tide of humanity came too close and the trustees moved the seminary to "safer ground."

I had never seen a ghetto before. The buildings were so shabby that I could scarcely describe them. The air was heavy with a foul odor of too many people crowded together for too long. Every one was black. Litter crowded empty lots and gutters. Rosemary turned to me and asked, "How do people live like this?" I looked and I was suddenly aware how out of place we were. I felt like a peeled banana in this new environment. It was culture shock for each of us.

We moved into the old brick seminary and were shown our rooms. Suzanne and Stephen and the other children were placed in one building, adults in another. Other young ministerial families arrived all day long, and soon our building was full to capacity. We quickly became a community of equals, as we were all white, while the world outside was all black.

The Ecumenical Institute referred to us as a new breed of Christians who were called to be agents of change in the Chicago ghetto. Experiencing it first hand confirmed what we had been told. I could not imagine a more desperate existence. The all-white staff that lived nearby in their own community welcomed us to our new home. They had lived here for years and had a network of colleagues in the black community. The staff welcomed us as harbingers of change that could bring in a new day of race relations to the church.

Monday morning we were quickly oriented to what our leader, Dr. Joe Matthews, described as "intentional living." One of the seven families who were permanent staff members walked down the hall at 5:30 am pounding on a Buddhist gong. It gave an unmistakable clarion call to hit the deck and get dressed. Breakfast was a bowl of cereal, a banana, and a cup of coffee or orange juice. It was the same every morning. Meanwhile, the kids in their unit dressed in jeans and striped red and white T-shirts. No deviation from that rule. They had to be clearly recognizable as staff took them on learning trips throughout downtown Chicago.

The kids visited some of the outstanding sites in Chicago, such as the Shedd Museum, that helped them understand the oceans. They visited the museum of Science and Industry and saw the captured German submarine from WWII. The Adler Planetarium showed them the universe, and the Field Museum opened its treasures of natural history. These trips opened their eyes to the world.

Joe Matthews was appointed by the National Council of Churches to establish the Ecumenical Institute in the heart of the Chicago ghetto. They also helped fund this unique experiment in social change. Many churches, such as my former church at Lamont had tried to cut off our apportionment that went to the National Council of Churches. They were unsuccessful. Now, however, I was living testimony as to why some churches chafed at paying dues to the National Council. These churches detested this departure from the old style of evangelism, and what they perceived as a subversive organization.

After breakfast we walked a block to an abandoned warehouse where worship services were held. We sat on old crates and listened to Dr. Joe preach a sermon. Joe was a preacher unlike any I had heard before. The word charismatic comes to mind. Joe could put you on the edge of your seat in a matter of minutes. When we worshipped in that warehouse it was as holy as Westminster Abbey. Only now the sermons were to send us out into the community that Dr. Joe designated as "5th City," an area of about eight city blocks, chosen for renewal. We put a mere penny in the offering plate, as Joe encouraged us to do.

Our real offering was to put our lives "on the line" revealing our commitment to go forth and serve God in the community. We sang new songs and avoided the old evangelical songs. We sang the Doxology to the tune of "Hernando's Hideaway." We sang another song that began, "Oh When the Trend Begins to Bend," to the tune, "When the Saints Go Marching In." And of course we sang Martin Luther King's "We Shall Overcome." Between Joe's charismatic preaching and our songs of a new urban Christianity, we left the warehouse ready to burn our spiritual candles at both ends. Is it possible to imagine how on fire we were to serve Christ and turn the west side around? We truly believed that we were the ones who could do it.

We took our study papers with us to the morning workshops. Papers by Dietrich Bonhoeffer, Paul Tillich, H. Richard Niebuhr, and Karl Barth were the staples that we studied in depth. By depth I mean we examined their theology of life in the world with a microscope. We left no stone unturned to understand exactly what they said and meant. Those papers were to be our theological building blocks for all of our work in 5th City. We were given the ideas we needed to meet black people as equals, to create a new community in the ghetto where white and black could build what I called Paul's concept of fellowship,

> "In Christ there is neither slave nor free, neither Jew nor Greek, neither male or female, but all are one in Christ Jesus." (Gal. 3:28).

In our morning study sessions we learned the theology on which 5th City was created. There was an atmosphere in our study sessions almost impossible to explain. We saw ourselves as the vanguard of a new generation of Christians who were going to turn the world upside down. We were going to make urban America a new community where all could live together productively. To do that, Joe and his training staff created an eclectic convergence of theology, philosophy, and what they called "practices" with which to train us.

The staff taught us that suburban Chicago was the enemy of west side renewal. Suburbia siphoned off resources for themselves that should have been shared with the black community. Suburbia made sure that the black community stayed isolated on the west side. Evangelical Christianity was also demonized because they preached the concept of an individualistic salvation. That concept failed to come to terms with communal life in our big cities. Of course, liberalism came in for a share of criticism. Liberalism was seen as a spent force, no longer relevant to Christianity. It was perceived as highlighting individual religious experience, while forgetting about a desperate world.

We studied selections especially from Bonhoeffer. But we also read selections from Tillich and H. Richard Niebuhr that were led by members of the permanent staff. Bonhoeffer chose to see things "from below" as he did when he visited black Harlem, witnessed segregated black America at first hand, and turned to the concepts of "sin and grace, and the love of God." There would be a new engagement with the world of black people.

Bonhoeffer spoke of "a world come of age," even as Allied aircraft were dropping tons of bombs around his prison cell in Berlin. His letters, which survived his death on a Nazi gallows, came to be a call to re-examine Christianity's relationship to the world. We were called to act in the world. According to Tillich, Christians were to create "structures of justice." That was seen as our immortality, that is, what lived on beyond our earthly life. Bonhoeffer also created the phrase, "religionless Christianity." That phrase led to an attack on traditional Christianity, and on liberal churches in suburbia. Later the "Death of God" movement emerged and the Bonhoeffer idea was carried far beyond its original intent.

When Joe preached the morning service in the warehouse he would challenge us to re-think our role as Christians. He proclaimed that Jesus chose to live and die on behalf of all mankind, revealing how to be the "man for others." If we choose to die on behalf of mankind, accepting our suffering, we would fulfill our purpose to the world. Thus, Joe would say, "Charles, George, Harry, you can each become a Christ. Live your life on behalf of others, and you can complete your mission in the world." Joe invited us to rename Jesus "Charley."

One of his favorite scriptures was taken from Mark 2:11. In that episode four friends brought a paralytic to Jesus for healing. After a back and forth dialogue with religious leaders Jesus said to the paralytic, "Rise, take up your bed and walk!" Joe gave it a new inflection. It wasn't an invitation, it was a command. Joe then challenged us to, "Pick up your lives and live them. If you don't want to get out of bed, get up anyway. There is a world out there waiting for you." Joe's preaching was compelling, like a thunderclap in the warehouse, and we left the service ready to go forth and spend ourselves in the new community that was emerging.

As I listened to Joe and our staff facilitators I heard overtones of a philosophy called "Existentialism." Developed by a Frenchman named Jean Paul Sartre, he taught that humans "Are doomed to be free persons in a meaningless universe." Sartre taught that we create our own values and meanings because we are alone in the universe. Our leaders took that seriously. For the Ecumenical Institute all the creeds of the ancient church had lost their significance. So had the theologies that emerged along with them. There was a convergence of existentialism with Bonhoeffer's theology.

We also studied Pablo Picasso's dramatic sketch, "Guernica", where German bombers blasted a Spanish village by that name. Old theological concepts no longer had meaning in a world where civilians were the objects of annihilation. Hitler along with General Franco, had made a mockery of the rules of war. Men and beasts alike showed the agony caused by war in Picasso's drawing. Paul Tillich, the foremost theologian of our era, wrote that Picasso's "Guernica" was the single most important piece of art of the 20th century. It symbolized the torments of our world, and the end of old theologies. Guernica was a foretaste of indiscriminate mass destruction that was to come in WWII.

We bought a copy of "Guernica" and hung it in our room. Tillich wrote that the GOD concept must now be translated as "The Ground of Being." The way was open for 20th century theologians to create a new understanding of how to live in this century. Evangelical Christianity had failed to penetrate our new urban centers. Evangelicals had been successful on the frontier of America, but had lost their way in the new urban centers. So had liberal churches. We in 5th City, on the other hand, were called to sally forth and build an inclusive urban core based on the new theology. Joe liked to quote the noted German philosopher, Martin Heidegger, who said there are only two realities in this world: you and me. A desperate west side called for a desperate gospel, and Ecumenical Institute provided it.

The philosophy that Joe was preaching was heady material. I absorbed it like a sponge. Like the Jewish kosher wine that we served at our communion services, it went straight to my brain. As with Jason and his Argonauts, the sirens were calling, the sirens of Joe's preaching. If I was not careful my ship would be on the rocks. At the same time I felt invincible. It was an amazing contradiction. Isn't that one of the reasons why Jason had to plug his ears when the sirens sang? That is what I failed to do, and it cost me later. That was as close as I ever came to agnosticism.

The sense of invincibility was one of the dangers of our community. Joe's philosophy was so persuasive that it penetrated to the deepest part of me. We were creating a community of black and white while America was tearing itself apart in race riots. But I was slowly losing my family. Wasn't that too high a price to pay? Wasn't the sense of invincibility a tip-off that I was in over my head? Because of my zeal, I missed the warning signs to leave while I could.

We saw both sides of the ghetto as we walked to and from classes. Down the street from the warehouse was another brick building purchased by EI. We held our morning study sessions there. To get there we had to walk by a whorehouse. Out front, early in the morning, a pride of black men lounged. An awning shaded the entrance, and they gathered in the shade waiting a turn to visit one of the ladies upstairs. We kept to our side of the street and they to theirs. We eyed each other cautiously, knowing it was better to say nothing and keep moving. We had on our black berets that identified us as friends who wanted to serve in their community. As we passed by we held our breath. They said nothing. With our black berets we were accepted. Perhaps the reality was that we were tolerated. Along the way we passed bars, pool halls, and storefront churches. Already they had customers. This was a new world to us.

One new reality took time to assimilate. When young blacks addressed each other they called one another, "Nigger." I never got used to that name. They threw it about all day long as a common form of address. Males were addressed as N… as a matter of course. To me it was the ultimate put-down. Usually it was preceded by the "F" word. Women were called "girl," "woman," "broad," or "bitch." It was no wonder this was a boiling cauldron ready to explode into a riot, as later happened in Chicago and in Detroit.

There was rage just beneath the surface. Joe told us "Even Martin King received some boos when he came here." It seemed to me that blacks had been segregated for so long, and treated as clowns by our society, that the message hit home and came out in their speech and self-concept.

The other segment of 5th City was an inspiration to us. On some evenings of the week we got to visit the homes of blacks that joined with EI in rebuilding 5th City. They were Christians, and they met in the evening in their homes. These were house churches. At our morning sessions we were alerted that though we were primed with theological skills, we were to let local blacks take the lead at their house churches.

They served us coffee and cookies, and offered us the right hand of fellowship. We got to listen to their dream for a renewed West Side. They did not want to go on living in such depressing surroundings. Their testimony stood in stark contrast to what we had heard at our family's BBQ. Our host summed up their feelings, "We want our children to go to college, raise families, and build churches." They pledged to work with us and pave the way for us in their (not our) community. Those house churches gave us hope that EI was on the right track.

They shared with us another new reality called, "Block busting." Realtors took advantage of the fears between blacks and whites. If a white family living on the edge of a black area could be coaxed to move out, they would be paid a good price for their unit. Then it could be sold at a higher price to a black family wanting to move into a white community. Suddenly, when other white families realized that a black had moved in to their neighborhood, panic broke out, and the remaining white families fled, selling their properties at cut-rate prices. Then black families wanting in could be charged a high price. Thus, realtors profited from these tactics.

Afternoons and Saturdays we worked within the boundaries of 5th City. We painted store fronts weathered by snow and ice, and now by the intense summer heat. My group was assigned an empty lot by one of the house churches. The lot was covered with the detritus of civilization: broken glass, cans, paper, and chunks of old furniture. We raked it and put it all into a dumpster, while singing songs of urban renewal. Then we were provided with playground equipment to mount and install in the lot. We put down a layer of wood chips to provide an attractive surface.

Suddenly, a cavalcade of limousines drove up. Mayor Daley stepped forward from a shiny black limousine to greet us. His staff, and a bevy of photographers flanked him. He greeted us with, "Good afternoon. How are you?" Then he looked at our project, took it into his gaze, and smiled. "This looks like fine work you are doing here. Have my people supplied you with enough equipment to do your job?" "Yes," we replied, "and thanks for your help, Mr. Mayor." He was an impressive looking man and dressed to fit his august status among us. Everyone treated him with deference and called him "Mr. Mayor" or "His Honor."

We were impressed by his visit and several of us stepped forward to shake his hand while the photographers took numerous pictures. Mayor Daley remarked, "While America is burning there are good things happening here in Chicago." Mayor Daley wanted to be seen as part of the renewal of the west side. Sargent Shriver, the architect of President

Johnson's "War on Poverty" also dropped by to see our work. We were in the national spotlight.

Saturday nights were special. Large BBQs made out of 50-gallon oil drums were hauled out and filled with briquettes. Huge loads of chicken were layered on the grills, and soon the smoke and the fragrance of BBQ chicken filled the air. Contemporary music of the black community rang out over loudspeakers, and the residents of 5th City arrived in clusters to join in the celebration. Everywhere blacks and whites talked, shared, laughed, and sang songs. This was a dream come true. This was the kind of community that I had wanted to see emerge in Lamont. Now we were part of a miracle in the making.

Rosemary, Suzanne and Stephen, however, were having trouble adapting to the west side. Even though the kids enjoyed the marvels of downtown Chicago, on the west side they frequently collided with street-wise black children. The black kids learned how to survive the mean streets by becoming tough. Suzanne and Steve were "PK's" (preacher kids) who were raised in small town America, and given special treatment by our churches. Now they were being pushed and shoved by black kids. They felt threatened.

Rosemary's dilemma went deeper. She felt overwhelmed by our morning study sessions. All of the radical new theology was more than she could internalize. She felt as though she was having a "nervous breakdown." Rosemary pleaded with me to fly her and the kids home. They had experienced enough. But, I was immersed in listening and learning all I could to build an inclusive west side. I was pumped up and ready to complete our commitment for the whole month of July at EI. Rosemary wept as she poured out her sorrow to me.

Rosemary and I went up to our room and talked. I listened and then responded to her. I asked if she had it available to remain through the last week of July. Then, I promised, we could fly directly to Oakland and catch a bus to Martinez, our new appointment. She reluctantly agreed, and wiped her eyes. But something silent happened between us. She had pleaded with me at Lamont for more help raising the children. I let her down. Now she was appealing to go home, and I gave reasons why we should stay. Something in the nature of what I call "trust" was slowly being fractured. I was on the edge of a volcano and did not see how precarious was my position as a husband.

I had some real learning to do in order to maintain a proper balance between the church and my family. Later, as the possibility of a divorce became evident I began to see my error. It dawned on me that my call to ministry was to serve Christ, not the church. I also had a calling to protect my wife and family. And I needed to protect a quiet time between the Lord and myself.

There must have been 50 ministerial couples at the Institute that summer. We had a farewell party and promised to get in touch with those who lived near us. We wanted to extend this work wherever we went. We had created a new community and it was now time to extend it to our church locations. The Methodist Church at Martinez was eager and ready to get started. But they knew nothing of the theology with which I was saturated. If they did find out I think they would have been horrified.

We quickly moved into our new parsonage, and I met with the lay leaders to begin looking at programs for the coming year. They wanted to hold an evangelistic crusade, bring in a revivalist preacher, and begin to win souls to Christ. How could I tell them that this was the very opposite of what we learned in Chicago? My focus was on building a new community that would include the urban core of Martinez. But they were not interested in that. I began work on an alternative plan that I hoped would set a new tone in the church. With the help of the Methodist Men's group, I invited the All Pro center of the Oakland Raiders football team to come to our church and speak to a father and son banquet. Our women prepared a special dinner for the occasion.

"Big Jim" Otto was the Raiders' center that year. He came as promised, and yes, he was BIG. He filled our fellowship hall with his presence. He spoke to the fathers reminding them of this, "You have a huge responsibility to raise your sons with values that will honor God." Then, he spoke to the sons who were present, "I want to remind you how important it is to listen to your dads and learn from them."

Stephen was sitting beside me and his eyes were wide open as he listened to this huge football player speak from the heart regarding his personal faith in God. Afterwards I took Steve over to Big Jim and introduced Stephen to him. Jim bent over and greeted him, and Steve was speechless. It was a defining moment for Steve and he never forgot that encounter. He became a staunch Raider fan that night.

Meanwhile with the training I had received in Chicago I became aware of racial tensions that were brewing in Martinez and Contra Costa County. There were ugly race riots in Chicago and Detroit. The "Kerner Report" was released with great fanfare and I read it through. It detailed the nightmare that took place in our race riots, beginning in Watts. I determined to do something about that nightmare. I was bold. I called on the chairperson of our County Supervisors. I pleaded with him to form what is known as a "Human Relations Commission" for the County.

If the Commission was created the members would be charged with investigating and responding to racial problems within the county and dealing with them quickly and fairly before they became a riot. The "Supes" had read the headlines of the newspapers. The chairman responded with "Bring a proposal to the next Board of Supervisors meeting. We will talk about it." I did so, and to my amazement they adopted it! I felt as though this was one of my major achievements at Martinez.

Rosemary, the kids and I made a major decision as to how we could impact Martinez as a family. We chose to take in a foster child named Jackie. His father, incarcerated across the bay in San Quentin Prison, and his young mother, unable to care for him, turned him over to Contra Costa County officials. We were thoroughly vetted, and passed a County review with flying colors. Jackie was given to us, a five-year-old boy with tousled blond hair, a big smile, and a desire to be loved. We took him in and loved him. Suzanne and Stephen played with him every day after school. We went for drives together and walked together. We bonded into a family of five. After two months, we were ready to begin the adoption process and make him a permanent part of our family.

But it was not to be. His mother had experienced separation anxiety while Jackie was with us. She went back to the County and asked that her original decision be reversed. She was ready to take Jackie back. As his mother, she was within her legal rights to do this. A County official came to our home with papers showing that Jackie was to be returned to his birth mother. We wept as we turned him over to the Social Worker and tried to explain to Jackie what was happening. Jackie cried, but was soon in the hands of the worker who drove him away. There was a huge gap in our family without him. We grieved over his loss, feeling sad without him.

Something also happened between Rosemary and myself. The erosion of trust, and the gap between us finally was too powerful to ignore. Our relationship was on the rocks and we needed help. Here I was a pastor who preached sermons to families seeking guidance, and my own family now needed counseling. *Whom could we tell? Who would give us the support we needed? We couldn't go to our church.*

Truth be told, I was living a double life. One side of me was thoroughly dedicated to the new urban theology of EI. The other side was still a Methodist pastor who was appointed to be a shepherd of the sheep and the guardian of my family. I could not preach the gospel of Christ on Sunday morning, and live by modernistic theology the rest of the week. That theology denied the very gospel and ministry that I was ordained to uphold. Something had to give. Finally we called my District Superintendent, Sargent Wright, and requested an appointment with him.

"Sarge," as he was known, graciously heard our story, and listened to what had torn our family apart. He then made a suggestion, "Take a Sabbatical leave from the ministry for one year. The two of you could then get professional counseling, put your marriage back together, and return to ministry the following year." Rosemary and I agreed that it was the right thing to do. I sent out a letter to our congregation that we would take a sabbatical leave. "The Bishop," I said, "would appoint a new pastor to Martinez in June." I got approval for the plan from the Conference Board of Ministry. In June of 1968 I took formal leave of the

Martinez church, and a Sabbatical from the Methodist Conference, and we moved into an apartment in San Pablo, several miles away.

The words of the Ecumenical Institute were ringing in my ears, "Pick up your life and live it!" Yes, I thought, but what about my wife, and my kids? Part of me felt like a failure for allowing our marriage to collapse while I immersed myself with avant-garde theology. Meanwhile, all that aside, I had no money and no income. I desperately needed a job. Royal Sherwood, one of the Martinez church lay leaders, got me a job at the Fruitvale Cannery in Oakland. There I took a place on the production line preparing fruit cocktail for canning. Now we had a breathing space for Rosemary and me to try to rebuild our marriage.

Fruitvale Cannery was in the industrial flatlands of Oakland. From the moment I arrived there was the noise of tin cans coming down the production line, ready to be filled with fruit cocktail, lids put on, and then cooked. I was assigned to a line of workers standing along a conveyor belt loaded with a never-ending stream of fruit chunks that needed to be picked over before they were canned. We went through the motions for eight dreary hours. We watched the clock as an unspoken tradition, for all of us looked forward to break time to ease the monotony of work. When the five o'clock whistle blew we made a beeline to punch our time cards and get out of the noise. In the cannery life was like a loud treadmill, endlessly noisy and boring. The one thing I could say for it was that it provided me with a paycheck.

An epilogue is in order here. Forty years later my daughter Suzanne and I went for a drive through west side Chicago. We wanted to see 5th City where we had lived such a significant chapter of our lives. We carefully followed a map that took us to the corner of 5th Street and Kedzie, the starting point of all of our work. We drove through the community. We tried to find the old seminary. It was not to be found. We tried to find the park we had built for the children of the ghetto. It was gone, returned now to an empty, trash-filled lot. The bars and pool halls were filled with customers. Everywhere the paint was once again cracked and peeling. Trash littered the sidewalks. There was nothing to give us any kind of reminder that once upon a time this was one of the greatest social and theological experiments in the world.

Once this was a vibrant center for the renewal of the black ghetto. Now it was all gone. Like a Faustian legend all our work was washed away, as though we had never lived and labored there. We sang our songs of urban renewal here, laid down our lives on behalf of this community, and now the streets defaulted to an ugly ghetto. Can the reader step in with imagination and sense our disappointment and disillusionment? Love's labors lost? Yes, our work was gone, swept away, and this part of America reverted to status quo ante. Here there were still two America's, one white and one black. And they did not accept each other. I suspect it was the same in other urban centers like Detroit and New York.

What were we, idealistic fools? We came here believing that a new inclusive Christian community could be built, one that put racism into the trash bin of history. Was our dream really possible? Once upon a time our little band of brothers came to Chicago with all our flags flying, hope springing eternal. Now, forty years later, it was gone. I thought of the book of Ecclesiastes, "Vanity of vanities, says the Preacher…All is vanity."(Ecclesiastes 1:2) That put into words what I was feeling.

It also raised the question, is it possible for we humans to make a difference in the world? St. Paul said there are principalities and powers arrayed against us. Today wealthy corporations and empires of greed dominate both our political parties. Apathy takes hold of many citizens. Yet as a Christian I am called to live a life of faith, a faith that says there is meaning and purpose here, and that God has called us to be coworkers with Him in this world He created.

What did Bonhoeffer mean when he wrote from his prison cell in Berlin, "A world come of age," and his striking concept of "religionless Christianity?" When I read his book I did not draw the same conclusion as did Dr. Matthews. I took it to mean that Bonhoeffer was deeply disappointed that his German Lutheran Church had so easily made peace with Adolph Hitler. I took it to mean that he formed his "Confessing Church" as a protest against Nazism. I don't think he wanted to abandon

Lutheranism in Germany, but simply show what it meant to be a Christian in a world come of age. He had a love for the church, but not for a church that did Hitler's bidding. Bonhoeffer was taken out of context and made to serve the Ecumenical Institute's purpose.

Years before I had read much about Albert Schweitzer. He said that one of the problems with new ideas is that they get carried too far beyond their original meaning. That is what I think happened with Bonhoeffer in Chicago. When he was wedded to existentialism, Bonhoeffer the Christian became Bonhoeffer the rebel. Joe Matthews and the Institute made enemies of evangelicals, of liberals, and of suburbia. We could have better done our work in the ghetto if we let it be a co-operative demonstration of Christ at work in the world. It seemed to me that we needed to find support wherever we could.

We all need to face the reality of the ghettos of America. Is there any cure for this scar on our claim to be free and equal? Can Christians come together to solve this problem? It still remains an open question. I believe we will once again face the Refiner's fire on this question.

Twenty-Three

Moving On

Fruitvale cannery was a dull place to work. Standing on the production line for eight hours a day was the ultimate boredom. Sometimes I was tempted to fall asleep while standing there. Once I actually did fall asleep, and dropped my pitting tool on to the conveyor belt. When it reached the end of the line it fouled the engine that was driving the belt. Embarrassed, I promised my supervisor not to let that happen again.

I knew of a certainty that I would not spend the rest of my life here. How did my fellow Americans put up with such meaningless labor? The Department of Labor published statistics on how many people are at work, but they did not ask, "Are you satisfied with your work?" Out of a cacophony of tin cans rattling, and a river of chopped fruit flowing by me, headed for an island of fruit cocktail, I made a decision to move on. Like Abraham of old I heard a call to leave this place and go forth to a country that He would show me.

At home in the evenings I got a whole new awareness of the power of television. So many programs were what Newton Minnow called a "wasteland." It seemed to me that TV was a form of escapism where Americans fled from the boredom of their work. Now I was a part of the great American escape.

Rosemary and I had some long, helpful talks. Her question to me was: "What are you going to do with the rest of your life?" I spent hours thinking through that question. One night when the lights were out and everyone was asleep I had an epiphany. The one thing I could do that was similar to ministry was to teach. At UC Davis I never imagined myself as a teacher. Rather, anything but that. Now it became a live option. I was not going to stay on line trimming chunks of fruit, or removing pits for canned fruit cocktail. I would gladly give my job to someone else.

The song "Born Free" was a hit that year. I played it and sang it as I worked the fruit cocktail line. I experienced a new freedom to rethink my life and what I wanted to do with the rest of my life. Reality training on the fruit cocktail line was just what I needed to get my life in order. Teaching suddenly seemed like a live option to me. I thought, *I could get a Master's Degree, teach history, and work part time for a church as a teacher or counselor.*

Ecumenical Institute was still a part of my thinking. Imagine for a moment: I still awakened Suzanne and Steve each morning with a Buddhist gong, just as we had done at EI. "Hey Dad," they cried out, "can't you try something else?" But it worked. It got them out of bed and when they did I stopped banging on it. I missed the ministry, and I was aware that I was now in a new country with many unknowns. But the song "Born Free" kept me thinking about the goal of a new future. Someone said that we go into the future looking backward through a rear view mirror. That described me in 1968.

As a pastor on sabbatical leave I wrote to universities and colleges in the Bay Area. I described my situation and asked if any tuition scholarships were available for a person like me. Amazingly, one college responded with an offer rather than an apology. My hopes soared when I read that letter. A Catholic all-girls college in the Oakland hills called "College of the Holy Names" wrote and offered me a full tuition scholarship if I would come study with them. What an act of grace and an answer to prayer! There was one hesitation, however. It was an all-girls college, but the Board voted to begin taking men into their Masters program.

With some trepidation I went to the Dean and explored the offer with her. She was a sister in their teaching order. I had never associated myself with Catholicism before nor had I ever known a "sister" or a nun. Now I was going to get a full experience of both. I accepted their offer and signed up for a summer session toward a Master's Degree with them to be followed in the fall with a full course of studies in history. I was going to train to be a historian and hopefully get a teaching job in a community college.

I was the only male student on campus. It may sound like a dream world, but in reality I was uncomfortable being so different from the rest of the students. When I entered the west side of Chicago for the first time I felt like a peeled banana. Now it was déjà vu once again. One of my friends asked, "Should we be worried about the girls or about you?"

Into this delicate situation I warily took my place in each class. However, the lectures were so interesting that I soon forgot the discomfort of being the only male student and settled into the new learning environment. The co-eds accepted me and I accepted them. Rosemary got a job at an elementary school and between my tuition scholarship and her wages we had a living income. We entered Suzanne and Stephen into an after school program where we could pick them up on our way home.

To my great delight the sisters were effective teachers. Suddenly, Catholicism was not so bad after all. In fact most of my teachers were outstanding in their communication skills. By knowing their subject they made their classes compelling. I studied hard and made good grades. But that became an issue between Rosemary and me. I still carried a torch for the Ecumenical Institute. I spent many hours in the library. Rosemary and I did not have enough quality time together.

One class impressed me above the others. "Black History" introduced me to the story of black people in America. I got a good look at how the ghetto in Chicago came to be. America has had a long history of slavery followed by segregation. In my imagination I could see how the very apartments built by my grandfather at the turn of the century became the ghettos of west side Chicago. My family was deeply enmeshed in the fabric of America, and willy-nilly, in its racism.

Black people fled segregation of the south only to find it again in the cities of the north. Our teacher assigned us to read books like, "Malcolm X". What an eye opener! Malcolm X was tormented as he tried everything in his power to become acceptable to white America. He found that no matter how hard he tried, he could not shed the stereotype of blackness. He came to hate white people. We read James Baldwin's, "The Fire Next Time". Eldridge Cleaver, a leader in Oakland's new Black Panther Party, wrote his story that year, "Soul On Ice."

New information kept pouring in through our class lectures. Slavery in America, Civil War and Reconstruction, The emergence of Jim Crow and lynching mobs, The Black exodus from cotton culture and the blasting of any hopes for a better life in cities of the north, then Race riots. It was all there. No wonder that 1968 was the year American cities were burning. No wonder Martin Luther King was assassinated, and the Democratic Party was torn apart when Mississippi blacks wanted to participate in the party. The United States was two countries struggling to find a way to a more perfect union.

It should not have been surprising to find that the teaching order of sisters were so adept at teaching Black History. But it was surprising to me. They were living a sheltered life at the college, yet understood clearly the distorted world of race relations in America. Sometimes our old assumptions have to fall in the light of new information. I was impressed with their skills. They seemed ready to deal with the fact that America faced the Refiner's fire.

Being a part of an all-girls college was a bit of a conundrum. The girls were from middle class homes and were carefully selected by the Dean to be achievers. Their faculty was the best. One day in our English History class we presented oral reports to the class. One girl gave her report and sat down. The sister stopped and asked her: "Where did you get your information?" Her response was: "In the library." Sister: "What books did you use?" There was a long pause with no response. This time the sister raised her voice in stern rebuke, pointed at the student and said, "You got that report by copying it out of an encyclopedia; the very thing I told you that you cannot do. Leave this class at once!" (Nowadays it is copying reports from a computer). The girl picked up her books, slouched to the door, and in tears left the class. These sisters had a high standard for the teaching-learning process. We respected them.

But the gender of this college affected me. When I told friends that I was back in school for a Master's Degree, I received plaudits. Then came the question, "What school?" After I told them the answer they would guffaw and tease me about being in a Catholic girls college. One person quipped, "Do you know why they call those teachers nuns? Because they don't get none!" It was jesting in good fun, and perhaps they were a tad bit jealous. But I asked myself, *Do I want to spend the rest of my life explaining how and why I went to an all-girls college?*

My response was to reach out to the University of the Pacific (UOP) in Stockton, at that time a Methodist college, and ask for financial help to study there. To my amazement I received another positive response. They too offered me a full tuition scholarship to matriculate toward a master's degree. Perhaps being a Methodist minister on sabbatical leave helped gain my acceptance. I thanked the sisters for taking me in when I was desperate for a break, when I stood wavering between the ministry and a new future as a teacher. In December 1968 I wrapped up my fall course of studies at Holy Names and we moved to Stockton.

Stockton looked like the armpit of California. Downtown was a dreary sight of crumbling buildings and homeless men. A kind of hopelessness permeated the air. We rented a cheap house three blocks from the University. That way I could walk to school every day. I parked my VW Bug in our primitive garage, cancelled my car insurance, and walked. The money available from PL 550 was all used up. We cut corners every way we could. Rosemary got a teaching job with Stockton Unified Schools, and drove to work in a Chevy Impala that her dad gave to her.

I took a full load of classes in History. In one class I was the only student. Dr. Paul Hauban, the instructor, would sit behind his desk and dialogue with me about European History. I had to be 100% prepared each week for such a demanding class. "Well, Mr. Bastear," he would ask, "Why did the French and Germans go to war in 1870?" In another History class Dr. Don Grubbs asked us to read Herman Melville's classic "Moby Dick." The story awakened in us the destructive obsession of Captain Ahab as he relentlessly pursued the great white whale. For us Captain Ahab was a symbol of how Americans destroyed the beauty of the frontier in order to conquer it. Didn't the same thing happen in Viet Nam?

Dr. Van Alstyne, a scholar from USC, taught us that American history is clouded with visions of empire that began in colonial days and stretched into our modern age. Those were exciting ideas. I was eagerly looking forward to becoming the very best teacher I could be.

On Sundays we helped found a new mission church. On Eighth Street in south Stockton, Tom McCoy, a young Methodist pastor, was eager to start a mission church based on the model of the Ecumenical Institute. Tom was an "Oreo cookie" in reverse. He was white on the outside and black on the inside. He did not fit in with traditional Methodist churches. Thus the Bishop sent him to our area to work on the south side. We gathered together a Filipino family, a black family, two white families from UOP, and a Hispanic family. Together we became a church. We called ourselves, "St. Peter's Church." Our plan was to reach out to the black community on the south side, and become interracial, just as we did in Chicago.

Tom conducted services like the ones Joe Matthews had led at the warehouse in Chicago. It was a carefully crafted service pointing us to service in the community outside. We sang the new songs from Chicago as we praised God each Sunday. What a sight we made! We were five families and a pastor determined to impact south Stockton. But was south Stockton ready for us? Several of us also became active in the South Stockton Parish, a cluster of churches banded together to promote peace and justice in South Stockton.

South Stockton was in a deep sleep. We went door to door. We let people know of our services. It was a poor neighborhood, yet that is why we chose it. There were broken homes and enough social problems to wilt any caring citizen. Single moms with children came to the door to answer our knocks. Residents verbally showed an interest in our church, but did not come on Sunday morning to worship with us. Our five families met and worshipped God Sunday by Sunday. We did not have enough of an offering to support Tom's full time ministry. Thus, our Northern California Methodist Conference graciously made up the difference in his salary so Tom could have a living wage.

We continued through 1969 and 1970. But by 1971 the financial reserves of our Conference were strained and the Bishop decided that the Conference could not continue to support a church that did not grow. We had to close our church, and Tom moved on.

This was another learning experience. I concluded that some white folks with high ideals of service could not enter the black community at will and expect to make a change. A new perspective would have to come from within the community itself. I don't think our neighbors were able to trust us with their future. Rosemary and I turned to Central Methodist across the street from UOP.

I graduated from UOP in January 1970 with a Master's Degree in History. I was primed and ready to go forth to teach in a community college. I sent letters to scores of colleges in northern California. Inside was a resume about my skills and background. Most of the colleges did not even reply. I think they filed such letters away in a back room and forgot about them.

Finally, in desperation I began calling on Deans of Instruction in nearby colleges. One dean in Sacramento said to me, "History teachers are a dime a dozen. You are not going to get a job teaching history. Why are you wasting your time? Do something else." He didn't mind crushing my dream with his negativism. In his eyes he was simply giving me a "reality" check. My anxiety level rose to new heights, like grease sizzling in a hot frying pan. I asked Rosemary, "Where does my future lie? Do I go back to ministry or forward into teaching?" I did not know. My anxiety level zoomed upwards.

I did a practical thing in response. Delta Community College was next door to UOP. I went to the department chair of the Social Science Division and offered my services free of charge to their History teachers. Some of them held seminars for their students and I offered to fill in for them when they couldn't make it. As I worked for my California Credential in teaching I needed opportunities to "student teach." That filled the bill very nicely.

Then Edison High School in south Stockton called. The principal's secretary spoke and told me, "We need a full time substitute right now. Are you available?" Am I available? What a question! I was salivating for work. She called in early April and offered me the classroom of a pregnant teacher who had to take a maternity leave of absence. Never before was I so glad for a pregnancy. Praise God! They offered me a real teaching job.

Opening day was frozen in time. My class was made up of black and brown kids from poor South side neighborhoods. I was in my suit and tie, and armed with my briefcase of lesson plans. I was going to impress those kids with the stature of their new, long-term substitute teacher. Yes, I was ready to make a good impression.

Over the intercom came a commanding voice, "All rise and recite the Pledge of Allegiance." I stood and faced the flag behind me. I closed the Pledge with the immortal words ringing in my ears, "With liberty and justice for all." I turned and with my hands signaled for the students to sit down. But I was shocked. Not one student stood! They sat at their desks in a rebellious mode daring me to do something about it. In desperation I asked, "Why don't you stand up and show respect to the flag?" One black student shouted out his response, "That pledge stuff is a lie. Justice is "just us" white folks. It ain't for us. It's a bad joke!" What a start to my opening day as a teacher.

Something else was going on besides the rebelliousness. They were testing my mettle as a teacher. I was put to the ultimate test that day. It was a clear signal of what April, May and June would be like. Eventually we reached an understanding on how to work together. We even closed out the semester with a trip to Yosemite National Park in June. We began as antagonists and ended as friends. But it took immense patience and hard work to get there. God was watching out for me to get me through that final three months of the semester.

The students taught me some lessons. Let go of your briefcase. Ease up on your suit and tie. Talk to us at our level, not the level of UOP professors. Speak to us in a language we can understand without condescending. Have a passion for the teaching-learning process and some of us will pick up on it. Later I also discovered that underneath their anger was fear. Wasn't I learning once again from the Refiner's fire? God was burning off the dross from my soul in order to make me a better teacher.

Del McComb, a history teacher at Delta College, offered to let me teach his summer class in Western Civilization. He was going to travel that summer. I seized on the offer. In my dream plan I wanted to teach at Delta College and remain in Stockton. I had not had a class in Western Civilization, but I trusted my background and my zeal to carry me through the summer session. The textbook was a masterpiece of information and illustrations. I sweated through that hot summer preparing lesson plans where I tried to stay one step ahead of my students. Barely, just barely, I was able to do it.

But I worked night and day to keep ahead of them, and thus generated another wedge between Rosemary and me. What Rosemary needed was quality time together. First at College of the Holy Names, and now at UOP and Delta College, I felt the pressure to perform at my highest level. I did so, but again Rosemary needed me to help with the kids. I was giving my best time to my lesson plans, and Rosemary had to carry on without me. It was difficult for her.

During the fall I taught a class in American History for Stockton firefighters. I taught about 30 of them in the ready room of a nearby fire station. They were good students. They listened, took notes and passed their examinations. I was covering material in American History that I loved. It was a dream job, and I was glad that none of the regular faculty at Delta wanted to teach it. However, I noticed that all my students were white. There were no black or Hispanic firefighters in class, and yet Stockton was full of such people hungry for work. Stockton showed its segregation patterns in that class.

By this time it did not surprise me that Stockton had segregated schools and institutions. Yet that awareness left me with a lingering frustration that so few people seemed to see it. There were the typical rationalizations as to why minorities couldn't perform at acceptable levels. My question was, *how long would it take for Stockton to see itself and take action?*

In the spring I was still teaching part time for classes that regular faculty did not want, and happy to turn such classes over to me. Delta's Social Science Division announced a June opening for a full time teaching position in History. I pounced on it and sent my resume and an application to the Dean of Instruction. To my dismay hundreds of other teachers also applied. That opening was a dream job to me.

I wanted it so badly that my imagination burst forth with tantalizing images, *We could buy our first home. I could stop searching for work, pay off my student loan at UOP, and take my family on a vacation.* I wanted that job. I prayed for an opening. Fortunately, I had the good sense to do no lobbying with the regular faculty. I waited as the Selection Committee did their work.

In June 1971 the Committee had culled through hundreds of names and turned over to the Board of Trustees the names of their three final selections. My name was one of those three. I held my breath while the Board debated the merits of each candidate. I dared not go inside and listen to the debate since my emotions were at fever pitch. Finally, Harlan Hague, a faculty member, came out and told me my name had been selected for the job. Ecstasy! What a wonderful, amazing outcome. What an answer to prayer. God and His angels were looking out for me once again.

But another finalist named Doug Carter, a rising young politician in the area, took the news in anger. He stood before the trustees and charged that the deck was stacked against him. "There must have been collusion between the Committee and Mr. Bastear to come up with their choice," he insisted. After he had riled the Board with his spurious charges, he then wrote a letter to the editor of the "Stockton Record" making such charges public.

He claimed that there was cronyism between the Social Science faculty and me. He said the committee was biased against him as a conservative, and for me as some kind of flaming liberal. The whole thing, he wrote, had a very bad odor. I felt embarrassed to be the object of such charges, especially since all of this was made public information, and none of the charges were true. I decided it was better to make no reply. In my mind all the charges were baseless. The Trustees quietly let the charges fade into the background.

That didn't prevent me from inviting Rosemary and the kids for a dinner date. We celebrated the beginning of the rest of my life. My contract with the college called for a salary of $10,000 a year. That seemed fantastic to me, for it doubled what I had made as a pastor at Lamont. Now we rejoiced. Rosemary chirped, "Now we can buy our first home, go on vacation, and perhaps even buy a car." Using my veteran's status for a loan, I bought our first home for $23,000, a king's ransom to us. We moved in at the end of June 1971. The die was cast: I would be a teacher and not a preacher.

In my heart, however, I was still a pastor, but in my mind I was now a teacher. I would live with both images tucked inside. It looked as though my mid-life crisis was over. But subtle tensions between Rosemary and me still lingered. I had hopes of starting over as I began my new job.

I received a summons from Delta College to go to President Blanchard's office. There would be no formal contract for me until he signed on. An ex-marine, he directed the college with military precision. His secretary ushered me into his office. He looked up from studying my resume. "You were a minister, is that correct?" I replied, "Yes, it is." We discussed the ministry for a while, and then he said, "You must be used to speaking to large groups." I didn't disagree, although my congregations in the valley averaged between 35-50 persons. "Are you willing to teach large classes here?" I sensed his drift. The college had built several large lecture halls called, "The Forums," that could seat 150 students, and another could seat 175 students. The college stood to make a good income from the state with a student-teacher ratio like that.

I wanted that teaching contract and I replied, "I'll be willing to try large lecture classes and see how they work." Within a semester I was teaching large lecture classes, and the college was getting a good return on their investment in me.

Within months a fly in the ointment appeared. I was informed that the history position had been given to someone else. My department chair asked, "Would you be willing to teach Political Science?" I could say "No" and start looking elsewhere for a job, going through another grueling search. If I said "Yes" it meant scrambling to make myself proficient in a new subject. I had a degree from UC Davis in Political Science, but it had not prepared me to teach college classes. I responded, "I will take it." But for the next seven years I was busy studying hard. I also took a class at UOP, and prepared once again to become a first class teacher of Political Science. It meant more time away from Rosemary and the kids as I studied to teach. But what we needed was time together, not more time apart.

Teaching a brand new subject was a challenge for me. For instance, when students asked me a question in class that I could not answer I would often fake a reply. Funny thing, but students could see through that. I tried to look competent when in reality I did not feel that way. Some times they giggled as they saw me struggling to answer questions for which I had no answer. After a while I responded to such questions with "I don't know the answer, but I will look it up and have an answer ready for you at the next class session." I found that as I followed through and did my homework, the students respected that kind of honesty. Eventually through trial and error I became a better teacher. Years later I was elected by the students to be one of the top ten teachers on campus.

The Methodist Conference gave me an appointment to continue my ministerial relationship with them by giving me an "Appointment Beyond the Local Church." Thus, I kept my ordination, but no longer served in the pulpit. Rosemary, the kids and I became active at Central Methodist Church, across the street from UOP. We planned a trip to New Mexico during the summer of 1971 to visit Socorro where Rosemary grew up. We camped along the way, visited Indian villages of the southwest, and got as far as El Paso before we headed for home. Finally, we had time to have fun together. A sense of hope emerged as we shared together at the Gallup Indian Festival, camped out, and shared exotic foods in Albuquerque.

At home, I gave the kids more time. Steve and I joined the YMCA and took canoe lessons. We practiced guiding our Grumman aluminum canoe under the new Interstate 5 freeway over Fourteen-Mile Slough. We learned to weave between the concrete pillars that supported the freeway over the slough. Steve laughed when we hit a pillar saying: "Hey Dad, keep it straight. You can do better than that." Then we shifted positions and Steve sat in the rear guiding the canoe. After we hit a pillar or two I shouted back, "Hey, Steve, there is a pillar ahead. Could you please miss it?"

Our director took us to the Kjeldsen Pool at UOP and we learned to capsize canoes and kayaks, right them, and climb back in. We were having fun. Our graduation came on Memorial Day 1973. Our YMCA director towed the canoes and kayaks on a trailer and we headed north, following in a rented bus. We unloaded our boats north of Yuba City, put our canoes and kayaks in the water and headed down the Sacramento River.

What a weekend of fun. We hit rapids. Steve and I shouted, "Yippee! Look out below. We're coming through!" Have you ever had an adventure that you cannot forget? This was it. The air was hot. But the water was a deep blue and cool, punctuated with quiet pools and modest rapids. In the evening we camped along the banks of the river. We cooked our meals over an open fire. I caught a fish that kept me busy for five minutes hauling it in. It was an inedible sucker, and I threw it back into the river. The songs we sang around an open fire that night drew us together into a fellowship. We didn't haul out of the water until Monday when we were just north of Sacramento.

Our director now thought we were ready for the next challenge. We set a weekend date in June to drive to a place on the Mokelumne River just outside of Jackson called The Electra. The water, gushing out of the Sierra Nevada Mountains, was fast, icy cold, with a sharp drop in elevation that created numerous rapids and white water. With great excitement we unloaded our canoes and kayaks, and set them down at the edge of the white water.

What was it about adventure that always attracted me? I loved the sensation of challenging nature. But sometimes I was not careful enough in measuring the risks involved. I looked at the river, considered the skills we had learned and thought, *What an exciting challenge*! Our director had warned us about white water, but said we were ready for it. Those who felt unready could stay on shore and watch. Not me. Steve was now 14 and he and I would launch out and test our canoeing skills.

With my paddle I took the stern of the canoe, the steering position. "Wow. Here we go!" I dodged around numerous rocks. We moved swiftly in the fast water. In the front end of the canoe Steve paddled furiously to keep control as we dodged huge granite boulders. Suddenly, a great rock was in front of us and I felt like the helmsman of the Titanic. We could not avoid hitting it. We slammed into the rock, yawed crazily to the port side, and the canoe groaned as it rolled over and threw us into the river. Steve was thrown toward the side nearest the shore while I was thrown toward the center of the fast water.

Our life jackets kept us afloat. Steve made it ashore as I struggled in midstream. Steve cried out and pointed behind me. I turned to see the canoe, sunken to its gunwales, drifting straight at me. The director had warned us that such a canoe weighs over a ton, and can be very dangerous in fast water if it hits you. I grabbed on to the granite boulder, and the canoe came up behind me slamming me against the boulder.

The sheer power of the current held me wedged between the canoe and the boulder. Then the weight of the canoe pushed me under the water. I was now under the canoe, trapped in icy stream water that pressed me against the giant boulder. I panicked when I realized I could not push myself up. It was one of those moments that you read about. My life flashed before me just as I had read of others caught in a crisis situation. What I saw were the dramatic moments of my life: my conversion at Davis, my decision to become a minister, seminary, and now trapped in icy waters. This was really happening to me, and I was going to be the ultimate victim. I had 60 seconds to live or die. That awareness created a fear in me of Biblical proportions, like that of king Belshazzar seeing a prophecy of doom on his palace walls. But that panic served me well. I felt a shot of adrenalin enter my bloodstream.

In that moment I decided I did not want to die. I kicked against the rock as hard as I could and surfaced on the upstream side of the capsized canoe. Now, I headed toward shore. The bone-chilling water kept pushing me downstream. Exhausted, I kept my arms pumping the water for the safety of the shore. Hypothermia was setting in. Swimming frantically helped prevent hypothermia from taking over my body.

I made my way toward a sandy bar. When I finally reached it I was so weak I could not stand up. My legs shook violently. I felt like I was trying to stand on jello legs. I collapsed into the sand. One of the team members found me, and with my arm around his shoulder, I hobbled back to where Steve stood. I embraced him and held on, weeping and mumbling that I was still alive. Steve and I bonded in those moments. I cherished the bonding, but never again went canoeing in white water. I learned another valuable lesson about challenging the power of nature. There are limits, and I needed to respect them. I slowly began to learn the importance of boundaries.

Now I was finding ways to be with the kids on weekends. We went camping in the Sierras to places like Jackass Meadow and Florence Lake. I went to Steve's Little League baseball games. I took Suzanne to be with her friends at their parties. Fatherhood became a source of joy for me.

In 1971 I did something new and different with Steve. I fashioned backpacks for us out of surplus Army gear. We filled them with dehydrated foods, sleeping bags and such, and headed to Lake Edison in the Sierras. We had fun building a campsite near the lake, and then we gathered wood for a campfire. We had steaks cooked over an open fire, and enjoyed the myriad of stars that hovered overhead. The next day I went too fast on the trail up Cold Creek, and right after lunch he asked to stop. Suddenly he vomited his lunch. That was a signal to me to slow down. I apologized to Steve for the speed.

We followed the trail along Cold Creek, fishing wherever we camped. I taught him the art of trout fishing. Floyd Moon, Rosemary's father, had taught me how to fish at Rabbit Ear's Pass in Colorado. Now I passed along the skill to Steve. He became a fast learner. The brook trout were hungry and we caught a limit quickly. Steve pitched in and helped me gather wood for our fire. Then I shared skills of cooking over an open fire. Father and son were bonding, creating a relationship that I lacked with my father. Steve liked learning new wilderness skills, so well in fact, that we took a week out of every summer to backpack in the High Sierra. Over the next twenty years we hiked trails between Mt. Whitney on the south to Lake Tahoe on the northern stretch of the Sierras. One summer we also hiked along the spine of the Grand Tetons in Wyoming.

At the same time a different kind of relationship began between Suzanne and myself. While Steve and I did things together, Suzanne and I developed along the lines of being together. Father and daughter had a different quality to it than father and son. Sons tend to be emotionally closer to their moms, while daughters tend to idealize their fathers. So I could simply enjoy Suzanne's relationship, while I needed to work on Steve's relationship.

But Rosemary and I were floundering. We had never fully recovered from her letdown when she asked for more help with the kids while I ministered in Lamont. I had failed to address that request. The shock of the Chicago ghetto still weighed on her thinking. Now I spent significant blocks of time playing catch-up with Political Science. It was one thing after another driving wedges in our relationship. She went to Oregon to spend time with her parents. Later, when she returned, she asked me to move out and try a temporary separation. Then she invited me to return. Then, she asked me again to move out, later to return. This cycle of separation and reconciliation took a toll on both of us.

One day we decided to drive to Mt. Diablo and talk. We parked in a lovely spot over looking our valley. I had reached a decision. I told Rosemary in tears that I was ready to give up my lingering admiration for Ecumenical Institute. I would take down our Picasso drawing of "Guernica", and stop waking the kids each morning with a Buddhist gong. Those were symbolic acts, but they were very real to me. I told her, "I want to rejoin the human race, become active in Central Methodist Church, be a part of mainstream Christianity, and give up my relationship with EI and the South Stockton Parish." That decision and those promises were major motion to me, and I meant to keep them.

I was late with my appeal, but Rosemary had a suggestion. Two professors from UOP were offering a "Seminar at Sea." Dr. Walt Nyberg and his wife, and Dr. Helmut Reimer had booked a cruise line going to Cabo San Lucas, Mazatlan, and Puerto Vallarta. Their offer was to mix the joy of a cruise to the Mexican Riviera with some solid work on human relationships. We decided to join the cruise, and see if we could put our marriage back on secure footing once again.

We sailed out of San Pedro in June of 1974 with some cautious hope for what we could accomplish. We had about 20 persons in our group and we blended well together. Each morning our two leaders met us in a seminar room, and led us into discussion on, "What does it mean to be in relationship?" It sounded intellectual, but they kept it practical, at a level where we could interact with them and one another. Each of us was in some kind of relationship. One of their questions was, "How do you see your partner? Spend some time now sharing with your partner what do you like about your partner? Then, spend some time sharing where you are frustrated with them."

Another morning we dealt with the concept of touching. "Does your partner like your touch?" came the question. "Ask her now." Then, "Do you cling too close, or are you too distant?" Ask, "How she would like to be touched, and practice that with her now." Then we reversed roles. After lunch we wandered the decks, or if we were in port we went ashore and walked the waterfront of Mazatlan or Puerta Vallerta. We had a wonderful cruise. But Rosemary and I did not resolve the basic feelings between us.

Why didn't the cruise become a healing balm for us? For one thing Rosemary had already come to a decision about us. For instance, she asked that we go "Dutch treat." While in Mazatlan we stopped to buy a coke at a curbside vendor run by two sturdy, middle-aged senoras. Rosemary bought hers and I bought mine. The senoras did not have a clue that I could speak Spanish. I heard one senora say about me to the other, "No es un caballero." (He's not a gentleman) Not very complementary, but it did indicate the level of intimacy between us. I think Rosemary had already made up her mind that her relationship with me was now tentative. She decided to keep a certain amount of distance.

The summer of 1974 was a roller coaster ride for us. I was in, and then out again. In September Rosemary asked me to move out. My response was firm, "If I move out again I will never return." She did not change her mind. On October 1st, I moved into an apartment about a mile away and began life on my own.

It was a devastating move. I truly was alone. There is a temporary moment of exhilaration about being a "free man." Mostly, however, I missed my family, and I missed all the familiar routines of Rosemary and the kids. I believe it was hard on the kids. They sometimes rode their bicycles to my apartment to see how I was. I began to wonder,

How are we going to exist separately from each other? How am I ever going to put them through college? I had lived as a poor parson and now had no way to pay for their higher education.

Each night I cried myself to sleep, that is, if I could sleep. There had to be a "Balm in Gilead" for me. But churches in those days did not minister to singles. Singles were considered strange and different, a breed apart. Church members asked, "Weren't ministers supposed to stay married for life?"

I asked questions of friends and found that the Catholic Diocese of Stockton had begun a Saturday group counseling program for singles and married couples with relationship problems. Just as in Oakland with the College of Holy Names, so now it was the Catholics again who reached out to us in Stockton. The group met every Saturday morning from nine until noon at a rented building near downtown. The leader, Reid Cerney, a counselor and Catholic layman trained for such a ministry, became our leader.

Immediately I began attending. I had a huge wound in my self-esteem. After all, my wife had asked me to leave our home. That seemed shameful to me. I was a trained pastor and knew about psychology and relationships. Yet here I was, in effect, out on the streets and alone. Our group had a dozen members, some single, some married. We sat in a circle with Reid in a prominent position. He dialogued with us just as Dr. Reimer and Dr. Nyberg had done on board ship. The only difference now was that there was no Mexican Riviera waiting for us.

Reid used group dynamics as well as role-playing. We shared quite openly and healing began to take place. I found two special friends in our group. One was Al and the other was Ike. Al's marriage was on the rocks, and Ike was a single that was getting teased at work because he did not relate to women. We formed a life-long friendship, and became backpacking buddies.

After six months I was feeling back on my feet again. I joined Parents Without Partners, (PWP), and started making new friends there. Jim Robinson, an old timer on the singles scene, took me under his wing, and guided me through some danger spots. He warned me which of the women to keep at arm's length, whom to avoid altogether, and which might be good prospects. I attended the PWP parties and the Saturday night dances at the Union Hall. I took dance lessons again, but found out that most of the women at the PWP dances only knew the two-step and I reverted to that.

I began reading books written for singles, or books dealing with relationships. I was determined to rebuild my life as a single. I got so interested that I shared with other members what I was learning. Members would start asking me questions about what I was reading. They wanted to know more. I started a Tuesday night book club at my apartment under the rubric of PWP. On Tuesdays my front room filled with people. I led a discussion on the book "Games People Play," by Eric Berne.

What Berne was talking about was me. He listed and described the psychological games that we play in our relationships, and I found that at some time or another I played them all. How could I teach this to others if I could not recognize them in myself? To be a facilitator I had to take Berne's message to heart and make some changes.

I shared the concepts of Dr. Thomas Harris "I'm OK, You're OK." He built on the theory of Dr. Berne and created the concept of Parent, Adult, and Child, and how in our minds we play tapes from our past over again, all the way into adulthood. I reached out with Jess Lair's book "I Ain't Much Baby, But I'm All I Got." Jess kept it pretty simple and basic and his ideas resonated well with the members. One of the most challenging books I read was Eric Berne's "What Do You Say After You Say Hello?" It seemed to me that Berne was a seminal thinker for our generation. I spent hours trying to digest his concepts.

But, trying to communicate Eric Berne to the Tuesday night seekers was another stretch. I found that for most people to really apply it to their own person took more than simply reading a book and discussing it. It meant mentally grappling with a counselor who has been there, and going deeper into their own behavior.

I was a prime example of the failure to learn some of those concepts. My behavior changed and I am not sure I can fully explain the change. I slowly but surely became a womanizer. I became the very opposite of what I had learned. At the Saturday night dances I met all kinds of divorcées. Attracted to some of them, I would invite a lady to meet at a coffee shop on Pacific Avenue where a dozen other PWP members met after each dance, and we talked far into the night.

After coffee, perhaps an invitation to her apartment for more conversation followed. Conversation often turned to romance, and romance became sex. It had a familiar ring to it, as though I was reliving what I did with women in Trieste. It is hard to explain, but I was both attracted and repelled by my behavior at the same time. One part of me was attracted to the adventure of meeting a new woman. If we communicated well, I wanted to find if "she was the one I was looking for." Eventually the question became, "My place or your place?" The other part of me wanted to pull away from this behavior, because it was a repeat of my behavior with women in Trieste. But I continued with this pattern.

Sunday morning arrived and I got out of bed, shaved and put on my Sunday "Come to Jesus" clothes, and headed for church. I sat in a pew at Central Methodist Church where I could be by myself, and as we sang hymns of faith, I wept. *Hadn't my soul been touched by God's grace at UC Davis?* Tears rolled down my cheeks and I kept wiping them away with my handkerchief. I felt deeply convicted over my behavior with Saturday night ladies, but couldn't (wouldn't?) stop what I was doing. Was there anyone out there who could understand and explain my behavior? Finally, in desperation, I called my pastor, Dr. Robert Moon, and asked if I could have an appointment to talk to him.

We sat in his office and I tried to explain myself. I was quite clear that as a pastor I had not a leg to stand on. Jesus was clear in the gospels that sex belongs inside marriage. However, is not intimacy between divorcees a kind of grey area that needs clarification? I was a pastor on special appointment, committing acts that were contrary to my ministerial vows, but how contrary? Dr. Moon knew of my Methodist ordination. I asked, "Is it right to have sex with a divorcee? What does scripture call sex between two divorced, consenting adults?" Bob's response gave me some comfort. He replied: "Sex is all right if you love her. If you don't love her, you should refrain."

I left his office feeling better about myself. However, what I didn't say was equally important. That is, I wasn't really in love, but simply exploring for that perfect woman who would some day become my wife, and using that as an excuse to continue my behavior. I was rationalizing my behavior.

Some years earlier, while Rosemary and I we were still married, I went backpacking with Rosemary's father, Floyd, into the southern Sierra Nevada. We were climbing Mt. Whitney, and camped at a 10,000-foot lake to fish and rest. Mosquitoes hovered over a nearby lake, inviting golden trout to surface and feast. Within 30 minutes we easily caught a limit of these beautiful fish, tinted with a golden color over their bodies.

A cookout under the stars brought us together into male bonding. The Milky Way slowly arced across the chilly night, surrounding us like a diadem of silvery jewels in the sky. There were no trees at 10,000 feet, so we had no fire. To bring out the flavor of the trout I harvested wild onions from the banks of a nearby brook and chopped them into pieces to fry with the fish.

My one-burner camp stove ignited like a flamethrower. With my light aluminum skillet, we could cook anything in minutes. I knew when the golden trout was ready to eat: when the eyes popped out. Floyd cooked his the same way while I feasted on fresh trout and cowboy coffee. Both of us shed formalities. We got into guy talk, one of the neat things between men while backpacking. He asked me a question that was simmering in his mind. He said: "Dick, you're a pastor. You are a man of the cloth. Tell me, why did God make sex so good? Sometimes it makes me wonder…." and his voice trailed off, unable to complete his sentence. What he was trying to say, I think, was why did God make sex so wonderful that the male of the species is tempted to stray from monogamy?

What is the answer to Floyd's question? As a single male I was now experiencing the reality of that question in my behavior. I was not comfortable with my inability to stay within Christian guidelines for divorcees, yet I did not change. A conflict emerged inside of me that others could not see, but I could feel it bubbling in my soul. My higher self, or what Freud called the super ego, criticized my actions. The lower self, or what Freud called the Id, was determined to have his own way.

Freud added, however, that each person has to learn to do what he termed "sublimate." That is, we need to modify instinctual sexual urges into socially acceptable ways. In our culture sublimation means "monogamy." As a single I was cut off from the bonds of marriage. Was I capable of being a chaste single?

Was I becoming a case of Dr. Jekyll and Mr. Hyde? At times it seemed so. But something St. Paul said in his letter to the church at Rome rang even louder in my mind:

I do not understand my own actions. For I do not do what I want, but I do the very thing I hate---So then it is no longer I that do it, but sin which dwells within me. (Romans 7: 15-17).

I was now a classic case of what Paul called sin. I felt convicted and hypocritical. Becoming a fraud and knowing it created a tension inside my mind that did not go away. Paul cried out, "O wretched man that I am! Who will deliver me from this body of death?" (7:24) This struggle of the soul showed the importance once again of why I cried out to God for deliverance.

However, while my personal life was crumbling, my professional life started expanding. During spring vacation of 1975 my Division Chair, Bill Dofflemyer, invited me to go with him on a tour of east coast historical sites called "American Heritage East." Along with 50 Delta College students we toured from Boston down to Washington DC, celebrating in stops along the way the bicentennial of the American Revolution. I got a whole new picture of the story of America.

At the Old North Church in Boston we saw where the plotting and planning for revolution took place. At Breed's Hill, not Bunker Hill, the patriots faced the wrath of the British army, stood their ground and fought valiantly. At Lexington and Concord we found examples of more patriot courage as the Minute Men stood to fight the British army. There the enraged British troops bayoneted the rebels lying wounded on the ground. It was as if we could once again hear the sound of the shot heard round the world. This was living history. We weren't reading about it. We were reliving it. Our students came alive, and so did I, as we visited such historic places around Boston and then continued to Plymouth, Hartford, Constitution Hall in Philadelphia, Gettysburg Battle Field, Annapolis, and Washington DC.

Never again could I be prosaic in my teaching about America. We found that history is an ever-changing dialogue between the past and the present. My sense of the present was activated. We 50 "students" became involved learners of American history. I found a new dynamic existed in my teaching. Good teachers are good students; good students are good teachers.

I turned my photographs into slides, and projected them on a screen for my classes. Perhaps I could startle them awake as to the drama that is America. I used those photos each year in my classes. My mantra became, never let your classes be boring. There is so much to learn.

I started a class at Delta called "Sacramento Seminar." I traveled with a handful of Delta students to Sacramento, and we stayed for a week. I arranged a meeting with Governor Brown, and found it amazingly simple to secure the interview. The key that opened the door was to say "This is for my Delta College students." He instinctively knew that students would be easy to talk to. Even though I primed the class beforehand with questions they could ask, their first question to him was, "Did you have a good time in Africa traveling with Linda Ronstadt?" That brought laughter and an easing of the tensions they felt at meeting the governor. He was coy in his response and led us to believe that it was purely a platonic relationship. We did not believe him. Then came questions like, "Why do reporters call you "Governor Moonbeam?" He shared his criticism of the press. He felt that they failed to see what he was trying to accomplish for the state.

I followed the same technique to secure entrance to the chief justice of the California Supreme Court, Rose Bird. She was liberal in her interpretation of the Constitution. She handed down decisions that strengthened environmental oversight, and decisions that put a stop to carrying out the death penalty in California. She was often criticized as "soft on crime," and was later voted out of office. She was the first woman to serve on the high court. We felt humbled to be able to talk with her. She spoke in broad terms of her judicial philosophy, while we quietly listened. Meeting her impressed us, especially the girls in our group. Our female students saw her as a role model.

B.T. Collins, head of the California Conservation Corps, was unforgettable. A wounded soldier, he was nearly killed by a grenade blast in Viet Nam. He survived the loss of his arm and became unique in every way. He kept us laughing with his sharp critique of politicians in Sacramento. He turned the Corps into a first class environmental organization. B.T. gave funny nicknames to all the major players in Sacramento. He became so famous at this that everyone wanted a moniker from B.T. I was impressed with him and I encouraged my son Steve to join the Corps when he graduated from Delta College. Steve liked the Corps enough that he almost made it into a career. I suggested the Corps to Gayle's son Gary and he told me later the experience turned his life around.

I took my students to attend several candidate's fund raising cocktail parties. We were impressed with the quantity of good food, beautifully dressed women in low-slung cocktail gowns, and alcoholic drinks in abundance. I asked, "How do our political leaders keep their ethical standards in an atmosphere like this?" B.T. Collins was one of those people in Sacramento who did not become egotistical, and kept his focus on public service.

Willie Brown, speaker of the Assembly, was next on my agenda. He shared how he was born into a shanty in a cotton patch in Mineola, Texas. Raised by his feisty grandmother, she told him, "Willie, you can do anything you want. Don't let anyone tell you differently." Willie continued, "I took it in and believed her." Of course he did not mention that to make a living in the highly segregated town of Mineola his family brewed moonshine, and served it to select customers at their store. Now he emerged as the second most powerful man in Sacramento. The students listened intently to Willie. He was believable, and a real person.

I invited him to come to Delta College and speak at his first opportunity. His response was, "I'll make a note to my secretary and she will arrange it." But he never made it. These seminars proved to be the best series of classes in Political Science I ever taught. More and more I concluded that politics consisted of real people making real decisions that in turn impacted California. This was "living politics," rather than teaching it. My students told me as we wrapped up a week in Sacramento that this was the best class in politics that they had ever taken. I moved forward in my teaching.

I also planned trips to broaden my horizons. In 1976 I attended a seminar sponsored by the University of St. Mary's to spend Holy Week in Mexico City. We got an in-depth look at Mexican culture, beginning with the Spanish conquest, then colonialism, and finally, modern Mexico. All three were on view in the architecture of Mexico City. One of the ways that I did my viewing was to leave the group and walk across much of the city, including the poor barrios. (Our leader later warned me, "Don't try that again; there is too much crime in the city," he explained.)

In the barrios I saw frequent drunkenness or "borrachos," as they were called. Always, not far away, were the ubiquitous signs of the PRI, Mexico's ruling political party, urging the people to higher moral standards of living, especially the fathers. For example, one sign read, "Fathers, be good to you children. They look up to you."

I walked to the basilica of the Virgin of Guadalupe where, during "Santa Semana" or holy week, peasants came to the basilica on their hands and knees to worship God. Somehow this was both touching and repulsive to me. The poverty and simple faith of the peasants, versus the wealth of the upper class, drew a sharp contrast in my mind. Mexico was only slowly emerging out of its colonial past. Our leader quoted a popular proverb, "Poor Mexico; so far from God, so close to the United States." Out of all this experience I learned a deeper respect for Mexico and its people.

In the summer of 1977 I took a 22-day grand tour of South America to prepare myself to teach a class on Latin American Politics. We started in Rio de Janeiro, Brazil, and then went on to Buenos Aires, Santiago, Chile, and ended at Machu Picchu and Lima in Peru. In each capital I took time to visit the Political Affairs Officer at our American embassies. They briefed me on major happenings in their country.

The officer in Buenos Aires seemed to lie to me when I asked about the so- called "Dirty War" going on in Argentina. At least 30,000 Montonero rebels, or even suspected rebels, were summarily arrested, and then executed by dropping them out of military aircraft from 10,000 feet over the Atlantic. It was an open and dirty secret that no one wanted to talk about. The Political Affairs Officer claimed to have no such information. My political instincts told me that his so-called ignorance was pure mendacity.

I found a similar reluctance to speak frankly at our embassy in Santiago. Our hotel was next door to the presidential palace and I could see the bomb craters like open wounds where General Pinochet ordered his air force to bomb the palace. General Pinochet also ordered his troops to attack the democratically elected president Salvador Allende. All of this was planned with the cooperation of president Nixon working through the CIA. My regard for American foreign policy plummeted to an all time low. We were supporting the reactionary forces of the military across South America, all in the name of anti-communism. I came back from the trip discouraged regarding America's role in South America. I shared my appraisal with the students in my classes, and they too were disappointed. My patriotism took another hit on that trip.

The following summer I studied in the Soviet Union under the auspices of UC Berkeley, to prepare myself to teach a class called "Political Ideologies." We spent two weeks in St. Petersburg, (then called Leningrad), and two weeks in Moscow. Our leader arranged meetings with our equivalents in Russia, teachers with teachers, medical people met with their clinicians, and so forth. We found that we could make easy conversation with them. That is until political scientists met each other. There was an immediate sense that each side wanted an advantage, and we warily sought to proclaim the righteousness of our side against their side. Political conversation broke down.

Otherwise, I was impressed with Russian hospitality and friendliness. My hostess was a Russian lady, short and stout in size, a veteran of the Red Army who served during WWII. She proudly shared with us how she trained as a sniper, shooting and killing twelve Germans. That was my first time to meet a female veteran of combat. I believed what she told us.

Our facilitator from Berkeley urged us to bring along some luxury goods as gifts to our hosts. I gave my veteran hostess 2 pairs of nylon stockings. She clutched them joyously to her breast, as if I had given her gold. After seeing so many czarist palaces, grand museums, and the Kremlin, the image of our hostess clutching those precious nylons so exuberantly stands out in my mind. We visited her apartment in Moscow. The stark concrete walls, broken by an occasional piece of furniture, held some bric-a-brac, which softened only slightly the monotony of concrete. All apartments were the same, reflecting communist egalitarianism. By our standards they were equally depressing. There were no private homes in Moscow.

Out in the rural countryside Russian peasants still brought in the harvest in horse drawn vehicles. The Soviet Union was two worlds in one: rural poverty in stark contrast to the backdrop of a more prosperous city life. I couldn't quite see how we treated them as such a formidable super power. Their structural weaknesses were obvious. With each trip I was getting experience as well as photographs to make my classes more interesting.

However, my personal life was languishing. I brought the world to the students in my classes, but on Saturday nights at PWP dances, I reverted to the same form I had shown in Trieste. Only now, I was relentless in my pursuit of a perfect woman. I know I hurt some women with that pursuit. I was using them for my own purposes, and rationalizing my behavior. If the Methodist Conference were to discover my behavior I would be asked to surrender my credentials and leave the ministry. Yet as fate would have it, the Annual Conference was concerned with other problems.

How ironic to begin life where sex was prohibited and now to find my sex life was out of control. How did that happen? It began as I tried to heal the wounds of divorce. Then at the Saturday night dances with PWP I began a relentless pursuit of divorcées.

Eventually my hubris began to sense the creeping presence of nemesis. To all appearances I was living the life of a happy single. But from the vantage point of my professional life and my Christian calling, I was a living lie. I contradicted everything I knew about being a Christian. I couldn't keep on living a double life. Something had to give.

This was an ethical quandary of the first order. *Was I trapped in it?* In Kierkegaard's words, I had "a sickness unto death." I needed a new standard of courage to find my way out of this dilemma.

By 1978, suicidal thoughts crossed my mind. That was a new and frightening phenomenon to me. I knew I was in deep trouble. I began questioning friends as to where a single could go for support. Several friends told me about a group in Stockton that met on a weekly basis. I was desperate. I needed help if I was to break my womanizing and get back on track with my personal life. I decided to find a solution to my double life. I was ready for a new start.

Twenty-Four

The Rhinoceros & The Pussy Cat

I am about to write the most difficult chapter of this book. I wish it was easier, but it is not. I feel compelled to be candid, and yet I know some one may get their feelings hurt in the process. But, why write this memoir if I cannot be candid? As so often is the case in life, there are many wonderful and painful things that happen together. Fascinating isn't it, that joy and sorrow are so often inseparably mixed? And can be blended into one person.

I called a woman named Carol, and asked for an appointment with her. She led a class in Transactional Analysis (TA) that met weekly at the Marina Gym, next door to the boat harbor on Benjamin Holt Drive in Stockton. I described my situation frankly, for it was too late to try and make myself look good. I wanted to invent a false reason for coming, but why do that? I was already living a double life. Remember T.S. Eliot's line, "(We are) the hollow men/the stuffed men." I thought: *I am that hollow man, as empty as a drum.*

I had been living with a hamper full of excuses for my womanizing. I had taken a vow at my ordination to live an exemplary life for Christ, doing nothing that would bring disrespect on his ministry. Yet here I was doing the very thing I vowed never to do. I deserved to have my ordination revoked and my Conference membership terminated. Floyd, Rosemary's Dad, once said that preachers who use women for their own purposes, "Ought to be horsewhipped." He could have been talking about me.

But I figured out ways to escape the terrible truth about me. I developed some huge rationalizations, the biggest of which I used to cover my sins and transgressions. It was that God's grace and mercy were wide enough and deep enough to forgive my behavior. That worked all week. Yet when I went to Central Methodist on Sunday mornings and began to weep, the wall I built between my conscience and my lifestyle broke down. I knew it was time to listen to Carol. She invited me to come to her group.

Carol always dressed like a woman on a mission, and was the obvious leader. She walked with assurance, stood tall, and spoke confidently. Her long blond hair stood in sharp contrast to her darker blouses, pants and boots. She opened her class with the simple words, "What's happening? Can we talk?" There must have been thirty people there, sitting in a large circle so that we could each see one another face-to-face. Someone would open with a situation at home or at work with which they struggled and could not solve.

Members of the group would respond to the dilemma that was presented, and speak frankly about that person's style of handling their crisis, that is indeed, if they could handle it. I was impressed with the candor in the group. To me it was like a "no holds barred" wrestling match. Now and then Carol stepped in if someone got hurt in the dialogue, or if we did not have a clear grasp of the issue.

I sat and listened and felt intimidated by the honesty with which they talked to one another. In everyday social affairs we often pass time by talking about the weather, some common sporting event, or the frustrations of the day. Voltaire put it succinctly when he said, "Speech was given to man to disguise his thoughts."

I grew up in a home where disguised thoughts were the order of the day. As a single male I reinforced that style and forgot my Christian teachings that we are to "speak the truth in love." Eventually, Carol asked, "What's happening with you, Dick?" Now I was invited to become a part of the conversation, and of course, with so many skeletons in my closet to hide, I bumbled my way into an introduction. The people in the group were aware that I did not reveal my real reasons for being there. I am not a good liar. They immediately heard my response and challenged me.

I shut the door tightly on my reasons for attending, and gave some trumped up ideas as to why I had come to group. It was too hard to be honest. In the process I tried to make myself look good. Here I was a pastor on special appointment, a teacher at Delta College, active at Central Methodist Church, and living a double life as a womanizer. It was a scandalous life, and I was skating on thin ice. Something had to give. But I wasn't ready quite yet to expose my wound and find healing.

It took me four meetings to finally be honest with the group. I felt like the drunkard at an AA meeting who simply did not know how to say the profound words, "I am an alcoholic." When an alcoholic can say those words after a lifetime of dodging the facts, that is his moment of truth. There are addictions to liquor, drugs, to food, and cigarettes. My addiction, however, was to sex. How could I stand before the class and say the profound words, "I am a sex addict." It seemed that if I blurted out those words I would enter Dante's hell, where carved on the entryway was an ominous warning "Lose all hope all ye who enter here." I was barely hanging on. *How could I let go of my last vestige of self-respect?*

Carol finally came to my aid. I shared with her my dilemma, that I did not know how to be as honest with the group as I was with her. I did not know my way out. She asked, "Have you ever felt like you are going crazy?" I thought about it for a moment and suddenly realized, "Yes, I have." She responded, "You are going crazy because you are living a double life, and you are no longer able to live that way. Share with the others what that is like for you, and they will listen to you." Implicit was the thought that when I did so my double life will be exposed, and like an act of repentance, I could begin the process of change and healing.

On the following Tuesday night I shared honestly with the group. I had never spoken so boldly and frankly about myself before. What a transition! What a relief! I felt like I shed a 50-pound weight off of my back. I had a new sense of freedom from my guilty past. It was sweeter than the honey in a honeycomb. The group heard me speak and quickly began asking me questions. They welcomed me into their camaraderie. From the moment that I shared more honestly with them I slowly began to shed my double life. I was grateful, and I was learning to share.

To drive home a point to me, Carol talked about my dog Mac Duff, a white and liver-spotted Springer Spaniel. He had a bad habit. He would hump anything that moved, including people. Carol asked one day, "Do you want to be like Mac Duff? You have been acting just like him. Do you really want to risk your inner child with strange women?" The fact of the matter was, "No, I do not." Then came the response, "Then behave differently!"

About twenty of the class members were attending the First Nazarene Church, the same church that Carol attended. I told my pastor at Central United Methodist in March of 1979 that I would like to take a brief leave of absence and attend there. The doctrines of the Nazarene church were deeply conservative, and I hesitated about attending. But I decided to set those doubts aside and go. Our Nazarene group filled two pews. Afterwards we went several blocks to a McDonalds and had lunch together. We had fun and laughter over our burgers.

We also had parties on Friday nights, and every effort was made to keep this from being a "meat market" as was sometimes the case at Parents Without Partners' parties. Boundaries were established at our class parties and we honored them. I made very sure not to invite anyone home afterwards. In fact, I decided to quit Parents Without Partners. The fellowship that we enjoyed at our TA group was centered on a code of honesty that asked each person to take a deeper look at who they were. I renewed my vow of chastity. Carol was a committed Christian, and we treated each other with respect.

Several women in the group told me they would like to see me dress with an eye to fashion, and replace the dull brown slacks that I had been wearing. I went to the mall with them, and under their guidance, I bought a leather jacket, a colorful Italian shirt, and some navy blue slacks. A new leather hand-held pouch that contained my wallet and personal items topped off my new look. I looked in the mirror and liked what I saw. I felt good as I shaped up my appearance.

Pastor Ray preached a dynamic sermon on the third Sunday of March and closed with an altar call. I sat in our pew and suddenly realized, *God is speaking to me*. It was an awesome feeling; I could not let it go. It was a God moment. But I froze in my place. I was so nailed to earth that I didn't know how to respond to such a moment. The Pastor invited us once again to come forward and pray. My inner prompting was to *Go forward, Go! Go now or you will forever regret it.* The prompting would not cease or be still. My heart was pounding. I thought surely everyone could see my chest pulsating. *But what will others think of me?* Then came an insistent voice, *Won't they judge me? What will they say about me? Now everyone will know how needy I am. They will know I am convicted by the message.*

I don't know how I did it, but I stood up in my pew. It was contrary to every instinct in me. My instinct was to stay frozen in place. *Pastors don't go forward for altar calls*, an inner voice said. *Only sinners do that. But Dick, you are a sinner.* I slowly moved down the seated row of worshippers. My heart was roaring as I moved down the aisle to the railing. I knelt down, cupped my head in my hands, and asked God to forgive me for all my sins, for all my failings.

My definition of sin is separation from God, as well as separation from your essential self, and separation from others. Some theologians say the separation is more apparent than real. For me it was very real. Suddenly, I felt my newfound friends at my side. They put their hands on my head and shoulders. They were praying for me. We all prayed together. When I stood up, we embraced, laughing and crying together. I was healed of the inner torment. Once again God delivered me from despair. I could fly free from the cage in which I had been living. It was a joy to be set free.

I had been saved at UC Davis over twenty years earlier. But now I was finding that my Davis conversion experience was a partial step forward. It was a beginning, not an ending. I found that salvation is an ongoing, life-long process. God was still with me after all those years. I had been through the Refiner's fire and now I was the better for it. Perhaps God was revealing to me that He had never left. Such was His promise.

Most of us in our class decided to participate in a program developed by Paul Meyer called "Dynamics of Personal Motivation." It consisted of a series of 14 lectures on audiotapes that we could listen to on our own time. With pencil and paper we created notebooks of our work. I purchased a tape recorder and began listening to lectures, writing my responses as I set goals for living, and wrote down my own personal affirmations to bolster my new decisions.

We set goals for our character development, and created another set of targets for home, work, and our spiritual life. With a new sense of enthusiasm, I spent my spare time listening to tapes and listing aspirations for myself. One program dealt with "Understanding Motivation," another with "Five Success Essentials," "The Art of Visualization," and "Your Personal Plan of Action." Even though my progress seemed like two steps forward and one step back, I pressed forward. I listened daily to the tapes as I drove my car.

Our group also had marathon sessions one Saturday a month. Sometimes we met for an entire weekend. On one of those weekend trips we went to Carol's cabin in the mountains above Porterville, at a place called Three Rivers. It was a beautiful location. We took breaks to walk in the nearby hills, along small streams. Otherwise we were in class together. On Sunday our group spent the morning one by one sitting in front of a large mirror. We spoke out loud as we shared what we used to be, and then what we were determined to become.

When it was my turn, I sat and faced myself in the mirror. I saw myself in a new light. In fact I began to see myself as whom I could become. I spoke of my time in Parents Without Partners when I used women for my own purposes. I became an addict to my own behavior.

Then there came a day when I could no longer live with myself. I leveled with the group, myself, and with God. Then I shared with them the man that I chose to become: warm, strong, and grounded in God. It seemed as though a new self emerged in me. There was power in the fellowship and in the truths spoken in that encounter. It was like what the philosopher Martin Buber called, *I-Thou*, a deeper way of knowing both you and another person.

After lunch we packed our things and said farewell. I climbed into my car and as I drove away I broke into songs of faith and joy. I affirmed from the depths of my being, *I will never go back to the womanizer that I used to be. That is over and done with. I am starting fresh again. Praise God!* I was so full of joy that happy tears streamed down my face on the way home. I thanked God for my new life.

In the New Testament there is chronos time and kairos time. Chronos time registers the passage of time as in a calendar. Time marches on and there is not much we can do about it. Kairos time, on the other hand, is meaningful time. I was now caught up in kairos time. Have you ever had the experience where time stands still? It is often an experience of the presence of God. Maybe it is what Christians call grace. Whatever I called it, my life came together into a wholeness of joy and peace. All I knew was that I was free to rejoice and sing, to live my life and praise God. I stepped outside myself, and it was glorious. A sobering thought emerged however. I would be a recovered sex addict for the rest of my life. But that was a small price to pay for the gift I had been given.

I began to think about marriage once again. The words of a popular song hit home with me, "Looking for Love in All the Wrong Places." It had been almost five years since Rosemary asked me to leave our home. However, instead of seeking a "perfect woman," I was now ready to look for a regular lady, but once again, she must be a Christian. I knelt in prayer and asked the Lord to guide me to a Christian woman.

Where better to seek a wife than in church? Two weeks later, in the front pew at the Nazarene church, sat two single ladies. I looked and I was interested. Friends told me one was Gayle and the other her friend

Peggy. Both had earlier belonged to Carol's group. After a Sunday service I asked if they would like to join us at McDonald's for a burger and some fun. They looked at each other and said, "Yes." We broke the ice at McDonalds.

I later asked Gayle if she would like to meet for lunch on Wednesdays at Lyon's Restaurant and she responded, "OK." We met for lunch once a week for several months. Nothing seemed to be happening between us. She told me later, "I was not interested in you. But I was ready to go along for a free lunch."

Friends told me about the Dicken's Fair at the Cow Palace in San Francisco. "Go," they said, "It's lots of fun." I asked Gayle and took her to the Fair. The Dickens Fair was unlike anything we had seen before. People strolled about in period costumes. English food was available in abundance, along with shows and quaint music. That night we arrived back in Stockton, sat in my front room, and reminisced. We looked at each other, and were both aware something was different. As she looked at me I met her gaze, and there was now a chemistry present that was absent before. Gayle said, "There is something going on here." Maybe some of my pheromones were pulsing through the air. Inside of both of us something was beginning to bubble up. From that moment on our relationship began to come alive.

What attracted me was her fun-loving nature. She enjoyed going out and seeing new things. She laughed easily. I liked the fact that she was a Christian and had joined the Nazarene Church after she gave her life to the Lord. I also liked the fact that she had been a part of our group and we had something in common that we could share. I could feel myself falling in love once again.

We began to go out more often with our friends. After a Friday night date we came back to her place to talk. I said something that agitated her temper. Suddenly, without warning she took a swing and hit me in the face, knocking me back. I was so shocked I did not know what to say. Never before had I been hit by a woman. I regained my balance, shook my head, and noticed that the anger in her eyes had turned to a look of,

"*O God, now I have done it!*" I said, "I'm out of here; I'll not be back." She pleaded, "Please don't leave," but I grabbed my coat and strode out the front door.

Over the next couple of days she called and said, "I'm sorry, it won't happen again." We both attended the TA group now and began to talk openly about what had happened. The upshot was that we both agreed to give it another try. I believed her words of apology. It was now spring and we took drives into the foothills for picnics at Daffodil Hill, near Jackson, and some of the foothill reservoirs. Despite the formidable punch, we were falling in love. On Mother's Day weekend she invited me over for dinner with her four kids, Mike, Gary, Jim and Lynette. Lynette was 10 and the others were teenagers. We had fun together and after dinner I presented Gayle with a small, boxed gift. Inside, an engagement ring, though tiny, sparkled brightly. Here was a surprise for her. I popped the question: "Will you marry me?" She was as excited as I was and tenderly replied, "Of course." Later that evening she asked, "When will we get married?" I sure wasn't ready for that question. I thought I had gone the maximum distance by giving her a ring. Now we had to set a date. I suggested August. She gasped and said, "Really?" I didn't know what I was doing. August 18 became our date with destiny.

Planning for the wedding brought out the best and worst in us. We each stubbornly wanted our own way. All the inevitable questions emerged with hassles over each detail, such as, big wedding, or small? Big cake or small? How much can we afford? Whom to invite? Some of our friends suggested that it is really the woman's day to be in the spotlight. The guy is simply along to play a role. I agreed, so she got to make the crucial decisions. All I had to do was figure out how to pay the bills.

I had grown confident after experiencing Three Rivers, TA, and the Nazarene Church. I thought, *I can handle a woman with four teen-age kids*. How wrong I was! Problems began almost immediately. Mike went to live with his dad. After numerous confrontations with Gayle and me, Gary ran away from home. I had frequent confrontations with Lynette and Jim. Steve and Suzanne decided to live with Rosemary. How fortunate I was that they made that decision. We would have had an impossible situation if they had come to live with us.

Both Lynette and Jim responded to my attempts at fatherly inputs with "You're not my father." In other words "Get out of my face." When we got into it Gayle's response was to become mother bear and protect her cubs from the big bad wolf. She had told them that I was now the man in her life and was entitled to respect. But when I called in question a behavior of theirs, they reacted, and that led to quarrels between Gayle and me. Wow! I was soon over my head with situations I was not prepared to handle. I found that in second marriages the problem was with the kids. They come between the new couple. I discovered that the only way to cool the situation was to stop trying to play dad, and let Gayle handle them.

But a deeper act of discovery was also going on. Two adults, former divorcees, have a whole lot of work to do to create a workable, happy home. There is an under-the-surface nature that quickly emerges in each partner, and we both had to face that new reality. Both of us soon became aware of the other's stubborn nature, and then by default, our own. Of course, you can always see the other's stubbornness quicker than you can see your own.

Another facet of this diamond in the rough soon appeared. When a diamond cutter in Amsterdam gets a rough gem, he has to hit it with his hammer in just the right place for the smaller diamonds to break loose. I think I hit her diamond in the right place, because soon enough, more facets appeared. I discovered that the nature of my wife was two-sided. One side I called the pussycat. The other side I called the rhinoceros. Both were very real and amazing to encounter.

We made a decision to have a weekend getaway each month. Our marriage was forever, and we would cement that choice by creating a quality weekend each month. We would take a break from the burdens of creating a new home. The first month I chose to go to a little town in the Sierras called Markleeville. It had the distinction of being the smallest county seat in the state. There was a hotel, gas station and restaurant, and small county buildings. I secured a room on the second floor of the hotel, and we went for a walk and then to dinner.

After dinner we got into an argument in our room. She decided to walk out. Gayle angrily slammed the door and went down the stairs to leave. The stairway ended at the bar-lounge, which was full of Saturday night cowboys. The cowboys spotted her at once as she emerged on to the dance floor. They began to make a beeline toward her. She panicked, turned around, and headed right back up the stairs to our room. She opened the door, quietly sat down, and we settled in for the night. That set the stage for more to come.

We busied ourselves creating a new home. She sold her previous home and I sold mine. With the proceeds we bought a new house and began to turn it into a home. We bought new furniture, venetian blinds, curtains, and all the other things that make a home. I put in a yard, planting grass, trees and shrubs. But I soon overspent and couldn't keep up with the bills. That led to arguments about how to pay off our debts. If Jim and Lynette had trouble at school we soon got involved and into arguments as to how to solve their problems. When the cubs weren't happy, momma bear came out of her den to protect them. That led to quarrels. Gayle put a memo on the refrigerator that read, "When momma isn't happy, ain't nobody happy." How true!

A typical quarrel began with her way of seeing a problem, followed by my interpretation. She then ratcheted up a defense of her side and I countered with mine. She was a warrior with words and could top my point of view. To reinforce her point she started using "you messages." Even though we both knew better, I reverted to "you" messages also. Then came name-calling followed by big trouble.

Once Gayle got really angry her eyes blazed with fury. She poised her face over against mine, called me a jerk, and suddenly let fly with a fist in my face, just like when we first dated. I was stunned. I felt a deep anger arising inside of me. I knew if I acted on it I would do something terrible to her. So I turned around and walked away, not for her sake, but to keep me from acting out my anger. I had now met the other side of her persona, and it was a rhinoceros.

The next day she called my office at Delta College. She knew my office hours. After asking if anyone was there with me, she purred like a kitten in a soft mellow voice and invited me home that night for her special stew called Beef Burgundy, and then perhaps some intimacy after that. Suddenly, fresh air washed over both of us, like a cool breeze on a hot summer day. I couldn't resist her tempting offer. There were no apologies, but this was her way of starting over. I now met her pussycat again. I felt relief as I let go of the tensions inside of me. Wow, I thought, *that's over with, isn't it?*

There was a reality to that pussycat. It wasn't just a game. On weekend getaways we drove to a small hotel, The Old Milano, outside Gualala on the Mendocino Coast. Our second story window looked out over the waves of the Pacific crashing at the foot of the cliffs below. We shared breakfast in bed, with hot coffee and fresh baked muffins. That scene cast a romantic mood over both of us.

At night after dinner we went out to the hot tub built on a cliff overlooking the Pacific. The moonlight cast shadows through the dark trees making them appear exotic, almost unreal. We took off our clothes and climbed into the hot tub, enjoying the idyllic scene of dark trees sprinkled with bright moonlight. Below us the waves washed ashore in a wonderful cadence. It doesn't get any better than that. We fell in love all over again.

We also found a motel in Aptos just a block from the beach. We bought sandwiches and Pepsi at a little deli, and wandered out on the beach to enjoy picnics. We found another place in Santa Cruz, one in Monterey, and then another in Carmel. Each had its unique charm.

I slowly found out a secret to her nature. She longed for softness and strength in a man, tender, yet a leader. More than anything else she wanted to crawl into my lap, feel warm and protected, and simply be a pussycat. Then she wanted me to take care of her, and drive away her fears, doubts and worries, "Make the world go away," went the popular song. That was a tall order and I sometimes fulfilled it quite ably, but not always. There were days when I came home from work and I needed to withdraw into my cave, and just be left alone.

Is there some kind of universal need in women to be protected and taken care of? It seemed that way to me. If only it was that simple. If one person could meet the deepest needs of the other, what a wonderful world this would be. That is the sense by which I understand the challenging words of Genesis 3:16, as God speaks to Eve in the Garden, "Your desire shall be for your husband, and he shall rule over you." But it seems to me that one person cannot meet all those needs of the spouse.

Much of the time there was a nature in Gayle that was beautiful to behold. She had a sense of humor, liked people, shared funny stories with her companions where she worked and then passed them along to me. When her kids had trouble she was there for them. She stood by Gary when no one else would. Her love and support for Jim and Lynette were boundless. When her kids got married she gave them wise counsel through the tight places, encouraging them each step of the way. I believe God gave her a gift of counseling. Many times after I listened to her support of her kids and to me I responded, "You are a natural counselor. It is a beautiful gift." There was in her a sweet, wise and caring persona.

Then came the surprising times of transition. A careless word from me, a foolish remark, and suddenly her rhinoceros appeared. Soft responses to her assertiveness did not work with Gayle. Another episode began. She would enter into her rhinoceros mode and move toward me, her eyes blazing. I stepped back so she couldn't hit me, but too late. She hit me in the face again. At first I didn't believe it. But my face was pulsating and red. I thought we had resolved that behavior.

I wanted to strike back as a rage erupted inside of me. But I knew that if I lashed out at her something awful would happen to her. The rage inside of me would emerge. I withdrew to prevent that from happening. I had never hit a woman. It was unthinkable. Whoever heard of a Christian man hitting his wife? This roller coaster ride continued, the rhinoceros and the pussycat. I couldn't quite adapt to this new reality, so unfamiliar to me. I also knew I couldn't go on this way. Something had to give. But to whom could I talk?

Who could comprehend a wife striking her husband? When our pastor preached on spousal abuse, his illustrations always centered on men who abused their wives, never the reverse. I felt like I couldn't talk to my pastor. Our close friends would be too shocked to reply. I never laid any of this information before our children, or before the church. I felt alone, even more alone than when I was single.

In desperation I went to talk to Carol. She confided in me to use "tough love" with Gayle. She advised me to do what I should have done much earlier. That is, take a stand by giving Gayle a point of reference as soon as possible. Once home I gave Gayle fair warning, "Do not ever hit me again. Do you understand me?" I decided at the next encounter to take a stand. Once again her anger emerged. But this time I did not back off. Sure enough, she hit me. In my mind I decided what tough love meant to me. I decided that I had two options. One was to simply turn, walk out, and not return. The second option was to strike back. I took my second option. I responded by slapping her face, and the sound of it echoed through our silent house like thunder. She stopped in her tracks with a look of total disbelief in her eyes.

The encounter stood out in bold relief. Time stood still. A stillness filled the house. Both of us were shocked, but for different reasons. I was stunned because I had done the unthinkable. I had hit a woman, and worse, it was my own wife. I had crossed some invisible, forbidden line, and I was in new territory. Gayle was shocked by the reality of what I did to her. I had taken the concept of what is a "stand" and translated it into my concept of tough love. It was outside my concept of reality, yet I did it.

We stood there in stony silence. Slowly, she put her hand to her face to feel the welt, looked at me as if I was a drunken abuser, and said in a shaken voice, "You hit me." "Didn't I warn you?" was my response. "But you hit me," she repeated in shock. She walked away nursing her face and her feelings. Several more times in succeeding months she became enraged, coming within inches of my face. I learned to look her in the eye and remind her of my vow. She thought about what I said and did not strike.

Where was all of this behavior coming from? Hadn't she gone to the altar at the Nazarene Church in July, 1976, and given her life to Christ? Sometimes in my classes at Delta College I suggested that civilization is but a thin veneer over our killer instinct. The students really got into that thought. But our behavior was at an even deeper level. John Calvin, the Reformation teacher at Geneva, and a source of inspiration to the Puritans, taught that our nature is "depraved" until redeemed by Christ. He also preached the concept of original sin. At our church we spoke of our fallen nature. Perhaps, I thought, both of us had been converted, but our conversion experience was partial, and not complete. Or was there something here that psychologists and theologians did not really understand?

I discovered something new about me at those times. I got so angry in my response that I experienced an impulse to murder. It was so scary that I moved away from her so I could not commit that ultimate act, for if I did I would regret it for the rest of my life. Bob Moon, one of the leading preachers of our Methodist Conference said the most common place for murder was in the kitchen of an American home. How right he was. It seemed to me that one of the risks of love is, each lover learns where the other is most vulnerable, and sometimes uses that knowledge as a weapon. That is when arguments become dangerous. Remember the ditty from childhood, "Sticks and stones may hurt my bones, but words can never harm me." That is a lie. Words can penetrate to your soul, cause pain and ultimately, retaliation.

On a weekend getaway to Monterey Gayle started to rag and nag. We were driving Interstate 5 to Santa Nella, and to the turnoff to State 156. She didn't stop ragging. Finally, I looked over and said, "If you don't stop, I will turn around and go home." She didn't believe me and continued unabated. At the next overpass I turned off the freeway, crossed the overpass, and headed back to Stockton. Suddenly she realized that I really meant what I said. She stopped her tirade. We drove on in silence. How golden it was. I spoke up and said, "If you are ready, we can continue to Monterey." She quietly replied, "OK." I turned again and headed back toward our romantic destination.

Does it surprise you that we then had a fun weekend? Gayle was the kind of woman who needed boundaries, strong and firm. The problem was how long it took me to learn these secrets of her feminine nature. For years I tried polite listening to no avail. What worked was the same technique I used with her rhinoceros, that is, give her a fair warning, and then follow through, say what I meant, and mean what I said. Only it was hard to hold into that. Both of us wanted to enjoy the moment. We romanced in Monterey. She was once again in her pussycat, and we had a romantic and fun weekend. I dropped into a mode where I thought everything was OK, once again. But the roller coaster was still there, waiting for me to dare to control it.

I know Gayle suffered bouts of clinical depression. But wouldn't it be better to use terms like manic depressive, or bi-polar, get a doctor's diagnosis and an Rx, and take the prescribed medication? A better take came from Carol. She told me that there was even a simpler explanation. Gayle's mother, Irene, treated her husband Ed exactly the same way. Gayle learned such behavior from her earliest childhood.

Before I proceed further with those thoughts, what about my behavior? I had taken vows of ordination to uphold the cause of Christ. My marriage vows lingered in my memory. I remembered my baptismal commitment to follow Christ the rest of my life. How far I wandered from those commitments was plainly visible. I had so many personal issues to deal with that I was in no position to cast aspersions.

So why stay together? That was a profound question. Because we loved one another was the simplest answer. Because we had wonderful times together. Because she was a fun person to be with. Because, though it is hard to understand, one facet of her nature was shyness. In her shyness she became transparent and was so easy to know. I loved that part of her little girl. Another side of her nature was boldness. Sometimes she took my breath away with her audacious ways. A professor at Stanford suggested that we have multiple selves. Now I met that theory face to face in my wife (and in myself). We humans are a mix of contraries. Is there really someone who understands how that happens? Heaven help us as we seek to build productive relationships. The vows we took at our wedding were freighted with a meaning that now became clearer. We pledged ourselves to love, honor, and obey till death us do part. We took those words quite seriously. We would not go through divorce again.

The people at our church loved her. She stood by her friends. She loved God and wanted to be His child as best she could, not perfect, but under construction. She found God in a new birth at the altar rail of the Nazarene Church 3 years before we met. She remained faithful to that calling. She was faithful to her children, even if they got in trouble. That was her motherly love.

I think some of that love rubbed off on Jim and Lynette. One day as we came home from a weekend trip I talked to Lynette about our adventures. She listened and then responded by calling me "Dad." That word at that moment took my breath away. I had wanted to hear that word so much, yet thought I never would. It was the breakthrough I had been longing for. Our relationship shifted and we began to treat each with respect and caring.

Through it all there was in Gayle a beautiful young woman that I loved. She decorated our home in country style that was warm and inviting. She loved little figurines and stuffed dolls that enhanced that motif. Her favorite figures were Dreamsicles. She began collecting them. I bought Dreamsicles for her each Christmas. She also cherished Austrian cut crystal figurines that I mounted for her in a glass case in the bedroom.

When we looked at those Dreamsicles they were so joyful, childlike, and innocent that we both smiled. Every time we went to the coast I also bought her a little animal figurine of Austrian cut crystal. She, in turn, would buy little comic figures that decorated my computer, my desk at home and at work. She bought a tiny stuffed duck that sat on the dashboard of my car. Sometimes while shopping she would return with a new shirt for me, or a sweater, or a new pair of slacks. They were always just right for me. Everywhere I was reminded of the joy we found in our love for one another. She was full of surprises both romantically and around the house. Those are the things that held us together.

She had bouts of depression that were unpredictable. If she could have found a medicine for that, it would have been wonderful. Her doctor prescribed Prozac, but if she used it there followed unpleasant side affects, such as weird sensations in her head, and an upset stomach. She didn't use it. If her friends at work and at church had known, I think some of them could have helped. But they did not know, and she did not tell. To say to me, "I'm sorry," was out of character for her. It was as if there was a part of her persona that was so different, so deep below the surface, a part of her unconscious mind, that she did not see it as part of her. Sometimes she went to her best friend, Carol, and the two would work out a plan for her happiness. But a short time later she reverted to her unpredictable behavior. The roller coaster began again.

Then, late in 1994, something happened that changed everything. A new chapter in our relationship opened.

Twenty-Five

The Beast

There are events in life that change our direction and our concept of who we are. Sometimes we can barely put such events into words. Death, divorce, and incurable disease come to mind. We dread them so much that we try to insure ourselves against the possibility of their striking us. But sometimes they creep up on us and we are blindsided. Then we have to meet such events face-to-face with all the faith and courage we have available.

In the fall of 1994 Gayle detected a lump in her breast. She had a dread of cancer as long as she could remember, especially breast cancer. Why that was so she could not explain. However, when she read articles by women cancer survivors she realized how dangerous it was. She had the lump X-rayed quickly. Sure enough, there was a suspicious growth there. Her surgeon set an appointment with her to come to his office. We went together and waited in his examination room.

He explained the procedure he would follow. He needed tissue samples to send to the lab. With Gayle's permission, he wanted a sample that morning. He took an enormous needle called an aspiration needle, the longest looking needle I had ever seen, and was going to use it to draw out a sample of breast tissue. I winced, and averted my eyes so I didn't have to look. But my curiosity got hold of me. I peeked.

The Beast

He treated Gayle's breast like a pincushion. He slammed the needle deep down into her breast in one fell swoop. Would he ever stop the thrusting motion? A short time later he pulled out the needle and sent a sample of her breast tissue to a lab for examination. Our job was to wait patiently for a report.

The wait was agonizing. Imagination worked overtime, from the very best scenario to the very worst, and back. Was it going to be a cancerous lump? We fidgeted and worried. Seven days slipped by with no call. Then 10 days. Gayle was as nervous as a teenaged girl waiting for her pregnancy review. Scripture reminded us hundreds of times to not fear situations like this. God would be with us all the way. Yet our active imaginations got the better of us. Gayle's call finally came on a day that I was teaching, and she drove home from the doctor's office to give me the results.

We sat in the front room much as we had the night we fell in love. She was on one side of the room and I on the other. In quiet, cadenced sentences she reported the results. She had breast cancer, and it was not benign. It was the dangerous kind that can explode into ugly growth. The doctor said she must have surgery immediately to remove the lump. There was a long silence as the news sank in. Neither one of us knew what to say. I had no idea of how this news would really affect us. I think I steeled myself against bad news. She was doing the same. Now her worst nightmare was unfolding. All I could say was, "I'm so sorry."

It was a lousy response. Sometimes guys really let their wives down, and I was that guy. We don't express our feelings very well. Here was news that devastated Gayle. I think she was in shock. Mom used to say, "Don't sit there like a bump on a log." Yet I sat there speechless. I was like the Missouri mule that needed a 2x4 across the nose to get its attention. I was meeting mortal danger and was barely aware of its seriousness. It didn't sink in yet. All I could say was three brief words in the face of her dreaded information. I wish I had it to do over. I would have gone over and held her in my arms to let her know I would stand by her all the way.

Her doctor gave Gayle two options. One was, mastectomy, a total removal of the infected breast. The other option was a lumpectomy, or a surgical removal of the cancerous lump within the breast. Gayle asked me, "Which should I request?" "Can you get equivalent results with both?" I asked. "The doctor said both would work," she responded. Cutting off her breast seemed too extreme. Yet we wanted to make a decision that would foster her long-term health. We settled on a lumpectomy.

In retrospect, was that a mistake? We simply do not know the answer to that question. We found out from her surgeon that during the lumpectomy surgery, the cancer had metastasized to her lymph nodes under her armpit. He had to strip most of the nodes away. The lymph nodes are an important part of her immune system. Thus, her body's ability to fight back was compromised, no matter what kind of surgery she requested. She was facing a dangerous cancer, and once it metastasized it was often incurable. We did not understand that at the time.

A round of chemotherapy followed surgery. She went to a clinic with rows of chairs where patients sat by tall stands that held clear bags of fluid roughly called "cocktails." Each cocktail contained toxins deadly to cancer cells, but also deadly for normal tissue. In the attempt to destroy cancer cells the cocktail had to destroy good cells too. "Wasn't there something better?" I asked. "No, this is the standard treatment," replied the staff. The doctors were doing the very best they knew. But it seemed medieval to me. To treat cancer they had to burn her body cells in order to kill the cancer cells.

Not long after that her body began to show the effect of chemotherapy. Gayle called me into the bathroom and tugged on a clump of her hair. Out came a huge wad of hair in her fist. Within weeks she lost all her hair. A woman's hair is her crown. She takes special care to present her hair at its best. Now she was stripped of her glory.

Cancer had a way of eroding her dignity, and invited her to feel like a medical freak. I'm sure Gayle felt that way. I looked at her and saw something so strange I hardly recognized her. Her baldhead shone like a full moon. Her face no longer held the sweet curves of the previous years. All the attractiveness was gone.

Sadly, the medical profession had no Rx for dealing with those terrible side effects of chemotherapy. Isn't it possible that research can discover a method of fighting cancer that replaces chemotherapy as a largely inefficient procedure? Far too many cancer patients derive little or no benefit from chemotherapy. Yet we had to choose chemotherapy because it was the only option available. It was time for us to call on our resources of faith in God to see us through this ordeal. That and authentic love held us together at a time like that.

There was nothing of beauty left to look at. Plaintively she asked, "Do you still love me?" I replied with, "Yes, sweetheart, I do love you." My task was to love her, and support her through this medical gauntlet. I had to redefine beauty. Beauty, I found, had to do with the courage to face down this beast of cancer and fight it. It is not a matter of attractiveness. *Fight back. Summon all the courage that you have, and stay faithful to God. Beauty is in not giving up or giving in. Beauty is in your will to live.* That is what shone through. I beheld it and admired it. We think of females as the weaker sex, but it is not so. Gayle gathered strength and resolve and began to fight back. It was the only way to survive. She showed her inner beauty.

I had to dig deep into myself to become the man she needed for such a time as this. What, for instance, is marriage all about? I had to go to the core of what we mean by love. It certainly wasn't simply an emotion. It didn't have anything to do with the romantic songs I had danced to all my life. In fact authentic love is the very negation of popular music. Popular music often invites us to focus on the self. It pleads for self-fulfillment and the good life. One of Frank Sinatra's hit songs was, "I Did It My Way." But, love has to do with learning to do things God's way. The vows we took at our wedding said it forcibly, "To have and to hold, from this day forward, for richer, for poorer, for better, for worse, in sickness and in health---till death us do part." I was being tested to the depths of my vow. I was learning a deeper meaning of love that involved my will, my commitments and my faith.

In my preaching days I often spoke of God's inestimable love, which the New Testament calls agape love. It is the love that Christ showed at the cross when he gave up his life for all humanity. Agape love is total self-giving. It puts other's needs above your own. As a young pastor I had preached that message for fourteen years. I had attempted to live it throughout my ministry, but I found that I could not duplicate God's love, only imitate it. My love was but a shadow of His love, but I was being asked to learn a sacrificial love and make it intensely personal on behalf of my wife.

Was it easy? Of course not. Was it the natural thing to do? No. Our natural instinct is self-preservation. The ego wants to be served, not serve others. But her cancer taught me the meaning of service to others in a whole new way. When she needed support I learned to be there for her.

There were many months of chemotherapy. Gayle ordered catalogues that sold wigs to women. Then we visited a shop that sold them. While she tried the sizes, colors, and styles, she asked me to look and see which was best for her. What a task! I wasn't good at it. The upshot was that she ordered at least three wigs and wore each on separate occasions.

Now came radiation. She was subjected to X ray treatments at St. Joseph's Hospital. Would this ever end? I was the bystander to these milestones in her life. She was living through it. My job was to be available for support. Now I was seeing what a monster cancer really was and how deeply it affects everyone in the family. It is like someone sticking a finger in your eye. It is painful. It demands your total attention. I began to call cancer "the beast."

Finally a day came when her oncologist held a meeting with us. He reported that Gayle was now "in remission." The chemotherapy and radiation had worked as all of us hoped. We rejoiced at the news. I was the optimist and shared the good news with our church friends. "Gayle is in remission," I declared, as if she was cancer free.

But Gayle was more the realist. She wasn't sure that is what was meant. Sometimes in the quiet of the night she would say, "Once you have had cancer you are always waiting for the other shoe to drop." What did remission mean? A cure? Not necessarily. Are there no detectable cancer cells, or merely a diminished amount of cancer cells? We tried to pin it down with the doctor, but he could not give us a definitive answer.

Now I know that "remission" simply means that the remaining cells are not growing. But he told us that if no more lumps appeared in the next five years he would declare her "cancer free."

We wanted to get our lives back to "normalcy." We were ready to take steps to live a healthy lifestyle. We signed up to begin nutrition classes at UC Davis Medical Center in Sacramento. One evening a week we drove there and an accredited nutritionist would teach us new skills in grocery shopping, vegetable and fruit selection, menu preparation, and preparation of a meal in their kitchen. The teacher would then give us a printout each month full of new recipes for healthy eating.

When we were done with that Gayle signed up for a program called *Women's Healthy Eating and Living*, or WHEL. It was sponsored through UC San Diego. Each month a trained technician at the university would call Gayle and talk to her for at least 30 minutes. The technician inquired exactly as to what Gayle had eaten and the size of her portions. Records were kept so that the information could feed into a study that the university was conducting. They wanted data that would show if there was indeed a relationship between proper nutrition and staying cancer free. The new cooking came back to one thing. Was she remaining cancer free?

Each activity came down to that fundamental question. Is what we were doing helping Gayle stay in remission? Our lives would be different from now on. We were in a deadly game. Gayle asked me if she could quit her job at the Foundation for Medical Care. I was well established now at Delta College and said yes. Later I came to regret that decision. It gave her time to worry about her health.

We changed churches. Our Nazarene Church conflicted over our pastor whom many members did not like and wanted to remove. Gayle was on the Board and felt the conflict intensely. She chose to support the pastor. The Board split into two factions and arguments broke out at each meeting. Ulcers began to appear in Gayle's stomach, so we decided to leave the church. We searched for months for a new church. Gayle liked First Baptist Church and urged me to come along even though I am an ordained Methodist. With some hesitation, I agreed.

First Baptist is a conservative church. Gayle and Pastor Jim connected immediately. I was slower to come around. I was a graduate of Pacific School of Religion in Berkeley, one of the more liberal seminaries in the Bay Area. I was a member of the Methodist Conference, and the California branch is the most liberal in the nation. What was I doing in a conservative Baptist church? Other than supporting Gayle and her healing, I had a hard time explaining that to myself. I kept on giving to Central Methodist Church so I could retain my membership in the Methodist Conference. But, I resolved to find a way at the Baptist Church to walk in their shoes and try to understand conservatism from their point of view. I tithed to them also.

We both joined the choir. Both of us love to sing. We attended all of the choir retreats in the Sierras or in a redwood grove on the coast. We toured northern California and sang at churches and institutions in the Bay Area, including our rendition of the national anthem for a San Francisco Giants ball game. We joined an adult Sunday school class studying the books of the Bible. I joined Promise Keepers, an all-male group who promised to serve the Lord. Gayle and I volunteered for a program at church called, Divorce Recovery Workshop. Facilitating a dialogue with recent divorcees was a natural for both of us. We helped them adjust to life after marriage.

I also committed to a program at church called Life Support Ministry. Five to six people would gather with me on Thursday nights and get into a workbook called "Search For Significance." We applied Christian principles to our lives to help solve the problems that each faced. One young woman came into our class a basket case, and in a puddle of tears. Her husband had left her. I applied the information that I had learned from my divorce and recovery. She took the information, digested it, and six weeks later left a changed woman. Cases like that kept alive my desire for more teaching.

We began to travel and test the idea that expanding our worldview was good medicine for the soul. We cruised the Hawaiian Islands, toured Great Britain and Europe, and visited places like Montreal and Quebec.

The Beast

We visited Branson, Missouri, and loved the music and the shows. We also tried something new to us. We wanted to do missionary service if we could find the right thing. The right thing happened when our church announced a mission to Kodiak Island in the Aleutian Islands. We signed on quickly and in July of 2003 we spent two weeks in Alaska. Gayle and I and three friends traveled to Denali Park the first week. Then we flew to Kodiak to meet the members of the work crew for the second week.

Gayle worked in the childcare center at the Baptist mission there. It was for kids whose fathers were out with the fishing fleet. I helped build a corral fence to hold horses in their pasture. Kids on the island could come for recreation and ride horses. We were serving the families who were waiting for their men to come home from a season of fishing.

The men of Kodiak were out on the stormy Gulf of Alaska catching king crab, salmon, and halibut. It was said to be the most dangerous job in the world. The fishermen drank heavily, and continued their habit when the boats returned to Kodiak late in the year. Wives were lonely and carried the burdens of the family. They needed the mission for support. I worked intensely hard that week, but it was worthy work. Besides putting in dozens of fence posts and barbed wire, I learned to support the consumption of wild salmon. That was my way of aiding the work of these fishing families. When back in the lower 48 I specifically ordered wild salmon when I went out to dinner. "Forget the farmed salmon," I told the waitress. I asked, "Is this sea caught salmon?" Usually she didn't know the difference, but I asked anyway.

In the summer of 2004 a member of our church named Joyce announced that her group of Gad-A-Bouts was going to Ashland, Oregon, for the Shakespeare Festival. We signed on. Joyce rented a touring bus that held 50 people. We stopped the first night at a lodge near the base of Mt. Shasta, and boarded a train for a ride around the mountain. The beauty of Mt. Shasta sticks with you. I loved the sights, sounds and the fragrance of the forest. How could it get any better than this?

The next day we drove on to Ashland. While we were viewing a play, Gayle began to have trouble breathing. I walked with her back to our room, but she only got worse. Both of us were beginning to panic. We had no doctor and no medicine for such a thing. I went to the room of a fellow traveler named George, a former firefighter who had lifesaving skills. He showed me how to prop her up in bed so her breathing was easier. She couldn't sleep that night, but at least she could breathe. I reported to Joyce what was happening. She reminded me that we would be boarding the bus in the morning to start our trip home.

In Stockton the first order of business was to call Gayle's oncologist. He gave us grave news. Her lungs were rapidly filling with fluid. She would have to go to the hospital to have her lungs drained. They would also perform tests to see what caused the fluid. Our worst fears were confirmed. Her cancer was back with a vengeance and had metastasized to her lungs. Lung cancer, one of the most dangerous kinds of cancer, had caused the fluid build-up in her lungs. Her oncologist gave orders that Gayle was to return immediately to chemotherapy. With chemo came all of the terrible side affects: losing her hair again, sick to her stomach, and a prolonged weakness. It looked to me that the so-called cure was worse than the disease.

At that point Gayle called her old friend Carol, who gave her some new information. Carol knew an oncologist named Dr. Purewal who treated some metastasized cancers with additional options. Gayle jumped on the suggestion to at least give him a try. She called his office and set up an appointment. He reported that since she had already been through surgery, chemo and radiation, he could now offer her a therapy that he called hormone blockers instead of killer cocktails. I looked at him and said, "It can't be that simple." His response was: "Oh, but it is. The cancer feeds on female estrogen hormones. We block those hormones and the cancer has nothing to nourish it." And he said, "The hormone blocker will not make her feel sick." Gayle was skeptical too, but it was worth a try. She agreed to become his patient and stepped into his examination room for a consultation and diagnosis.

While she was with the doctor, Carol and I stepped outside. Carol told me what I had learned in her TA group years before. "It is better for you to know than not to know." She then told me that metastasized lung cancer is almost always fatal. It was sobering information. Dr. Purewal's hormone blockers were a form of maintenance therapy. They added more years to Gayle's probable life span, but did not provide a cure. Later I found that the average patient gained another five to six years of life using hormone therapy.

I did the math in my mind and started imagining when the cancer would take her life. Carol and I also agreed that it would be better for Gayle if we did not tell her that she only had about five years left. I needed above all else to keep her hopes alive. It was my task to strengthen what I called her "will to live." She would need that for the struggle ahead.

Dr. Purewal's diagnosis was correct. Gayle did not have the terrible side effects with hormone therapy. We both rejoiced with that news and both of us announced to our friends that she was in remission again. They too were glad. But an awareness lingered in my mind. Sometimes I felt like a liar. I didn't tell anyone that Gayle was terminal, or at stage four cancer. If I told anyone, I knew that eventually it would rebound back to Gayle with dire consequences. I lived in two worlds at once. I knew the truth, but I shaded it in such a way that it was not the whole truth. Then I could tell myself I wasn't really a liar, but was following what the author of the book of Ephesians called, "Speaking the truth in love." (Eph.4:15). Love was the alchemy that would help promote life against death. I followed that way and told no one of the depth of her crisis. Was that the right thing to do? I can only hope so.

I decided to retire from Delta College. I formally retired in 1998, but continued teaching part time through the episode at Ashland. After Ashland I faced a whole new situation. I didn't want to give up teaching, but Gayle needed me at home. The spring of 2004 proved to be my last class. We made decisions to travel again. We cruised the inside passage to Alaska with our friends from church. We cruised to Jamaica and other islands of the Caribbean. Some of the activities were too much for Gayle and we would stand by and watch others at play.

At home we signed on for more Gad-A-Bout trips with our church friends. We traveled by bus to Banff Park in the Canadian Rockies. The scenery was unforgettable. Gayle gasped and said, "Have you ever seen anything so beautiful?" We stopped in Yellowstone to see the great falls. As Gayle stepped forward to the rim of the overlook, she instinctively reached backward with her hand to grasp my hand. But the leader of another tour bus stepped between us. She grabbed his hand by mistake, turned to exclaim the beauty of Yellowstone Falls, and realized it was not me, but a stranger. We all roared with laughter and shared that story all the way home. We also took in plays at the Sierra Repertory Theater and Stockton Civic Theater. We were holding back the night and keeping hope alive.

She began to lose weight, but not in the right places. I began to get the sense of how many women struggle to achieve a more perfect body, to the point of an obsession. When I talked to Gayle about that she would reply: "You civilians simply don't understand."

Oddly, she did not use the menus or the recipes that we labored for in the UC Davis Nutrition kitchen. There was a streak in Gayle of what I call laziness. She didn't want to work too hard at preparing nutritious meals. She started serving Weight Watcher frozen dinners each night of the week. She would say, "I've been cooking for my children all my life. Now I'm tired of it." That was a hard corner for me to turn. I loved home cooked meals.

Insistent questions began to emerge. In several articles I had read, cancer patients go through a predictable range of emotions. When they first get the news from a doctor that they have cancer, their first response is denial, "That can't be true. There must be some mistake." Gayle had already been through that phase in 1994-95. The next phase is anger, then grief, and finally acceptance. Gayle entered into the anger phase, and needed me to be her sounding board. With the training I have had on the skill of listening, I needed that training now more than ever.

She needed me. My full attention was just the beginning of dealing with the struggle inside of her. Her biggest question was, "Why does God allow cancer? Doesn't the Bible say that God created the world and called it good?"

The Beast

I soon found out that trying to apply theological answers to spiritual questions did not work. When facing a dreaded disease, intellectual answers miss their mark. We read together Rabbi Kushner's book, "When Bad Things Happen to Good People." That helped. She wanted an explanation that she could connect with. Kushner's story of losing his son while keeping his faith in God helped her. We also read numerous articles in "Guideposts."

Then her questions became intensely personal, "Why me?" She continued, "Doesn't God like me? Am I being punished? Have I done something wrong?" First I listened. Sometimes she didn't want a response. She simply wanted to know she could pour out her heart and I would be there, "Don't say anything. Just listen to me." Eventually she wanted me to give my feedback.

I fell back on the Baptist/Methodist preacher mode. That message asserts that Adam and Eve sinned in the Garden of Eden by eating the forbidden fruit. God then cast them out of the Garden. An angel with a flaming sword guarded the entrance so they could not come back to paradise, at least not in this life. That explanation continued with the statement that we now live in a fallen world where a rebellious angel called Lucifer (Satan) can wreck evil and disease upon us. I said that with tongue in cheek.

The problem of evil is the most intractable issue for the Christian faith. Theologians hold that if we admit to the reality of a "Satan," it will lead to a dualism in the nature of God. They point out that we hold to a monotheistic faith. God is a monism of one, not a dualism of two. My professor of Systematic Theology taught me that. Thus, we are back to the real question, which is, "What is the nature of God?" Let theologians try to explain that. A famous preacher likened the problem of evil this way: God has a crazy half-brother who lives out behind the barn. He is the one responsible for such suffering. Sometimes when Gayle was depressed, it seemed as though the crazy half-brother was living in our back bedroom. He was too close for comfort. My task was primal. Keep alive our faith in Christ who suffered and died for us, and who showed on the cross how much He loves us. Second, don't give in to the beast.

Gayle was a realist who thought of herself as streetwise. Normally she liked to get down to cases, but not so with cancer. Once I heard her say to Dr. Purewal, "How long do I have to live?" Then, reversing herself she said, "Don't tell me. I don't want to know." Dr. Purewal responded wisely, "The fact of the matter is, I don't know how long you will live. Only God knows that." Or she said to me, "Don't tell me if I look tired and worn. I don't want to know." My response was, "Honey, you are beautiful, but it radiates from the inside out." She wanted me to tell the truth, but shade it so that it didn't hurt. For her, cancer was a tug of war between faith and futility.

She had to constantly struggle with anger management. When she was depressed, despondency or anger soon followed. She was depressed more often now. She would say, "Why should I live? I am not getting any stronger." I reminded her of how much her children needed her. I needed her. Her grandchildren needed her. I asked, "Are you sure you want to end your life?" Dr. Purewal would say at their next consultation, "I want you to live. Go on a trip with Dick. Get on with living. Don't you realize that I am prolonging your life and giving you the gift of more time?"

I wanted a photo of Gayle and Dr. Purewal together. As Gayle sat on the examination table Dr. Purewal came over and put his arm around her, holding her close while I took their picture. Later, he recommended a psychiatrist for Gayle who could deal with her anger and depression. Gayle found a female psychologist and started seeing her regularly. Sometimes Gayle came home in tears, but she always wanted to go back again.

Part of her depression was, I believe, a God problem. It seems to me that for many cancer patients one dimension of the disease they face is "Why does God allow suffering?" Oncologists aren't prepared to deal with that. In childhood we were taught to believe in God, but as adults in their hour of need many experience His absence. That does not make sense, and as a result will they turn to hope or despair? Gayle was angry with God for allowing cancer. Or at a deeper level her anger was,

"Why doesn't He heal me? He heals others, why not me? Why do I still need hormone therapy?" Or, "With so many people praying for me why doesn't He heal me?"

That was another theological problem for me to try to answer. "Why does God seem to be selective with His gift of grace? He heals some but not others." St. Paul had a thorn in the flesh and asked God to remove it. But instead God said to him, "My grace is sufficient for you." (II Cor. 12:9) That is what a cancer patient must come to, the act of accepting God's grace. It is the power to see it through.

In our adult Sunday school class we discussed the problem of suffering often. One of the conclusions we drew was that God is sovereign. His time is not our time. But His timing is perfect. We want healing now, "Deo volante," God willing. But God may say, "Wait." If someone is not healed perhaps there is much we don't understand of His Will, but He does have a plan for us. Like Paul, we need to wait patiently for His will, and for a deeper understanding of the mind of God. One day we will meet Him face-to-face and we will understand.

I listened to Gayle as she poured out her heart. She told me, "I am not afraid to die." Her fear was, "Will it hurt when I die? Will Jesus be there to take my hand and take me across the Jordan River into Heaven?" "Yes," I said, "Jesus will be there for you. He will show you the way into Heaven." What she wanted now was to meet Jesus face-to-face, lean into his arms, and experience his healing touch. Forget my attempts at dealing with her questions. Just give her Jesus. One night as she was in bed she saw Jesus standing at the foot of our bed. His face was full of compassion. She was sure that he had come for her, and she wept for joy. She was unafraid of His presence, and clung to that image for the rest of her days.

Sometimes when we went to our adult Sunday school class, our teacher, Rock Sytsma, would seat Gayle in the center of our large class. Then we would circle around her, placing our hands on her head and shoulders. Each person offered a prayer on her behalf as they were moved to do so. She felt the touch of the Holy Spirit, and how much people cared for her. Her anger moderated, and it was waterworks all around. In ways that we did not always understand, those were healing moments. God was healing her spirit, but not her body. Slowly, I think, that perception had some good effect. She was slowly moving toward acceptance of her fatal condition.

Imagine for a moment what it must be like to have a dreaded disease from which only a few recover. I likened it to a miner in a cave. He is deep inside his cavern when suddenly there is a terrible crash. The cave entrance has collapsed, and there is no way out. He cannot go forward nor backward. He has only a limited amount of power in the batteries of his flashlight to light his way. There is no access for fresh air to come in. The oxygen will run out, and he will suffocate. Or he will die of dehydration. He is encircled by a deep gloom and no one has a way to reach him. He is alone. That awareness sinks in. He must come to terms with the fact that his time is limited and he will die. Imagine what that must feel like. That is how I conceive of the ultimate dilemma of cancer. There is often no way out but the way of faith in God, and the acceptance of your mortality. Otherwise you go mad.

Gayle got weaker. In November 2008 we went to the Sierra Repertory Theater outside Sonora, and on the way back she said, "This will be my last trip to this theater." At our next treatment with Dr. Purewal she requested a wheelchair. She felt exhausted. Dr. Purewal's response was a classic, "No, I will not prescribe a wheelchair. If I do, you will never get out of it." He wanted her to keep on moving.

Lynette rented her a wheelchair for her next appointment. Lynette and Jim wanted to come along. They sensed Gayle's need for support. We went together for an appointment with Dr. Purewal on December 10, 2008. As we walked by his office he gave us a look of tender compassion. In the examination room he measured his words in order to say exactly what he meant. They are the words that no patient ever wants to hear. But now he was required to give his final diagnosis, "Gayle, there is nothing more that I can do for you."

It was a raw-edged statement of reality. Quickly responding Gayle said, "But didn't you promise an alternative therapy?" She was desperately hoping for a cure. "Yes," came his reply, "but only if it works. Yours no longer works. You are a very sick person." Then he followed with, "I am calling Hospice now and they will send a team to your home to care for you." He stepped out to call Hospice while we gathered around Gayle, and prayed fervently for her. As we closed our prayer time it was waterworks amongst all of us in the room.

Within 24 hours our local Hospice sent two ladies to our house. Rosie was a nurse and she checked Gayle's vitals regularly. Josie was a social worker that helped Gayle with filling out papers for Social Security, insurance and prescriptions. Several days later a third worker appeared named Priscilla. With a Caribbean lilt in her voice such as you might hear in Jamaica, she went about her tasks cheerfully. She helped Gayle into our bathtub, shampooed her hair, changed bed sheets, and helped her apply makeup. She would proudly bring Gayle to the front room in a wheel chair and reveal her fresh appearance to me. Gayle smiled broadly. She felt better when she was clean and fresh.

Priscilla clipped her nails, and applied nail polish to brighten Gayle's day even more. Gayle, fastidious about her appearance, loved being taken care of. Priscilla came three days a week, and stayed several hours giving a lift to Gayle with her attitude. I felt so grateful for her. Sometimes when I used to go backpacking in the high Sierras, a gentle breeze would whisper through the pine and cedar trees. My sweat disappeared. I took off my hat, dropped my 45-pound pack, and allowed the beauty of the mountains to take my spirit into a moment of reverie. Priscilla was like that to our home. She made a positive difference when she was there. Those were profound moments in our home.

I entered into a new phase in our home. I now did the cooking, the cleaning, laundry, and management. I was called to perform Gayle's work in the home. It wasn't all that difficult, except for the physical demands placed on me. I looked forward to finding ways to be helpful. What could I do in the face of such urgent human need? I could get down and do the mundane things that make a home possible, mopping floors and doing dishes.

The New Testament is full of illustrations by Jesus where he speaks of being a servant. In Mark 9:35 Jesus says to the twelve, "If anyone wants to be first, he must be the very last, and the servant of all." Christ is not for the faint of heart. Jesus makes demands that run counter to our instincts of self-preservation, and self-service. Yet I found in Jesus' paradoxical statement the very nub of truth. When I let go of self and my demands, I found a release into a new sense of freedom. Becoming a servant was what I wanted to do.

Am I gilding the lily, making myself look good? Is that self-serving talk? I don't think so. I was at the point in life where I was ready to surrender to Christ my claims to my way. I was ready to learn His way. The Refiner's fire was at work in me. One of the decisions I made sounds simplistic, but it worked for me. I decided I would serve Gayle in her time of need not for her sake, but for Christ's sake. When I knew I was serving a larger purpose in obedience to God, serving Gayle became easy. I wasn't some galley slave pulling on my oar out of brutal necessity, but a servant of God called to duty. "Inasmuch as ye have done it unto one of the least of these my brethren, ye have done it unto me."(Mt.25:40) That made all the difference that I needed.

I found, however, that I still needed a getaway time, and so I went for an hour's workout at the gym three afternoons a week. That was my relaxation time, my time of renewal. I felt good when I worked out. However, Rosie told me in private never to leave Gayle alone. Rosie gave me orders to begin administering morphine to Gayle as needed. I called her kids, and my daughter Suzanne to come and "house sit" while I went for my workouts. Gayle reacted, and protested. Her response was "No!"

Here it is important to note why she reacted like that. In private she told me that when I was gone, she felt her level of anxiety rise to explosive levels. That helped me understand her response. I explained to her that I needed that time to come back refreshed and ready to serve. I developed a system where I called one of the kids to come while I slipped out of the house and went to the gym, or did some grocery shopping.

But as I left I always had to struggle with my own sense of guilt. Was it right on my part to take time away when her needs were so obvious?

Maybe if I was a better man…..? But, if I did not get that time away, I began to tighten up, and cabin fever began to emerge from somewhere within. Basically, I am an outdoors kind of guy. The reality of my human nature was colliding with her needs of the moment.

We each had our own kind of need. We were both "right." I struggled with my guilty feeling, and sometimes with a sense of anger that she did not understand such a simple request. Fighting for her life, however, her needs were paramount. Did being a caregiver allow me time to get away and refresh myself? I decided that it did. But it was always a tension between her needs and mine.

The church continued responding to her. Our class members sent cards daily to encourage Gayle in the fight of her life. Other members visited and brought DVD's of the Sunday service so we could participate in worship on our own TV. Some brought flowers and some brought dinner. It was a huge response to her needs. Always they asked how she was. I responded with, "She's hanging in there." Or "She's keeping her faith in God." How much of the ordeal did they really want to know? A precious few asked, "How are you doing, Dick?" I responded with a word of acknowledgement, and thanked them for their thoughtfulness.

Sometimes I got the impression that most people don't want to get too close to cancer. It's too scary. They don't know what to do or say. Others have an intuition of how awful it must be, and try their best to give comfort. Each is doing the best they know to address the person in need. But, after all is said and done, it seems to me that the person with cancer stands alone. We speak of the Spirit of God carrying that person in their time of need. There is truth to that. However, when all the people have left, the nurses have done their duty, the doctors have gone home, the person with the deadly disease has to face the fact of their approaching death in their heart. Like St. John of the Cross, they have their own "Dark Night of the Soul."

They have to ward off the demon of fear, the grim reaper of death who stands remorseless in the gloomy shadows of Hades by the River Styx, ready for his next victim. The cancer patient must instead, reach out to God, and even more, accept surrender into His will. They must dare to see Christ standing by the River Jordan, with love in his eyes, ready to receive them. That is the cancer victim's struggle, and it is a lonely one.

Pastor Jim called too. He shut the bedroom door and wanted to be alone with Gayle. He talked with her and prayed with her. When he re-entered the front room he had a request of me. He asked if I would be more direct in speaking of death with Gayle. Heretofore, I had been reluctant to speak of death because I wanted to help keep her hopes of a cure alive. But now he wanted me to be forthcoming with Gayle and speak of death as imminent. He asked that we invite the grandchildren to our home and let them ask Gayle about her death. "Let them ask all the questions that they want to," he said. "They need this kind of reality talk." After he left, Gayle and I both agreed to his suggestions, and yes, we did follow through.

But I got a puzzling response from Gayle when I opened a conversation about her coming death. Her response took me off balance. She replied: "That's not really going to happen to me, is it?" Once again, she was oscillating between hopefulness of a cure, and the reality of her oncoming death. At that point in time it was still too difficult for her to talk about it with me. Yet in a day or two, and in different circumstances, she wanted to talk about her death. I needed to be ready for anything.

One conversation took me completely by surprise. We were both in the bedroom, and she quietly said, part question and part statement of fact, "I haven't treated you very well, have I?" I was nonplussed. What do you say at a moment so freighted with meaning? One part of me wanted to say, "As a matter of fact, dear, no, you did not. Sometimes I felt violated in the depths of my soul. Sometimes your words stung with all the fury of angry hornets." But was I going to say that now to my wife who was dying? I don't think so. Or should I say in a shallow kind of way, "Oh, it was nothing. That is all in the past. Think nothing of it." That would have been a lie.

That was as close as Gayle ever came to saying the riveting words, "I'm sorry." Where was her "rhino self?" Gone, or now displaced by cancer? I questioned myself. Did I somehow invite her "rhino" outbursts by some fault in my subconscious that spoke out of turn? I wasn't sure. But one thing I knew. Now off balance, I said nothing. She reached out to me and offered in her own way to transcend old wounds. It was my turn to respond to her, to redeem this moment in time, and say, "Yes, I forgive you. I was at fault too. Forgive me."

The fact that I did not say that reflects on how hard it was for me to let go of the hurt caused by her behavior. She had hit me below the belt many times. Now in this moment, with the tables turned, the old memories surfaced, like a specter out of a swamp. I had not let go of some of those memories. It was hard to let go when the wound had not healed. I had nursed it and rehearsed it. It was mine. Strange, isn't it, yet sad, how we hang on to things like that.

Quo vadis? (Where are you going?). *Were those words directed to me? Are you asking me, Lord, to let go of the old hurt? Don't ask me to do that. Anything but that.* When nailed to the cross and dying a cruel death Jesus said, "Father, forgive them for they know not what they do."(Lk. 23:34) The Hound of Heaven was reminding me of what I needed to do: forgive Gayle so that I am forgiven too.

The difficulty lay in what Christians call "sin." Dr. Buttrick, one of my Homiletics professors, likened sin to someone slashing DaVinci's "Mona Lisa." The damage is irreparable, like a knife slashing Truth. Yes, a touch-up artist can cover the tear so it no longer shows. But, if you turn the painting over, the gash is still there. That is the terrible reality of sin. Thus, sin can be forgiven, and repairs made, but there are consequences that reach beyond the deed.

What Gayle and I were dealing with were the consequences of our behavior. We not only damaged our relationship, but we grieved the Holy Spirit of God. Truth be told, I think both of us had done some amount of withdrawal from one another, a kind of Freudian defense mechanism to protect ourselves from further hurt. Those were the consequences of our behavior. Our relationship had moved into the shallows as a result. We missed some of the benefits of the deeper waters of intimacy.

Some say words are cheap, but not at that moment. Words can carry all the deepest freight of our one precious life. I have godly sorrow that

I did not immediately break through my barrier and say those forgiving words to her. God knows she needed them. Just think of the power of these words, "All our sins were nailed to the Cross of Christ. As He spilled out his life blood for us, so we are forgiven and are reconciled to God."

We did draw near to God. I refused to live with anger for the rest of my life. I let go so we could be free of the curse of anger. I told her that I love her. But the hard part was to end the defense mechanism that I had built. The blows we had both exacted took their toll in consequences. I had built defenses brick by brick, and now the Lord was asking me to take them down, brick by brick. Easy? No. But, I made a decision that those hurtful incidents were in the past and it was time to move on with all deliberate speed. Time was running short.

Later, remembering Pastor Jim's words to me, I said to Gayle more healing words that were special between us, "Will you promise to meet me at the Eastern Gate of the New Jerusalem? Will you wait for me there? I will come to you." St. Paul spoke to me when he wrote to the Church at Rome, "God causes all things to work together for good for those who love him."(Rom. 8:28) I came to that faith now through my fallen nature and reached out to grasp God's good news. This line from a poet has always grabbed me,

"And ever and anon' a trumpet sounds from the hid battlements of Eternity."

The trumpet sounded now. This was God's grace at the heart of reality. The wound was healing. I was letting go of my defense mechanisms.

Gayle was failing fast. Christmas was coming and we had no way that we could shop or prepare food for our annual holiday festivities. Her kids saw Gayle's condition and could read the signs of her oncoming death. They rushed to fill the breach. They came on Saturdays and brightened our home with all of our Christmas décor. Suzanne came down from Petaluma and spent weekends helping care for Gayle. Gayle's kids worked out a rotating system so that each took turns standing in the gap. I was so proud of them. In the past when we had BBQ's sometimes they barely had time for Gayle because they had so much fun together. Now they doted on her.

Gayle took it in, but only marginally. There was that part of her that still wanted to be in charge, making things happen, and working out plans. It was not easy for her to give up her role as master planner. Now she had to surrender her self-concept. On Christmas Eve we all gathered together and shared as we had always done, only now with the unspoken awareness that this would be our last family Christmas. Gayle whispered in my ear, "This will be my last Christmas with you."

That was a poignant moment. We had almost 30 years together. I reached out and held her close. Words cannot begin to express how I felt. Not only did Gayle have to let go of the precious things of this life, our marriage, her children and grandchildren, but also let go of all the special mementoes that she had collected. I too was going through a process of letting go. I had to let go of my wife, and all the things that we created together in our home, all the things we held dear. We both had to deal with the awareness of how we had misused the time that we had together. Now, soon enough, all of that would be gone. We both felt the shortness of time.

I began giving her larger doses of morphine as Rosie directed me. I had been using a wheelchair to take her from bed to the bathroom. Fortunately, the wheelchair just barely fit through the doors of the bathroom. Then I would walk her to the toilet, and finally back to bed. One night at 2:00 am I was walking her from the wheelchair to the toilet. Suddenly, without warning, her legs failed her and she collapsed to the floor. There she lay, sprawled on the tile floor, and try as I might, I could not lift her. She had no strength with which to lift herself, and even though she had lost weight, I could not get her off the floor.

We looked at each other in panic. *Should I call paramedics? Should I call 911?* I had to do something. Finally, I remembered that my firefighter friends, George and Bill, had once taught me their version of an emergency lift. I got down on my hands and knees, told Gayle to form her arms in an arc over her chest, and clasp her hands tightly together. Then I put my head through the circle and slowly began to lift her. It worked.

Rosie, alarmed when she heard the news, gave strict orders. "No more trips to the bathroom for Gayle. From now on," she insisted, "Gayle must be confined to bed." She would have to start using a bedpan. Later, Rosie inserted a colostomy device that collected Gayle's feces and urine into a plastic bag. Now I learned to take care of that also. Rosie told me once again to further increase her dosage of morphine. But those doses of morphine had a nasty side affect. Remember the Centaur of Greek mythology, half horse and half man? Now the Centaur took a new configuration. Gayle slowly morphed into a different Centaur, half Gayle, half zombie.

Morphine is a two-edged sword. It kills pain, but robs the patient of their identity, and leaves a terrible void in its place. Now she spent large portions of each day sleeping. When she awoke she was only half present, her eyes appearing vacant. The old fire was gone. Handling her bedpan, and later emptying her bag, I was given the strength to do the very things I never imagined I would have to do. Once again I remembered the words of my wedding vow, "in sickness and in health,...until death us do part." That vow is the most daring covenant that a man and woman ever make.

I now brought her meals to her in bed. When I served her "Cream of Wheat" in the morning, as much reached her mouth as the front of her nightgown. It was painful to watch. She had been so fastidious with her eating habits. She kept her clothes spotlessly clean at all times. She could not imagine spilling food on her blouse. Now it was a regular occurrence. I was witnessing the demise of her life force. Only marginally did she show the presence that had once animated her life. As she inched toward death, she became more and more like an infant, needing constant attention.

Her weight dropped precipitously low. What irony! She had wanted desperately to lose weight. Now she was down to less than 100 pounds, and looked pale and sickly. Priscilla did her best to make her look presentable.

Her hair was back, but was now a short, silvery sward atop her head. Priscilla combed it so as to create some waves. The waves in her shallow, silver hair looked amazingly attractive. However, the wavy hair created a sharp contrast between her hair and her face, for her face now appeared gaunt. Priscilla polished her nails, and applied lipstick, anything that would give a hint of her vanishing femininity. Thank God for Priscilla's tender touch, for it helped revitalize Gayle when she needed it most. Priscilla would put her in a wheel chair, and proudly bring her to the front room so Gayle could greet us and give us her famous smile. Her kids and grandkids shouted their approval and came forward to kiss her. One look at her and they knew without being told that there wasn't much time left.

How many times are there when we have opportunities to say a word of encouragement to someone we love, but do not? Then we come to speak to the one who is dying and we hardly know what to say. We fumble for the right words. "Get better soon," someone says, and it is so obsequious that we let it pass. I like St. Paul when he said, "The last enemy to be destroyed is death." (I Cor. 15:26) Or the Puritan divine, Richard Baxter when he wrote "I speak as a dying man to dying men." We may rail against the old Puritans and their legalistic religion, but some of them knew how to find grace for living, and grace for dying.

The grandkids in their youthful ardor groped for the right words with their grandma. We often chuckle because they seem so young and immature in their knowledge of life and death. But these kids came through with flying colors. They bent over, some going down on their knees, holding her as she sat in her wheelchair, and saying so simply and beautifully, "I love you Grandma." Then they kissed, with tears flowing down their faces. I loved them so deeply in those moments. There was no embarrassment as they wiped away the tears with whatever they had--hands, handkerchiefs, or sleeves. That is transcendent time, kairos time, God's time, when we come close to both life and death, and find new meaning in the life of the person we love. And yes, we find new meaning within ourselves.

Dr. Joe Matthews in Chicago used to say, "We are unrepeatable historical events. There has never been someone just like us ever before and there will never be another like us ever again." He was affirming that there is transcendence in our humanity, or as I like to say, something of God in each of us. We were finding that "something of God" in those brief moments with Gayle.

One of my students at Delta showed me his biology textbook. It defined humans as "self-balancing bi-peds." But there is a description in the book of Genesis that is best of all, "So God created man in his own image, in the image of God He created him; male and female He created them."(Gen. 1:27) The ancient Hebrew writer-priest saw something in us that revealed the God dimension in us. Our farewells with Gayle confirmed that truth to us.

Near the end of January Rosie said to me in whispered tones, "Gayle only has seven to ten days left. Make sure everything is in order." Rosie knew a lot about death and dying. I trusted her wisdom. I made a decision that cut my conscience to the quick. I went to a mortician in Lodi and opened negotiations for Gayle's funeral service and the burial in plots I had purchased years earlier. Once again I felt guilty doing this duty while she was still alive, but somehow it had to be done.

While she got weaker there were more anxious phone calls from our friends at church, and a stream of cards, gifts, and flowers soon followed. Pastor Jim came and prayed with her. On the night of February 5th, 2009, our friend Carol came and wanted time alone with Gayle. She shut herself into the bedroom and remained with Gayle for 30-45 minutes. When she came out she gave me a resume' of what she said. It went like this, "Gayle, you have been fighting cancer for 15 years. You have put up a good fight and given your best to it. Now I want to share personally with you. It is now time to let go. There is nothing more you can do. You can now go home to your Heavenly Father. He's waiting for you. You can rest now in His arms." Then they prayed together, and Carol left. When I heard what Carol had said my heart overflowed with thanksgiving. Those were the words that I knew Gayle needed. I hugged Carol and thanked her for coming.

Gayle's kids came too. After Carol left we gathered around Gayle's bed. We sang hymns and then we prayed. I prepared a simple communion of bread and grape juice. Ralph, Lynette's husband, served the bread, and I served the juice. In Jesus' last supper on the night of his arrest, after dinner, he served his disciples bread and wine. He said to them, "Do this in remembrance of me." Now we shared together for the Lord and for Gayle. Lynette sang a beautiful gospel hymn, "Standing on Holy Ground." At that moment in time we all knew that this was holy ground.

That night Gayle slept fitfully. At 4:00 am in the morning I heard a sound that I have never actually heard before. Once I heard it my skin tightened and I froze in place. Gayle gave off what is known as a death rattle. I had heard of it, and now I recognized it immediately. It is an ungodly sound, almost beyond description, but so intense that you know instinctively that death is near. Like a broken foghorn and a train wreck at the same time, the sounds ricocheted across the room. I listened and waited. From 4:00 until 6:00 am the sound shook the bedroom, and went up through the ceiling. Rosie had given me a booklet that showed what to do at a time like this. Once again I reviewed it, and wiped her lips. I remembered, *help her clear the phlegm in her throat. Help her get comfortable.* Then, I waited.

We had signed an Advanced Medical Directive years earlier, thank God. In it we both agreed that when death was imminent, no extraordinary measures were to be taken that would prolong life. Let nature take its course. I called her kids and told them what was happening. I did not call a doctor, nor did I call emergency services. The kids rushed to our home and waited anxiously. At 9:00 am Mike, her oldest son, asked me to call her doctor. I stepped out of the room to place a call. When I returned, Gayle was dead. I looked at her face, for she had turned white and cold. Her eyes were vacant and saw nothing. They stared at the ceiling, motionless.

At that moment of truth I caught my breath. It took a second to grasp what had just happened. I would never talk to her again. I would not see her again except at the Eastern Gate to the Heavenly Jerusalem. She was dead and suddenly gone. I thought I was prepared for this crisis, but I was not. I was a kindergartner looking into the face of death. It was like standing on the edge of a vast universe and gazing out into the Milky Way, trying to make sense of it all. She was utterly cold and gone.

Out of my mouth came a response so spontaneous, so unpremeditated, earthy, and crude that I couldn't believe it. "Shit!" That was the creature in me, "the natural man" as Paul described it. The Psalmist helped me find better words when he cried: "Out of the depths I cry to you, O Lord; O Lord, hear my voice." (Psalm 130:1) Then tears flooded my eyes.

Events unfolded quickly and had a momentum all their own. Rosie came and formally pronounced Gayle dead, and signed the appropriate papers. Then came the mortician who lifted her body out of bed, mounted it on a gurney, covered her with a sheet, and wheeled her out to a van. There was an eerie silence in our home. The sounds of Christmas mirth were gone. Then we formed for action. A million details required our attention. Everyone jumped to be a part of the helping action. We made it all happen.

Sometimes we say jokingly to one another that we all know what is the world's oldest profession. And everyone laughs at the apparent truism. But I disagree. It seems to me that the world's oldest profession is that of building monuments for the dead. We grieve for them. We want to say that death should not be the end. But we are faced with a stark reality. And we want to soften the blow by building memorials for them. We choose to remember them. Perhaps by doing so we ease the pain in our hearts just a bit.

Pastor Jim conducted her memorial service. Many of her friends were there. All of her kids and grandkids were present and we sat together in the front row. Everyone who wanted to speak on her behalf stood up and gave their testimony. There were many memories and copious tears as we remembered her life and her long battle with cancer. Pastor Jim told us that Gayle was a personal inspiration to him, and also to the entire congregation. Sharing with us he said, "For 15 years she fought a good fight and kept the faith. Now she is with Jesus where He welcomed her into an Eternal life so glorious that only the Bible can describe it." Our director of music, Pastor Steve, sang a solo, "I Can Only Imagine." We closed by singing "Amazing Grace." Years before, on our way to our cabin at Agate Cove in Mendocino, our favorite get-away, she requested some songs for her funeral. Right at the top of the list was "Amazing Grace." I wrote down the songs so I could not forget them. Now I poured forth tears as the reality of her death and the empty future now facing me became so very real.

The weather was overcast on the day we buried her. A light rain fell as we stood beside her casket. Deciduous trees were stark against the cloudy skies, but the droplets of water that sparkled on the bare branches softened their outlines. The flowers on top of the casket shimmered with the coating of raindrops forming on their petals. Pastor Jim intoned a prayer. It was ironic to have the rain falling. Gayle had shared with me her fear of lying in the stone cold ground, getting wet and cold in her grave. Those fears to the living don't make sense, but they were very real to her as she was dying. Pastor Jim put the matter in context for us. He reminded us that we were burying only her shell. "Her spirit," he said, "is with God in Heaven." Now it was time to go home and begin the grieving process.

Twenty-Six

Recovery

At home alone, the reality of her absence set in. I had a devastating feeling that I had fallen into a well. The well had no bottom and I kept sinking deeper into water, not like a rock, but like a heavy ball. I couldn't reverse the inexorable downward spiral. At night while trying to sleep I dreamed of sinking in a well. During the day as I tried to return to a "normal" life I had the sensation of sinking. Where was the bottom? I couldn't find it. I knew I needed help. I called our local Hospice and found out that they were starting a Grief Workshop in March. I signed up.

I could hardly wait for the Workshop to begin. Twelve of us met together in early March, nine widows, and three widowers, including me. We had two facilitators from Hospice, Connie and Laura Ann, who led us with questions, and then tried to guide us through painful dialogue laced with memories. Several of the widows were basket cases. Shaken to their foundations by the death of their husbands they wept uncontrollably, and then their tears turned to bawling. The other widows, faced with this outpouring of grief picked up the emotions and also burst into tears, creating a crescendo of tears. Connie and Laura were busy handing out Kleenex, and finally passed the box of Kleenex around the circle.

When I realized how desperate the widows were I reached out to them. I shared memories of Gayle, but in their grief that did not mean anything to them. They didn't really hear me. So I turned to something else. I entered into their concept of reality and tried to understand where they were coming from. I asked questions like, "What kind of man was your husband? What was his favorite hobby? What kind of relationship did you have? Did you travel together?" And so it went. Instead of telling them about Gayle and me, I opened opportunities for them to talk about their beloved husband and the deep sense of loss they experienced at his death.

I think those questions enabled a healing process to begin. I know that it did for me. As I stepped outside myself and entered their world, I began to heal. When the workshop ended I no longer had that sinking feeling. I finally touched the bottom of the well, kicked off of the bottom, and began to rise toward the surface. Connie asked me afterwards if I had ever considered being a facilitator. I considered her request, but decided that other issues were priority for me. I wanted to return to choir. Pastor Doug had asked me to help him in his ministry to seniors. I also wanted to be part of a Bible Study group.

Another pathway to healing opened up. A member of our Sunday school class named Lynda Botiller had begun a breakfast feeding ministry in Stockton outside the Homeless Shelter under the freeway. Single handedly she fed the homeless who gathered under the cross-town freeway. In March she asked our class for help. I volunteered. A group of Christians met each Saturday morning and began cooking breakfast in massive quantities. I helped crack 80 dozen eggs. We served scrambled eggs, cottage potatoes, fruit, sweet breads, coffee and juice.

We served the families in the Shelter first, and then took the leftovers out to the street and served homeless souls who waited patiently for their breakfast. Three to four hundred people formed a line in the sweltering heat of summer, or under the overcast, chilly days of winter. I liked to serve oatmeal to those who waited in line. Tiredness crept through my body as I bent over the huge kettle of hot cereal. But it was a good feeling. If ever there was an effective therapy to deal with grief, this was it. I liked being a servant, feeding those who had no way to return the favor.

Irony was part of the scene also. Across the street was a waste paper processing plant where trash blew out into the street. Consequently, the area was a constant mess of waste paper trash, and homeless people, all mixed together. The scene was right out of a Dickens' novel. These people and this trash were the cast-offs of society, refugees from a capitalistic system that had failed them. Or perhaps it is fair to say that they tried, and then quit the system. To a casual observer the scene looked like the poorest of the poor mixed with the detritus of civilization, to some a fitting union. Some of the people were mentally ill. Others showed obvious signs of drug abuse. Some were veterans. And some were simply out of work and out of luck.

We sallied forth, taking our food out to the mean street. I took off my hat, and in a booming voice called for prayer. The hungry and the homeless lined up, took off their hats and joined me in prayer. We treated them with courtesy, using latex gloves to serve them breakfast. We treated them like real people, with respect. They responded in kind and a simple bond took place between us. We liked meeting them and serving them. I don't know about the others, but I liked my new role.

There was a crazy chaos on the street. Here we were on the shabbiest street in Stockton, littered with debris, and laughter broke out with the food. If I served oatmeal I would say, "Here, this will put hair on your chest." The man in front of me would put his hand on his baldhead and respond, "Can this stuff grow hair on my head?" We both shared a laugh as he moved down the line. When I served bread and sweet bread I would say to the Hispanics, "pan or pan dulce?" (bread or coffeecake?). I got smiles this way when they realized that a gringo knew some Spanish. To a gruff, bearded man, whose clothes were worn to a frazzle, covering an unwashed body, I said "Here, this coffee cake will sweeten you up." Most would produce a grin and reply, "I'll try it." There was humor even in the grim situations of life. I liked to make them smile, if only for a brief few minutes. That was a gift God gave to me, inviting people to laugh. I did so with increasing frequency now and enjoyed using my new found talent with others.

It's funny, but when I was younger I did not have such a gift. When I pastored at Lamont I could barely use humor in the pulpit. Maybe I was afraid that no one would laugh. I had fun with my kids and Rosemary, and we laughed freely together, but not so much with others. Now, however, as I drew closer to God something blossomed in me. I found joy by inviting others to laugh. Each day became another opportunity to rejoice and be glad and share that with others.

Something else was happening at the same time. At first I thought I would never marry again. *Why bother? I could be a bachelor for the rest of my life*. But something stirred within and said *It is not good that man should be alone.* However, I knew I had more grief work to do before I was ready for anything or anyone.

Was it a mere coincidence that I saw an ad for a trip to the Canadian Rockies? At times like that the word "coincidence" seemed unreal to me. Is it not more true to say that somehow, some way, the Creator of the universe was acting on my behalf? God had placed an opportunity before me. The thought gripped my imagination. I called the tour company, and by their persuasion I was convinced I would not be out of place as a single mingling with married couples. I signed on for the trip.

My plane flew out of Sacramento on July 20, 2009, and landed in Calgary, Canada later that afternoon. Our group met one another, and got our traveling instructions at our hotel. Yes, the group of 50 was all couples and I was the only single. I made a decision to make the best of it. The next morning after breakfast a touring bus met us at the hotel and we began our drive to the Rockies.

The Canadian Rockies stood out in all their grandeur just as I remembered from my trip with Gayle. Only now something was different. I was alone, though surrounded by 50 people. My challenge was to enter into the beauty of these mountains, and come alive as a single. The people I was with were friendly, and I had learned years before how to deal with new groups. I introduced myself, asked if I could join them for meals, and struck up conversations on the bus. Soon enough, I was not alone any more. It was simple to do once I made a decision to get into their concepts and their way of thinking. I made new friends.

There were three couples in particular with whom I shared many meals. We would sit in a large booth in a restaurant by our hotel. Often the conversation turned to vignettes that reflected who we are, and our situation in life. The most obvious issue with me was why I was there without a partner. That gave me a chance to share with them the story of Gayle's long struggle with cancer, and her recent death. That took the spotlight off of me and put it instead on her brave fight against cancer.

That message was consistently received with empathy that was revealed in their response. They wanted to know more details. They asked many questions. Sometimes I felt alone. But they sensed through our conversations that I was coping productively to move out of despair and into hope. With their level of caring, I soon realized that we were creating a community of shared meaning. We began to feel a kinship with one another.

The highlight in Banff Park was a helicopter flight high into the mountains. Up, up, we rose out of the great valley, a valley laced with waterways. The spires of the mountains were now outside our windows. I had climbed mountains like these in the Sierra Nevada, but now I was flying among them. How gorgeous! Their majesty spoke with eloquent silence. We rose over the tops of the mountains. We could look down on a wonderland of forests, and a giant hotel here or there, coaxing space among the trees.

A river cut a path through the valley below. Taking the appearance of a thread of blue, it slowly carved its way through the valley that was formed eons ago by slow moving glaciers. Streams here and there flowed out of the mountains from melting snow, creating a kind of web with the river. That web gave the valley a connectedness to all of life, just as I was reconnecting to life.

To increase the sensation of flight, the pilot descended into the next valley, reversing the imagery of the upward flight. Up and down we went until the whole range of the Rockies belonged to us.

The high snow-covered mountains whispered to me as they always have done. What I heard was

> *You have been here before. You have spent 35 years hiking the Sierra Nevada of California, and you and Steve traversed the range of the Grand Tetons in Wyoming. You have endured the worst storms that nature can conjure, and you survived. You sat and watched a red/orange sunset glow over Vogelsang in Yosemite and from atop Mt. Whitney. You came home with the joy of confidence. You handled those situations well, and will do so again.*

Several days later we went out to the Columbia Glacier. After lunch we mounted huge vehicles with tires that seemed six feet tall, dwarfing us, but giving us security as the driver took us out on the surface of the glacier. Warning us after we stopped, he asked us not to walk too far away from the vehicle. There were crevasses in the ice that could swallow a person alive, leaving not a trace behind.

Water flowed out of openings in the ice. "Crystal clear," the guide told us, "this water is absolutely pure and drinkable. It is the melt from ice below us that predates the Industrial Revolution." I filled a bottle with the water and sipped on it for the next two days. This seemed to me to be the most unique water in the world.

How do you describe water that is 250 years old, yet fresher and clearer than anything that comes from our faucets? It is an anomaly. This shouldn't be. It was like stepping back in time and savoring the pureness and freshness of what early pioneers and explorers experienced on entering the New World. They could scarcely describe the wonders of this new world: an abundance of fish, birds, wild life and forests that stretched to the far horizons. They drank deeply of its water, and ended by polluting it with their notions of progress. Now I got to peel away 250 years and taste what they savored. I felt a kinship with the explorers who opened this new world. Yet along with it came a sense of how badly we have abused it. *"We can do better,"* I thought.

There was now a different kind of awareness emerging in me. More humble, a decision slowly emerged and gained momentum. I did not want to spend the rest of my life alone. I wasn't going to saunter out on the singles scene ever again to look for a companion. But I would stay active, in touch with God's will for my life, and follow His leading instead of trying to show Him the way. I was ready to open the next chapter in my life.

Making a decision that I no longer wanted to live alone was one thing. But how do you start over again? I stayed close to my church and kept my social antennae up. I tried relating to our Single Adult Ministry at our church. but they were much younger than I was. That wasn't going to work.

In the fall of 2009 I traveled to Apple Hill alone. The leaves on the apple trees were turning color, from bright green to a mottled yellow and a hint of orange. The crisp air caused me to button up my jacket. Roadside stands overflowed with harvested apples. After a delicious piece of pie and a cup of coffee at High Hill Ranch, I purchased a basket of apples to carry home. Following a simple recipe, I turned them into applesauce. Two boxes of Mason jars full of homemade applesauce soon crowded the shelves in my garage. *Surely, I can share this bounty with someone*. That someone was Marilyn and her friend Jane.

Marilyn had been a good friend of Gayle's while we were attending First Baptist Church. We often traveled together on the Gad-A-Bout trips as well as trips to Great Britain and Germany. We traveled together to Denali Park in Alaska, and then spent a week at the Kodiak Baptist Mission ministering to the fishing families there. We had known each other for twenty years. Her husband had been institutionalized with schizophrenia and asked for a divorce. Marilyn agreed and the paperwork began.

On a balmy October evening while white puffy clouds lazily floated across the sky and the temperature was cooling from summer, I invited

Marilyn and Jane over to share coffee, a choir fundraiser dinner, and cups of homemade applesauce. We gathered on my back patio seated on comfortable lawn chairs. Stockton has wonderful color in the fall. The leaves of the liquid amber trees turn into a kaleidoscope of colors: yellow, orange and red highlight the change of seasons. What a wonderful evening to share and reminisce with my friends. How many romances begin in such an inconsequential way? We had a delightful time and talked far into the evening. The ice was broken.

Christmas was coming, and our friend Ken asked a group of us to participate in a simple Christmas musical. We were videotaped as we performed our parts. Afterward, Ken thanked us by giving each of us a gift certificate to the Olive Garden Restaurant. I called Marilyn and asked if she would like to go together to the restaurant. Her answer was a simple, "Sure." We had chicken dinners, along with a host of memories for table talk that day. Marilyn reciprocated by inviting me for a second lunch using her gift certificate. As we left the restaurant we turned to the parking lot to say goodbye. At that moment I reached out and gently, with a feather edged touch, brushed my lips against hers. I surprised us both. Suddenly, that kiss was a tip-off that I cared about her. For her part she now realized that this dinner date was more than a casual invitation. From that moment on we began to see each other whenever we could. Romance was in the air.

Marilyn invited me to her house for lunch and other times for dinner. I responded by preparing meals at my house and inviting her over. The more we exchanged meals, the more we both realized that a deeper relationship was emerging. We were both falling in love. Marilyn asked me to define my thoughts and feelings, sometimes verbally, and other times in writing. I found that to be difficult. Part of me was afraid to get involved in marriage again. Gayle's death was still too close for comfort. But the other side of me wanted to be close to Marilyn. I liked our time together, and conversation flowed naturally between us. We laughed easily. She was fun to be with. I knew in my heart that I wanted to spend the rest of my life with a fun person. She was also a Christian, sensitive, and smart. God had led me to the right person.

I put my thoughts into words, and she did the same for me. I was in love with Marilyn, and though it was scary, I told her about my love. I also confessed my past problems with my two marriages, and my sexual addiction. We were both aware of our hesitation about marrying again. As I was honest about who I was, she was open to sharing her past. Honesty was either going to help create a new relationship or destroy it.

We drove to Mendocino. I proposed with the finesse I had available. The ambience of the place, our location in a beauty spot on the coast, and my honesty all worked together to speed my words to her heart. She accepted my proposal.

When we returned to Stockton I called her son Ken, and asked him to join me for coffee at Starbucks. Sipping our espressos I posed a question to him. "I am in love with your mom. I want to marry her. Can you give your consent to that?" His response was a classic one, "It's all good. Go ahead." We closed with smiles, a handshake, and hugs.

For years as a Methodist minister I used a marriage manual to counsel couples preparing for marriage. Most couples told me they didn't need counseling, "They were in love," they said. Nevertheless, I would not marry couples without at least four counseling sessions. By the time we finished the four sessions they thanked me for our time together. Titled "Growing Love in Christian Marriage," Marilyn and I would now use it for ourselves. We discussed it after meals, and took it with us in the car whenever we traveled during 2010. While I drove the car Marilyn read key paragraphs out loud, and then we discussed the questions that the authors posed.

Every issue facing couples preparing for marriage was up for discussion: money, family relationships, sex, personal values, and faith in God. Our discussions took us deeper into relationship. We also took an on-line survey that our pastor, Jim Dunn, gave to us. He had the results professionally scored, and then gave us the results. We found that we were more closely matched than any other couple Pastor Jim had married. We already felt that way, but the survey confirmed it.

We were married at the First Baptist Church on February 12, 2011. What a glorious wedding day! The air outside was chilly, but the temperature inside was warm and cozy. Almost all the family was there, and Pastor Jim did a masterful job as he conducted the ceremony. He blended together humor and decorum. He told the story of Adam and Eve with a new twist. God created Eve from one of Adam's ribs so that Adam would not be alone in paradise. When Adam awoke from his sleep, the Lord asked Adam, "Well, what do you think of her?" According to our pastor, Adam's first response was, "*Wow!*" We were alternately laughing and crying as we finally recited our wedding vows. After the wedding we stayed at the Wine and Roses Inn in Lodi and then flew from San Francisco to Maui, Hawaii.

In August I was sent to the hospital with a heart fibrillation. There Dr. Lim, my cardiologist, told me I had to have open-heart surgery. *Is this really happening to me? I just got married seven months ago.* Open-heart surgery was scheduled for Stanford University Hospital on October 6th. Cracks in my faith yawned before me and I could not put my fears out of my mind. The thought of a surgeon sawing open my chest and then lifting my heart into his hands disturbed me. Unsettled by my fears, an inner voice repeated to me, *I don't want to die; I am not ready to die*. I was a mature Christian, yet engulfed in my own fears.

After surgery, my fears dissipated. I was left with a strong desire to draw closer to Christ. God had been good to me. I wanted very much to serve Him. It seemed to me that writing my story was one way I could do that. I hoped that my children and grandchildren would benefit from reading my struggles and successes. By February 1, 2012, I was at St. Joseph's Hospital doing exercise routines in their Rehabilitation Center three times a week. Then, I was back at my computer each morning to continue writing or editing my story, doing what I felt God was calling me to do.

How did I know what God was calling me to do, you may ask? *Isn't it presumptive to think God speaks to me?* Yes, I hear that. But an indelible feeling had been growing in me that I wanted and needed to confess my faith through my story. I am not an evangelist. But I was convinced that there were others like me, who have fallen from grace, have experienced life in its deepest despair and in its highest heights of redemption and want to try to explain that experience to others. I asked myself,

> *Who do we thank for everything of this life? Are we aliens upon the earth, wanderers who are lost? Or does God reach out to us and seek to guide us? I am convinced He is there, and His presence surrounds us. There are those who are looking for a more excellent way with God. So now, I thought, tell your story.*

I joined with a fellowship of Christian men from our church for lunch on Tuesdays. Later, I proposed that we turn it into a Bible study. They agreed, and made me chairperson! I vowed to learn to love God with my whole heart, "for His love," as St. John said, "casts out fear." "We know that we have passed from death into life," St. John's letter reads, "because we love the brethren." My aim was that kind of love.

Epilogue

I write now from a vantage point of age and experience. Retired, I can take time to walk my dog Brandi each morning. She is so eager to go. She whimpers for joy as she waits for me to buckle her into her harness. What excitement awaits her! She salutes each tree or lamppost along the way. Overhead a mockingbird trills and tweets a song for this new day. It is the music of God's creation. Creation is so beautiful that I marvel at what God has given us. I whisper, "This is the day that the Lord has made, let us rejoice and be glad in it."

I let my mind roam free of shoulds and oughts. I look back on my life, and I am humbled to think God has given me these many years (86). He has brought me through a furnace of existence to purge the dross from my soul. I was so naïve and self-centered as a youth. Only slowly did I begin to see a golden thread in my life that when spooled out led to the heart of God.

Somehow, in ways that I did not completely understand, I grew up with a fracture in my soul. My youthful nightmares, bed-wetting episodes, nocturnal emissions and childhood sicknesses reminded me that something was wrong. I had my first panic attack at age 13. As if that was not enough, I was shy and socially awkward. Over time I learned a coping mechanism; I looked inward so I could see how I was doing. My persistent question was, "How do I feel? Do people like me? What can I do to fit in and be inconspicuous?"

Yet, I was also impulsive, doing things my way, and not particularly concerned how my behavior affected other people. In El Sereno I earned the nickname of Daredevil. I was stubborn, and refused to seek help.

I attempted to integrate all these disparate parts of me into one consistent self. How could I become the person I wanted to be? Later this became a question of how to be the person God wanted me to be.

In the introduction I pointed out that telling the story of how I became a person was one of my goals in this book. My poor self-confidence was a constant hindrance, as was the contrary blend of selves within me.

Early on a neighbor, Mr. Rutledge, began offering me rides on Sunday mornings to a little Presbyterian Church on Main Street in San Gabriel. I was the only member of our household to get up and go with him to Sunday school, and then to church. I looked forward to going. I enjoyed my Sunday school class. Not that I got any specific help for what afflicted me, but I did receive reminders that God was there. A portrait of Jesus was in view, and we sang the song, "Jesus Loves Me."

Growing up was not easy. I recall hitchhiking to Mexico with my friend Mel. I took a risk, but it was my personal declaration of independence from Mom. Do people understand how it feels to lack self-confidence, to be shy and awkward, to be a momma's boy? I took risks in order to try to shake loose those demons in my mind. I joined the tennis squad at U.C. Davis and got burned on the first day of practice and quit. At Pasadena City College I decided to compete in a speech tourney and in one fell swoop erase the image of an awkward youth. My speech ended as a disaster. Only my decision to join Toastmasters helped me rebuild from that failure.

Then God's love began to be more real to me. There was the Sunday when I went to the little chapel in San Gabriel and the pastor preached surrender to God's will, and then baptized me. At U.C. Davis I read Paul Tillich's sermon "You are Accepted." My heart leaped for joy when I was forgiven for my sins of the flesh, and my guilt vanished. There was also the day I was ordained a Methodist minister in the chapel at the University of the Pacific. All of that should tie this story together, but it does not. There is more.

After my Army service was completed, I finally realized I needed personal help. I went to a counselor named Herb in Sacramento. He took me in, and counseled me as a person of worth. He became the father I had always wanted. I experienced his strength. Pieces of a giant jigsaw puzzle slowly began to come together. That process continued when I worked with Stan in our young minister's group in Fresno. He taught us how to spot the hidden obstacles in our personality that held us back from successful relationships. Also, the puzzle pieces came together when I worked with Carol here in Stockton. She taught us even more about relationships and how to build the attitudes that fostered confidence.

For purposes of writing this autobiography it appears that these events occurred separately and distinctly. In reality, however, my learning happened at the same time as God's will became more clear to me. As I inched toward self-understanding, I found that "God" was not simply a concept, but a Presence in my life.

How do I explain that? In reality I find it very difficult. In God's great scheme of things, my search for myself was really a way to learn self-surrender to God. Thus when my wife Gayle was dying of cancer I found strength taking care of her out of my love for Christ. That in turn became a service to her. I learned to be grateful to God as I took care of her. That is a conundrum of the first order. My long search for myself ended when I learned to be a servant. I find joy in sharing that mystery with you.

My story is also a testament of faith. It is about what I have found to be true in growing up. For instance, I look back to the early morning Easter hike to the top of Mt. Roubidoux near Riverside. As the sunrise split the pre-dawn darkness we joyously sang Easter hymns. That was the most significant sunrise service I have ever attended. It became a holy moment for me at the tender age of ten. That sunrise service awakened in me an awareness of God's Presence. It was the first of many. Did my skeptical father have any idea what that sunrise service would mean to me?

There were special nights in the Trinity Alps after our campfire burned down and the fellowship around the fire was stilled. A tired crew went to their sleeping bags, to their own thoughts, and to some sleep. I looked up at the Milky Way as it arced across the mountains and made the sky seem alive. The brightness of the Milky Way invited me to wonder about my place in the universe. Then I thought of my bear encounter, and of my many fears when I got lost overnight in the woods. I had profound relief when I found my way back to our crew the next morning. Gaining close friends in Charley and George showed me that I was accepted among these mountain men, and that touched my heart. I did some growing up that summer, but even more importantly, I began to sense that there was Someone in the stars above watching out and caring for me.

Of course, a life-changing moment happened just at the time I needed it most. I came home from Trieste burdened with guilt that weighed me down. Freud said avoid guilt at all costs. But it clung to me like a nightmare, and that "damned spot" on my conscience would not go away. Alone, while reading in my room from Paul Tillich's sermon "You Are Accepted" turned my life inside out. God forgave me and a huge weight fell away from my soul. I felt so light I could dance, and joyously did just that. That was the decisive turning point in my life. From that point on I knew I was a Christian and wanted to learn what Christ had to teach me.

Learning to love my parents just as they were was a big step for me. I needed to change my behavior to reflect my values as a Christian. I gave them big hugs when I came home and said to each of them, "I love you," and meant it. Dad could not respond to my offer of unconditional love, but I gave it to him nevertheless.

Shooting seagulls on the beach in front of Mr. Hearst's "castle" was an epiphany for me when I realized how gross was my behavior. I decided then to never shoot another animal so needlessly. I slowly learned to respect all life.

Along with cautious attempts at growing in faith, two steps forward and one step backward, came a dim, but growing social consciousness. I could no longer accept segregation or discrimination. I remember the day that I suddenly realized why Mexicans lived on the south side of the tracks in my hometown of San Gabriel. The fact that they lived there was not an accident. When I attended Washington Elementary there was not a single Hispanic in attendance. The same scene repeated itself at Alhambra High School. We were segregated as a result of decisions made on the Anglo side. I soon realized that we were all poorer because of segregation. When I took Spanish classes in school, and when I chose to learn from the Hispanics with whom I worked at Hines Nursery and at the Del Monte Peach Ranch, I became a better man for it. The Mexican men taught me how human they are, how much alike we are, and how much segregation hurts both sides. Part of loving God was learning to love my neighbor.

A similar thing happened at the Ecumenical Institute in Chicago. We had to step outside our concept of reality, and become like peeled bananas in order to understand the depths of segregation on the West Side Chicago. I was shocked by what I saw, and how I felt. There seemed to be an utter disregard for human life on the West Side. I began to feel a sense of shame at what our dominant white culture had done to perpetuate black inferiority, and structure blacks into second-class citizenship. Our work that summer was a daring attempt to create a true community of blacks and whites.

My Catholic teachers at College of the Holy Names in Oakland confirmed all this in my class on Black History. They brought solid information on the history of black culture since the Civil War. What a wake-up call! President Jefferson said that he feared a "fire bell in the night" for America, of blacks and whites confronting one another in a race war. That fire bell now seems to be going off again and again. I was growing in my social consciousness and praying for a wake-up call for America. I found it difficult sometimes to deal with pervasive prejudice in our white culture. That was a constant challenge to my Biblical ethic to love my brother as I loved myself. I still have to work at it.

My meeting with a transvestite at Glide Methodist Church was a failure in communication. I discovered that I was not ready for such an engagement. My own prejudice got in the way. But out of that experience came a desire to learn more about the gay community and what they think. I found how much Rosemary's brother Jim suffered by being dishonorably discharged from the Navy, and how he finally died in a mental institution. I realized something needed to change in our understanding of these people. A change began with me.

My testament of faith also includes a spiritual gift that I believe God has given me. It is the gift of accepting others where they are. I now believe that each person is doing the best they can. It is also the gift of inviting people to smile, or laugh. When I stand in front of a clerk at a store, I try to understand them and find something I can say to brighten their day. I have become good at it and most accept my invitation to look up and smile. I make their day and mine a little brighter. I do the same thing on the Saturday when I feed the homeless under the Crosstown Freeway. I don't say this casually. Serving others for Christ's sake is a joy.

Part of my testament of faith includes my struggle to deal candidly with the Bible. In seminary we were presented with modern research used to re-examine the Bible. German scholars for the past 200 years, and now American scholars, have researched scriptures, making the Bible the most cross-examined book in the world. All of this was necessary to correct my simplistic understanding of scriptures. But at the same time it raised deep questions for me about the authority of the Bible, and created merely an intellectual understanding of the Bible. That meant that as a pastor and teacher I faced a long struggle to learn how to once again use the Bible as the Word of God. I did so, and at some cost of searching my own soul for truth in scripture.

What I have found as an answer to this difficult situation is this: with my head I read what the scholars have to say, while with my heart I follow a path to the Christ of faith. When reading the first five books of the Bible (Pentateuch) I understand it as the story of salvation, God reaching out to us. I interpret it as not literally true, but figuratively true. However, when I pray, it is to the God and Father of our Lord Jesus Christ. When I intercede for the sick and the dying I plead for healing through Christ. When I attend services on Sunday morning I sing gratefully of what Christ has done on my behalf. I give thanks I can be Christian for such a time as this. All that and more is part of my testament of faith.

Then there is the issue of how the Refiner's fire has shaped me. Let me first explain what I consider the Refiner's fire to be. It is the experience of facing our pretenses, arrogance, timidity and fears in the light of God. He desires to purify us from all that contradicts His nature. Often the only way we learn is the hard way of stubborn refusals. He allows us to face the consequences for that response, not out of anger, but out of His Love. That is the Refiner's fire.

So often when I was young I considered my actions merely from my own point of view. When I was into myself not only was I separated from God, but I was separated from others as well. It seems to me that God is constantly asking us the same question that He asked Adam and Eve in the Garden of Eden: "Where are you?" "Why do you crawl into yourself and hide from me?" Someone needs to get our attention and get it quickly, or we limp through life out of touch with others and God.

"Come out of your cave, your hiding place, and learn of me." That is what God is calling us to do. Why are we timid and reserved about such a magnificent call? Since I became aware of God working in my life through the Refiner's fire everything has changed. He changes me for the better. There has been a constant invitation to see the world through new eyes: eyes of faith, joy, and yes, the eyes of Christ. How could I have been blind for so long? John Newton's song "Amazing Grace" is my companion:

Amazing grace! How sweet the sound That saved a wretch like me!
I once was lost, but now am found, Was blind, but now I see.
I will sing that song for the rest of my life.

There were times when I charged forward with my own ideas, could have been seriously injured, and was not. Many times I have thanked God for the injuries that never happened! St. Paul says in his letter to Corinth that God's response to us is always a divine "Yes." (II Cor. 1:19-20). I think I experienced that Yes when I really didn't deserve it. In the quote from Isaiah 48 that I used for the title of this book, God said He refined his people out of His deep love for them. He reminded them that He is compassionate not for their sake, but because He wants to demonstrate His Love, and show His people as pure silver. We go through a process of refinement so we can shine as a light in the world. By undeserved grace I am learning that and will not turn back from this pathway.

Where do I go from here? As I finish my story I do not know what lies ahead. But once again I will buckle Brandi into her shoulder harness, take a handful of poop bags, grab the leash and head for the front door. Opening the door I will find cool morning air, a bright sunshiny day, "the day the Lord has made" (Ps.118: 24), and God waiting to reveal Himself once more through His marvelous Creation. The walk continues, and so does life.

Bibliography

Ambrose, Stephen E. *The Wild Blue: The Men and Boys Who Flew the B-24s over Germany.* New York: Simon & Schuster, 2001.

Augustine of Hippo. *The Confessions of St. Augustine.* New York: Paulist Press. 1984.

Bauer, Walter, Wilbur Gingrich, Arndt, William, Frederick W. Danker, and. *A Greek-English Lexicon of the New Testament and Other Early Christian Literature, 2nd Edition.* Chicago: U of Chicago, 1979.

Berne, Eric. *What Do You Say after You Say Hello?* New York: Grove Press, 1972.

Berne, Eric. *Games People Play; the Psychology of Human Relationships.* New York: Grove Press, 1964.

Baldwin, James. *The Fire Next Time. New York:* Dial Press, 1963.

Cleaver, Eldridge. *Soul on Ice. New York:* McGraw-Hill, 1967.

Bonhoeffer, Dietrich. *Letters and Papers from Prison.* New York: Touchstone, 1953, 1967.

Bonhoeffer, Dietrich. *Life Together.* Harper & Row, 1954.

Book of Discipline of the United Methodist Church. Nashville, Tenn.: United Methodist Publishing House, 1984.

Fosdick, Harry Emerson. *On Being a Real Person.* Harper and Brothers, 1943.

Fromm, Erich. *The Art of Loving*. Harper and Brothers, 2006.

Fromm, Erich. *Escape From Freedom*. New York: Holt Paperbacks, 1941.

Handlin, Oscar. *The Uprooted*. Little, Boston: Brown and Company, 1951.

Herberg, Will. *Protestant, Catholic, Jew*. Garden City: Doubleday, 1956.

Hessler, Peter. "Tomb Soldiers in China, BC 221-220 AD." National Geographic Magazine, Vol. 200, Issue 4, October, (2001): 48.

Hobsbawm, E. J. *The Age of Revolution 1789-1848*. New York: Mentor Book, 1962.

Holy Bible - Revised Standard Version. New York: Thomas Nelson & Sons, 1953.

Hoover, J. Edgar. *Masters of Deceit*. New York: Holt, 1958.

Horney, Karen. *Neurotic Personality of Our Time*. New York: W.W. Norton, 1937.

Hunt, Joan and Richard. *Growing Love in a Christian Marriage*. Abingdon Press, 1981.

Kerner, Otto, et al. *Report of the National Advisory Commission on Civil Disorders*. Dutton, 1968.

Kierkegaard, Soren. *Either/Or*. Garden City, New York: Doubleday, 1959.

King, Martin Luther Jr. *Stride toward Freedom*. Harper & Harper, 1958.

Kushner, Harold S. *When Bad Things Happen to Good People*. Schocken Books, 1981.

Lair, Jess. *I Ain't Much, Baby-But I'm All I've Got*. Bantam Doubleday Dell, 1971.

Langer, William L., General Editor. *Western Civilization*. New York: Harper & Row, 1968.

Methodist Hymnal, 59, 138. Nashville, Tenn.: United Methodist Publishing House, 1966.

McGee, Robert S. *Search for Significance*. Lifeway Press, 1993.

Melville, Herman. *Moby-Dick*. New York: Bantam Classics, 1967.

Malcolm X. *The Autobiography of Malcolm X*. New York: Ballantine, 1992.

May, Rollo. *Man's Search for Himself*. New York: W. W. Norton & Company, June 1953.

Morris, Jan. *Trieste and the Meaning of Nowhere*. New York: Simon & Schuster, 2001.

Paine, Ralph D. *Four Bells: A Tale of the Caribbean*. Boston: Houghton Mifflin, 1924.

Pawel, Miriam. *The Crusades of Cesar Chavez*. Bloomsbury Press, 2014.

Paton, Alan. *Cry, the Beloved Country*. New York: Scribners, 1959.

Paz, Octavio. *The Labyrinth of Solitude Life*. Random House, 1980.

Quiller, Arthur, ed 1919. *The Oxford Book of English Verse, Wm. Ernest Henley, 1849-1903*. Oxford: Clarendon, 1919.

Ritual of the United Methodist Church. Nashville, Tenn.: The United Methodist Publishing House, 1964.

Rogers, Carl R. *Client-Centered Therapy*. Boston: Houghton Mifflin, 1965.

Service, Robert W. *The Spell of the Yukon and Other Verses*. New York: Barse and Hopkins, 1907.

Smith, Huston. *Religions of Man*. New York, Perennial Library: Harper & Row, 1958.

Steinbeck, John. *The Grapes of Wrath*. New York: Viking Press, 1958.

Sylvester, Charles H. *Journeys through Bookland*, 1922. Vol. 10. Chicago: Bellows-Reeve Company, 1909.

Tillich, Paul. *The Shaking of the Foundations*. New York: Scribner Sons, 1948.

White, William Lindsay. *Queens Die Proudly*. Harcourt Brace and Company, 1943.

White, William Lindsay. *They Were Expendable*. New York; Harcourt Brace and Company, 1942.